DATE DUE		
GAYLORD			PRINTED IN U.S.A.

Addendum

All of Appendix A is taken from Leon Nemoy's translation of the book *The Karaites and the Rabbanites* written in Arabic by Murād Farag. The translation is published in *Revue des Etudes Juives,* Janvier-Septembre, 1976.

Errata

Page	Mistake	Correction
Acknowledgement	May their soul be bound	May their soul be bound up
13 :line 5	12,000	1,200
26 :line 28	"Les Ecoles...de Caire"	"Les Ecoles...du Caire"
63 :line 34	Ibrāhīm Mangbī	Ibrāhīm Mangūbī
65 :line 7	$ 4,100	$ 4,200
65 :line 15	$ 4,400	$ 4,600
69 :upper photo	Welcoming al-Ra'īs	Welcoming al-Ra'īs
110 :line 2	al-'Imān	al-'Imām
136 :line 1	According to Samuel ben Moses al-Maghribī (15th century)	According to Israel ben Samuel al-Maghribī 13-14 century)
152 :line 9	Footnote 28	Footnote 26
169 :photo	Printed backward	Corrected on back of this page "Karaite act of marriage"
182 :line 13	Psalm No. 81	Psalm No. 91
186 :line 24	Me'aliyah	Me'aliyah
213 :line 6	al-Isrā'īlyīn	al-Isrā'īliyīn
219 :line 11	Moreh Sedq	Moreh Ṣēdeq
241 :Plate No. 8	English characters are in Italic	Should be in Roman characters
270 :line 8	Umm al-'agā'ib	Umm al-'agā'ib
279 :lower photo	'Isā Manūm	'Isa Manūn
332 :Appendix C	Blessing for the New Moon	Blessing for the New Month
Back cover flap last three words	Far Eastern studies	Near Eastern studies

Karaite Act of Marriage

The Karaite Jews of Egypt

The Karaite Jews of Egypt
1882-1986

By
Mourad El-Kodsi

Wilprint, Inc., Lyons, N.Y.
1987

University of Charleston Library
Charleston, WV 25304

Copyright 1988, by Mourad El-Kodsi ©
Printed in the United States of America by
Wilprint, Inc.
83-89 Broad Street, Lyons, New York 14489

All rights reserved. This book may not be reproduced, in whole or in part, in any form, without written permission from Mourad El-Kodsi.

LC 87-91038

ISBN 0-9620052-0-7

Printed in the United States of America

To all the communities that once existed but are
now part of the history
To all the communities that vanished because of
racial, religious, or political prejudice
I offer this book.

THE KARAITES

"If it was only for the Karaites that they freed Judaism from the deformities of popular superstition and rendered it a well-defined and logically constituted system of ideas and tenents, then that would be more than enough."

   Goitein S.D.

The Karaite Jews of Egypt from 1882 to 1986

Contents

Preface	Objective of the Book
Introduction	Who Are the Karaites. A Quick Review of Their History in Egypt
Chapter I	The Karaites of Egypt: Their Population, Their Occupation
	al-Ṣāghah
	Ḥārat al-Yahūd
	Their Relation with the Karaites Abroad
	Their Relation with the Mainstream Jewish Community
	Their Relation with Other Communities
Chapter II	How the Community Was Governed
	The Religious Council
	The Religious Courts
	The Internal Code
	The Personal Status Code
	History
Chapter III	Community Establishments
	The Schools, The Lottery
	Places of Worship
	Cemeteries
Chapter IV	Caring for the Needy
	The Role of the Various Religious Councils
	The Role of the Various Organizations
Chapter V	A Brief Discussion of Karaite Liturgy
Chapter VI	Customs and Traditions
	Saturdays
	Holy Days
	Rites of Passage
	Food
Chapter VII	Cultural and Social Activities
	The Various Organizations and their Achievements
	Literary Output
	Leading Men
	Murād Farag
	Dā'ūd Ḥusnī
Chapter VII	Chief Rabbis
Chapter IX	Karaites and Zionism
Chapter X	The 20th Century Exodus. Where Did the Karaites Go?
	The Karaites in Israel, Their Future
Epilogue	
Appendixes	A, B, C, D, E and F
Glossary	
Bibliography	
Index	

Preface

The major objective of this book is to record the history of the Karaite Community of Egypt during the last one hundred years. It covers all aspects of this community from 1882 until today. The material on the chief rabbis goes back even further than that, as I was able to find the needed information and I saw no harm in recording it in this book.

The period for which I had much trouble finding reliable information on certain activities of the community was the one from 1882 until 1901. There was no record of the events of that period anywhere. To be sure, there were visitors from time to time from other countries who wrote what they could see or what they heard about the community, but that did not cover much.[1]

Ḥākhām Shabbethāi Elīyāhū Mangūbī, the chief rabbi of the Karaite community of Egypt from 1876 until 1906, kept a log in which he recorded in detail the events of the community. That log could have been of great help, but like many other manuscripts and famous Torahs, no one was able to locate it.[2]

In recording the history of the community in this book, I felt that this history would not be lost to future scholars.

---

1. E.N. Adler, *Jews in Many Lands* (J.P.S.A.: 1905), pp. 23-25
2. *Al-Kalīm* no. 94, February 1949, indicates that the "log" was still in the library of the Karaite Bēt-Dīn. The library of the Karaite community of Cairo was a small one, yet it contained hundreds of priceless manuscripts, many famous, and unique Torahs. Unfortunately, during the years 1976-1982 many art collectors from Europe and the U.S.A. spent a great deal of money and effort to put their hands on this treasure — and they succeeded. Now in the Magnus museum of San Francisco there are many priceless manuscripts that were taken from the Karaite community of Egypt. Another well known rare book collector in Long Island, New York, has already acquired one of the most beautiful Torahs ever written.

As a member of the community who was active in its various organizations; as a member, secretary and chairman for over twenty years, and who served the community in his youth as a principal of its schools for 12 years, and as a member and a secretary of its religious council for 10 years, I feel that no one is more qualified to record its history than I.

My main sources of information are:

1. The minutes of the Karaite religious councils from 1901 to 1972 (6 volumes);
2. The issues of the five Karaite magazines that appeared from 1901 to 1957 (19 volumes);
3. The archives of the Karaite Bēt-Dīn, which fortunately were intact, and with which I am familiar;
4. Pictures and documents that I was able to gather during my visits to Cairo and Israel in 1979, 1982, 1984, and 1987;
5. Books written by Rabbanite or Karaite scholars that are related to the subject of the book;.
6. My personal memoirs that I wrote down from 1944 to 1959.

While this work reflects my own experience and efforts, yet it gives me great pleasure to acknowledge here my deep gratitude to Professor Leon Nemoy, one of the leading authorities on Karaitica, as he was the first to suggest the idea of the book, and continued his assistance and kindly guidance for many years, to Leonard Fox for several suggestions and for editing the text, to Marcy Gamzon of the English department of the University of Rochester, and Kathryn Pinto of the Associated University Press of New Jersey for their help in editing the text and proof reading it, and to my wife who was very patient with me during the endless hours I was busy working on this book.

Acknowledgement

The publishing of this book would have been incomplete without the cooperation of the following institutes: Société des Etudes Juives, Paris, France; Henoch, Torino, Italy; Annenberg Research Institute, Pennsylvania, U.S.A.; Yale University Press, New Haven, U.S.A. It would have been also very difficult if it was not for the generous contribution of Mr. Elie Haroun of Lausanne, Switzerland, in memory of his beloved brother Jacques Haroun, who died in a car accident in California in November 1984, and a contribution in memory of the benevolent man, Mūsā Pessaḥ, who died in May 1987. May their souls be bound in the bonds of eternal life and their memory ever be for a blessing. Finally, my deep gratitude to both Karaite communities in Israel and in San Francisco, as they both shared a good part of the cost of publishing the book.

The Karaite Jews of Egypt

Introduction

Judaism, like Christianity and Islam, has developed throughout the years different ideas and beliefs by members of the Jewish communities who, at the time, were dissatisfied with the "status quo."

In general this dissatisfaction could be traced to political and socio-economic reasons, as well as to different religious beliefs. As a result, many Jewish sects appeared, preaching their beliefs and hoping to carry out the changes they felt were necessary.

Of all the Jewish sects that appeared during the long history of Judaism — and they were many — none was able to have as serious an effect on the Jewish mainstream as the sect of Karaism. Karaism, whose adherents are called Karaites, strongly challenged the mainstream and, to some extent, threatened its existence, and was able at times to attract 40 percent of the whole Jewish population. Karaism is the only Jewish sect besides that of the Samaritans that still exists today.

Who are the Karaites:

"The Karaites are a Jewish sect which does not recognize the authority of the post-Biblical tradition incorporated in the Talmud and in the latter Rabbinic works."[1]

"Rejection of the authority of the Talmud does not mean that the Karaites consider it unlawful to consult it or to rely on it; it means only that they deny its heavenly origin and regard it as an original work of the Sages in interpretation of the written Torah, and therefore subject to the shortcomings inherent in any handiwork of mortal men uninspired by heaven."[2] There are a number of reasons why Karaites cannot acknowledge the authority of the oral Torah:

1. The word "Torah" (in the sense of Divine Instruction) is always used in the singular. Were the Mishnah a genuine (oral) Torah, surely somewhere in Scripture the existence of two Torahs would have been mentioned at least once.

---

1. *Encyclopedia of Islam*, 2nd ed. (1975), Vol. VI, p. 63.
2. See footnote 3.

2. Since the Mishnah is a commentary on the written Torah, what reason was there for the original injunction to preserve it only orally? Surely writing it down would have benefited Jewry by promoting agreement among the later Sages and reducing disagreement.

3. If the Tannaitic Sages have received their tradition through an interrupted chain of tradents going back to Moses himself, how could disagreement arise among them? They should have been of one mind in every particular.

4. The Torah is called *perfect* (Ps. 19:8). The Rabbanites say that it is perfect along with the Mishnah that accompanied it. If this is so, then the Mishnah is a completion of the written Torah. Why then did God order it not to be written down?

5. God surely had foreknown that someday the oral Torah would be in danger of being forgotten, and that it would become vital for its preservation to set it down in writing. Why then did He at first forbid its recording and thus expose His people to the dreadful risk of losing it altogether? The truth must be in the opposite direction: When the Sages saw that the unity of the people and the preservation of the oral Torah was in jeopardy, they invented the fiction of its having been revealed to Moses simultaneously with the written Torah, and of the ordained delay in its recording until that time, when circumstances made it imperative to reduce it to writing in order to prevent its loss.[3]

"Aside from the rejection of the authority of the post-Biblical tradition, there is no basic divergence between the Karaite and the Rabbanite dogmatic."[4] (For a detailed list of these differences, see Appendix A).

When Did the Movement Start?

The theory that Karaism began in the middle of the eighth century is now questionable. The Karaite community in Egypt had in its possession, until the end of the 19th century, a legal document stamped by the palm of 'Amr Ibn al-'Aṣ, the first Islamic governor of Egypt, in which he ordered the leaders of the Rabbanite community not to interfere in the way of life of the Karaites nor with the way they celebrate their holidays. This document is dated 20.A.H. (641 A.D.), more than one hundred years before 'Anān. If that document really existed, and there is no reason to suggest otherwise, does that not indicate that the word "Karaite" was known long before 'Anān?[5]

Leo Baeck, in the Preface to the book *Karaite Liturgy,* by Rabbi P. Selvin Goldberg (Manchester University Press, 1957), wrote: "Karaism, when it was a ferment in Judaism and had not yet become a mere sect, did play an important part

---

3. The material between footnotes 2 and 3 is from: *The Karaites and the Rabbanites* in Arabic by Murād Farag, printed in Cairo, 1918, pages 47, 53, 54, 55. Leon Nemoy translated parts of the book into English, and it was published in *Revue des Etudes Juives,* Janvier-Septembre, 1976, pp. 91-92.
4. *Encyclopedia of Islam,* 2nd ed. (1975), Vol. VI, p. 66.
5. *Al-Tahdhīb* No. 38, 5 Sept. 1902, p. 158. *Al-Shubbān Al Quarrā'īn* 4, 2 June 1937, p. 8

in the formation of medieval Jewish philosophy." No doubt, this is an indication that the word Karaite refers to certain Jews who were not satisfied with the way things were going on among Jews, and that was long before 'Anān.

Al-Qirqisānī (in the first half of the tenth century) in his book *Kitāb al Anwār Wal-Marāqib* refers to the "Karaites" and the "people of 'Anān" as two different sects. In *KA VII*, 1, Vol. IV, p. 790, he writes, "This is the faith of 'Anān, the majority of the ancient Karaites, and all Karaites of today.[6] In *KA II*, 18, 1, Vol. 1. p. 141, he mentions the Ananites and the Benjaminites (followers of Benjamin al-Nahāwandī: second quarter of the 9th century) as two separate groups.[7]

What does all this mean? It simply indicates that until the second half of the tenth century, at which time al-Qirqisānī was writing his book, there was more than one group that had almost the same religious beliefs and practice, although under different names: Karaites, Ananites, and Benjaminites. This also indicates that the word "Ananites" was added to designate the followers of 'Anān, and the word "Benjaminites" to designate the followers of Benjamin, in order to separate them from the "original Karaites." Until that time all groups who opposed the divinity of the Talmud had their ideology still in the making and they had not yet come under one name. Later, the word "Karaites" prevailed and became the name associated with all those who had an almost identical ideology and did not accept the idea of the divinity of the Talmud.

To conclude this point I quote what D. Chwolson wrote in his book *Beiträge Zur Entwicklungsgeschichte*: "It is a fact that in the 9th and 10th centuries there developed among the Karaites an abundant and diversified literature, so that one can conclude that a long time before 'Anān the Karaites were already in possession of a great inheritance of knowledge and scientific scholarship, since a literature as important as the Karaite literature of the 9th and 10th centuries does not fall from the sky nor does it grow on the sand. Karaism was not a new sect founded by 'Anān but was erected on the basis of an old law."[8] And thus 'Anān's role was not that of a founder of the sect, but that of the one who was the main figure in the "split" of the Karaites from the Rabbanites.

From Bagdad the movement penetrated eastward to Persia and westward to Syria, Palestine (especially Jerusalem and Ramlah), Egypt, and North Africa. By the 10th century there were Karaite communities in Byzantium and parts of central Europe.

Earlier, and in several cities in Spain, the Karaites were part of the larger Jewish community that flourished and helped establish the golden age in the history of Jews

---

6. "وَ هو مَذْهَبُ عانان و أَكْثَرِ القرائين القدماء و جميع قرائين هذا العصر"

7. "أفاريق اليهود وم الربانيّون و العانانيّة و البنيْاميْنيّة و غيرم من الفِرَق"

8. Simon Szyszman, *Le Karaïsme*, (Lausanne: L'Age d'Homme, 1980), n. 5, p. 18.

in Spain. By the 12th century there were many influential Karaite communities in the Crimea, Lithuania, and Poland.

The history of the Karaites in Egypt before and after 'Anān until Aḥmad ibn Ṭūlūn established the Tulunid dynasty (868-969) is shrouded in obscurity and will stay this way until all the documents of the Cairo genizah and those that Abraham Firkovitch took from the Karaite Bēt-Dīn of Cairo in 1864 and gave to the National Library of Leningrad are fully studied.

We will try here to offer some suggestions on the subsequent history of the Karaites, using what has already been written on the subject and whatever documents still exist in the headquarters of the Karaite community in Ramlah, Israel.

Because of the aforementioned facts about the origin of the Karaites, Karaism quickly expanded in Egypt, and new Karaite communities were found in Alexandria and in Fusṭāṭ by the first quarter of the 9th century, along with the older Karaite community in Fusṭāṭ.

At first there was peaceful coexistence between the two communities, the Rabbanite and the Karaite. During the time of Karaite ascendancy (9th to 12th century) there were frequent cases of intermarriage between members of both communities.[9]

During the Tulunid dynasty the Karaites, for many reasons, were able to exert much influence. In Jerusalem they established a Karaite center, which forced the Rabbanites to move to Ramlah.

At times also some influential Karaite leaders in Fusṭāṭ took an active part in the communal affairs of the Rabbanite community.[10] According to Graetz, there existed in Cairo a Karaite congregation which is said to have been more numerous than that of the Rabbanites. It also had a chief rabbi who possessed plenary power in religious and judicial matters, and bore the title of Prince *(nāsī;ra'īs)*. During this period (1160-1200) many Karaites in Egypt enjoyed the favor of the court, and were, in general, more influential than the Rabbanites.[11]

Nevertheless, on some occasions the relations between the two communities became so tense as to result in violence, which forced the Muslim authorities to interfere.

In the year 1024 A.D. the Fatimid Caliph al-Ẓāhir issued an edict of religious tolerance and freedom of action. Part of the edict states that "...at the same time all are prohibited from interfering with the sect -Ṭā'ifat- of the Karaites in their synagogue, which belongs to them to the exclusion of all others" (Pl. 1). In the same edict the caliph orders the chief of his armies and the governors *(Wulāh)* to protect members of the two sects and to care for them.[12]

---

9. Mann, *Texts and Studies,* Vol II, Preface.
10. Mann, *Texts and Studies,* Vol. II, p. 122.
11. Graetz, *History of Jews,* Vol. III, 1984, p. 444.
12. Mann, *The Jews in Egypt and Palestine under the Fatimids,* Vol. I, p. 135.

Al-Ẓāhir was the fourth Fatimid caliph. The Fatimid dynasty ruled Egypt, Palestine, North Africa and parts of Syria from 969 A.D., which coincided with the time of Karaite ascendancy, especially in Egypt. The Fatimid caliphs — with the exception of al-Ḥākim — treated the Jews in general with much tolerance.

During the reign of al-Ẓāhir (1021-1036) and the first years of his son al-Mustanṣir (1036-1094), two Karaite brothers known as Abū Sa'd and Abū Naṣr Ibrāhīm al-Tustārī occupied a most prominent position within the Jewry of the Fatimid. They were loved and respected by all Jews. They were the refuge of every Jew in trouble or need. When the Rabbanite Jews of Tripoli, Lebanon, wanted to rebuild their synagogue, they wrote to the two brothers to help them obtain permission. Jews in general and Karaites in particular were at the peak of prosperity, which prompted a Muslim poet to write a poem urging his fellow Muslims to adopt the Jewish religion, as heaven itself had become Jewish. Unfortunately, due to jealousy and feuding among members of the Fatimid court, the two brothers were assassinated in 1048. The Gaon writes to Saḥtān Allūf B. Ibrāhīm, the spiritual leader of the Babylonian community of Fusṭāṭ, about the death of the two righteous men *(shnei ha-Ṣaddiqīm)*. They were the upholders of religion.

Ṣalāḥ al-Dīn put an end to the Fatimid dynasty in 1171. He and his successors, heads of the Ayyubid Dynasty, ruled from 1171 to 1250 A.D. Jews in general, Rabbanites and Karaites, enjoyed good relations with the Ayyubids. Maimonides, the great Rabbanite scholar, was the court physician of Ṣalāḥ al-Dīn and his son al-Afḍal. When Ṣalāḥ recaptured Jerusalem from the Crusaders in 1187 A.D., he helped the Karaite community of Egypt to redeem the codex of Ben Asher which remains in their possession until today.

The Mamelukes took over from the Ayyubids in 1250 A.D. and stayed in power until 1517 A.D. During their rule the Jews in general suffered a great deal. The Mamelukes were of various races and various cultures. They were Muslims, but Islam never was deep in their hearts. They were greedy, thirsty for money to buy other Mamelukes, and to stay in power.[13]

From a legal document dated 29 Ramaḍān 684 A.H. (1258 A.D.), we learn of a transaction between a certain "Maḥāsin ibn Thābit" on behalf of himself and his brother "Abū al-'Izz" and three women "Sadīdah, Ẓarīfah and Rashīdah, daughters of Wahbah ibn Thābit" who sold to a Mameluke "Shams al-Dīn Toghuz, son of the prince Toghus" their house in Ḥārat Zuwaylah in the place called "Ruḥbat Surūr al-Lu'lu'ī; the house was known as "dār al Nakhlah." From its description

---

13. From the time of the establishment of Cairo in 969 A.D., and al-Azhar mosque a year later, Cairo, and especially the area around al-Azhar, became the center of the government and the residence of the rich people and the elites. The neighborhood of al-Khurunfish, of which Ḥārat al-Yahūd al-Quarrā'īn is a part, was in walking distance from al-Azhar. It was then very natural to find it attract some of the elites. Until today in al-Khurunfish one can find houses built by some rich Mamelukes that are considered to be masterpieces of Arabesque architecture.

one can learn that some of the houses in that area were well-built and furnished with complete facilities on every level, even the one at the top which was called "al-Suṭūḥ."

Ḥārat Zuwaylah, part of Ḥārat al Yahūd at the time, was inhabited by members of both communities, Rabbanite and Karaite, as well as by Samaritans. Many Karaites owned the houses they lived in, while poor members of the Karaite community lived in houses acquired by the community through endowment.

It appears that all Jewish communities preferred to live together and the majority of them lived in Fusṭāṭ or in Ḥārat al Yahūd in Cairo.

In spite of the strict attitude of the Mamelukes towards non-Muslims, it appears that the Karaite community held its own. During the second half of the 13th century and the first decade of the 14th century, we hear of the Karaite scholar Israel ben Samuel al Maghribī. He was the judge *(dayyan)* of the Karaite community, and the teacher of Yefeth ben Saghīr, the "famous physician." Samuel ben Moses al Maghribī, the well-known scholar and physician of the 15th century, was also his disciple.

The discovery of the route to India around the west coast of Africa at the end of the 15th century (1497 A.D.) was a blow to the economy in Egypt, as the Mamelukes lost a great deal in trade taxes. To cover that loss, as was always the way in such cases, the Mamelukes had to extort money from members of the Jewish community at large.

From certain documents of the 15th and 16th centuries we learn that the Karaites in Egypt had more than one synagogue; they had one in al-Maṣṣāṣah near the Mosque of 'Amr ibn al-'Aṣ in Fusṭāṭ, one in the neighborhood of "al-Gudriyah" near al-Ḥusayn mosque and two in "Ḥārat Zuwaylah." The one in al-Gudriyah, which was not a part of the Jewish neighborhood, was completely burned during the time of al-Ḥākim, the third Fatimid caliph (996-1021 A.D.), and Jews — including Karaites — never returned to live in that neighborhood again. By the end of the 16th century the synagogue in Ḥārat Zuwaylah that was near the place called "Al Khōkhah" was in ruins. The other one was kept in use until the 18th century, at which time many Christians moved to that area which would be considered later not as a part of Ḥārat al-Yahūd.

A document dated 19 Ṣafar 919 A.H. (1512 A.D.) tells us that there were Karaites still living around their synagogue of al Maṣṣāṣah, as Dā'ūd ibn Shamwāl ibn Ibrāhīm, the Karaite Jew who was the "Shaykh" of the Karaite community, had endowed a certain place that he had just bought so that its revenue would be spent on the poor *(ṣa'ālīq)* among Karaites who lived near the synagogue of al-Maṣṣāṣah.

By the end of the 16th century the number of Karaites living in Fusṭāṭ dwindled, and we know little about the fate of their synagogue there. Jews, and Christians as well, under Islamic rule were not permitted to add anything to the existing building of a synagogue or a church. They could only repair falling parts as long as they did not change the original structure. Once the building was in ruins it had to stay that way until permission to rebuild it was granted.

A document dated 9 Ṣafar 860 A.H. (1455 A.D.) states that Jews and Christians had agreed to the aforementioned rules 800 years before. The same document indicates that Samaritans were still living in Egypt. From all these documents we learn that Karaites used to work as goldsmiths, money changers, merchants in woollen cloth and in spices. They used to bury their dead in the village of al-Basātīn, which had been in their possession for a very long time. From a document dated 15 Muḥarram 980 (1571 A.D.), we learn that the Rabbanite community, the Maghribī Jews, and the Egyptian Arabized Jews had legally acquired a piece of land in al-Basātīn to bury their dead, from al-Mu'allim Shamwāl, the Karaite, known as al-Dustūrī, who at the time, 6 Rabī' al Awwal 945 A.H. (1538 A.D., was the representative of the Karaite community *(al Mutakallim 'an Ṭa'ifat al Qarrā' īn)*. The document goes on to state the responsibility of each community for the care of its property in al-Basātīn. It also holds the leaders of these communities responsible in case any member or any party from the Rabbanites or the Karaites infringes on the other.

The Ottoman Turks took over in 1517 A.D., and conditions for non-Muslims improved, especially when the principles of Islamic rule, which they called the Millet system, were enforced. Yet for many reasons — and most importantly because of the weakness of the central government in Turkey — the Mamelukes were able to regain most of their authority and again non-Muslim communities were burdened with taxes.

From several documents dated 980 A.H. (1571 A.D.), 1058 A.H. (1646 A.D.), 1091 A.H. (1679 A.D.), and 1201 A.H. (1786 A.D.), it is clear that some members of the Rabbanite community in Cairo used to infringe on members of the Karaite community. The frequency of such incidents leaves no doubt that the relations between the two communities were not smooth.

In the year 1150 A.H. (1747 A.D.) four 'Ulamā' of al-Azhar, one Shāfi'ī one Mālikī, one Ḥanbalī, and the fourth Ḥanafī pleaded with the authorities to care of the Karaites as they are few *(qillah)* and not rich, and to ask all officials to relieve them from injustice.

Less than thirty years later matters must have improved somehow, because Samuel ha-Levi, the Chief Karaite Ḥākhām, fled from Jerusalem to Egypt to ask for financial help and support for the Karaite community in Jerusalem. Mann in his book, *Texts and Studies,* did not mention whether Samuel returned with any money, yet he mentions that the Karaite community gave Samuel a letter from prominent Muslims in Cairo to the Pasha of Jerusalem to defend the rights of the Jerusalem Karaites until the promised aid from the Crimea would arrive.[14] Such

---

14. Mann, *Texts and Studies,* Vol. I, pp. 324-236.

a letter must have cost the Karaites of Egypt quite a lot of money; besides, it indicates that they could still ask for "favors."

The turning point for the Jews — including the Karaites — came in 1804 A.D., when Muḥammad 'Alī became governor of Egypt *(Walī Miṣr)*. He was the first governor to be able to put a permanent end to the Mamelukes. As a result of a strong government and many reforms in industry, agriculture, health, and education, Egypt enjoyed a strong economy.

Christians and Jews experienced better times, especially when the government treated them on terms of equality with the Muslims.[15] With the British occupation of Egypt in 1882, both Rabbanites and Karaites were able to improve their status and enlarge their community. The number of Karaites grew from fifteen hundred during the time of Muḥammad 'Alī to almost five thousand in 1952.

Relations between Karaites and Rabbanites started to improve, and by the first quarter of the 20th century, there was a strong rapprochement between the two communities. Both communities continued to work together with mutual respect and joint efforts to face the problems that threatened them.

In the long history of Judaism, both the Rabbanites and the Karaites shared the same fate and suffered much of the same persecution, whether in Egypt, in Europe, or other parts of the world.

Until the first quarter of the 20th century there were strong Karaite communities in Russia, Poland, in parts of central Europe, and in Turkey (Pl. 2). After World War II the only Karaite community left was that of Poland, which survived until the 1950's. In Egypt there was a flourishing Karaite community until the 1960's, when the Arab-Israeli war of 1967 put an end to it, as well as to the large Rabbanite community. In Istanbūl, Turkey, there is still a Karaite community.[16]

The Karaite community in Israel numbers ten thousand. Its headquarters are in Ramlah. There are Karaite communities in Ashdod, Mushav Maṣliyaḥ, Mushav Rannîn, and in other cities in Israel.

---

15. Asad J. Rustum, *The Royal Archives of Egypt and the Disturbances in Palestine in 1834,* Beirut 1938, "And by announcing a policy of equality between Muslims and non-Muslims." p. 19.
16. Until today there are still some Karaites in various parts of Russia where Karaites used to live.

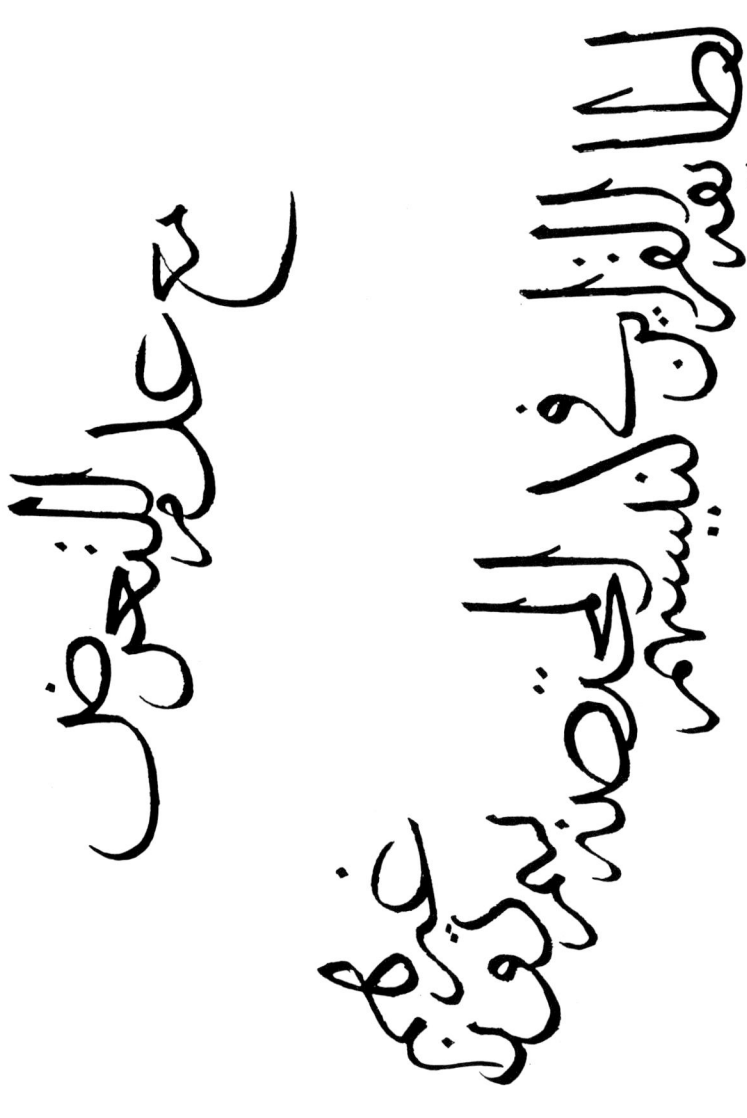

PLATE 1: Part of the edict issued by al-Ẓāhir, the Fatimid caliph, in the year 1024 A.D. The edict was examined in the late 1950s by Professor P. Kahle. The edict is now in the library of the Karaite community in Ramlah, Israel.

"without interfering with the sect of the Karaites in their synagogue, which belongs to them to the exclusion of all others."

(٥٠٥٠ روبل)

توفي منذ شهرين ونصف يهوديٌ من القرائين بسنفروبل من بلاد الروسيا اسمه شلومو (سليمان) بن يهوذا شيتان وترك وصية باربعة الآف وخمماية روبل وهو يوازي عندنا عشرة قروش صاغ . اوصى بهذا المبلغ الى كنائس وجمعيات خيرية للقرائين بمصر والآستانة والقدس وبعدة بلاد بالروسيا واضاف اليه ورثته وبعض اقاربه ٥٠٠ روبل زيادةً من عندهم قسموها على اصل ما هو مخصص في الوصية لكل كنيسةٍ وجمعية من تلك الكنائس والجمعيات تقسيما مناسبًا فكان المجموع ٥٠٥٠ روبل

ونحن نأتي هنا على ذكر هذه الوصية نشرًا لهذا الفضل والكرم وتعطيرًا للذكر بهذا النشر وطلبًا للمغفرة والرحمة والثواب على هذا الاحسان ونأتي على ذكر بيان تلك البلاد للعلم بها ولمعرفة الجهات والبلاد التي بها يهود قراؤن ومعرفة انه حتى السيدات منهم هناك لهن جمعيات خيرية

روبل

١٥٠٠	لوقف سنفروبل		بلاد الروسيا	
٥٠٠	لكنيسة سنفروبل			
٢٠٠	»	اياتوريا	»	
٢٠٠	»	خركوه	«	
١٠٠	»	سفاستوبل	«	
١٠٠	»	ثؤدوسيا	«	
١٠٠	»	بقجه سراي وقلعه	«	
١٠٠	»	اوديسا	«	
١٠٠	»	نكولايف	«	
١٠٠	»	خرسون	«	
١٠٠	»	كيوف	«
١٠٠	»	يكترنسلاف	«	
٥٠	»	اور	«	
٥٠	»	بطرسبورج	«	
٥٠	»	موسكو	«	
٥٠	لكنيسة يلطه		بلاد الروسيا	
٥٠	»	برده	«	
٥٠	»	كرمنشوك	«	
٥٠	»	مليتوبل	«	
٥٠	»	كاراسو	«	
٢٥	»	اليزابيت جراد	«	
٢٥	»	بولطوه	«	
٢٥	»	الآستانة		
٢٥	»	مصر		
١٠٠	القدس الشريف			
٥٠٠	للجمعية الخيرية بسنفروبل			
٢٠٠	للجمعية الخيرية باياتوريا			
٢٠٠	للجمعية الخيرية التي للسيدات باوديسا			
٢٠٠	»	»	في خركوفه	
١٠٠	»	»	في ثؤديسا	
٥٠	»	»	في بقجه سراي	
٥٠٥٠				

PLATE 2: From *al-Tahdhīb*, no. 37 22 May 1902; no. 38, 29 May 1902.
A Karaite from Simferopol in Russia died a few months ago (1901). He was Shlomoh ibn Shitan. In his will he left 4500 rubles to be distributed to the Karaite synagogues and benevolent associations in Cairo, Istambūl, Jerusalem and Russia. The donor's relatives added 550 to the original amount, and the total amount of 5050 rubles was shared by the following synagogues and associations:
In mentioning this we ask a blessing and a forgiveness for the donor.
1500 rubles Endowment for Simferopol in Russia.
 500 rubles Synagogues of Simferopol.
 500 rubles Benevolent Association of Simferopol.
 200 rubles Benevolent Association of Women in Odessa.
 200 rubles Benevolent Association in Eupatoria.
 200 rubles Benevolent Association in Kharkov
 200 rubles to each of the following synagogues: Eupatoria, Sebastopol, and Kharkov.
 100 rubles to each of the following synagogues: Theodosia, Odessa, Nikolaiev, Kherson, Kiev, and the Benevolent Association in Theodosia, Jerusalem and Ekaterinoslav.
  50 rubles to each of the following synagogues: Yalta, Berdichev, Kremenchug, Melitopol, Karasu, and the Benevolent Association in Bakhchisarai, and/or Moscow, and St. Petersburg.
  25 rubles to each of the following synagogues: Cairo, Istanbūl, and Elisavetgrad.

Chapter I

The Karaites of Egypt
   Their Population
   Their Socio-Economic Status
   Al-Ṣāghah
   Ḥārat al-Yahūd

   Relations with People of
   Authority and with the Natives

   Relations with the Karaites
   Abroad

   Relations with the Mainstream
   Jewish Community

   Relations with Other
   Communities

Their Population

The Karaite community of Cairo was one of the oldest communities in Egypt, having existed there for over fourteen hundred years. In spite of that long history, the Karaite community was among the smallest communities in Egypt. Their total population is unknown. There are few data as to their number and one has to be very careful in using them because, as we will see, they are not reliable. One of the most dependable sources of data about the number of Jews in Egypt is the annual census taken by the Department of Census every ten years. Yet even this source is not of any help in our case, as it puts all the Jews living in Egypt into one group, with no distinction between Rabbanites and Karaites.[1]

Historians, as well as the travellers who wrote about Jews in Egypt, including Karaites, have given us unreliable data about their number. Adler, in his book *Jews of Many Lands,* put the number of Karaites at five hundred in the last quarter of the 19th century, while Clot Bey a few decades earlier put the figure at 12,00 ,[2] while J. C. McGoan states in his book *Egypt as It Is* (p. 35) that in 1877 the number of Karaites rose to two thousand. When Muḥammad Nagīb visited the Karaite synagogue in 1952, the reporter from *al-Balāgh* who covered the event put the number of Karaites at ten thousand; we can rightly assume that this number was based on hearsay rather than on reliable sources of information.[3]

Hayyim Cohen, in his book *The Jews of the Middle East: 1860-1972,* put the number of Karaites in Egypt at 4,507 during the 1950's. He did not say how he had arrived at that figure.

A few months before the census of 1927 was to begin, the organization of "The Israelite Union" asked the department of census to include in the census sheets what indicates the faith among Jews of Egypt, as is the case with the Christians. The department agreed and sent a letter of confirmation to the organization. Both letters are published in *al-Ittiḥād* No. 20, 25 January 1927. Unfortunately the department never carried out that promise.

In 1939 the Karaite community tried to take a census to determine the number of its members in Egypt, but failed in spite of the advice and assistance of a high-ranking Karaite in the department of census.[4] There were simply no volunteers and no cooperation among the members. On 19 December 1944, the Karaite religious council, at the request of one of its members, formed a committee to take the census. The committee was headed by a high-ranking engineer in the central government (Elīyāhū Ya'qūb Aṣlān). He prepared in detail all the steps to be taken for this task. Twelve volunteers agreed to work with him to take the census of all the Karaites living in Cairo and its suburbs. Letters were sent to all members of the community living in other cities. At the same time the clerk of the Karaite Bēt-Dīn prepared a list of all Karaite families. No doubt the plan was well-prepared, but as we will see, it was not executed as the planner had hoped. Most of the volunteers did not care to carry out their responsibilities and returned the census sheets incomplete or blank. Some of them did not bother to return the sheets. Mr. Aṣlān had no choice but to do the work alone, which he did. From the list of families and from the families' records, he completed as much as he could from all the census sheets. It is a fact that he obtained most of his data from these sheets. When the

---

1. Number of Jews in 1917 was 59,000, compared to 66,000 in 1947.
2. Clot Bey, A.B. *Aperçu Général sur L'Egypte,* p. 243.
3. *Al-Balāgh* No. 9528, 30th year, 6 Ṣafar, 1372 A.H. 25 October 1952.
4. He is Yūsuf Kohen.

work was completed he published it in *al-Kalīm* in 5 parts, from No. 33 to No. 37, 16 June 1946 to 16 August 1946. Mr. Aṣlān put the total number of males at 1,930 and the females at 1,904, with a total of 3,834 Karaites in Egypt.

In the first report he explains the steps taken to carry out the census; he also mentions the many difficulties he encountered and how he solved some of the problems. In the second part of his report he gave much interesting data about the Karaite families: how many there were and how many members in each. In Part 3 he wrote about the weddings from 1901 to 1945. He indicates that the month of June is the month during which most Karaites preferred to get married, and in fact more weddings took place during that month than during any other month. Next to June was March, as Purim always falls during it. He also mentions that as a result of the economic boom in Egypt during World War II more marriages were performed during 1945 than any other year before. In Part 4 he writes about Karaite names and the tendencies involved in choosing a name. Unfortunately, he examined only male names and he concluded that the most popular names among Karaites were in this order: Ibrāhīm or Albert, Elīyāhū or Elie, Mūsā or Morris and so on. He also mentions that there are names that were used only once, such as Stalin, Manṣūr, Luṭfī, and others.

In his report he promised to write about family and individual names, their meaning, and how they were adopted, but he never did. In Part 5 he put illiteracy among males at 17% compared to 30% among females, and he explained why, aside from other interesting data. It is a fact that the percentage of educated Karaites and those who held a higher degree in education was much higher than in any other community during the first half of the 20th century.

According to Mr. Aṣlān's census, then, the number of Karaites living in Egypt in 1946 was 3,834. I will discuss this report later, but first I would like to give other data regarding the number of Karaites in Egypt in 1952.

In 1952, I was the chairman of the Maṣṣōt Committee and the supervisor of the whole operation.[5] After consulting some former chairmen of that committee, the clerk of the Karaite Bēt-Dīn, and members of the religious council, it was decided that 35,000 maṣṣōt should be made, on the basis of the fact that there were around 5,000 Karaites, and the consumption of each member, on the average, is 7 maṣṣōt during the 7 days of the feast.[6]

There is no doubt that Mr. Aṣlān put tremendous effort into his project, and he himself had to work alone because all the volunteers had left, yet we have to give the following facts some consideration:

---

5. The Karaite School of which I was the principal was in walking distance from the bakery, which enabled me to do the supervising.
6. The Karaites in Egypt depended more on a special maṣṣōt they made at home, aside from rice, potatoes and eggs, so the consumption of the regular maṣṣōt was very limited.

1. In 1946 there was a fair number of Karaites living in cities other than Cairo: Port Sa'īd, Alexandria, al-Maḥallah al-Kubrā, Aswān, and others, aside from some other Karaites working in the central government who could be found in still other cities. I wonder whether Mr. Aṣlān was able to contact them and — more importantly — (knowing the habits of some Karaites) whether he received the needed response.

2. In Part 2 of his report he states that there are 68 main families. Of these families, 23 make up a total of 2,731, people while 45 make up a total of 1,103. This might be possible, yet a person well informed on Karaite families would question these findings, especially if we mention that, for example, families like al-Qudsī, Darwīsh, Yomtōb, Shamwel, Uziel, Fīrūz, Siyāhū, 'Abd al-Wāḥid, and others not included in the report among the families of the first group, supposedly had, on the average, less than 60 persons, which is not true.

3. There were some families (not too many) that were not known to everyone, and these were either the very rich or the very poor, and again I wonder whether Mr. Aṣlān was able to get the needed data about such families.

4. We must keep in mind that the Karaites, even in the 20th century, had the bad habit of not reporting the new-born to the bēt-dīn if it was a girl. That leads us to suggest that for this reason, not having all the females' names, Mr. Aṣlān was not able to analyze their names as he did with the males.

If we take all these points into consideration, then the total number of the Karaites in Egypt should be higher than 4,000. Mr. Aṣlān is not with us anymore, in order to check with him the details of his report and examine with him the sources of his data.

As for myself, I still remember vividly that in 1952, after the whole operation of the Maṣṣōt was completed, I personally checked at random some receipts of maṣṣōt sales to compare the number of maṣṣōt bought and the number of members of the family on each receipts, and I found, in accordance with our estimates, that each member used to consume 7 maṣṣōt during the holy day.

However, if we bear in mind that some Karaites used to buy more than they used to consume, in order to give their Egyptian friends some maṣṣōt (usually a package of 5 or 10) as a gift, or because they liked to keep them until the holiday is over, to prepare a favorite dish made of maṣṣōt and cheese (Karaites do not eat cheese during Passover), and some wealthy Rabbanite preferred the Karaite handmade maṣṣōt to the Rabbanite machine-made ones, then we can rightly assume that the number of Karaites in 1952 was somewhat less than 5,000, but not less than 4,000, as Mr. Aṣlān states in his report. We may safely round the figure off and make it 5,000.

Their Socio-Economic Status:

During the 19th century Jews in general, as well as all other minorities, witnessed a big improvement in their socio-economic status. Towards the end of that century money-changing became the function of the banks, and so Karaites, many of whom were money-changers, had to change their trade. More Karaites became gold- or silversmiths.

By the end of the 19th century most of the stores in al-Ṣāghah were owned by Karaites. The majority of the Karaites at that time used to live in the Jewish neighborhood known as "Ḥārat al-Yahūd al-Qarrā'īn," while few lived in what was then considered the fashionable parts of Cairo: 'Abbāsiyah, Ghamrah, Sakākīnī, and al-Ḍāhir.

At the turn of the century members of the community took steps to improve their status, and the local newspapers *Miṣr* and *al-Liwā'* took note of the improvement (*al-Tahdib* No. 2, 10 October 1902).

By the first quarter of the 20th century many young men graduated from Egyptian and European universities as doctors, lawyers, engineers, and teachers. From 1901 to 1956 there were more than 40 doctors, 50 engineers, 25 lawyers, and 25 teachers in this small community,[7] aside from many others who graduated from the faculties of commerce, science, agriculture, and from other academies.

Women had their share in education. They too, like men, worked for the central government.[8] As was always the case with minority members, they had to work for some time in small towns before they were transferred to large cities.

Gradually, the community began to enjoy prosperity, and some members became quite rich. Certain families acquired farmland in addition to their businesses.[9] The 'Abd-al-Wāḥid family was nicknamed "the Gold Kings." The Murād "Mordokh" family owned the largest and most modern of the gold-plated jewelry plants.[10] Among the best known jewellers were members of the Mas'ūdah and the Līsha' families. Another member of the Mas'ūdah family, Lieto Bārūkh Mas'ūdah, owned the largest recording company in the East, "Odéon." They were the sole contractors for — among others — Umm-Kulthūm, the "superstar of Egypt and the Arab world," for over fifty years.

A silver and metal factory owned by the two brothers Nagīb and Thābit furnished the mosques of Saudi Arabia for years with chandeliers and similar items. This factory was the best of its kind in the Middle East.

Two members of the Darwīsh family were able to establish the most modern facilities to process shrimps for export to Europe and the United States. The facilities were completed in 1957, and in 1961 they were sequestered by the government.

---

7. This figure was arrived at after careful examination of several records in the Karaite Bēt-Dīn and all Karaite periodicals during this period.
8. Rachel Marzūq was among the first women teachers in the country.
9. Among these families were the Līsha', Mas'ūdah, and the 'Abd-Allah families. (It was not easy for non-Muslims or non-Egyptians to acquire farmlands.)
10. Sharikat al-Gamal al-Miṣriyah.

Shālōm Mūsā Pessaḥ was credited with providing Egypt, as well as other countries of the Middle East, with "Primus stoves" when, at the time (during World War II), it was almost impossible to import them from any other country. ("Primus stoves" were the most common kitchen appliances at the time).

Few Karaites were in the financial field, although some were accountants or officers in banks. Jacques Mangūbī was considered one of the founders of the Bank Miṣr.

Al-Ṣāghah

In spite of changes and the fact that by the 1940's fewer Karaites were working as gold- or silversmiths, al-Ṣāghah was always associated with the word Karaite. Al-Ṣāghah was and still is the center of gold- and silversmithing, and also of jewellers. It is a neighborhood of less than one half square mile surrounded by Ḥārat al-Yahūd al-Quarrā'īn and Ḥārat al-Yahūd al-Rabbāniyīn. It had many shops that used to be owned by Karaites. In fact it was like a Karaite "town." During the first 40 years of the 20th century, most of the clientele came from among the Egyptian farmers. For this reason most of the gold and silver jewelry was fashioned to meet their taste and demands. After selling their crops the farmers preferred to save some money from their profits and, because they had no faith in banks at the time, they invested their savings in gold. They used to load their wives with heavy gold ankle-rings, heavy gold bracelets, necklaces and earrings.

In the 1940's during and after World War II jewellers and goldsmiths had to accommodate the "gold-diggers" who profited from the presence of the Allied forces in Cairo.

In al-Ṣāghah, shops used to open in the early morning and close at sunset. A good number of Karaite peddlers used to earn their living providing clean and Kasher food for their more fortunate brothers. In the morning they sold "fūl" (cooked fava beans), boiled eggs and "simīṭ" (a very large ring-shaped roll made with special flour). Fūl, prepared with olive oil, lime juice, chopped onions, tomatoes, and cucumber, is a dish that is hard to resist. For lunch they used to sell "pasta," fried fish, and shish-kabāb. Some Karaites used to bring their lunch with them in the morning, or a servant (usually Nubian) would deliver it to his master in a special container at noon-time. Between breakfast and lunch, as well as after lunch, the peddlers used to sell fruits, home-made cookies, coffee, tea, and cold drinks.

Friday was a good day for the peddlers, as they used to sell many items liked by Karaites: candies, chocolate, roasted seeds and fruits. Some poor members of the community, as well as from other communities, used to ask for charity, which they received.

On Saturday and on Sunday, activities in al-Ṣāghah, until the late 1940's, were at a minimum. Among the gold- and silversmiths of al-Ṣāghah a code was used that included some Hebrew words, especially numbers. Until today that code is used among silver- and goldsmiths, though none of them is Jewish.

Accompanying this bright picture of the community there was another, somber, one. There were more than one hundred-fifty members on the welfare list. The majority of them lived in "Ḥārat al-Yahūd" which for centuries was the neighborhood where most Jews — Rabbanites, Samaritans, and Karaites — lived.

This neighborhood was called "al-Ḥārah," and it will be referred to as such in the detailed discussion which follows.

Ḥārat al-Yahūd al-Qarrā'īn:

For many centuries there were Ḥārat al-Yahūd al-Rabbāniyīn, and Ḥārat al-Yahūd al-Qarrā'īn. The history of both is not a part of our work, yet it is important to know that both were a part of one large neighborhood and both were adjacent to each other.

During the period under discussion, both neighborhoods were considered parts of the al-Gamāliyah district, and they still are.

Ḥārat al-Qarrā'īn in the 19th and 20th centuries was about half a square mile. Its main road was " 'Aṭfit al-Yahūd al-Qarrā'īn," which during the 1970's and after the Karaites had left became " 'Aṭfit al-Miṣriyīn." It has many alleys and lanes, some of which still carry the names of the Karaite families that used to live there: 'Aṭfit Menashah, 'Aṭfit al Dabbāḥ, 'Aṭfit al-Muṣaffī. Until the 1930's Ḥārat al-Yahūd al-Qarrā'īn was inhabited by Karaites only.

The main road of al-Ḥārah was paved, but the alleys and the lanes were not. They were cleaned daily; nevertheless, they were always dusty and muddy, and eventually unclean.

The ugly look of the houses from outside was no indication of their condition inside. That was true at least until the 1940's. Usually each house has an open court around which the house was built. Windows that look out on the court are wider than the windows that look out on the road.

Most of the houses had all the necessary facilities: kitchens, bathrooms, running water, electricity. Few houses had natural gas.

Until World War I each house used to belong to one family, and until the 1960's, while walking with an elderly person through the alleys and lanes of al-Ḥārah, he or she would tell you "Līsha' al-Kabīr" used to live here, this house used to belong to "al-Shaykh Menashah," and so on. Little by little, at the turn of the century, some members of the community left al-Ḥārah to live in other more fashionable districts. Poor members of the community replaced them, and by the 1930's most of the residents were low-income families. However, until the 1950's there were some middle class families, and even the very well-to-do Shamwel family was still living there. This family took care of Nāṣir during the 1930's when his father remarried.

There were few shops: two or three groceries, a few cafes, one Kasher butcher, one European tailor and one Arab tailor, as most of the men and young men preferred the galabiyah and the quftān. Some owners of these shops were Muslims.

Because many men and young men among the residents of al-Ḥārah used to work for the Karaites of al-Ṣāghah, they used to get up very early, and so by six o'clock in the morning al-Ḥārah was almost in full activity. During the day it was relatively quiet, but in the evening it was different. When the men returned from work they met in the cafes to listen to the radio or to play backgammon. Sometimes gambling took place and the cafes stayed open until the early hours of the morning.

Until the turn of the century al-Ḥārah, on Friday nights, was completely dark; no lights outside or inside were permitted. Intruders took advantage of the situation, which forced the residents to ask the authorities to light the street lamps on Friday nights.

Among the Karaites there were several musicians who provided entertainment groups which usually performed on Saturday nights, as well as during the holy days. Dā'ūd Ḥusnī, the well-known Karaite composer and musician, started his career in al-Ḥārah. Such entertainment parties included belly dancers to begin with, then by ten o'clock in the evening the main event (the singing) began.

During the first quarter of the 20th century certain Karaites were experts at making fireworks. They used to make a good profit during Purim, Muslim and national holidays. But because of incidents where some Karaites were blinded, maimed or even killed, the government outlawed making or selling fireworks.

The chief of police of the al-Gamāliyah district was the person responsible for enforcing the law. It was not an easy task, as al-Ḥārah was considered a fortress.

During the holy days — and especially Purim and Passover — al-Ḥārah used to get a face lift. If it was Purim, then it was because many members of the community wanted to visit the old neighborhood and join their friends and relatives in the festivities. If it was Passover, it was because everything should be cleaned.[11]

The uniqueness of al-Ḥārah was the atmosphere that prevailed during the holidays and Saturdays. In the morning almost everyone attended the morning services. Some members of the community living in other neighborhoods would come to Rab-Simḥah synagogue to attend the service and to visit their relatives living in al-Ḥārah.

During lunch, wherever you went, you could smell the aroma of good food mixed with the piercing smells of thyme and ouzo. In the afternoon people used to congregate in the courtyards of the houses or the synagogue, or in the cafes. It was the custom that while congregating they used to nibble on cured lupines or roasted seeds. Karaites were known for roasting certain kinds of seeds in a special way that rendered them very tasty. Natives used to call these seeds "leb yahūdy" (Jewish seeds).

Residents of al-Ḥārah used to care about each other; they were all like one big family and in fact they were. All Karaites, in one way or another, are related to each other.

The *Shaykh al-Ḥārah* was a government official whose responsibility was to be able to identify every resident in the area of his jurisdiction. Until the early 1940's,

---

11. See under "Customs and Traditions" the activities in al-Ḥārah during Passover and Purim.

the *Shaykh Ḥārat al-Qarrā'īn* was a Karaite. He was the liaison between the authorities, especially the police, and the residents of al-Ḥārah. He also had other responsibilities, among which was reporting to the police any suspicious activity in his district. In the 1940's, when *Shaykh al-Ḥārah* was not a Karaite, he acted like a spy for the government.

A story about the *Shaykh al-Ḥārah* that goes back to the first half of the 19th century gives us an idea of the risk involved in this position. An ordinance was issued not to charge any fee when changing *al-Magīdī*, a coin honoring the Sulṭān 'Abd al-Magīd of Turkey (1839-1861). One Friday, while al-Muḥtasib was returning from al-Azhar mosque after the Friday noon prayer, he noticed a commotion. When he asked about it he was told that some Jews had broken the law and charged fees for changing *al-Magīdī*. He immediately called for their arrest. Most of the money-changers, at that time, used to have their businesses at Ḥārat al-Ṣayārifah (the money-changers district) which was at the entrance of Ḥārat al-Yahūd al-Rabbāniyīn from al-Muskī Street, which leads to al-Azhar mosque. The minute the money-changers sensed trouble they ran, followed by the agent of al-Muḥtasib. Two Rabbanites were caught; the third one, who was said to be a Karaite, fled to his neighborhood, Ḥārat al-Qarrā'īn. Residents of al-Ḥārah started to scream. When the Shaykh al-Ḥārah looked from his window and saw the agents of al-Muḥtasib, he came down quickly. When he was told the story he assured the agents that he would bring the Karaite to the authorities. Being afraid of al-Muḥtasib, the agents took the Shaykh al-Ḥārah, Yūsuf al-Baṣīr, with them. The three Jews were hanged at the entrance of Ḥārat al-Ṣayārifah.

The wife of the Shaykh al-Ḥārah, whose name was Mas'ūdah, took good care of her children, who became the grandparents of members of the Mas'ūdah families of today.

The Karaites and Their Relation with the Authorities and the Native Population:

Although Muḥammad 'Alī, the governor of Egypt from 1805 until 1848, granted the Christians and the Jews equal rights with the Muslims, still the majority of them were not treated so.

When the British occupied Egypt in 1882, Jews, like all other minorities, were granted and practiced equal rights with the Muslims. From that time on, the Jews enjoyed more freedom in all aspects of life.

The authorities, as well as the natives, willingly or unwillingly, changed their attitude towards the Jews. If a Jew had Egyptian nationality, then under the law of the land he had equal rights with an Egyptian Muslim. If a Jew had foreign protection, then he was protected under the system of capitulation.

As we have seen, most Karaites lived in Cairo and its suburbs. Some lived in other big cities, such as Alexandria, Ṭanṭā, and al-Manṣūrah. That, of course, does not include the central government employees who could be found in any city. Thus, when we talk about the Karaites of Egypt, we mean, in fact, the community of Cairo.

Small as the number of Karaites was, they were well known to almost everyone: the Muslim natives, the wealthy, the authorities and to all other communities.

The natives who had contact with the Karaites liked them because they felt that they, too, were natives; that is, they understood them and considered them Egyptians. (The Muslim natives felt that only Muslims could be considered true Egyptians.) It was common to hear one of them saying to a Karaite "Ya-khusartak fil-Yahūd" — "too bad you are a Jew" — a remark that was regarded by them as a compliment.

In general the Karaite is honest and a hard worker. He is naive in the sense that he is plain, good-hearted and that he trusts everyone. And while that caused trouble for some individuals, yet it also helped many to keep out of trouble during hard times.

By birth, the Karaite is an Egyptian. Most, if not all, his ancestors were born in Egypt. He is Egyptian by virtue of his physical characteristics, the way he talks, acts, and even the way he dresses.

Karaites used to send their children to Egyptian schools. Those who graduated from the universities as lawyers, doctors, teachers, engineers or another profession had their own share in serving the country with honesty and devotion. It is to the credit of the dedicated Karaite employee in the central government that the Karaite community enjoyed a good reputation among the people in authority.

The Karaites considered themselves part of the nation, sharing with it its struggle and its hope for a better future. When the head of the most popular political party (al-Wafd), Sa'd Zaghlūl Basha, died in 1927 the whole nation mourned him. The Karaite community joined the nation in sending representatives to attend the funeral. Many members of the community and the boy scouts participated in the funeral (al-Ittiḥād No. 10, 4th year, 1927).

The head of the Karaite community was invited to participate in all major events.[12] From the time of Ḥākhām Mangūbī, in 1876, until the last days of Ḥākhām Tobiah Babovitch, in 1956, the head of the Karaite community participated in almost all the national ceremonies. All invitations were formal and his place was always among the dignitaries (Pls 1-2).

During the High Holy days, a representative of the king, of the Prime Minister, and of the Governor of Cairo used to attend Karaite and Rabbanite services and deliver messages of good will.

When Passover approached, the government, upon request, would provide the community with the best wheat available to make maṣṣōt (unleavened bread for

---

12. In general, in all celebrations of national holidays, laying the foundation of new institutes, universities, projects, military parades, etc.

Passover). Even during World War II, when all commodities were scarce, that tradition was kept up.[13] A well-known mill used to kasher everything before grinding the wheat and bag it in special kasher bags for Passover, under the supervision of representatives from both communities.[14]

Under the law of the country, Muslims, Christians and Jews were equal, and in all practical respects they were equal. Yet in some cases the situation depended on the identity of the local authorities. In large cities the law was upheld, whereas in small towns a more provincial attitude was often found.

On the other hand Jews, including Karaites, were looked on as second-class citizens. During periods of political unrest it was common not to find Jews among the crowd; they were looked upon as "foreigners" *(khawagāt).*

Jews were not allowed to join the military or the police. The only exception to that was the case of four Karaites who were in the police force during the 1940's and the 1950's.

Jews were often the scapegoats for mishaps. In the last quarter of the 19th century and in the first decade of the 20th century, there were still false accusations of blood libels *(tuhmat al-dam).*

During World War II, when many commodities were in short supply, among them small change, kerosene, oil, rice, and sugar, everyone blamed the Jews for it.

A number of Karaites worked for the central government. It was an unwritten law to promote those employees only up to a certain grade, after which they had to choose between early retirement or remaining in that grade until retirement would normally occur.

During the Arab-Israeli wars of 1956 and 1967 many Karaites and Rabbanites were put into protective custody without trial or even interrogation. Many, especially younger people, suffered a great deal.

To sum up this part, one can say that during the last 100 years (1882-1986) three distinct periods are easily discernible. From 1882 until 1922 the Jews, Karaites included, were in a transitional period; there was not too much change. To be sure, some became rich, a few held high position in the central government, but the majority did not enjoy much prosperity, nonetheless changes — at the time — started to take place.

The golden years for the Karaites and the Rabbanites alike was the period from 1925 until 1945. During these 20 years Jews in general reached the peak of prosperity, of political and economic power. The Rabbanites considered themselves superior to the rest of the population. Rabbanites and Karaites alike did not care to apply for Egyptian nationality when, during the early 1940's, the law was changed to render

---

13. The Ministry of Provision used to double the ration of oil, sugar, and kerosene for members of the Jewish communities.
14. Maṭāḥin al-Rimālī — Rimali Mills.

it easier to obtain this nationality.

From 1948 until 1986 most of the Jews left the country; the "good old days" belonged to the past, and the future was never certain. Their number dwindled, their condition started to deterioriate, the property of those who left was confiscated, and many were left penniless.

To complete the picture about the Karaites of Egypt in the 20th century, one must mention three members of the community who left Egypt in the early years of the century and served with honor in three different countries.

Dr. Bārūkh Yūsuf Mas'ūdah: Left Cairo in 1914, when he was only thirteen years old, for the United States of America. A few years later he joined the army and became a naturalized citizen.

In 1922 he returned to Egypt after he had finished his higher education in the school of agriculture. His uncle asked him to manage his farm in al-Sharqiyah, in the eastern part of the Delta, but Bārūkh declined and instead accepted a teaching job at the American University in Cairo.

Three years later he returned to the United States to earn a doctoral degree in dentistry and later became one of the leading dentists in the country.

In 1955 he served his profession as the Chairman of the Dental Association of Philadelphia.

In 1956 he visited Cairo, Rome and Paris, where he lectured to dentists in these three capitals. He died in January 1986.

Dr. Shālōm Ibrāhīm Aṣlān: Born in Cairo in 1910. When he completed his secondary education he left for Paris.

In 1937 he earned a doctoral degree in medicine. Two years later, as a doctor, he joined the French army in Toulon where he was captured.

After the war he opened his own medical clinic in Ampus Var. While working in his profession he continued his education and earned a degree in tropical diseases.

Among his colleagues, Dr. Shālōm enjoyed a high reputation for his dedication. He died in 1984.

Ḥabīb Yūsuf Mas'ūdah (1919-1945): Left Cairo after he had completed his secondary education. In England he joined the British Royal Navy and became an engineer. Early in 1945 his mother was informed that her son Ḥabīb was missing in action.

Relations with the Karaite Abroad:

During the 18th and the 19th centuries, there was continual communication between the Karaites community in Egypt and the Karaite communities in the Crimea, Istanbūl, and Jerusalem.[15] This concerned mainly matters of common in-

---

15. Jacob Mann, *Texts and Studies in Jewish History and Literature,* J.P.S.A. 1935, pp. 321-333.

terest, legal affairs and financial help.

The community that received the greatest outside attention was the one in Jerusalem. As early as the 14th century, the Karaite community of Egypt, by way of endowments, had acquired some real estate in the heart of Jerusalem, around the old synagogue of 'Anān. In the 20th century, the Karaite community in Jerusalem was very small and most of its members were living in the old settlement around the synagogue of 'Anān. The Karaite community of Egypt was responsible for looking after this settlement and the Karaite members living in it. The persons appointed by the Karaite religious council in Cairo in the early years of the 20th century to be in charge of this settlement caused trouble and misunderstanding, and the minutes of the religious council from 1901 until 1945 explain why such a small community took up such a great deal of time at the meetings of the Cairo religious council during that period.

The Jersulaem Karaite community was one among dozens of Karaite communities that existed during most of the period we are covering: there were communities in Russia, Poland, Lithuania, parts of central Europe, in Turkey and in Bagdad. During that period anti-Semitism was always widespread, and Jews in general suffered from it. Jewish organizations played a major role in helping thousands of Jews escape to freedom. The Rabbanite community in Egypt, aided by several world Jewish organizations, was able to help those immigrants settle there.[16]

That was not the case with the Karaites. After examining carefully the minutes of the religious council and all Karaite publications during that period, it can be stated that the relationship was limited to the exchange of letters with members of other Karaite communities. And even that activity was promoted mostly by members of Karaite organizations in Cairo and not by the religious council (Pls. 3, 4 and 5).

The Cairo Karaite community could have set up a plan to study the situation of those communities that were in trouble and might have found a way to help them, or bring those who wished to Egypt.

It is my judgement that the various Karaite religious councils which governed the community during that period failed to take any steps to save the other Karaite communities or even to help some of its members. After World War I the Karaite community learned from two Russian Rabbanite officers about the plight of some Karaite officers in the Russian prisoner-of-war camp in Tal al-Kabīr in Egypt (Pl. 6). A member of the community who spoke Russian went there, and was able to locate a few Karaite officers.[17] They returned with him to Cairo and lived with him until he ran out of donated money. There is no record about the fate of these officers anywhere. I do not recall any Russians living among the Karaites of Egypt.

---

16. Landau J., *Jews in 19th Century Egypt*, pp. 23-25.
17. He was Elie Bārūkh Mas'ūdah.

It is not surprising, therefore, to hear nothing of Karaite immigrants in the Egyptian community.

In 1909, the Karaite community in Jerusalem, at that time numbering twenty-five persons, was in severe financial distress. They asked for help, and got twenty-five dollars, one dollar per person.[18] During World War II the same thing happened, and the Government of Palestine interfered on behalf of two Karaite sisters who were in distress (Pl. 7).

In 1910, the Karaite community in Hasköy, in Istanbūl, planned to build a new school. When they asked for help, they got the equivalent of thirty dollars.[19]

In 1925 the Karaite community in Istanbūl asked for support and received an apologetic refusal.[20] This happened again in 1942: the head of the Turkish Karaite community asked for one thousand Egyptian pounds (a little over two thousand five hundred dollars) to help pay the poll tax levied on all non-Muslims, and for the second time the Karaite community of Egypt denied the request. In that year, 1942, there were hundreds of Karaites in Cairo who could each have well afforded to contribute the money.[21]

In 1935 a Karaite rabbi in Theodosia in the Crimea asked for support. He received ten dollars.[22]

In 1945, Simon Szyszman, a Karaite scholar from a well-known family in Poland, fled to Italy, where he lived for a while. From there he sent a letter to the Karaite community in Egypt asking if they could help him enter the country, though not to live there permanently. Their reply was, "We cannot do anything."

In 1952, S. Szyszman wrote a strong letter urging the Karaite religious council to take all needed steps to send three young men to Paris so that he could help them study to become rabbis. Unfortunately, the efforts put into that request by the council were minimal.

These are just a few examples out of many that lead us to the conclusion that those who were administering the Karaite community chose to do nothing to help the Karaites abroad, nor even to help Karaite immigrants come to Egypt.

In the word of Simon Szyszman, "cependant, bien que saine et viable, cette communauté qui n'avait plus de relation avec les communautés soeurs, ne put tenir compte de leur expériences, ne sut comment se préserver, et subit le même sort que les autres."[23]

---

18. Minutes of March 1909.
19. Minutes of 5 May 1910.
20. Minutes of 22 October 1925.
21. Minutes of 31 December 1942.
22. Minutes of 14 January 1935.
23. S. Szyszman: *Le Karaïsme*, p. 102. (Although sound and viable, this community, which no longer had relations with its sisters-communities, was unable to understand their experience, did not know how to survive, and suffered the same fate as the others.)

Although I agree with Szyszman in his comment, I must, however, state here that the fate of the Karaite community in Egypt was the result of the political unrest in the Middle East which had begun in 1948, as was the fate of all the other non-Muslim or non-Egyptian communities, including, of course, the powerful and wealthy Rabbanite community.

Relations with the Jewish Mainstream:

As Leon Nemoy states, during the early period of Karaism, "a more or less amicable *modus vivendi* prevailed for a long time between the schism and the Rabbanic mother-synagogue, but in the first half of the 10th century, this peaceful situation came to an abrupt end when Sa'ādiah al-Fayyūmī condemned the Karaites as outright heretics."[24] Later, however, Maimonides stated his view that the Karaites "should be treated with respect, honor, kindness, and humility, as long as they do not slander the authorities of the Mishnah and the Talmud. They may be associated with, and one may enter their home, circumcise their children, bury their dead, and comfort their mourners."[25]

During the centuries that followed, there were periods of hostility and periods of rapprochement.[26] At times the Rabbanites tried to force the Karaites to join them in celebration of the holidays on particular dates, although the Karaite calendar prescribed other dates.[27] At that time also there was only one officially recognized religious head for all of the three communities, Rabbanite, Karaite and Samaritan.

In 1890, the Egyptian government acknowledged the Karaite community as separate and independent from the Rabbanite community.[28] From that time on, relations beween the two communities improved, reaching its peak at the end of the first quarter of the 20th century.

At that time the whole country was in a constructive mood. The Rabbanite community built schools (Les Lycées Juifs), dispensaries, and a modern hospital. Those institutions always favored Karaites when they were available. During the 1940's and the 1950's "Les Ecoles de la Communauté Israelite de Caire" had many Karaite teachers. The Jewish hospital at Ghamrah in Cairo had at least six Karaite doctors. The names Līsha', Mas'ūdah, Menasha, Marzūq, and al-Qudsī were well known in both institutions. During the period between the 1920's and the 1950's many Rabbanite welfare organizations had wealthy Karaites among their board members and sponsors. The names Mas'ūdah and Līsha' were at the top of these

---

24. *Encyclopedia of Islam,* 2nd ed., IV, 604.
25. *Encyclopedia Judaica,* (English, X, p. 781).
26. See Introduction.
27. The Karaite community in Ramlah has many documents indicating this fact.
28. *al-Irshād* No. 12, 11-1-1908.

lists[29] (Pl. 8). In fact, relations between the communities were so harmonious that rumors spread that the leaders of both communities were privately discussing unification.[30] Other members from both communities vehemently opposed such a movement (Pls. 9a and b).

The chief rabbis of both communities respected each other and were on very good terms. Ḥākhām Mangūbī was liked and respected by members of the Rabbanite community. They always invited him to all their ceremonies. He had a close relationship with their Ḥākhām Pāshā Raphael Ahārūn Simon.[31] The chief rabbi of the Karaite community Ḥākhām Kohen and the chief rabbi of the Rabbanite community Ḥākhām Nāḥūm had known each other prior to their coming to Cairo; they had both been born in Istanbūl.[32]

It is safe to say here that the friendly relationship between wealthy members of both communities helped produce smooth relations between the two communities. In 1940 Yūsuf Qaṭṭāwī Bāshā sent a letter of thanks to the Karaite religious council for offering the girls' school as a home for Jewish immigrants.

For almost 30 years (1926-1956) over 200 Karaite students studied in Rabbanite schools each year. Many paid full tuition, and the Karaite Bēt-Dīn paid over 800 dollars each year to cover those who qualified for free or reduced tuition (Pl. 10).

Almost all poor Karaites in need of health care were able to receive it at the Jewish hospital. The Karaite Bēt-Dīn, in this case also, sent yearly financial help. It was traditional during the holiday of Simḥāt Torah to collect money in both Karaite synagogues for the Jewish Hosiptal.

During the first half of the 20th century leaders of both communities worked together to face the common problem of changing the civil code and the judiciary system on those matters that affected the minorities: religious courts, probate courts, laws of inheritance, and public notaries.

Rabbanite writers wrote in Karaite periodicals.[33] Dr. Hillel Farḥī and Dr. Alfred Yalūz were well known to the Karaite reader. In addition to their writings, both lectured regularly at the headquarters of various associations (Pl. 11). Conversely, as early as 1906, Murād Farag, the prominent Karaite author and poet, wrote in *Israel,* a Rabbanite magazine published in Egypt in Arabic, Hebrew, and French.

The Rabbanite community depended on members of the Karaite community to train performing companies in the Rabbanite schools. The orchestra of the Young Men's Karaite Association participated in almost all related Rabbanite activities (Pl. 12).

---

29. Al-Shubbān al-Qarrā'īn No. 2, p. 10, 5-2-1937.
30. *Al-Ittiḥād* No. 20, 12-28-1924, No. 11, 3rd year, p. 6. 9-7-1926.
31. *Al-Irshād* No. 12, 11-1-1908, p. 90
32. *Al-Ittiḥād* #1 Second year. 4-25-1925
33. *Al-Irshād, al-Ittiḥād, al-Shubbān al-Qarrā'īn,* and *al-Kalīm.*

Starting in 1956, the Rabbanite Bēt-Dīn took care of all necessary steps for immigration for all Jews, regardless of their religious affiliation.

Relations with Other Communities

Since the Arab conquest of Egypt in 641 A.D., Jews and Christians, or *ahl al-dhimmah* or *ahl al-kitāb,* as they were called, were treated equally. It is a fact that during certain periods of that long history the Copts, who are the Orthodox Egyptian Christians, and who consider themselves the descendants of the Pharaohs, were entrusted with many influential positions in the Muslim administration, and it is also a fact that when the Copts were in a position of power they mistreated the Jews. At times, the Jews held key positions in the government and during such times they favoured their own people.

Relations between Jews and Christians were never, in general, smooth. Besides the religious factor there was also the economic one: Jews were rivals to the Christians in trade.

In the period we are covering there was no apparent animosity between the Jews and the Christians, but the true feeling between these groups was known to everyone. Yet it is strange enough to state here that most, if not all, the Karaites of al-Ṣāghah, as well as many Egyptian Rabbanite businessmen of al-Ḥamzāwī, al-Muskī, and al-Azhar (neighborhoods near al-Ṣāghah), entrusted Copt bookkeepers with their bookkeeping. These Copts in most cases inherited the businesses of their employers when the latter left the country.

In Egypt, and especially in Cairo, Alexandria, and most major cities, there were other large non-Muslim communities, among the more important of which were the Greek and the Italian communities.

In the common interest, representatives of all the non-Muslim communities met regularly to share views and ideas. The Karaite religious leaders always maintained a good relationship with the religious leaders of those communities.

It was the custom that no member of any community could change his faith without going through certain procedures.

If, for example, a Karaite wished to become affiliated with the Rabbanite faith, he would first apply to the Rabbanite Bēt-Dīn, which would then inform the governor of Cairo. He, in turn, would inform the Karaite Bēt-Dīn, which would send a ḥākhām or any well-informed member of the faith to try to persuade that person to change his mind. That custom was never broken, even if the person wanted to convert to Islam.

Bārūkh Lisha', and his wife Mas'ad Farag Mas'ūdah. Both from well known Karaite families.

Lieto Bārūkh Mas'ūdah — during the last quarter of the 19th century.

A typical well-to-do Karaite family. The picture is of Bārūkh Kohen, his wife Fortuné Mas'ūdah, and their daughter and sons. The picture was taken in 1914.

A unique photo of Karaite gathering. The pictures were taken in the farm of the Mas'ūdah family (les Bārūkh) in their farm in al-Sharqiyah in the eastern part of the Nile Delta. Both pictures were taken in April celebrating Yom Sham al-Nassīm, a national holy day. The first one was taken in April of 1917, the second in April of 1937 in which we can identify members of the Mas'ūdah, Iīsha', Kohen, 'Abd al-Wāḥid, and al-Qudsī families.

Members of the Darwīsh, Maṣliyaḥ, Marzūq, Līshaʿ, Mordokh, and al-Qudsī families in a family gathering (1956).

Members of the Līshaʿ, al-Qudsī, Kohen, and Masʿūdah families in a wedding party. (1960)

Lieto Yūsuf al-Qudsī (in the middle) with his sons and daughters, his sons-and daughters-in-law, and his grand-children. (1958)

A Karaite gathering: from left to right ... Dr. Elie Līshaʿ, a very well known eye specialist; Joseph Bārūkh Masʿūdah, Zaki Bārūkh Līshaʿ, both jewelers; Dr. Albert B. Līshaʿ, a gynecologist; Murād Yūsuf al-Qudsī, a high-ranking engineer in the central government. (1960)

Dr. Bārūkh L. Masʿūdah

Dr. Shālōm Aṣlān

Ḥabīb Masʿūdah

Members of the Karaite community in Jerusalem in 1925. The picture was taken in front of the old synagogue of ʿAnān in the old part of the city. In the middle is Elīyāhū Sinānī, the superintendent of the Karaite real estate in Jerusalem. To the far left and right are the two daughters of Ḥākhām David al-Dimashqī, brother of Ḥākhām Mosheh al-Qudsī II, the ḥākhām akbar of the Karaite community of Cairo.

يتشرف وزير الأشغال العمومية بأن يدعو جناب الحترم
رئيس طائفة الإسرائيليين القرائيين

الى الحفلة الرسمية التي سيتفضل بتشريفها حضرة صاحب الجلالة الملك لافتتاح محطة الأميرية لرفع مياه مجاري مدينة القاهرة في الساعة ٤-٣٠ بعد ظهر يوم الخميس ٢٥ أبريل سنة ١٩٢٩.

ملاحظة: هذه التذكرة شخصية والحضور يكون بالردنجوت لغير ذوى الملابس البلدية

a-

يتشرف وزير الأشغال العمومية بأن يدعو جناب الحترم رئيس طائفة القرائيين
محضوره في صيوان البوفيه الخصوصي الذى سيتفضل بتشريفه حضرة صاحب الجلالة الملك عقب الحفلة الرسمية التي ستقام في الساعة ٤-٣٠ بعد ظهر يوم الخميس الموافق ٢٥ أبريل ١٩٢٩ لافتتاح محطة الأميرية التي أنشئت لرفع مياه مجاري مدينة القاهرة.

b-

PLATE 1: The Minister of Public Works invites the Head of the Karaite Community:
a) To attend the official ceremony that will be honored by King Fu'ād to celebrate the inauguration of a sanitary project;
b) To attend the Private Buffet that will be held immediately after the ceremony and which will be honored by King Fu'ād. Thursday April 25, 1929 at 4:30 P.M.

(ج)

محافظة مصر

برسم حضرة المحترم الخواجة يوسف ابراهيم مرزوق
لدخول محطة مصر بمناسبة تشريف حضرة صاحب
الجلالة الملك فاروق الأول مدينة القاهرة فى يوم الأربعاء
٦ مايو سنة ١٩٣٦ الساعة ١٢ والدقيقة ٣٥

الملابس — الردنجوت

والحضور للمحطة يكون الساعة ١٢ والدقيقة ١٥ والدخول والخروج من
الباب الشرقى الكائن بجوار المحطة
والمرجو تقديم هذه التذكرة عند دخول المحطة

a-

يتشرف اللواء أركان الحرب عبد الحكيم عامر القائد العام للقوات المسلحة
بدعوة حضرة ....
لمشاهدة العرض العسكرى الذى سيجرى احتفاء بحضرة صاحب الجلالة

الملك سعود بن عبد العزيز آل سعود

بميدان الجمهورية فى الساعة العاشرة صباح يوم الأحد ٢١ مارس سنة ١٩٥٤

b-

PLATE 2: An invitation from the Governor of Cairo to the acting chairman of the Karaite community, Yūsuf Ibrāhīm Marzūq, to be at main railway station of Cairo to welcome King Fārūq.
May 6, 1936, 12:35 A.M.* (a)

*Ḥākhām Tobiah Babovitch had not yet been acknowledged by the Egyptian government as the Ḥākhām Akbar of the Karaite Community of Egypt.

'Abd al-Ḥakīm 'Amir, Commanding General of the Egyptian Armed Forces, invites Ḥākhām Tobiah Babovitch, the Ḥākhām Akbar of the Karaite Jews, to attend the military parade that will be held on 21 March 1954 in honor of King Sa'ūd ibn 'Abd al-'Azīz Al-Sa'ūd. (b)

القراؤون في الخارج   تركيا (١)

تكونت في جمعية الشبان الاسرائيليين القرائين بمصر لجنة باسم « القراؤون في الخارج » ، غرضها ايجاد رابطة دينية وثقافية واجتماعية بين جميع قرائي العالم . وتتكون اللجنة من حضرات الافندية ايلي يوسف مرزوق وبركات أمين الجبل وجهاد رحمن وزكريا وفرج يعقوب أصلان . وقد بدأت اللجنة عملها وعقدت عدة اجتماعات لذلك راسلت اللجنة من عناوين قرائية قديمة كانت لدى الجمعية منذ عام ١٩٣٩ . وبلغت عدد الرسائل المصدرة ٣٥ رسالة إلى جميع أنحاء العالم الا أن الردود التي وصلت كانت من استانبول (تركيا) وهيت (العراق) والقدس (فلسطين) ولوزان (سويسرا) وباريس (فرنسا) . وسيلخص كل عضو باللجنة أهم محتويات الرسائل المتبادلة وذلك الى أن يتوفر لدى اللجنة عدة عناوين في جهة معينة فستعلن اللجنة عن ذلك للطائفة لمن يرغب في مراسلتها ومعرفتها .
وكانت اللجنة تأمل أن يساعدها كل من لديه عناوين لقرائين بالخارج ولكن بالأسف الشديد امتنع بعضهم عن المساعدة وادلى بهذه البيانات لها . ونأمل أن يعدل هؤلاء الافراد عن مسلكهم هذا ويساعدون اللجنة بالعناوين الموجودة طرفهم.
ونلخص في هذا العدد رسالتين متبادلتين بين سيادة الحاخام الاكبر اسحق كريم بتركيا وبين اللجنة

ورسالة تركيا الأولى التي هي رد على نداء اللجنة مكتوبة باللغة العبرية الفصحى محطة يد على المنهج القرائي استهلها سيادته بالسلام والتحية والبركة لقرائي مصر وقرائي العالم وسرور الطائفة بتركيا بغرض اللجنة الشريف الذى تسعى اليه وذكر أنه في عام ٦٨٧ عبرية كان قد أرسل نداءات لعائلة لقرائي العالم بهذا المغزى ومنها طائفتنا في مصر ولكنه بالأسف الشديد لم يحظ برد ما آلمه كثيرا ولذلك كان نداء اللجنة كالبلسم الشافي لجراحه . وقد جاء في الرسالة أنه على أتم استعداد لموافاة اللجنة بأسماء وعناوين جميع القرائين الذين يعرفهم سواء في تركيا أو الخارج وطلب بالحاح منا أن نداوم على مراسلته وعدم قطع هذه الصلة مطلقا واختتم رسالته بتشجيع اللجنة والدعاء لها بأن نصحبنا بأعلى النصائح وطلب أيضا تبلغ سلام طائفته لكل قرائي مصر وتبليغ سلامه الشخصي لسيادة حاخامنا الأكبر وللحضرة الأستاذ مراد بك فرج والوجيه أبد زكى ليشع حفظه الله وكل قرائي مصر كبيرا وصغيرا .

وقد قام حضرة الحاخام يوسف فرج حيينا بترجمة هذا الخطاب الى اللغة العربية كما قام بتحرير وترجمة الرد الى اللغة العبرية أيضا فله منا جزيل الشكر .

وردت اللجنة على خطاب سيادته بتحية أحسن وتبليغ سلامه إلى كل القرائين في تركيا والخارج وأبلغته أن وصول الخطاب البنا من تركيا ليعتبر فاتحة باب خير وصلاح للطائفة كلها في العالم .

وطلبت اللجنة من حضرته موافاتها بيانات أسماء وعناوين القرائين حسب ما وعدها مؤكدة له استمرار المراسلة بيننا وابلاغه أن مجلة الطائفة بمصر « مجلة الكليم » ترسل اليه منذ صدورها
واختتمت اللجنة خطابها بالدعاء وابلاغ سلامه الى من ذكرهم في مصر مرحبة باستمرار الكتابة إلى قرائي تركيا .

وسننشر في العدد القادم انشاء الله مراسلات قرائي سويسرا

بقلم الزميل بركات أمين الجبل أفندى   اللجنة

PLATE 3: The Karaites Abroad: Turkey
In 1947 some members of the "Young Men's Israelite Karaite Association" formed a committee with one goal in mind: to establish a relationship with as many Karaites abroad as possible. The committee sent 39 letters to various countries. It received answers from Istanbūl, Jerusalem, Lausanne, Hīt in Iraq, and from Paris.
This is the first letter received from the Ḥākhām Akbar of Turkey, Ishac Kirimi, in which he mentions that he had carried out earlier attempts to communicate, but was unsuccessful. He wishes the committee good luck and asked to convey his best regards to Ḥākhām Tobiah, to Murād Farag, and to David Līsha'.
Yūsuf Hayyīnah translated Kirimi's letter into Arabic and the committee's letter into Hebrew. *al-Kalīm,* no. 49, February 16, 1947.

MARCONI RADIO TELEGRAPH COMPANY OF EGYPT, S.A.E.
ASSOCIATED WITH
THE EASTERN TELEGRAPH COMPANY LIMITED.

11.4.49

ADDRESS:
LC
ISHAC KIRLMI
183 BAHRIYA CADDESSI KASSIMPAZA
ISTANBUL

PAQUE JEUDI

Tovia Babovitch

Signature and Address of Sender: TOVIA BABOVITCH
50, RUE K' ONFISH, LE CAIRE

PLATE 4: A telegram sent by Ḥākhām Tobiah Babovitch, Ḥākhām Akbar of the Karaite community of Cairo, to Ishac Kirimi, the head of the Karaite community in Turkey, informing him that the first day of Passover (1949) is on Thursday.

القراؤون في الخارج

كتبنا في عدد مضى ملخص الرسالتين المتبادلتين بين قراي تركيا وبين لجنة القرائين في الخارج التي كونتها جمعية الشبان القرائين ونكتب اليوم ملخص خطاب بيننا وبين المسيو ليون صديق المقيم بلوزان بسويسرا - ترجمها ونقلها إلى اللغة العربية حضرة الزميل بركات افندي امين الجيل .

حضرات المحترمين

تسلمت بمزيد السرور خطابكم الدوري الذي وجهتموه إلى جميع قراي العالم وأني أبلغكم أني على استعداد تام للمساهمة في غرضكم الشريف الثقافي والانساني والاجتماعي الذي تنشدونه

أنكم تسألوني عن القرائين الموجودين الآن في أنحاء العالم فأخبركم :

اني قد عدت الآن من رحلة طويلة جبت أثناءها انجلترا وهولندا وبلجيكا وايطاليا وغيرها من دول أوروبا وأنه لا يوجد في الوقت الحاضر طائفة بمعنى الكلمة في الغرب الا في باريس مدينة النور اذ انه يوجد بها حوالي ٢٠٠ قراي اغلبهم من الروس وبعضهم من اسطنبول ، وهذه الطائفة للاسف مفرقة في جميع أنحاء باريس وينقصها حاخام وأحزان ليلم شملها في أيام السبت والاعياد والمواسم الدينية . اما في الدول الاخرى فانه يوجد على ما اعلم عدد قليل في لندن (انجلترا) وفي برلين (المانيا) وفي ميلانو (ايطاليا) وعدة اشخاص في السويد هربوا في أثناء الحرب من دول البلطيق . وقليل منا في سويسرا من عائلة صديق التي انتمي اليها ونحن مقيمون فيها من حوالي ٣٠ سنة .

وقد مر علي في العام الماضي وأنا بجنيف أحد افراد عائلة صديق - وهي عائلة لا تنتمي الى عائلتنا باية قرابة - ويدعى يونيا صديق وهو من بلاد العراق واخبرني أنه يوجد في العراق

عائلة صديق ماير التي تقطن بغداد والموصل والبصرة وعمرة وهي عائلة قرائية وأني أرجو من حضرتكم التكرم بافادتي عما اذا كنتم على علم بهذه العائلة التي اعتقد أنها لا تؤمن الا بالتوراة فقط .

وفي انتظار خطابكم تفضلوا ايها الاصدقاء والزملاء سلاما أخويا .
امضاء (ليون صديق)

فردت عليه اللجنة بما يأتي :

حضرة المحترم

لقد تسلمنا خطابكم المؤرخ في ٢٥ - ١٢ - ١٩٤٦ بمزيد السرور ونحن نرجو منكم كي نستطيع أن نراسل جميع القرائين في العالم ان تدلونا على عناوين القرائين المقيمين بباريس ولندن وبرلين وايطاليا والسويد والبلاد الاخرى .

واننا لا نعلم شيئاً عن عائلة صديق التي تقيم بالعراق والمشار اليهم في خطابكم غير أننا نعلم أن قراي العراق مقيمون بقرية (هيت ، ولنا معهم اتصال ولقد طلبنا منهم استعلامات عن هذه العائلة ونكون شاكرين لو تفضلتم بموافاتنا باسم وعنوان الشخص الذي مر عليكم بجنيف لكي نتمكن من مراسلته .

هذا وقد أرسلنا اليكم مجلة ، الكليم ، التي تنشرها جمعيتنا كتذكار لكم من قراي القاهرة ولو أنها تصدر باللغة العربية . ولا مانع عندنا من نشر أخبار القرائين بسويسرا ونشر صورهم . ونأمل أن تتوالى الخطابات بيننا وبين قراي العالم .

وفي انتظار خطابكم تفضلوا بقبول فائق الاحترام ؟
امضاء (لجنة القرائين بالخارج)

وسننشر في العدد القادم ان شاء الله القرائين في العراق
(هيت) بقلم حضرة الزميل ابلي يوسف مرزوق افندي :

PLATE 5: The Karaite Abroad: Switzerland
A letter from Leon Ṣaddīq indicating that at the time (1946) there were a few Karaites in London, Milan, Berlin, and Sweden.
The letter indicates also that a family by the name Ṣaddīq, though not related, lives in Mosul, Baṣrah, and 'Amrah in Iraq.
The committee replied to Mr. Ṣaddīq's letter requesting some addresses.

V.—CONSULAT DE RUSSIE
AU CAIRE

Dated 5 June 1920

N° 824

Sir,

Will you kindly give necessary instructions to allow to Mr. E. B Massoude to visit the Russian camp and hospital of Tel-el-Kebir

I am, Sir,
Yours truly
I. Malex
Russian Consul

Inspector
Prisoners of war
Egypt

Mr Massoude has permission to visit the Russian Camp & Hospital of Tel-el-Kebir.

7. 6'. 20

LIEUT. CO...
INSPECTOR
PRISONERS OF WAR CAMPS. E...

PLATE 6: A letter to the Inspector, Prisoners of War, Egypt, requesting permission to visit the Russian camps and hospital of Tel-el-kebir.

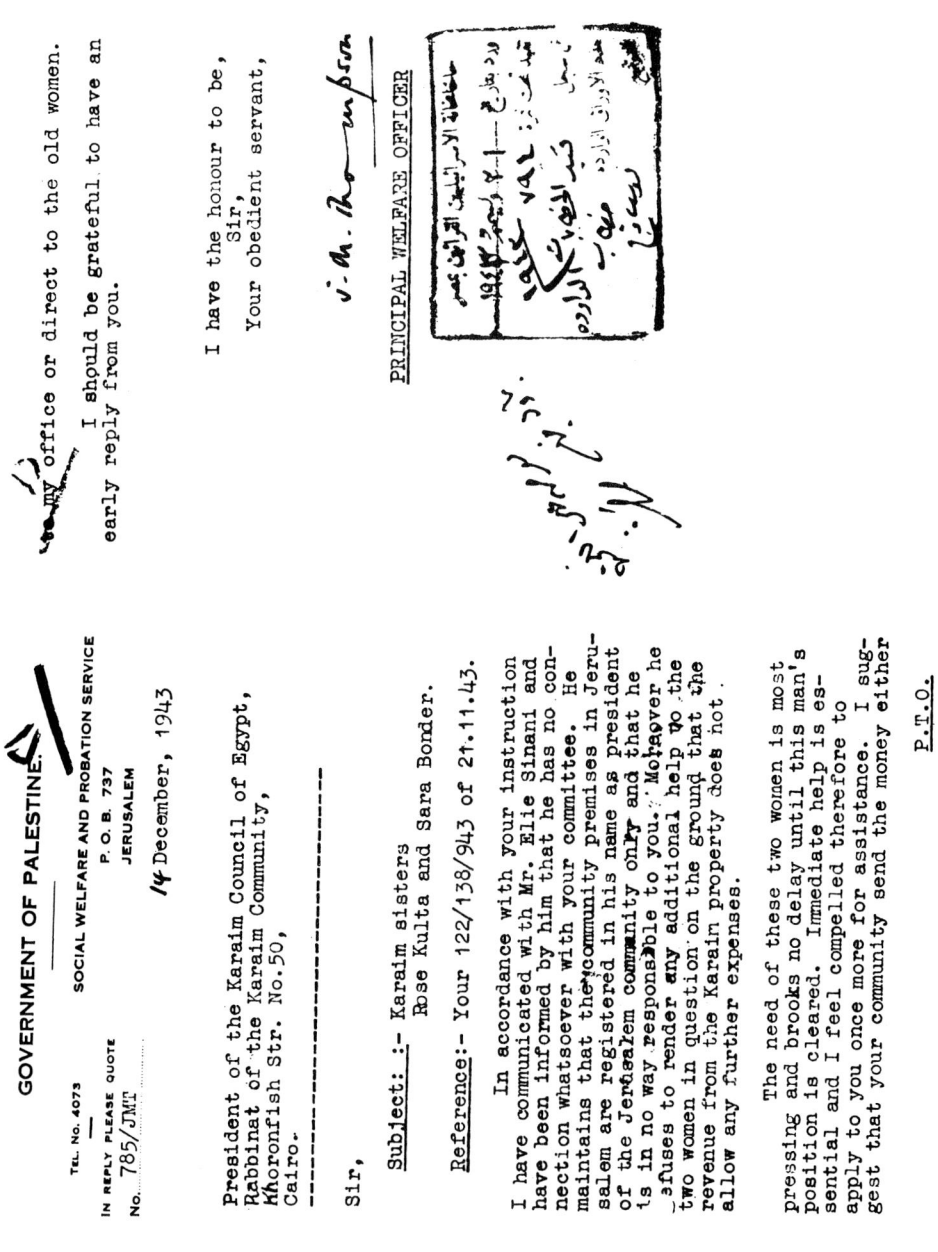

PLATE 7: A letter from the Principal Welfare Officer of the Government of Palestine to the Karaite Religious Council of Egypt requesting financial help to the two Karaite sisters Rose Kulta and Sara Bonder.

The Karaite Religious Council sent 8 Egyptian pounds. The amount includes two Egyptian pounds, a donation from two (very wealthy) members!!!

A LA GOUTTE DU LAIT

Dimanche 25 Avril 1937

Chaque année à pareille date la Goutte du Lait, œuvre philanthropique de la plus grande importance, abritant les orphelins et les pauvres de toutes les races et de toutes les religions, leur donnant une éducation morale et intellectuelle suffisante pour leur permettre plus tard de pourvoir à leur besoin quotidien, donnait Dimanche dernier 25 courant, dans ses vastes jardins un Tea-Party des plus réussis, qui comprenait dans son programme plusieurs sketchs, et prit fin dans la gaîté générale par un small Dance.—

Parmi les personnalités Caraïtes qui s'y trouvaient, nous citons au hasard du crayon : Mr. & Mme Baroukh Liéto Baroukh, Mme. Khadr Yaphet Massouda & Melle, Dr. Joseph Tawil, Dr. Albert Lichaa, Mr. Joseph Zaki Lichaa, Mr. Albert Sadik d'Istamboul, et Melle. Sarah Cohen.

Nous nous faisons un devoir de rappeler à nos chers correligionnaires que l'Institut de la Goutte de Lait abrite une cinquantaine de nos garçons et filles, à titre purement gratuit.

Nous prions les dirigeants de la Goutte du Lait de croire à notre sympathie, et que nous remerçons pour leur bienveillance

Notons que Mr. Baroukh Liéto Baroukh est Vice-Président de la Goutte du Lait. —

Jos. Cohen

PLATE 8: Some rich members of the Karaite Community were active in the various benevolent associations of the Rabbanite Community. Among these was the "Goutte du Lait" ("The Drop of Milk").

In the first issue of *al-Shubbān al-Qarrā'īn,* 2 May 1937, this article appeared.

القرّاؤون في مصر
هل من خطر يهدد كيانهم الملي؟؟

تحت هذا العنوان كتب المسيو سام ليڤي صاحب ومحرر
دليل سام ..السنوي..كلمة عن القرائين في مصر سنة ١٩٢٥ الماضية
ونقلناها في حينه علي صفحات هذه المجلة تحت عنوان ذو كيان
الطائفة الملي في خطر.. وحملنا فيها علي أعيان الطائفة الذين
يدعون انهم يمثلون مجموع الطائفة في ابدائهم التصريحات التي
جاءت في هذه الكلمة واستنكرنا الاعمال التي نسبها اليهم
صاحب الدليل

PLATE 9a: " 'The Karaites of Egpyt.'

Is there any danger threatening their religious status? Under this title Sam Levy, the owner and editor of the annual guide 'Sam's Guide,' wrote an article about the Karaites of Egypt in 1925. We published the article in due time under the title 'The Religious Status of the Community is in Danger.' We criticized the leaders of the community who claimed that they represented the whole community in making the declarations that were included in the article, as we disapproved of the acts attributed to them by the owner of the Guide."

al-Ittiḥād, no. 11, 3rd year, 7 September 1926.

الاتحاد

كيان الطائفة الملّى فى خطر
أغنياؤنا المفكرون يقررون ضم الطائفة

نلخص فيما يلى بعض ماقاتله زميلتنا الاورور فى العدد ٤٢ بتاريخ ٥ الجارى عن دليل سام لسنة ١٩٢٥ الذى صنفه المسيو سام لفى فى باريس خاصا بنا نحن القرائين المصريين نظراً لخطورته وربما عربنا ونشر ناجيم ما جاء فى هذا الدليل خاصا بنا

«من مدة ربع قرن تقريباً هبت روح جديدة على طائفة القرائين بمصر فالمدارس من جهة وحالة الطوائف اليهودية الشرقية والغربية التى تأسست واستقرت فى هذه البلاد من جهة أخرى دفعت بالقرائين المصريين الى الارتقاء والتمدن الحديث. فالكثيرون من طبقة الاغنياء الموسرين بينهم هجروا حى أسلافهم الاولين وهرعوا الى سكنى الاحياء الجديدة وهم يرسلون أولادهم الى المدارس الاوروبية وحتى الى بلاد أوروبا ويسيرون بعزم وثبات نحو تحرير أنفسهم والاحسن من ذلك (اسمعوا اسمعوا) استولت على نفوسهم أفكار وبدع جديدة اذ يوجد بين القرائين بمصر الان الكثيرون من الاغنياء المفكرين الجديرين بكل اعتبار واحترام يسرون من وقت لاخر من مزيد تأخرهم واضطرابهم

من تلك الفوارق القليلة التى تفصل مذهبهم عن باقى اليهود ولكى يصلوا الى تقريب ـ مسافة الافتراق بل قل الى ضم طائفتهم بحثوا عن الطرق التى تمكنهم من ازالة الفواصل التى وضعت فى طريق انضمامهم الى اخوانهم اليهود الاخرين ولتحقيق هذه الغاية أو أى شكوا ألجنة خاصة منهم كلفوها بمفاوضة اخواننا فى ايجاد حل لهذه المسألة. ولغاية الان لم تصل هذه اللجنة الاولى فى نوعها الى تحقيق الغرض التى كلفت به ولكن على كل حال قد مهدت الطريق وقريبا باذن الله نرى أنفسنا بانضمام هذه الطائفة» اه

وفى هذا القدر الكفاية للدلالة على خطورة الحالة التى أوصلتنا اليها تصرفات أعيانا القابضين على زمام ادارة مصالحنا بالحاخامخانة

PLATE 9b: The Religious Status of the Community is in Danger
Our Concerned Rich Decide to be Affiliated with the Rabbanites

A summary of what was published in *L'Aurore,* no. 42, 5 December 1925, which was taken from *Sam's Guide,* written in Paris by Sam Levy. The article is about the "Karaites."

"A quarter of a century ago a new spirit filled the air among the Karaites of Egypt. The improved situation of the Sephardic and Ashkenazic Jews forced the Karaites to follow the path of modern civilization. A large number of their rich people left the Jewish neighborhood, where their ancestors used to live, and moved to Heliopolis. They have made up their minds to liberate themselves.

More importantly (listen to this) they were possessed by these new ideas and innovations. Among the Karaites now there are many rich people worthy of our respect who express their unhappiness because of the few little differences that separate them from the Jewish mainstream. They have already formed a committee to look into ways to narrow the gap between the two communities and to carry on negotiations to find a solution. Shortly we hope to congratulate ourselves when the Karaites join us."

اعلان

من لجنة مساعدة الطلبة غير القادرين على دفع المصروفات بمدارس الطائفة الاسرائيلية

ليكن في علم جميع أبناء الطائفة الذين يرغبون في الحصول على اعانات لالحاق أبنائهم بمدارس الطائفة الاسرائيلية في العام المقبل (٥٢ / ١٩٥٣) أن اللجنة ستطبق بكل دقة قرارات المجلس الملي في شأن إعانات الطلبة في المصاريف المدرسية

هذا ولن تمنح اللجنة أية إعانة للطلبة : ـ

١ ـ الملتحقون بقسم الحضانة (ماترنيل) ٢ ـ الراسبون في الامتحان عام ٥١ / ١٩٥٢

كما أن اللجنة قررت منع المجانية منعاً باتاً

اللجنة

مراد موسى القدسى ـ فرج يعقوب وأصحابه

أما عن الطلبة القرائين بمدارس الطائفة الاسرائيلية فعددهم قد بلغ ٢٤١ طالباً منهم ٦٨ طالبا يدفعون مصاريف كاملة ، و ٧٢ طالبا يدفعون مصاريف مخفضة . و ١٠٦ طالب معانين من الطائفة .

ونحن ما زلنا سائرين على احترام اتفاقنا مع مدارس إخواننا الاسرائليين .

ولا ننسى أن نذكر هنا بمناسبة الكلام عن المدارس أن المجلس الملي لا يألو جهداً في مساعدة كل من يرغب في إتمام دراسته العالية والمعاهد الخاصة ولا تسمح ظروفه المالية بتحقيق هذا الغرض .

PLATE 10: There were over two hundred Karaite boys and girls studying each year in the "Lycée Juifs" of the Rabbanite Community in Cairo. Some of these students were on reduced or free tuitions. The Karaite Bēt-Dīn used to pay the yearly difference. This ad appeared in al-Kalīm for the boys and girls who were not paying full tuitions.
al-Kalīm, no. 169, 8th year, 1 August 1952. (a)

According to the Annual Report of the Karaite Community of Cairo for the year 1952, there were 241 Karaite students studying in the "Lycée Juifs," 63 paying full tuition, 72 on reduced tuition and 106 on free tuition.
al-Kalīm, no. 180, 1 March 1953. (b)

القى الدكتور الفريد يلوز .محاضرة قيمة عن « فضل اليهود على حضارة العالم » وذلك بدار جمعية الشبان الاسرائيليين القرائين وبها اختتم موسم المحاضرات فى هذه السنة .

PLATE 11: Dr. Alfred Yalūz gave a lecture on "The Contribution of the Jews to World Civilization" at the headquarters of the Young Men's Karaite Association.
al-Shubbān, no. 6, 2 July 1937.

يلقى حضرة العالم الكبير الدكتور هلال فارحى من مشاهير الادبا. الباحثين محاضرة شائقه فى الساعة الثامنة من مسا. السبت 5 يونية سنة 1937 وذلك بدار جمعية الشبان الاسرائيليين القرائين ، موضوعها (عصر مملكة اليهود الذهبي فى عهدى داود وسليمان) والدعوة ، عامة للجميع .

Dr. Hillel Farḥī will deliver on Saturday evening, at 8:00 o'clock, at the headquarters of the Young Men's Israelite Karaite Association, an interesting lecture on "The Golden Age of the Jewish Kingdom" during the time of David and Solomon. All are invited.
al-Shubbān, no. 4, 2 June 1937

حفلة مدرسة الليسيه الاسرائيلى

كان يوم الاحد الماضى الحفلة السنوية لمدرسة الليسيه الاسرائيلى وقد كان الاقبال عليها كبيرا مما يدل على ماتتمتع به هذه المدرسة من التشجيع والحب والعطف . وقد نجحت الحفلة نجاحا كبيرا ولاقت هتافا منقطع النظير وقد كان أوركستر نادى الشبان الاسرائيليين القرائين رياسة المايسترو الياهو أصلان بهجة هذه الحفلة . وكذلك درب طلبة المدرسة وأخرج الروايات الاستاذ ابراهيم حسنى رئيس فرقة التمثيل بالنادى فنحن نهنى. ادارة هذه المدرسة الناشئة ونتمنى لها دوام التقدم والنجاح .

PLATE 12: The Annual Festival of the "Lycée Juif"
Last Sunday (27 June 1937) the "Lycée Juif" celebrated its annual festival. Many participated, an indication of the respect and encouragement the school enjoys. The festival was a great success. The orchestra of the Young Men's Israelite Karaite Association was the chief joy of the festival. Ibrāhīm Ḥusnī, head of the acting group in the association, directed all the numbers.
al-Shubbān, no. 6, 2 July 1937.

Chapter II

How the Community Was Governed

The Religious Council

The Religious Court

The Internal Code

The Personal Status Code

History

Financing the Community

During the last quarter of the 19th century, the ḥākhām akbar, or chief rabbi, was considered the head of the community, responsible for its welfare and activities. But, since the ḥākhām akbar did not have his own financial means to run the community, he depended on wealthy members of the community for support. It was in this way that Ḥākhām Shabbethāi Elīyāhū Mangūbī was appointed ḥākhām akbar of the Karaite community in Egypt in 1876.

Authority, then, was in the hands of the ḥākhām akbar and the leaders of the community, and one can rightly assume that during the 19th century, a patriarchal system was the base of governing the community.[1]

In 1882, the British, in a move to protect the reigning Khudaywī of Egypt at the time, Tawfīq (1879-1892), occupied the country. Several months later, the head of the American missionaries, Dr. Linson, was able to help Ḥākhām Mangūbī establish good relations with the British consul, Sir Evelyn Baring (Lord Cromer).[2]

Ḥākhām Mangūbī also had a good relationship with the Khudaywī of Egypt, Tawfīq. In view of this, it was not difficult then for Lord Cromer to help Ḥākhām Mangūbī obtain recognition from the Egyptian government that the Karaite community was an independent one, and Ḥākhām Mangūbī its head.[3] When 'Abbās, the son of Tawfīq, became governor of Egypt in 1892, Ḥākhām Mangūbī found no difficulty in obtaining his support. It is my judgement that Tawfīq, 'Abbās, and also Lord Cromer found in Ḥākhām Mangūbī a helpful friend, as he was born and educated in Turkey, whose Sulṭān at the time still considered Egypt part of the Turkish Empire. It is safe to assume that this relationship helped Ḥākhām Mangūbī introduce his administrative reforms. In 1900, Ḥākhām Mangūbī succeeded in getting together enough leaders and members of the community to form what could be considered a general assembly that "chose" and "elected" the members of the first religious council the community ever had. However, no mention was made as to how those members were chosen or elected. This "general assembly" had another task to accomplish: to write down the first internal code for the community (Pl. 1).

There are 26 articles in this code: articles 1 and 2 state that the community had elected the aforementioned members to represent them and that their election is an admission by the whole community that those elected members, headed by the Ḥākhām Akbar Shabbethāi Elīyāhū Mangūbī, form the "religious committee" *al-lagnah al-milliyah*. In case of death or resignation, the elected members have the right to appoint a new member of the committee (article 3).

Article 4 states that the elected members have to take an oath for their new office in the main synagogue in Ḥārat al-yahūd in Khurunfish. The text of the oath is: "On this Holy Torah I swear to carry out my duty, for which my community has elected me, truthfully and honestly" (Pl. 2).

The responsibilities of the "committee" were defined in articles 5 to 13. It is clearly understood that this "committee" was at the time like a government within a government. It was responsible for all administrative, religious, and judicial mat-

---

1. It is interesting to note that from the 15th century until the end of the 19th century, each one of the community leaders in Egypt assumed the title *al-Mu'allim*. In the library of the Karaite community in Ramlah, Israel, there are many documents to indicate this.
2. In a bulletin written and distributed by Farag Rāṣōn al-Sirgānī, one of the members of the religious council of 1901 stated this fact. In late September of 1883 Lord Cromer visited Ḥākhām Mangūbī in his office in the Karaite Bēt-Dīn in Khūrūnfish (Cairo).
3. In Egypt, until 1890, there was only one recognized head — *Ra'īs* — for both the Rabbanite and the Karaite communities.

ters of the community.

Articles 14 to 19 state the sources of revenue: what they are, how to keep records of revenues and expenditures.

How to keep records of births, engagements, marriages, divorces, and deaths is mentioned in article 20.

Articles 21 and 22 explain how to acquire certain certificates and their charges.

As for taxes levied on performing certain religious responsibilities, such as engagements, marriages, circumcisions, and deaths, it was left to the committee to decide the amount levied on each, according to the person's financial status, and the amount had to be recorded in special records (articles 23 to 25).

Article 26 indicates how to amend the code. Finally, the code states that the head of the community is Ḥākhām Shabbethāi Elīyāhū Mangūbī, and that all revenues must be kept in the care of Dā' ūd Isḥāq Līsha', who was also the *gabbāy* of Rab Simḥah synagogue.

From 1901 until 1940, when the religious courts were formed, the religious council was the only body responsible for all community activities: birth and death certificates, marriage and divorce documents, operation of the synagogues and the schools, the welfare of the community, which included health and the educational needs of the poor, and providing the community with the needed rabbis — *ḥākhāmīm,* cantors — *ḥazzānīm,* circumcisers — *mohelīm,* and ritual slaughterers — *shoḥetīm.*

During the period between 1901 and 1940, the religious council acted as civil court, religious court, conciliation committee, and even probate court.[4]

In 1940 a religious court was formed, followed by a religious court of appeal in 1947. Both courts were chaired by Ḥākhām Tobiah Levi Babovitch; each had two regular judges and two alternates.

The religious council and the religious courts were guided in their acts and rulings by the laws of the land, the internal and personal status codes, and the laws of the Torah.

Until the first quarter of the 20th century, Karaites preferred to take their disputes to the religious council. In rare cases, when one or both parties had foreign protection, they preferred to have their cases adjudicated by the consulate of their home country. In some cases when a Muslim or Christian native had a case against a member of the Karaite community, he would take his case to the religious council, knowing well that the council would be fair.[5]

For 40 years, the minutes of the religious council were filled with legal disputes between members of the community: cases of verbal and physical assault, maltreat-

---

4. Minutes of 3 November 1901; 21 June 1921; 27 March 1923; 9 February 926; and 7 January 1935, respectively.
5. Minutes of 28 February 1910.

ment, divorce, broken engagements,[6] inheritance, endowments, and the desire to marry a second wife.[7]

The religious council would normally meet weekly but, if necessary, twice or three times a week. In some cases the minutes were fully recorded, especially when the council was looking into legal matters. On other occasions, reference to the topic was considered sufficient. The minutes were recorded in Arabic, although on one occasion, during the time of Ḥākhām Abrāhām Kohen, the language of discussion and parts of the minutes were recorded in French.[8] The council was looking into an important legal issue and wanted to be sure that the ḥākhām understood every word said. The council was investigating article 63 of the first draft of the personal status code of Murād Farag which states that it is forbidden for Karaites to marry non-Karaites (Pl. 3).

The schools and the lottery dominated most of the sessions of the religious council until 1929. One example is a detailed record of an incident in which a Karaite lottery vendor tricked the winner of the first prize on 19 May into believing that the ticket was worthless, obtained the ticket from him, and cashed it himself. The investigation was completed in two long sessions, after which the winner, who was a Muslim barber, obtained the money and the vendor received a penalty.[9]

At each session of the council, a member was chosen to record the minutes.[10] It was up to the understanding of that member to record correctly the proceedings of the council, which until 1940 used to be simply an administrative council, a religious council or even a religious court. Usually, both Hebrew and Gregorian dates were recorded, but in a very few cases either one only was used.

There are six volumes of the minutes from 1901 until 1971; from 1971 until the present time, the minutes have been recorded in a kind of notebook. No details of matters discussed were recorded.

From the beginning in 1901, the elections had to be supervised by the deputy governor of Cairo. The internal and personal status codes had to be approved by the Ministry of the Interior.

In many cases communication with the Ministry of the Interior was direct, while in other cases, it was through the governor of Cairo (Pl. 4).

On Monday, 2 April 1906, Ḥākhām Mangūbī died. Farag 'Abd-Allah, a member of the council was asked to carry out the legal and religious responsibilities

---

6. Engagements were entered in a special record, and were considered a legal step towards marriage.
7. That was common practice for Karaites as well as Rabbanites in the Muslim East (minutes of 7 January 1935). Rabbanite practice, however, ended much earlier (1914).
8. Minutes of 29 May 1924.
9. Minutes of 21 and 22 May 1901. The vendor was ordered to clean the area around Rab-Simḥah synagogue and around the Karaite Bēt-Dīn for one week during which he was put under ḥērem (ban). He was not allowed to speak to anyone, nor was anyone else allowed to speak to him.
10. Ths is clear from the style of writing. From 1916 a secretary for each council was elected or nominated.

of the ḥakhām, *al-mas' ūliyāt al-shar 'iyah wal-dīniyah,* which he proceeded to do very effectively and without pay. Dā' ūd Isḥāq Līsha', also a member of the council, acted as chairman of the religious council and to the community at large. A letter was sent to the governor of Cairo informing him of the change, and another letter was sent to Russia requesting a new ḥakhām.[11]

On 1 February 1907, Ahārūn Kefīlī became ḥakhām akbar for a three-year term, but he did not stay long in office. The religious council felt that Kefīlī had given a written consultation in a matter of inheritance that contradicted the written law and the Karaite tradition. The council terminated his responsibilities and settled with him all financial matters, whereupon Ḥakhām Kefīlī returned to Russia.[12]

In Egypt at that time there were more than twenty members of the Karaite community who were very well educated in the field of the law, and could have effectively carried out the responsibilities of the ḥakhām akbar. Yet it was common and even preferred among Karaites and Rabbanites to look for a ḥakhām from another country. So Ḥakhām Berākhāh Kohen was called in from Jerusalem, and was appointed by the general assembly on 5 December 1907.

When Ḥakhām Kohen died on 15 March 1915, Abrāhām Mangūbī, the son of Ḥakhām Shabbethāi Mangūbī was appointed acting ḥakhām; he also became responsible for all the community affairs in the Karaite Bēt-Dīn.

At that time (1915), it was felt that new elections were due and, of course, the internal code needed to be changed. That was exactly what happened. A new internal code entitled "The Religious Council Code" *(Qānūn al-Maglis al-Millī)* was drafted by a committee. According to this code, elections were held on 13 August 1916. The new code contains 58 articles:

Article 1 states that the community had a religious council of twelve members elected from among those who received the majority of votes. They were responsible for looking into the community affairs and to run them in a manner that will be mentioned later.

Articles 2 to 23 are all about electors and candidates, and the formation of the religious council. Article 2 gave the right to vote to every member of the community 18 years or older, of proper conduct and with no police record. To be a candidate, however, one had to be at least 25 years old, of proper conduct, and with no police record, and must know how to read and write.

Article 17 states that the term of the council is three years, while article 18 made it clear that elections should be held thirty days before the end of the term. The chairman of the council is the one who receives the majority of the votes (article 22).

Articles 24 to 39 define the rights and responsibilities of the religious council.

---

11. Only the ḥakhām akbar was regarded by the authorities as the head of the community and the religious council.
12. Minutes of 12 September 1907.

Article 24 states that the council is responsible for looking into and administrating all that the community owns, including real estate or otherwise. The council is also responsible for the welfare of the whole community from both the cultural and religious points of view. The council has to look into the religious duties according to the Karaite law and the law of the country in a fair and just manner. Article 25 gave the religious council the right to investigate civil suits between members of the community when both parties agree that the council arbitrates between them.

For the first time the term "general assembly" was mentioned: how it is formed, how often it meets, and what are its responsibilities. The code defines clearly when the religious council abides by the decisions of the general assembly and when these decisions are on a consultative basis only (articles 40 to 45).

Articles 46 to 57 are about the "general chairman," al-Ra'īs al-'Am. It is surprising that while in all the code there was no mention of the word ḥākhām akbar, which is very unusual, article 46 states that the "general chairman" is appointed by the general assembly by a majority of votes, and article 47 states that "that chairman" is the person responsible for officiating marriages and for looking into divorce cases, as well as other religious duties. Why then did they avoid mentioning the word ḥākhām akbar, when all the aforementioned duties are carried out only by him? Articles 50 to 57 define precisely what the "general chairman" can or cannot do.

Article 58 shows how to amend the internal code.

Comparing the two codes, one can notice that the second one clarified some of the ambiguities in the first code: as to who is eligible to be a candidate, who has the right to vote, the responsibilities of the general assembly and that of the "general chairman" (ḥākhām akbar).

According to the new code, elections were held on 13 August 1916. And on 2 March 1917, the general assembly was formed of twenty-eight members representing most of the main Karaite families.

Because of personal disputes, however, the council was unable to do effective work, and some members refused to attend the sessions. The remaining members of the council continued on, while efforts were made to put an end to the misunderstanding between some of the members. The council dragged its feet until new elections were held on 2 January 1921.

The first item on the council's agenda was the monthly payments, known to Rabbanites and Karaites alike as a 'Arīkhāh.[13] At the meeting it was decided that during Passover each member of the community should double his donations (dues) to help poor families meet their holiday needs.

With the new council, there was also a new ḥākhām akbar. Abrāhām Kohen, who came from Turkey at the end of 1920 and became ḥākhām akbar of the Karaite

---

13. Every financially capable male over 18 years old had to pay to the Karaite Bēt-Dīn whatever amount he could afford. The revenue from the 'Arīkhāh was an important part of the budget.

community in Egypt. In fact, he was the ḥakhām who headed the elections committee at the time.

As the community's affairs began to become more complicated, and as the ḥakhām did not know Arabic, the religious council decided on 1 January 1924 to consider its chairman the responsible member to deal with community affairs. A letter outlining the decision was sent to the governor of Cairo.

In 1922, Egypt succeeded in gaining its independence and became a sovereign country. New reforms took place in all branches of the government and throughout the country.[14] The same spirit of reform was felt in the minority communities.[15] It was timely then, under pressure from the "Israelite Union Association," that efforts were made to hold new elections on Sunday, 31 December 1924. The new religious council was faced with many problems, one of which was the Karaite settlements in Jerusalem. This problem persisted until Jerusalem was lost to the Arabs. When, after the Six Day War, Israel regained the old city, it started to renovate its buildings and returned the renovated synagogue of ʿAnān to the Karaite community in Israel, but refused other claims, because the Karaites had no deeds to support their claims. Where are those deeds? Who is to be blamed for their loss? The people who were in charge of these settlements in Israel or the various councils that governed the Karaite community in Egypt, which had owned these settlements through endowments since the 14th century. The council of 1924 as well as the councils that preceded or followed could have acted more firmly to preserve the community rights in these settlements.

Another related problem arose in 1924 and again in 1934. Ten Karaite families requested financial help to move to Jerusalem and settle in the Karaite settlements there. The council, claiming financial hardship, did not take any action. In both cases one rich member of the council or of the community could have covered all the expenses needed with no trouble, or at least the council could have started a campaign to collect money for those who wanted to leave.[16]

It was during the time of this religious council that some legal problems arose, and again the council failed to act intelligently. Some members of the Rabbanite community expressed the desire to be affiliated with the Karaite community and to marry Karaites.[17] The religious council and the general assembly met several times, but failed to reach a decision on the request. Murād Farag was the head of a group that called for better understanding and closer relationships with the Rabbanite com-

---

14. Egypt was declared a sovereign country in 1922.
15. During this period, the Rabbanite community built an ultra-modern hospital in Ghamrah, in the western part of Cairo, and an ultra-modern school in ʿAbbāsiyah, in the eastern part of Cairo.
16. Minutes of 12 October 1925 and 30 May 1934.
17. One case was recorded in the minutes of 31 May 1926; another case was published in detail in the local newspapers and also in *al-Ittiḥād* (a Karaite magazine) from 16 June to 14 July 1925, Nos. 5, 6, 7. These are only two out of twelve cases, all recorded in the minutes of the religious council.

munity. Ḥakhām Kohen agreed completely with this group, yet he made it clear that as the ḥakhām akbar of the Karaite community of Egypt, he had to abide by the decisions of the Eupatoria convention.[18]

Polygamy was another legal problem. Ḥakhām Kohen found great understanding from Murād Farag in solving this problem (see below under "Chief Rabbis").

Another problem was the need to rewrite the internal code and to compile, for the community, a complete and accepted personal status code, especially in view of the various judicial reforms that took place in Egypt at the time. Efforts to do just that had already begun earlier, and while a committee was working on the internal code, Murād Farag was busy translating from Hebrew and compiling the items of the personal status code.[19] As an authority on both languages, Hebew and Arabic, Murād Farag was the best qualified member of the community for the job, which he did without any delay.

Yet one subject in that code, dealing with the legality of marrying non-Karaites, became the center of heated discussion among well-informed members of the community. Unfortunately, the uneducated and, of course, the uncontrolled were dragged into this emotional issue, and the situation became very dangerous.[20] The reader would be very surprised to know that the community wasted more than ten years on this problem, along with the problem of the internal code. During this time, Ḥākhām Abrāhām Kohen died (1933), and almost a year later, Ḥākhām Tobiah Levi Babovitch, who came from Russia, became ḥakhām akbar for the Karaite community in 1934.

Details about the new internal code leaked during the time the council was examining its articles. Both Murād Farag and members of the religious council became the target of a vicious attack from various groups of the community. Dozens of circulars were distributed accusing Murād Farag of heresy, and of trying to change the "written laws" and the Karaite traditions. Members of the council were accused of ignoring the rights of members of the community especially the poor among them, and of protecting the interests of certain groups, and the council was asked to resign. Many parties were involved in the subject and dozens of brochures were published to express the point of view of each party (Pl. 5).

---

18. The Eupatoria convention of 1910, when the Karaites of Russia closed the door to anyone who wished to become affiliated with the Karaite faith.
19. Before Murād Farag an attempt was made to codify the personal status code. Farag Rāṣōn al-Sirgānī, a well-informed member of the community, wrote a complete code in Hebrew. Also Ḥākhām Abrāhām Kohen wrote another personal status code in Hebrew. Unfortunately, I was not able to find either one.
20. In the meeting of the religious council on 29 May 1924, the article in question was discussed. When the code was printed in 1935, another article also caused much trouble. It was article 273. A child born to a Karaite woman from a non-Karaite father is considered a Karaite, but if the father is unknown the child is considered a bastard.

The office of the governor of Cairo was flooded with complaints about the religious council, which forced him to intervene (Pl. 6a). The council had to resign and was replaced by two temporary committees, one after the other (April 1936, June 1937) (Pl. 6b). The second committee was able to do what the first one failed to do: to draft an acceptable internal code which was sent to the Ministry of the Interior on 16 December 1937 to be approved.

This third internal code served the community without any major changes until the last election, which was held in 1966.

For the first time the "quiddity" of the Karaite community in Egypt was clearly defined (article 1).

Articles 2 to 7 define the rights and responsibilities of the ḥākhām akbar, who was still considered the head of the community.

The ḥākhām akbar was forbidden from interfering in the financial and administrative affairs of the community (article 7). One can notice the change in running the community's affairs: while the first code gave Ḥākhām Mangūbī wide financial and administrative powers, this code relieved the ḥākhām akbar from those responsibilities. Yet that did not prevent Ḥākham Tobiah Babovitch (1934 1956) from expressing his opinion on both matters in the pages of al-Kalīm (a Karaite magazine) and during Saturday ceremonies, without causing much trouble.

Twenty-six articles (8-33) addressed the electors and candidates. The right to vote was limited to those who were 21 years of age or older, of proper conduct, with no police records, and among those who pay the 'Arīkhāh.

The candidate for the council must be 35 years or older, of proper conduct, with no police record, a regular contributor to the 'Arīkhāh and must be a resident of Egypt.

The above articles (8-33) explain all about the election committee, how the elections are conducted, when a ballot is considered valid, and that the elections must be under the supervision of the deputy of the governor of Cairo.

The formation of the religious council and the protocol of the meetings and the duration of the council (three years from the day the members take the oath) were mentioned in articles 34 to 53.

The responsibilities of the religious council are defined in articles 54 to 57. Article 54 defines the responsibilities as:

Representing the community... forming the religious courts... appointing and discharging of all employees... appropriating taxes to be levied on the performance of the religious and administrative duties... forming the committees needed to run the community affairs... preparing the yearly budget... buying and selling the community real estates... accepting the endowments and the wills... fixing monthly payment on community members... In short, the religious council is the body responsible for guarding the community's interests.

Articles 58 to 62 are about the religious courts. For the first time, the religious courts replace the religious council in dealing with all religious matters. As previously mentioned the religious court and religious court of appeal are headed by the ḥākhām akbar. Each of the two members of the court must be 35 years of age or older, well informed about the faith, married or previously married, of proper conduct, with no police record, and, finally, of Egyptian nationality. The term of each member as a judge in the religious court is one year only, but subject to renewal (articles 58-62).

Articles 63 to 68 are about the protocol that must be followed when looking into religious lawsuits.

Article 86 indicates the sources of revenues:

1. Monthly payments, *'Arīkhāh*.
2. Interests on bonds, real estate and other investments.
3. Revenues from both synagogues.
4. Taxes levied on performing religious duties such as circumcision, engagement, marriage and death.
5. Revenues from the *gabalāh*.
6. Wills and endowments.
7. Community lottery.
8. Whatever enters into the budget as revenue.

The *'Arīkhāh,* who pays it, how much, when due, how it is collected, who is exempted from payment — everything in connection with the *'Arīkhāh* is defined in articles 87 to 93.

Finally, article 94, the last one, states how and when the code can be amended.

It is clear that the community was more aware now of its rights. Yet surprisingly, there is no mention of the "general assembly" which used to help the religious council with its decisions.

As mentioned above, on 16 December 1937, a letter was sent to the governor of Cairo along with 20 copies of the internal code. Almost three years later, in March 1940, the governor returned the internal code with the approval of the Minister of the Interior. The only explanation for such a delay that I can think of is for personal reasons: the acting chairman of the community, Yūsuf Ibrāhīm Marzūq, did not try to press for quick approval. During this time, he was in charge of everything: education, health, all community records — in short, running the community's affairs.

During this period (1937-1940), there was no religious council, no temporary committee, so there were no records of any activity of the community except from April to November 1937 when *al-Shubbān* (a Karaite magazine) was published.

In accordance with the newly approved internal code, elections were held in May 1940. The ballots numbered only 134, an indication that the elections were boycotted. In 1940 there were almost 800 members of the community who had the right to vote.[21]

After almost seven years since his arrival in Egypt, Ḥākhām Tobiah Babovitch was given Egyptian nationality and was acknowledged by the authorities as the ḥākhām akbar of the Karaite community (1941).

At the request of the Justice Department, a copy of the personal status code compiled earlier by Murād Farag was sent.

In May 1943, Yaʿqūb ʿAbd-Allah, the chairman of the religious council, died suddenly. On Sunday, 25 July 1943, elections were held under the supervision of Muṣṭafā Ṣādiq, the deputy governor.

The new council had every opportunity to move the community forward and accomplish major needed reforms. The economic situation in the country was never better: in Cairo alone there were about one million Allied troops who, especially the Americans, were pouring money into the economy. Yet almost nothing was done; rich members of the council and the community ignored this opportunity and were busy getting richer. The only good thing that was accomplished was the building of a home for elderly and poor members of the community. The home replaced a very old and decrepit one known as "al-Warshah." The home was named "Raḥmīn Līshaʿ (Benevolent Home) because Mr. Līshaʿ's daughter, the wife of the chairman of the council, donated most of the money. The home was officially opened on 6 January 1945.

An interesting point should be mentioned here: on 13 June 1944, Ḥākhām Tobiah Babovitch requested that the council send a delegation consisting of the ḥākhām as chairman, a lawyer, a doctor, and a social worker to the Jewish community in Ethiopia. The Jews there, called *Falashas* or the *Falakh,* were by all reports using only the Written Laws (i.e., the Torah), and had no knowledge of the Rabbinic oral laws. This suggested the possibility that they might be Karaites. As usual, promises were given but were never carried out.

Another interesting point is that the council requested that Ḥākhām Tobiah submit to the council copies of the Sabbath and Holiday ceremonies. The ḥākhām told the council that his ceremonies were extemporaneous.[22]

On Sunday 27 October 1946, elections were held under the supervision of Zakariya Ḥāmid Bey, the deputy governor. One month later, a new round began between the Minister of Justice and the non-Muslim minorities. At times, each community acted alone, but again they often found it more advantageous to work together. For this reason, representatives of most non-Muslim communities met in the headquarters of the Orthodox Copts (the largest non-Muslim community) in Faggālah, in Cairo, on 3 January 1947. Telegrams were sent to the president of

---

21. In the history of the community elections, no more than 35% of those who had the right to vote exercised their rights.
22. A similar situation had occurred in the Rabbanite community of Alexandria with its chief Rabbi Mosheh Ventura (*al-Kalīm* No. 71, 16 January 1948).

the senate and to King Fārūq asking for the withdrawal of the bill concerning minorities from the senate floor, to be rewritten so as to assure no interference in all personal status codes of any non-Muslim community.

Meanwhile, the new council had many projects to execute, and things started to move forward — always with a struggle against red tape. The community, however, was not to be lucky for long.

On 20 June 1948, the Muslim brothers, *al-Ikhwān al-Muslimūn,* bombed both the Karaite and the Rabbanite neighborhoods. Many were killed. The Karaite School for Boys was completely demolished. The newspapers blamed the incident on the feud between the two communities, but they knew better. Both communities, the Rabbanite and the Karaite, and the Rabbanite community of Alexandria, sent a joint plea to the king and the cabinet to take the necessary steps to ensure the lives and the safety of the Jews.[23]

The first Arab-Israeli war of 1948 did not affect the relations between the Egyptian authorities and the Jews. Members of both communities continued to enjoy the same manner of living as before, in spite of the tense relations with some Muslim organizations.

In the Karaite community elections were held in 1950 and the new council did not waste any time. It started working from the moment the members were sworn in.

After the first Arab-Israeli war the situation in Egypt became very tense. Deep struggles between certain organizations and King Fārūq could be noticed everywhere. The army, or more accurately certain army officers, were not happy with the way King Fārūq was running the country, nor with his personal behavior as an Islamic leader.

In July 1952, a group of Egyptian officers undertook a coup d'état which resulted in establishing the Arab Republic of Egypt.

Muḥammad Nagīb was the first president. On 1 October 1952, Ḥākhām Tobiah Babovitch, Lieto B. Masʻūdah, the vice chairman of the council, and Murād al-Qudsī, a member of the council, met with Muḥammad Nagīb in his office. The meeting was so successful that Nagīb promised to visit the Karaite synagogue in ʻAbbāsiyah, in Cairo, on 25 October 1953. The visit took more than an hour and the affair was covered in great detail by the local and foreign newspapers (Pls. 7, 8a and b).

On 26 April 1953, new elections took place and the new members took their oath the following Sunday. Although nine of the members had served in the previous council, everyone hoped the new one would do better.

The situation in Egypt seemed to be calm, but everyone knew that Nagīb and Nāṣir were struggling for power. Nagīb felt that the country needed peace and internal reforms; Nāṣir, among other views, advocated hostility towards Israel. Finally

---

23. Minutes of 26 June 1948.

Nāṣir won and became the most powerful man in the country, and later among all Muslim leaders.

On 1 January 1956, state courts replaced all religious courts, including those of the Muslims. This was the result of Law No. 426.[24] It was a continuation of a move to unify all kinds of courts (Pls. 9a and b).

The second Arab-Israeli war of 1956 marked the beginning of the end of most of the minorities, especially the Jews, in Egypt. In Cairo, along with major cities, thousands of Rabbanites and Karaite were detained. When they were released five months later, they were taken to the secret police headquarters and were told that they had been detained for their safety.

During the crisis, Jacques Mangūbī, the chairman of the council, did his best to keep things going. On 12 March 1957, the religious council met for the first time since October 1956. It was decided that all actions taken by J. Mangūbī from October 1956 till March 1957 should be considered legal. Unfortunately, some members of the council were very reluctant to meet and so the council did not convene until May 1959.

During this period, Jacques Mangūbī, the chairman, and Murād al-Qudsī, the secretary, assumed all responsibilities and used to meet every Sunday in the Karaite Bēt-Dīn to take care of community affairs.

The next elections were held on 27 December 1959, and on 2 January 1960 the new council held its first meeting.

The emigration waves among the Jews of Egypt, which had started in November 1956, did not wane. Yet the various councils did their best to cope with the new situation and with the problems that accompanied it.

The last election, however, took place in October 1966, at which time there were less than 1,000 Karaites left in Cairo.

The third Arab-Israeli war of 1967 gave the strongest signal to those who were still in Egypt that it was time to leave. In April 1970, there were about 200 Karaites left in Cairo, compared to only 24 in 1984.

Final Note

To sum up this part, one can say that in the 19th century, the community was governed by the ḥākhām akbar and the leaders of the community. From 1901 until 1940, the various religious councils governed the community according to the approved internal codes. From 1940 until 1956, the religious courts assumed certain legal responsibilities according to the approved personal status code.

As for the religious councils that governed the community from 1901 until 1970 they all had one positive aspect that may be mentioned here: without them the Karaite

---

24. *al-Waqā'i' al-'Miṣriyah:* 24 September 1955.

community in Egypt would have fallen apart.

Other than that, I cannot find anything worth mentioning. From the very beginning, when the council became the body responsible for governing the community, until 1970, there was no set policy to be followed nor any long-range plan for all the needed projects and reforms, and when one member of the council called for that, nothing was done.[25]

The various religious councils dealt with the problems as they occurred, and because there were too many problems, there was not time for needed projects or reforms. There was no comparison between what the councils accomplished and what the community needed.

In 1890 the community had one synagogue and some real estate. In 1960, after 70 years, the community had another synagogue, two schools, a new home for the elderly, and much real estate. The new synagogue was built mostly as a result of the honest efforts of some members.

As for the schools, though, there were times when they were the pride of the community, yet the various councils looked at the schools as a source of revenue more than anything else. And when they became a financial burden, the council did not hesitate to try to close them. The minutes of the religious council are full of many decisions to close the school. The community needed schools in 'Abbāsiyah, where there were more than 600 Karaite boys and girls learning in the various Rabbanite and public schools. Late in 1947, the community lost a golden opportunity to acquire a beautiful building near the synagogue of 'Abbāsiyah, suitable for the schools, simply because some rich members of the council refused to contribute less than two thousand dollars to close the deal.[26]

The Karaite neighborhood of Ḥārat al-Yahūd al-Qarrā'īn needed a dispensary to care for its poor residents. The doctors were there; in fact, more than four Karaite doctors worked on a voluntary basis in the neighboring Rabbanite dispensaries.

Day-care centers were badly needed, but that was not even on the agenda of the religious councils.

From the turn of the century until 1950, many members of the community called for the establishment of a higher religious institute. During this period there were more than twenty well-schooled members of the faith qualified to teach in such an institute. Among them were: all the chief rabbis, Murād Farag, Farag Rāṣōn al-Sirgānī, Yūsuf Yomtōb, Yūsuf Farag Ḥayyīnah, Yūsaf Marzūq, Ibrāhīm Mangbī, Mūsā Ibrāhīm Menashah, Farag 'Abd-Allah, Ya'qūb Farag 'abd-Allah and David Līsha'.

All the religious institutes that existed at the time were run by some Karaite associations, and their goal was to teach the language, the principles of the faith

---

25. He was Farag Ibrāhīm Levi. Minutes of 7 November 1944.
26. *al-Kalīm* #68, third year, 1 December 1947.

and how to pray.

There were dozens of poor Karaite families that were living in unhealthy apartments belonging to the community. There was enough accumulated money in the treasury of the community to reconstruct all these apartments and to allow members of these families to live in much better conditions.

Many members of the community, however, share the blame; rich members were never generous, and some members refused to pay the ‛Arīkhāh. One member filed a lawsuit against the religious council, challenging its right to impose such "taxes."[27]

It is my judgement that all the religious councils failed to carry out any project to raise the cultural and religious standards of the members of the community.

One final comment: in all the councils that governed the community, there was no place for the women who wanted to serve.

Financing the Community

Since I began the collection of data for my book, I have been unable to find any information about the financial situation of the community in Egypt during the last quarter of the 19th century.

On my visit to Egypt in the summer of 1984, I found some documents, among which was a brochure printed in August 1916 entitled "An Imperative Declaration about the Karaite Jewish Community Affairs in Egypt" *(Biān lā-Budda minhu 'An shu'ūn Ṭā'ifat al-Isrā'īliyīn al-Qarrā'īn bi-Miṣr).*[28]

A few lines on page 2 (page 1 is the cover) help us learn about the financial situation of the Karaite community in Egypt in the 19th century. The only sources of revenue at the time were limited to: 1) the charges collected on the performance of some religious duties such as circumcision and marriage; 2) the revenues from the real estate owned by the community through endowments. The salaries of the ḥākhām and the beadle, the maintenance of the synagogue and the real estate accounted for all the expenditures.

The *gabbāy* of the synagogue served also as the treasurer of the community. He was entrusted with all the revenues and was responsible for all the expenditures. This may help us understand why the Karaites of Egypt always choose the gabbāy from a rich or well-to-do family.

We can safely assume that, because most of the Karaites used to live in the

---

27. The court of appeal in 1929 ruled that "only the government" has the right to raise taxes.
28. The brochure was written by Farag Mūsā al-Sirgānī. Farag al-Sirgānī was well informed in the field of Karaite law, and one of the members of the first religious council. He served his community in many capacities: as the person in charge of the Karaite Bēt-Dīn from 1909 till 1915, and as the principal of the Karaite Schools from 1916. He published the brochure in an attempt to clear his name from the many false rumors spread by his opponents accusing him of mismanagement.

Jewish neighborhood, rich members of each family used to help needy members of their own.

In 1897 the lottery was introduced and quickly became a major source of revenue. Each year it yielded about one thousand Egyptian pounds, a great deal of money at that time, especially in Egypt. In 1903 the community published its first financial report. The report was in two pages, page 1 for the lottery and the school, page 2 for the Bēt-Dīn. The Bēt-Dīn revenues were almost $4,100, while expenditures were $2,000. The main sources of revenue were real estate, donations, the *gabalāh*, and charges on the performance of certain religious duties (Pl. 10a).

The salary of the ḥakhām and the other employees accounted for 50% of the expenditures. About $11.00 was given to welfare activities.

As for the lottery and the schools, revenues were $6,800. Revenue from the lottery was $5,200, tuition at almost $1,200. Salaries of all personnel were $3,600 (Pl. 10b).

Both the schools and the Bēt-Dīn yielded a surplus of almost $4,400.

The community had neither assets nor bonds. Wealthy members of the Līshaʿ and Masʿūdah families were entrusted with the money of the community. They used to pay a reasonable interest on that money. Other sources of revenue opened up slowly as more financial responsibilities were added. Able members of the community were asked to contribute monthly dues, known as the *ʿArīkhāh*, to the Karaite Bēt-Dīn. Donations to read certain parts of the Sabbath and Holy Days' prayers added to the revenues.[29] The revenue from the *gabalāh* was noticeable.

The next financial report I was able to find was that of 1927. There was not much change from the first budget except for the amount of money involved.

Revenues from the Bēt-Dīn were almost $10,200, while expenditures were $6,700. The main sources of revenue were in this order: the *ʿArīkhāh*, real estate, interest on savings and, finally, donations. Once again the salary of the ḥakhām, the employees, and money spent on welfare activities constituted 75% of the expenditures (Pl. 11).

The Karaite Bēt-Dīn had to help poor families left behind in the Karaite neighborhood. During the first quarter of the 20th century, many Karaites left the Karaite neighborhood to live in what was considered the suburbs of Cairo (ʿAbbāsiyah, Ghamrah, al-Ḍāhir, and al-Sakākīnī). A problem was created for those who were running the community's affairs: taking care of those poor who were left behind. Thus, new responsibilities were added in health care, education, and housing for the poor.

---

29. In the Karaite tradition, parts of the service on the Sabbath as well on Holy Days, are carried out by worshippers who contribute money for charitable activities, so in Cairo some rich members of the Karaite community used to acquire parts of the service and donate them to the poor so they could have their share in the prayers.

As for the schools and the lottery, revenues were $4,800, while expenditures were $5,600.

In the total budget, there was a surplus of $2,700.

Twenty years later, in 1947, we notice new items in the budget. Both synagogues yielded about $1,800, there was $800 interest on bonds owned by the community. The revenue from the 'Arīkhāh was $3,500, a little less than all that was spent on welfare activities. Revenue from the lottery started to decline. The budget showed $3,000 surplus (Pl. 12).

When the budget of 1955 was published it became clear that the community had become much richer than before. Money spent on education — on both Karaite schools, on the scholarship for Karaite students in the Rabbanite schools or public schools or colleges — reached $12,500. The 'Arīkhāh and the donations reached an all-time high, a little less than $5,500, almost double the amount of all welfare activities. The itemized budget was published in 8 full pages of *al-Kalīm*. Another page showed all the properties owned by the community (Pl. 13).

Besides the two synagogues, land for a third one in Heliopolis, north of Cairo, the Karaite Bēt-Dīn, the kasher bakery house, and the burial place in al-Baṣāṭīn, the community owned 22 pieces of property. The one in 'Abbāsiyah was worth $45,000.

Financially, the community was sound. There was a surplus each year. That was the result of the unwillingness of the various religious councils to carry on any major project, fearing not to be able to sponsor it in the future. The community was in bad need of many projects, none of which was carried out.

The Arab-Israeli war of 1956 marked the start of a declining trend in all sources of revenue. That, of course, forced those who were in charge of the community's affairs to sell some of these properties to meet the mounting demand for financial help.

Today, those who are considered the caretakers of the community's properties are doing nothing to save them from further deterioration.

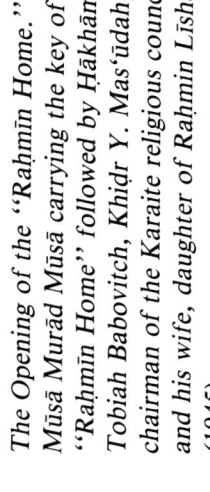

The Opening of the "Raḥmīn Home." Mūsā Murād Mūsā carrying the key of the "Raḥmīn Home" followed by Ḥākhām Tobiah Babovitch, Khiḍr Y. Masʿūdah, the chairman of the Karaite religious council, and his wife, daughter of Raḥmīn Līshaʿ. (1945)

The front of the "Raḥmīn Home" building for elderly and poor people. (The small picture is of Raḥmīn Līshaʿ)

This picture was taken in 1947 in the headquarters of the Coptic Orthodox Church at Faggālah, Cairo. In the middle is al-Anbā Yūsāb, the Coptic Orthodox Pope. To his left and to his right, some members of the Greek Orthodox and Catholic Churches, as well as of the Roman Catholic Church. Behind him, to the right, is Ḥākhām Tobiah Babovitch, the Ḥākhām Akbar of the Karaite community of Egypt.

Muḥammad Nagīb's visit to Mosheh al-Darʿī synagogue in Abbāsiyah Cairo in Saturday, October 25th, 1952

Members of the greeting committee welcoming "al-Raʾīs"

Muḥammad Nagīb enters the synagogue

And listens to the service of taking out the Torah

Hākhām Tobiah blesses the movement and its leaders

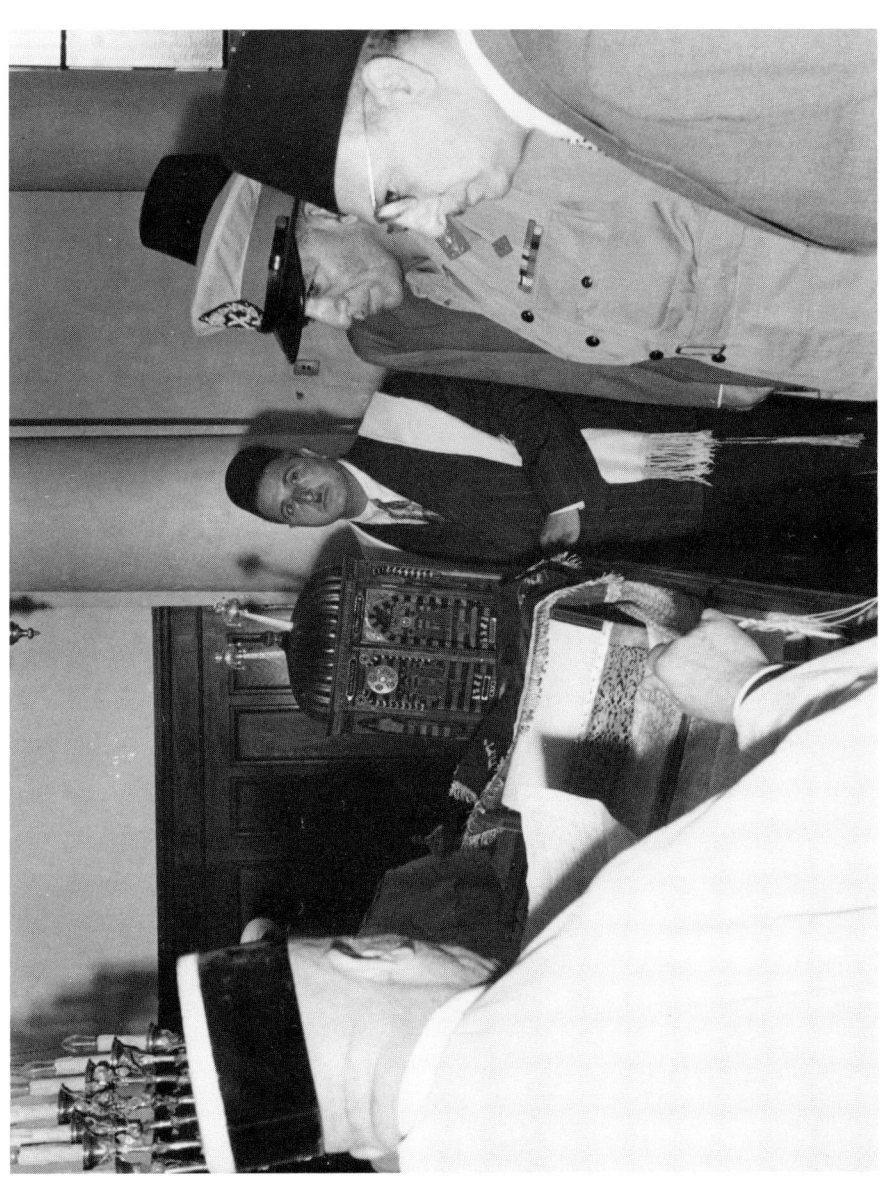

After the blessing he delivered a speech.

From the pulpit Nagīb assures the worshipers that religion is for God, but the nation is for everyone: Muslims, Christians, or Jews.

Murād al-Qudsī reads a poem written by Murād Farag.

Hākhām Tobiah expresses his point of view

And so does the vice chairman of the Karaite religious council, Lieto B. Mas'ūdah, and Nagīb is very attentive.

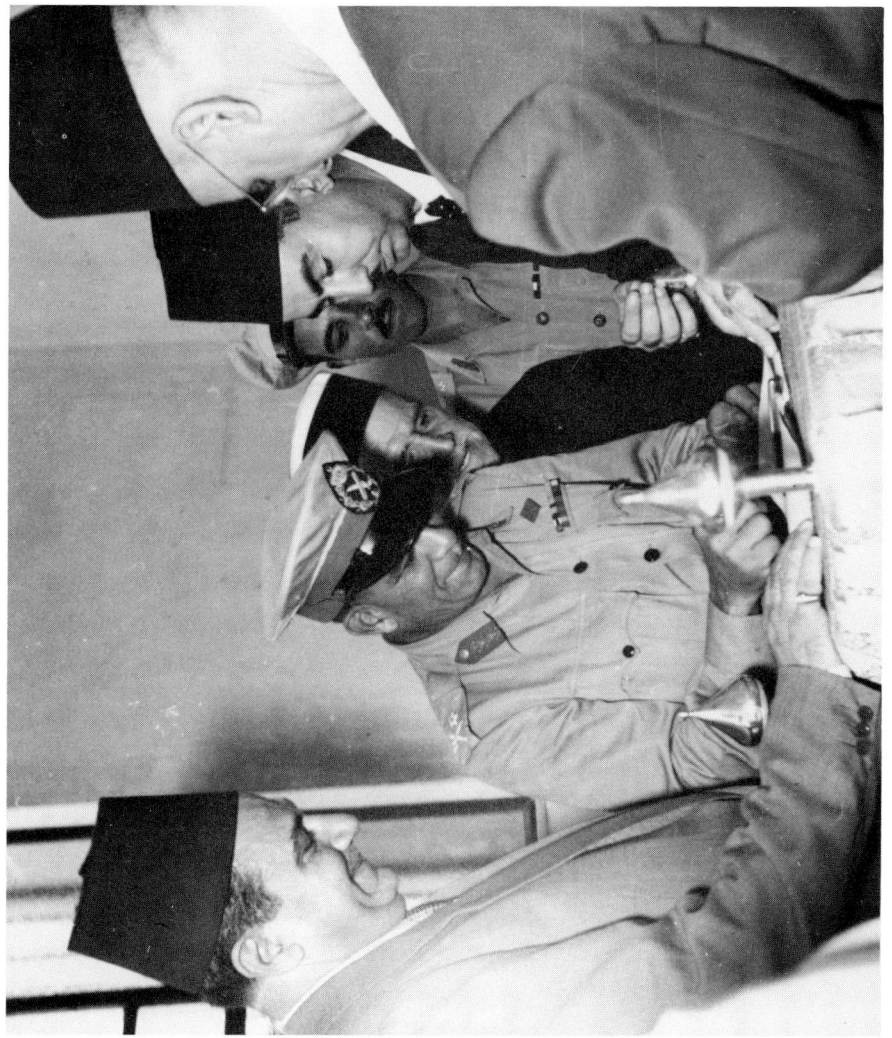

Nagib records his reactions in a special book.

A fatherly kiss to the young girls who presented flowers and gifts to Nagib.

Among the cheers of the crowd Muḥammad Nagīb leaves the synagogue.

The first session of the Karaite religious council of 1950. Sitting from right to left are: Elie al-Nāsī, Farag Aṣlān, Jacques Mangūbī, ʿAbd al-ʿAzīz ʿAbd al-Wāḥid, Tobiah Levi, the ḥākhām akbar, Tawfīq al-Gazzār, Thābit Yaʿqūb Khiḍr, Murād al-Qudsī, Zakī Menashah. Standing to the left is Kamāl Ḥusnī (representing al-Kalīm). Standing to the right in Lieto B. Masʿūdah.

The Election Committee of 1953. In the middle Ḥākhām Tobiah Babovitch. To his left Jacques Mangūbī and Elie 'Abd-Allah. To his right, the deputy of the governor of Cairo, Murād Lieto Murād, Zakī Menashah.

The deputy of the governor of Cairo (1), among members of the election committee of 1963, headed by the acting ḥākhām, Mūrad Hārūn (2). In the middle is Jaques Lieto Mangūbī, the president of the Karaite religious council.

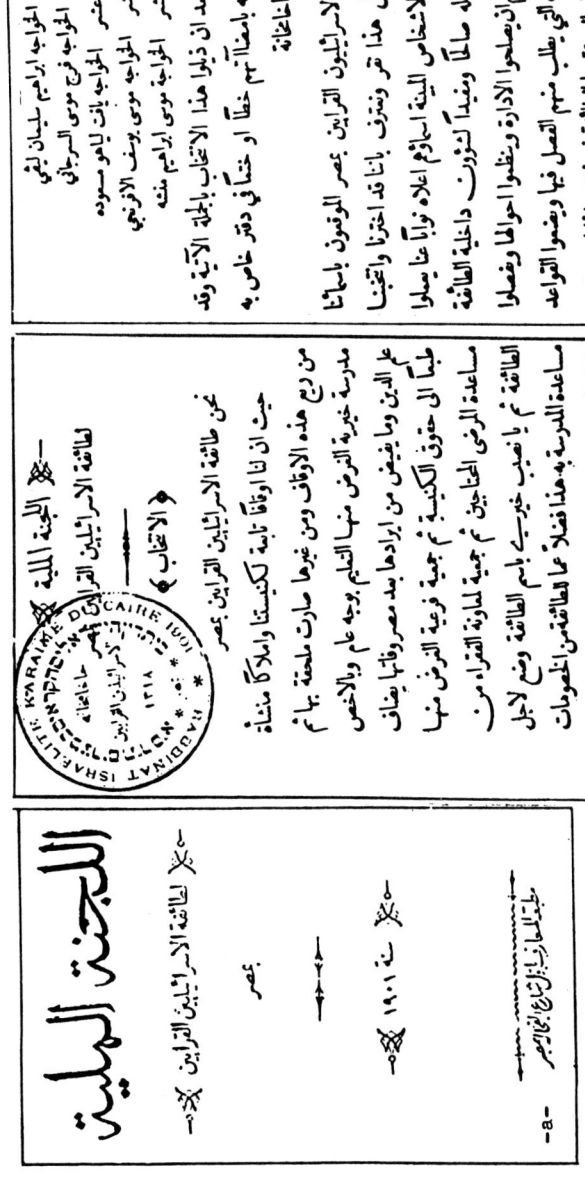

PLATE 1: The cover (a) and page 1 (b) of the first internal code of 1901. The introduction states the purpose of having this code. It mentions that the Community has endowments that belong to the community's congregation, and real-estate that the community acquired through the revenues from its real-estate. It also mentions that the community has a school and a lottery to help finance it, and an association to help the sick. Then it goes on to state that the community needs to have a religious council to run its affairs.

After mentioning the names of the members of the council on page 3 (c), the introduction goes on to state that "We, the Karaite Jews of Egypt, the undersigned, with our names and seals, declare and acknowledge that we have 'chosen' and 'elected' the members whose names are mentioned above to represent us and to do whatever they see fit for the welfare and the progress of our Community...."

نحن رؤساء ديانة طائفة اليهود القرائين ورئيس اللجنة الملية لهذه الطائفة اشهد بأنه بناءً على المادة الرابعة من اللائحة التي وضعت المنتخبون من هذه الطائفة وبناءً على
١٤ اول ١٦٦٠ يوم مارس سنة ١٩٠١ المشار اليه المعين لاجل حلف المنتخبين بحضرة هيئة الطائفة في الكنيس.

وبناءً على حضور معظم الطائفة في اليوم المذكور لاجل ذلك وحضور معظم المنتخبين ما عدا ثلوثة منهم وهم خواجه لتو يوسف مندوق وثابت اقنقه صالح وحموم بانه فند مشروه وقد اعتذر خواجه لوتو وثابت اقنقه عن عدم حضورهم هذا للكباد بأنه ارسل كل منهما خطاباً بأنه وقد تلي كلاً من هذين الخطابين علنية امام جميع الحاضرين

وبناءً على ادن من تخلف من المنتخبين عن الحضور في هذا اليوم العمومي يؤدي يمينه في وقت اخر اماما وحضور من حضر من باقي المنتخبين ومن الطائفة

بناءً على كل ذلك قد أدق ما حضر من المنتخبين الحميد بالتوراة بالصيغة الآتية (احلف بربي التوراة المقدسة اني اودي مأموريتي التي انتخبت من اجلها طالما في بالذمة والصداقه)
ثم قررنا بايصال خطابات لبقية المنتخبين لتسأل استدعاء الحميث نحو ورعة في الكاله لتنفيذ العمل بهذه اللائحة وإثبات لذلك حرر هذا المحضر وتم توقيعه على ذلك من حاضرين من المنتخبين ومن بعض من الطائفة

PLATE 2: Elected members of the first religious council took the oath in the main synagogue, Rab-Simḥāh, on 3 March 1901 A.D.

This tradition was kept until 1960 when it was decided to take the oath in Mosheh al-Darʿī synagogue in ʿAbbāsiyah.

حضرة المحترم الملي السعيد في يوم الاربعا ٢٨ مايو ١٩٢٤

بجلسة المجلس الملي المنعقدة مساء لدى سعادة الحاخام ومنزل الخواجه
ليتو يوسف مرزوق برياسة سيادة الحاخام وحضور كل من حضرات الخواجات
بارون ليتو سعود، والحخ جرمي ليتسم والخواجه ليتو يوسف مرزوق والخواجه
ابراهيم شنجربي والمحامي ميسير يوسف صالح ودكتور ابراهيم مرزوق

للنظر فيما اشيع بالسنة من لعدة اشخاص وهم حضرة الوكلاء
يوسف مسعود و مراد يوسف القدسي و داود زكي الستي وجبل الستير مجولي
و ابنه بارون الجمبي بان ممن قانونه للاحوال الشخصيه تدوينه قد تم
اشياء ومنها لم لشريعتنا وعلى الأخص اباحة الزراج مع اخواتنا
الربانيه وانهم قد حرروا نفسهم بعريضه تقديمها لهذا المصري ذكر
فيها ان المواد المذكوره ارفضم على قبولها حتى تمت الحاخام وبسلا لوزارة الداخليه
وحيث ان اساءة تذرعت بمس الملي وعلى الصاحه
الحاخام مبنى المجلس لتعقيد ما ذكر واستدعى لذلك حضر
مراد بك زرج الذي سعيد تكلقى سيد المجنه نجبه - قد نفى حضرة الحاخام
يومهم قانون الاحوال الشخصيه

ابتدا المجلس باستجواب حضرة الحاخام فيه ذكر وصراحة لا
يوسف على ان يسأل بالفم الغربي و في لعدم معرفه اللغة العربيه
كتابة

— Avez vous examiné et verifié la codifi-
cation du projet du code du Statut personnel
préparé par Moral Bey Faraq?

PLATE 3: On Wednesday, 28 May 1924, members of the religious council met to discuss rumors that Ḥākhām Abrāhām Kohen had agreed on accepting the principle of intermarriage, especially with Rabbanites. Ḥākhām Kohen denied that he ever expressed such an opinion and that as the head of the Karaite community he had to abide with the decisions taken in the Eupatoria of convention of 1910.

— Oui j'ai examiné le dit projet, en plusieurs séances et en présence de Mr. Baroukh Liéto Massouda, Rahmin Léochaa, et la première séance, il a assisté également Liéto Cohen, Avocat. et aux autres séances, en présence de Mr. Chonmeul Cohen. Après chaque séance, j'approuvais au fur et à mesure le travail fait, sur sa traduction en langue Hébraïque.

— Souvenez-vous qu'à la première séance, sous le chapitre "Étrangers," il figure à l'Art. 63 l'empêchement de mariage avec tout étranger, conformément à la décision prise ~~tou~~ par le grand Consistoire d'Ipatoria?

— Oui, je me souviens qu'après l'art. 62 qui à l'origine autorisait le mariage avec l'Étranger, à condition de se convertir à notre rite, il a été par l'art. 63, selon à la dite décision interdit tout mariage avec un étranger. —

— Est-il vrai que vous auriez déclaré à un ou plusieurs membres de la Communauté que l'approbation du projet vous a été imposée, malgré votre opposition?

— Non, je n'ai jamais fait une telle déclaration à aucune personne; toutefois, j'ai déclaré que le code sera soumis à certaines personnes compétentes, avant d'être définitivement admis.

— Donc, le bruit et le fait des personnes sus-indiquées sur les deux questions ci-dessus, savoir : 1° celle du non empêchement du mariage avec un étranger et notamment les Rabanites, 2° celle d'avoir été forcé d'approuver le projet dont il s'agit ne sont pas exacts

— Oui — c'est absolument inexact, et je proteste énergiquement contre les faits ci-dessus qui sont de nature à mettre le trouble dans la communauté, en dehors de l'humiliation, en ma qualité de Rabbin.

D'ailleurs, j'ai déjà fait par un discours à la Sinagogue, Samedi dernier, déclaré formellement, devant le public, l'inexactitude des bruits dont il s'agit et j'ai énergiquement protesté contre les faits ci-dessus.

Aléha

ثم بعد ذلك طلب المجلس بعض مراد عليه فزع الاطلاع على
المواد المذكورة سواء كانه بالشرعي لمجرى الموضح على سيادة الحاخام
اوا التشريع العربي الرئيس على سيادة الحاخام وهذا نصا الذى رآى بالعربية

(בה הדין דאזול דף ס. ע.ב. דיבור המתחיל אתא
ע. ש. ב. ל. ע.ה. הכ"מ.)

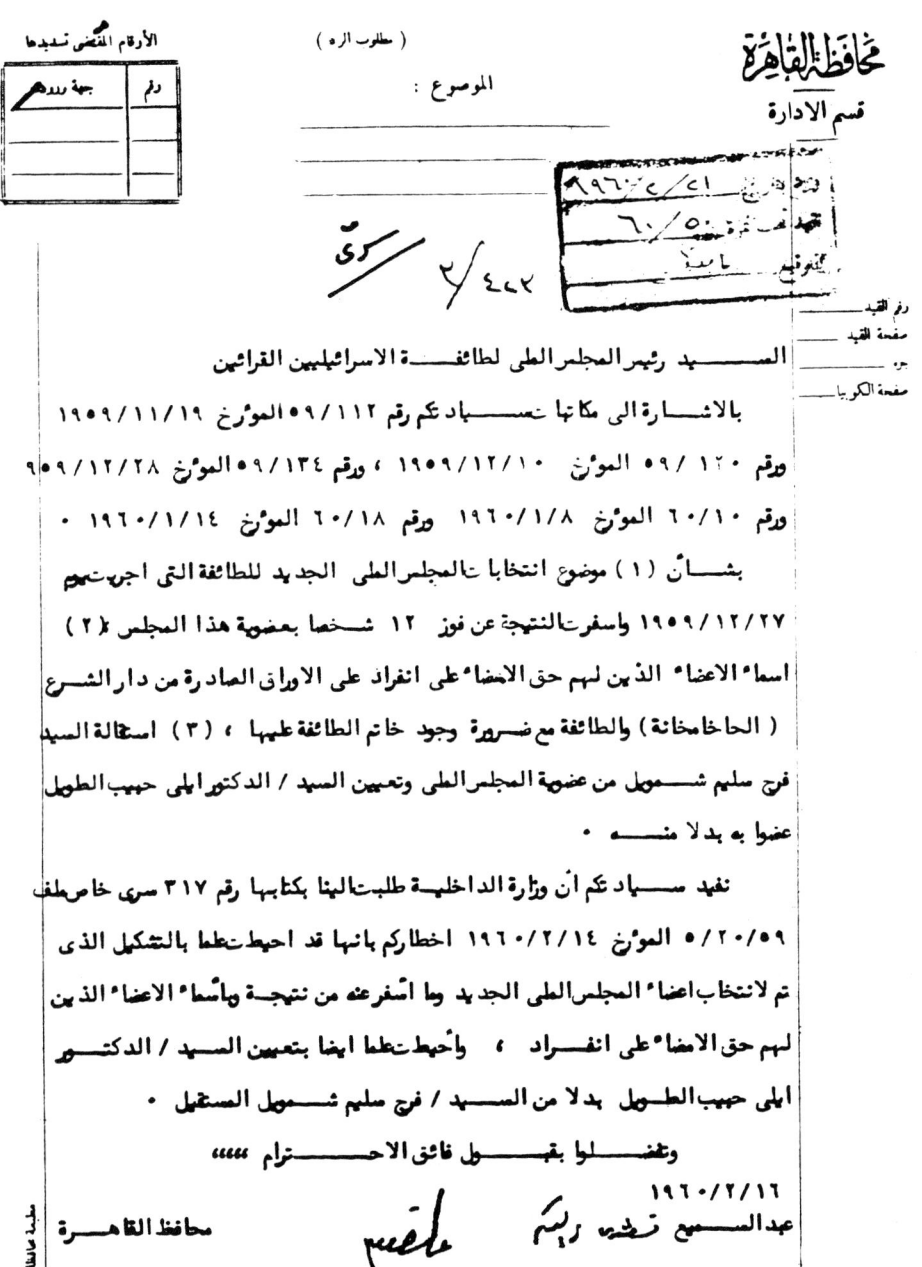

PLATE 4: A confidential letter from the Governor of Cairo to the chairman of the religious council of the Israelite Karaite Community.
The Governor took notice of the results of the new elections held on 27 December 1959.
He also acknowledged the names of members who had the right to sign the official papers of the community.
The governor   signature   date: 2/16/1960

الى ابناء طائفة الاسرائيليين القرائيين
لاتصدقوا وعود المجلس الملي !!

اصدر المجلس الملي بتاريخ ٢٧ مارس سنة ١٩٣٥ منشوراً بعد فيه وعودا طالما سمعناها منه ولم ينفذ منها شيئاً كما هي عادته وتعلمون يا ابناء الطائفة ان المجلس الملي كان يجب ان يتجدد قانونا في اواخر سنة ١٩٣٣ ومن هذا التاريخ استبد المجلس الملي ولم يعمل انتخابات رغم العرائض الكبيرة التي كانت تقدم من الطائفة واخر هذه العرائض تلك التي قدمت من جمعية الاصلاح الاجتماعي بتاريخ ٤ يناير سنة ١٩٣٥ حيث وعدها المجلس بعمل انتخابات بعد شهرين من هذا التاريخ . واخيرا اصدر المجلس المنشور السالف الذكر بالنظر في لائحة الانتخابات الجديدة يوم ٢١ ابريل سنة ١٩٣٥ فلا ترون ان كل هذه وعود ومراوغة ؟!

لا مناقشة في كتاب الاحوال الشخصية الا بعد حل المجلس الملي الحالي

الا ترون يا ابناء الطائفة ان المجلس الملي كان يريد تنفيذ هذا الكتاب رغم انف الطائفة والدليل على ذلك ان الكتاب صدر من دار الشرع . واذا قرر المجلس النظر في امر الكتاب بتاريخ لم يحدد بعد ـ لامر الذي يثبت سوء النيه ـ فان هذا تحت تأثير الحركة التي قامت بها جمعية الدفاع عن مصالح الطائفة اذن يجب المحازرة من الاجتماع الذي ينوي المجلس الملي عقده بشأن الكتاب بأنه سيجمع المحاسيب والانصار والاقارب للتصديق على ما جاء به الكتاب من المتناقضات للدين

لا نقبل لائحة جديدة الا ﻣ....ن المجلس الملي الجديد

اجتمع المجلس الملي بجلسة ٢٦ مارس سنة ١٩٣٥ تحت تأثير الحركة التي قامت بها جمعية الدفاع عن مصالح الطائفة وقرر المجلس عرض اللائحة الجديدة على الجمعية العمومية فاعلموا يا ابناء الطائفة انه ليس من حق هذا المجلس الملي ولا من حق الجمعية العمومية ومنع لائحة جديدة لان الطائفة فقدت ثقتها فيهم وليس من المعقول ان مجلس ملي له في ادارة الطائفة ١٠ سنة يعمل لائحة انتخابات فانها بلا شك ـ هو الواقع ـ تكون من مصالحهم وجمعية الدفاع عن مصالح الطائفة ترى ان عليها واجبا مقدسا وهو لفت نظر الطائفة انه يجب ان تجرى الانتخابات بمقتضى اللائحة القديمة وباقرب سرعة

سئمناك يا مجلس فاستقـــــــل

يحرمون علينا الخطابة في الكنيس اليس هذا حق من حقوق كل قرائي خصوصا وان الخطب لا تحتوي الا عن مواضيع اصلاح العوج من امور الطائفة وحفظ كيان الدين . يطلبون منا السكون والهدوء وان يكون هذا الاستقلال منهم وعودا كاذبة

ان المجلس الملي الذي يدعي انه صاحب الشأن وانه يريد ان يعمل الصالح ما هو الائقة لا تسعى الا لاغراضها الشخصية فنصيحتنا اليهم بالاستقالة في اقرب وقت

ايها القرائي العزيز

ضع ثقتك في جمعية الدفاع عن مصالح الطائفة فانها جادة في عمل ما فيه الصالح للطائفة ؟

٢٨ مارس سنة ١٩٣٥   جمعية الدفاع عن مصالح الطائفة

PLATE 5: One of the many circulars by "The Association for Defending the Community's Interest" condemning the Personal Status Code written by Murād Farag.
The circular calls for:
    No discussion in the book "Personal Status Code" written by Murād Farag unless the religious council is dissolved.
    Only the new elected religious council can submit the new Internal Code to the authorities.
    The community is fed up with members of the religious council. They should resign.

March 28, 1935

شكوى الاسرائيليين القرائين

والطعن في مجلسهم الملي وطلب تعيين لجنة لادارة شؤون الطائفة

كتب ابناء طائفة الاسرائيليين القرائين الى وزارة الداخلية يطعنون في انتخاب مجلسهم الملي وقد جرى في سنة ١٩٣٤ وقدموا عريضتين احداهما في اوائل الشهر الماضي ممضاة من نحو ٤٠٠ عين من اعيان الطائفة بالطعن في تأليف هذا المجلس وفي تصرفاته وسحب ثقتهم منه والثانية في آخر الشهر الماضي يعني الشكوى الاولى واضافوا اليها رغبتهم في تعيين لجنة مؤقتة لادارة شؤون الطائفة حتى يتم انتخاب المجلس الجديد وسردوا في عريضتهم الاسماء التي وقع اختيارهم عليها لتأليف هذه اللجنة

وأرسل جناب وكيل الطائفة اخيرا الى محافظة مصر كتابا طلب فيه سرعة البت في مشروع اللائحة النظامية الجديد وقد قدمت منه وهي التي يدرسها الآن قسم قضايا وزارة الداخلية وطلب جنابه الترخيص له باجراء انتخابات جديدة طبقا لهذه اللائحة بصفة استثنائية وذلك بحلول ميعاد الانتخاب

وأحالت وزارة الداخلية الموضوع الى قسم القضايا التابع لها لا بداء الرأي فيه والمفهوم من محادثة ذوي الشأن انه لا محل لتدخل ولاة الامور في الموضوع حيث ان اللائحة التي اجريت بموجبها هذه الانتخابات لم تصدق عليها الحكومة كما انه لم يطلب من الحكومة اعتماد الانتخاب للطعون فيه

PLATE 6a: Complaint of the Israelite Karaites
Defamation of their Religious Council and the demand to appoint a committee to run the community's affairs.
Members of the Karaite community wrote twice to the Ministry of the Interior charging that the 1934 election was not legal.[1] They submitted two petitions signed by 400 members of the community defaming the Council and declaring no confidence in its members.
They requested the formation of a temporary committee to run the community's daily affairs until new elections were held. The deputy of the Community wrote to the Governor requesting permission to hold new elections but his request was denied.

1- No elections were held in 1934. In 1934 one member of the Council died, and two members resigned. Instead, the Council appointed three members, according to the approved Internal Code.
al-Muqaṭṭam, 3 January 1936.

في النزاع القائم
بين افراد طائفة
الاسرائيليين القرائين

رأينا قبلا خبر النزاع القائم بشأن مشروع اللائحة النظامية الجديدة لطائفة الاسرائيليين القرائين بين افراد الطائفة ونضيف اليوم الى ذلك ان محافظة العاصمة دعت اعيان الفريقين المتنازعين ونالت منهم موافقتهم الصريحة على تأليف لجنة وقتية تدير مصالح الطائفة التي ستقدم مشروعها الى الحكومة للموافقة عليها على ان تجري الانتخابات بعد ذلك طبقا لهذه اللائحة بإشراف وزارة الداخلية

واتصل بنا ان كلا من الفريقين اختار ثلاثة من انصاره لتأليف اللجنة الوقتية المشار اليها وذهب الجميع الى محافظة العاصمة ووقعوا على محضر الاتفاق

PLATE 6b: About the Division Among the Karaite of Egypt
The Governor of Cairo met with the leaders of both parties of the Karaite Community. They all agreed to form a temporary committee to draft a new Internal Code on the basis of which elections would be held.
Later, each party elected three members and they all met with the Governor and signed a Procès Verbal of agreement.
al-Muqaṭṭam, 19 April 1936

السبت المبارك

حشفان سنة ٥٧١٣ ع

٦ صفر سنة ١٣٧٢ هـ

٢٥ اكتوبر سنة ١٩٥٢ م

إنه هذا اليوم ليوم سعيد لأنني قد سعدت بالحظ بالتواجد
بين اخواني وابنائي ، بنا ، طائفة الاسرائيلية القرائيين
وباركني السيد الحاخام كما بارك حركة الجيـش
التي تشبه الى حدٍ كبير حركة الطائفة. نفرع --
والذي احب ان اؤكده ان جميع ابنا ، مصر على
اختلاف ديانا تهم ومذاهبهم ، ما هم جميعا اخوة
في الوطن لا فارق بينه اسرائيلي او مسلم او مسيحي
فالدين لله والوطن للجميع وليحيا الاتحاد والنظام
والعمل ح موحديد لواء أ ع.

٢٥/١٠/١٩٥٢

PLATE 7

The Blessed Saturday·

Ḥeshvan 5713　　　　　　　　　　　　　　　　　　Ṣafar 1372

October 25, 1952

This is indeed a happy day, as I was lucky to be among my brothers and children, members of the Jewish Karaite Community.

His Excellency the Ḥākhām blessed me as he blessed the Army movement which is similar to a great extent to the Karaite movement.

I would like to emphasize here that all the children of Egypt are brothers, regardless of their religions or faiths, there is no difference between Jews, Muslims or Christians. Religion is for God. The nation is for all. Long live Unity....Discipline and Action.

Major-general Muḥammad Nagīb　　　　　　　　　　　　　　　　10/25/1952

Le lewa Mohamed Naguib visite le Temple des Israélites Karaïtes où il assiste au service religieux

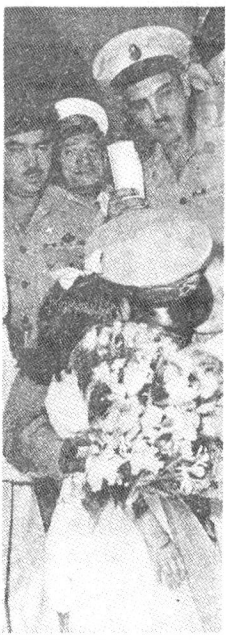

A gauche : le lewa Naguib prononçant son allocution devant les membres de la communauté. A ses côtés le Grand-Rabbin Tobia Lévi. Ci-dessus: le président embrassant paternellement une fillette qui vient de lui offrir une magnifique gerbe de fleurs. En bas : le chef du gouvernement s'entretenant amicalement avec le Grand-Rabbin des Karaïtes.

Il affirme: « Tous les Egyptiens sont égaux et frères, quelle que soit leur religion »
...Ajoutant que le mouvement de l'armée ignore totalement le fanatisme religieux ou racial

La devise de l'ère nouvelle — telle que l'a proclamée le lewa Mohamed Naguib — est l'Union, l'Ordre, le Travail.

Pour la réalisation de ces principes et afin d'assurer l'union de la nation, le président a entrepris une série de visites aux diverses communautés de la nation. Il a déjà rendu visite au recteur d'El-Azhar, au patriarche copte-orthodoxe, à la communauté israélite et au patriarche grec-catholique. Hier, il a visité le temple des Israélites Karaïtes, répondant à l'invitation que lui avait adressée il y a quelque temps le Grand-Rabbin Tobia Lévi.

LE SERVICE RELIGIEUX

A son arrivée, le lewa Naguib fut salué par les notables de la communauté et par les ovations et les applaudissements prolongés de la foule massée devant la synagogue. Ayant enlevé ses chaussures — car telles sont les traditions de la communauté — il pénétra dans le temple où il assista à l'action de grâces célébrée par le Grand-Rabbin. A l'issue du service religieux, le Grand-Rabbin forma des vœux pour qu'il plaise à Dieu de donner la victoire à Mohamed Naguib et à ses officiers et de couronner leur œuvre de succès, pour la plus grande gloire de l'Egypte.

(LIRE LA SUITE EN PAGE 4)

PLATE 8a: Muḥammad Nagīb visits the Karaite synagogue Mosheh al-Darʿī.
Le Journal d'Egypte, Dimanche 26 Octobre 1952.

الرئيس نجيب يزور كنيس اليهود القرائين

صـــلاة الدعاء للحركة ولوحدة الوادي وللقائد العام وكلمته في المصلين
الدين لله والوطن للجميع والمصريون جميعاً اخوة متكاتفون

ابتدأت صــلاة الســبت فى كنيس اليهود القرائيـــن فى وقت شروق الشمس واستمعت ســماحة الحاخام كلمة وطن الصلوات فى أماكنهم لأن الحاخام طويني لبى أرغب أن يقيم صلاة دعاء ديركة

من الفوز
روج تركيا والعراق

للرئيس اللواء محمد نجيب بحركة الجيش المباركة .

وبلغت أصمح رسالة شفوية للاستاذ صلاح الشاهد تشريفاتى ديوان الرياسة بأن التقاليد المرعية عند اليهود القرائين عند دخول كنيستهم تشابه التقاليد المسلمين كضرورة الوضوء وخلع غطاء الرأس وخلع الحذاء عند دخول للمساجد
وفي التاسـعة تماماً وصل موكب الرئيس فاستقبله عند باب الكنيس السادة ليعا بارون دافيد وتوفيق الباهر الجزار وفرج اصلان وجاك ليتو مرزوقى وابراهيم داود حسنى ويوسف كمال رئيس تحرير مجلة الكليم لسان حال الطائفة وابراهيم الجزار ، وايل ابناس ومراد القمسى والمهندس موسى مراد مزوق
وخلع الرئيس ومن معه احذيتهم ثم دخل الكنيس فاستقبله الحاخام

الأكبر واعضاء المجلس الملى ولجنة أعيان الطائفة وصمد الحاخام الى الهيكل ومارس مراسمه الدينية لفتح الهيكل

واخراج سفط التوراة ثم صعد الرئيس الى الهيكل حيث صلى الحاخام آيات البركة للرئيس وللجيش المصري ووحدة وادي النيل .

واصطف حوله القراء واضعين على اكتافهم « الطليت » وهوعبارة عن شال ذى « شراشيب » تحتوي على عقدة عدد يوافق عدد كلمات آية التوحيد عندهم التي تقول « اسمعوا ياشعب اسرائيل » الرب الهنا إله واحد ...

وحين انتهت الصلاة دخل الرئيس بصحبه الحاخام وكبار رجال الطائفة الى حجرة جانبية وقدمت المرطبات ثم تقدم أحد الأعيان وقدم سجل الزيارات فكتب الرئيس فيه العبارة الآتية :

« إن هذا اليوم ليوم سعيد لأنفذ اسعدنى الحظ بالتواجد بين اخوانى وأبنائى أبناء طائفة الاسرائيليين القرائين وبارك المسيد الحاخام الأكبر كما بارك حركة الجيش وهى التى تشبه الى حد كبير حركة الطائفة نفسها والذى أحب أن أذكره لجميع أبناء مصر على اختلاف أديانهم ومذاهبهم هم جميعاً اخوة فى الوطن لأفارق بين اسرائيلى أو مسلم أو مسيحى ، فالدين

لله والوطن للجميع وليحى الاتحـــاد والنظام والعمل .

تم جرى الحديث بين الرئيس والموجودين فى صفاء ورد وقيل للرئيس إن اليهود القرائين فى مصر يبلغون عشرة آلاف شخص وهم أقل فى العدد من اخوانهم الربانيين الذين يبلغون حوالى ســتين ألفا والفرق الجوهرى بين الطائفتين هو أن القرائين متمسكون بالنصوص الاصلية كما وردت فى التوراة دون الارتباط بشروح أئمة الدين إذ لا يجتهد مع وجودنص وأنهم لايعترفون بالتلمود ، أى التفسير

وقال سيادة الحاخام : أنهم يأملون سيحتفلون فى السنة القادمة باليوبيل الفضى لهذا الكنيس ، أما الكنيس الاخر الموجود بالحرنفش فهو الكنيس الرئيسى له مئات السنين

ودخل الحجرة أحد افراد الشــعب الذي كان يصلى والدى طل واقفا فى الكنيس وطلب الى الرئيس أن يتفضــل ويلقى كلمة على افراد الشعب فخرج اليهم ... وقال :

هذا شرف لى أن أوجد بينكم ، وهذه فرصة سعيدة انتهزها لاهنئكم جميعاً بحركة الجيش وهى حركة الأمة جميعاً وأهنئكم بالخير الذى جلبته علينا جميعاً هذه الحركة .

اننا سائرون الى الأمام ولا نصل الا بوحى ضمائرنا مجردين عن كل غرض وغاية ، الا عن هدف اسمه الوطن فلنتجرد من المصلحة الشخصية ونكرس حبنا للوطن .

نحن مهما اختلفت أديانا فأنا اخوة فى الوطن لأن الذين والوطن للجميع وانتم جميعا مصريون فلا فرق بين مصرى وآخر تحلت تحتهم الظلم والارهاق فى العهد السابق وكلكم علمتم للحركة فشكرا لله الذى وحد بيننا صفوف هذه الأمة الكريمة

اننا جميعا نؤمن بالله وكل منارى الطريق الى الله من ناحية مدينه والكل فى النهاية يلتقون فى الايمان بالله ...

البقية ص 2

الغاء المحاكم الشرعية والملية

أصدر مجلس الوزراء فى جلسته المنعقدة فى ٢١ سبتمبر سنة ١٩٥٥ قانوناً بالغاء المحاكم الشرعية والمحاكم الملية وإحالة الدعاوى التى تكون منظورة أمامها إلى المحاكم الوطنية .

وقد نص القانون على الغاء المحاكم الشرعية والملية من أول يناير القادم وتحال الدعاوى المنظورة أمامها بجميع درجاتها إلى المحاكم الوطنية بجميع درجاتها لاستمرار النظر فيها وفقاً لأحكام قانون المرافعات وبدون رسوم جديدة .

وبالنسبة للمنازعات المتعلقة بالأحوال الشخصية للمصر بين غير المسلمين والمتحدى الطائفة والملة الذين لهم جهات قضائية ملية منظمة وقت صدور هذا القانون فتصدر الأحكام فى نطاق النظام العام طبقاً لشريعتهم .

PLATE 9a: The Abolition of the Religious Courts
The Egyptian Cabinet, in its meeting of 21 September 1955, issued an order to abolish all religious courts for Muslims and non-Muslims alike.
All pending law suits should be referred to Public Courts.
However, in all disputes between non-Muslim Egyptians of one faith, the ruling must be given according to their Personal Status Code existing at the time.
al-Kalīm, no. 233, 11th year, 1 October 1955.

بسم الله الرحمن الرحيم

الوقائع المصرية
جريدة رسمية للحكومة المصرية - عدد غير اعتيادي

(العدد ٧٣ مكرر "ب") الصادر في يوم السبت ٧ صفر سنة ١٣٧٥ - ٢٤ سبتمبر سنة ١٩٥٥ (السنة ١٢٧ ه)

محتويات العدد

رقم الصفحة		رقم الصفحة	
١٥	قانون رقم ٤٦٢ لسنة ١٩٥٥ بإلغاء المحاكم الشرعية والمحاكم الملية وإحالة الدعاوى التي تكون منظورة أمامها الى المحاكم الوطنية ...	٢	قانون رقم ٤٥٢ لسنة ١٩٥٥ بإعادة تنظيم مركز التنظيم والتدريب بقليوب ...
١٧	قانون رقم ٤٦٣ لسنة ١٩٥٥ بتعديل بعض أحكام القانون ٤١٩ لسنة ١٩٥٣ الخاص بنظام كلية البوليس ...	٣	قانون رقم ٤٥٣ لسنة ١٩٥٥ بتنظيم وزارة الخارجية ...
١٧	قانون رقم ٤٦٤ لسنة ١٩٥٥ بتعديل بعض أحكام القانون رقم ٥٠٨ لسنة ١٩٥٤ بإعادة تنظيم الجامعات المصرية ...	٥	قانون رقم ٤٥٤ لسنة ١٩٥٥ بالإذن لوزير الشئون البلدية والقروية في منح التزام استغلال أسواق عمومية ...
١٧	قانون رقم ٤٦٥ لسنة ١٩٥٥ بفتح اعتماد إضافي في ميزانية السنة المالية ١٩٥٥ - ١٩٥٦ ...	١٢	قانون رقم ٤٥٥ لسنة ١٩٥٥ بتعديل تأشيرة في ميزانية مجلس الدولة لسنة المالية ١٩٥٥ - ١٩٥٦ ...
١٨	قانون رقم ٤٦٦ لسنة ١٩٥٥ برفع درجة مدير عام "١" إلى وكيل وزارة مساعد في ميزانية وزارة الشئون الاجتماعية للسنة المالية ١٩٥٥ - ١٩٥٦ ...	١٣	قانون رقم ٤٥٦ لسنة ١٩٥٥ بفتح اعتماد إضافي في ميزانية السنة المالية ١٩٥٥ - ١٩٥٦ ...
١٨	قانون رقم ٤٦٧ لسنة ١٩٥٥ بفتح اعتماد إضافي في ميزانية السنة المالية ١٩٥٥ - ١٩٥٦ ...	١٣	قانون رقم ٤٥٧ لسنة ١٩٥٥ برفع عملية تقوية في الرياح التوفيقي من ٤٥,٠٠٠ ج الى ٨٥,٠٠٠ ج في ميزانية السنة المالية ١٩٥٥ - ١٩٥٦ ...
١٩	قانون رقم ٤٦٨ لسنة ١٩٥٥ بتعديل جدول الوظائف والمرتبات الملحق بالقانون رقم ١٦٦ لسنة ١٩٥٤ بنظام السلكين الدبلوماسي والقنصلي ...	١٣	قانون رقم ٤٥٨ لسنة ١٩٥٥ بإنشاء وظيفة مستشار فني في ميزانية وزارة التربية والتعليم للسنة المالية ١٩٥٥ - ١٩٥٦ ...
١٩	قانون رقم ٤٦٩ لسنة ١٩٥٥ بفتح اعتماد إضافي في ميزانية السنة المالية ١٩٥٥ - ١٩٥٦ ...	١٤	قانون رقم ٤٥٩ لسنة ١٩٥٥ بالإذن للحكومة في استبدال ٢٠٠,٠٠٠ ج من الأموال الموجودة تحت يدها تم توريل عملية استيراد منتجات بترولية ولفتح اعتماد إضافي في ميزانية السنة المالية ١٩٥٥ - ١٩٥٦ ...
٢٢	قرار مجلس الوزراء بتنظيم الديوان العام لوزارة الخارجية ...	١٤	قانون رقم ٤٦٠ لسنة ١٩٥٥ بالإذن للحكومة في أن تأخذ من الأموال الموجودة تحت يدها ما يعادل مبلغ ٥٩٠,٠٠٠ دولار أمريكي ...
٢٤	قرار بإنشاء فرع لجامعة القاهرة بمدينة الخرطوم بالسودان ...	١٤	قانون رقم ٤٦١ لسنة ١٩٥٥ بتعديل بعض أحكام القانون رقم ١٤٧ لسنة ١٩٤٩ بنظام القضاء ...

PLATE 9b: The front page of the official paper of the Egyptian Government, al-Waqā'i' al-Miṣriyah, 24 September 1955, in which law #462 is mentioned. Specifics of the law are explained on pages 15 and 16. The law calls for abolishing all religious courts for Muslims and non-Muslims and referring all cases to Public Courts.

PLATE 10a: Karaite Bēt-Dīn 1903

Revenues	$4,200
Expenditures	$2,000
Surplus	$2,200

Minutes of the Karaite Religious Council, February 1904.

In 1903 one Egyptian pound equaled five dollars.

PLATE 10b: Karaite Schools 1903

Revenues $6,800
Expenditures $4,400
Surplus $2,400

In 1903 revenue from the lottery was $5,200.

Minutes of the Karaite Religious Council, February 1904.

PLATE 11: Israelite Karaites Bēt-Dīn in Cairo
Ḥākhamkhānat al-Isrā'īliyīn al-Qarrā'īn bil-Qāhirah

Revenues and Expenditures of the Endowments and the
School of the Israelite Karaites bi-Miṣr 1927

Bēt-Dīn
Main source of revenue

Egyptian pound
548 800 'Arīkhāh
130 935 Donations
425 950 Real estate

Total of revenues
2573 549

Surplus 891 173

Main source of expenditure

Egyptian pound
330 000 Salary of the ḥākhām
133 200 Other salaries
378 250 Aid for the needy

Total of expenditures
1682 376

Schools and Lottery
Main sources of revenue
805 000 Lottery
371 930 School tuitions
 25 000 Donation from the
         lottery contractor

Main source of expenditure
938 550 Salaries of personnel
324 000 Rent for school building
 58 995 Miscellaneous

 50 000 Bonus for the principal
 30 000 Scholarship for two students

Total of revenues
1201 930

Total of expenditures
1401 545

Total of all revenues
3775 552

Surplus 691 631

Total of all expenditures
3083 921

In round figures:

	Revenue	Expenditure
Schools	$4,800	$5,600
Bēt-Dīn	$9,300	$6,700
Surplus	$2,700	

al-Ittiḥād, no. 18, 4th year, 27 December 1927

In 1927 one Egyptian pound equaled 4 dollars.

PLATE 12: The Israelite Karaite Community Ṭā'ifat al-Isrā'īliyīn al-Qarrā'īn Revenues and Expenditure of 1947

Item	Revenues	Expenditures
	Egyptian pound	*Egyptian pound*
Welfare activities	1364 120	1199 364
Welfare projects	110 450	50 000
Miscellaneous	286 650	273 843
Synagogues	732 919	427 327
Real estate	1583 475	2895 556
Bēt-Dīn	2655 889	1740 301
Bonds and Interest	321 318	38 048
Schools and Lottery	2800 367	3055 945
Total	10855 188	9644 384
Penny cash	22 487	
Surplus		1233 291
Total	10877 675	10877 675
In round figures Revenues were	$27,000	
Expenditures were	$24,000	
Surplus was	$ 3,000	

In 1947 one Egyptian pound equaled $2.50, either officially or on the free market.

al-Kalīm, no. 76, 4th year.

PLATE 13: The Karaite Jewish Community of Egypt
1955 budget, prepared by the Secretary of the Religious Council, Zakī Menashah, and reviewed by Elie 'Abd-Allah.

Item	Revenues	Expenditures
	pound	*pound*
Welfare activities	2225 450	1643 980
Home for elderly		177 745
Education	4933 933	6049 939
Synagogues	804 149	667 296
Bēt-Dīn	2119 705	2304 516
Real Estate	2190 444	567 730
Bonds	203 497	5 419
Tithe	100 000	
Securities	433 709	413 842
Money withdrawn from the bank	4405 054	
Money put in the bank		5683 018
Penny cash 1954	123 371	
Penny cash 1955		25 827
Total	17539 312	17539 312

Welfare activities	'Arīkhāh donations	Monthly payment for the poor. Emergency help during holy days.
Education	Financial help from the Ministry of Education. Revenue from the lottery.	Salaries of all personnel. Tuitions for students in all Rabbanite schools. Scholarship for students in other schools or colleges.
Bēt-Dīn	Money collected for the performance of religious duties. Charges on certificates issued, and fees for religious courts, *Gabalāh* and others.	Salaries of the Ḥākhām and his deputy as well as all other employees. Other needed expenses.

al-Kalīm, no. 244, 15 July 1956.

In 1956 the Egyptian pound equaled $2.50 officially. On the black market, one Egyptian pound equaled one dollar.

Chapter III

The Community Establishments

The Schools

The Lottery

Places of Worship

The Cemeteries

Education

In the last quarter of the 19th century education was limited to teaching the faith and the Hebrew language. All indications are that the level of that education was high, owing largely to the caliber of those who did the teaching. During the last decade of the 19th century and the first half of the 20th century, the Karaite community had over twenty men who were well versed in the faith and the language, each of them qualified to serve as a ḥākhām akbar.

When Ḥākhām Mangūbī became ḥākhām akbar, he apparently had in mind some plans for reforms. In 1896, with the help of the leaders of the community, a primary school was established, known as "the Benevolent Israelite Karaite School." To ensure financial means to operate the school, a lottery was established a year later, known to everyone as the "School's Lottery." The school and the lottery were run on the same budget[1] and were for a long time the main item on

---

1. Minutes of 3 February 1904.

the agenda of the religious council (See Pl.10b in Ch. 2).

From the minutes of the religious council, and from five well-known Karaite periodicals of the period, 1901-1957, it appears certain that there were three schools: one for boys, one for girls, and a third one serving as a kindergarten.[2] Yet in one place in *al-Kalīm* it was mentioned that the community had three schools in al-Ḥārah and three in 'Abbāsiyah, but in all the minutes of the religious council, there is nothing to confirm this statement. The only explanation may be that in the minutes, the word "schools" was used without mentioning their location or their number.[3]

The first data about the school system were recorded in a letter sent to the governor of Cairo, which justified the lottery[4] and stated that at that time the school had a principal, fifteen qualified teachers, a visiting physician, one secretary, and three custodians (Pl. 1). At all times the students were a mixture of Jews, Christians, and Muslims. In a very few years, however, the Jews were in the majority.

Both the School for Boys and the School for Girls were primary schools with first to fourth grades. In 1946, when the last year for primary education was changed to sixth grade, the School for Boys was expanded to six grades. At first the three schools were located in Ḥārat al Yahūd in Khurunfish. But when many Karaites moved to 'Abbāsiyah, Ghamrah, and al-Ḍāhir, the schools were also moved to 'Abbāsiyah. During the 1920's the schools fluctuated between 'Abbāsiyah and al-Ḥārah; in the early 1930's they moved to al-Ḥārah and remained there. In 1943 the School for Girls was closed and its building was used to house the expanded kindergarten.

From 1944 to 1956 the schools were run by a Karaite principal (Mourad el-Kodsi) and for the first time there were five Karaite teachers who were university graduates teaching mathematics, science, and art. During the Arab-Israeli War of 1956 the principal of the School for Boys, who also had the authority to supervise the kindergarden, was put into protective custody. This was an opportunity for the Egyptian teachers of the kindergarten to petition the Minister of Education to change the name of the schools, which then became "al-Nāṣiriyah" (after Nāṣir).

In the meantime, the Ministry of Education appointed a Muslim principal for the Karaite School for boys. From that time on, the Karaite community had no stake in the schools, except making good the deficit resulting from the difference between the revenue and the expenditure.

Later on, the authorities imposed unjustified regulations and financial burdens on the school; the school started to close on Friday and to open on Saturday, besides opening on Jewish holidays.

---

2. Minutes of the religious council from 1901-1957; *al-Tahdhīb, al-Irshād, al-Ittiḥāf, al-Shubbān al-Qarrā'īn, al-Kalīm,* for those years (1901-1957).

3. *Al-Kalīm* No. 94 (16 February 1949). In the minutes of 25 June 1914 the religious council raised the salary of Shmoel Kohen, the Hebrew teacher in the Karaite School in al-Ḥārah, providing that he taught Hebrew to one class in the Karaite School in 'Abbāsiyah.

4. *Al-Tahdhīb,* 19 February 1903.

The community was asked to pay real estate taxes from which all other schools were exempt. In 1962 the Ministry of Education put its hands on the schools and assumed full responsibility for running them. In the early 1970's the situation changed and the schools were returned to the Karaite community. The school buildings are now rented to an educator who runs them under a new name.

Education was not limited to the schools. From 1901 to 1960 there were night classes for the teaching of Hebrew and Arabic. The various organizations of the community took care of teaching the faith and Hebrew. From 1937 to 1949 there was the "Benevolent Workshop for Girls" which taught sewing to the girls of al-Ḥārah. In the 1950's the "Ahavāt ha-Torah" organization was responsible for providing the community with a number of circumcisers and ritual slaughterers.

It should be mentioned here that as early as 1901 the religious council offered financial help to members of the community who wanted to continue their education in high schools, vocational schools or universities. Also, when "Les Ecoles Juives du Caire" were established in 1920, the religious council used to help members of the community who wished to have their children educated there. That policy was carried on until these schools were closed.[5]

Quality of Education

Both the School for Girls and the School for Boys were at the primary level, at no time offering courses beyond that level. From the time the school was established, it offered English and French as foreign languages,[6] in addition to courses in Arabic. Other subjects offered included mathematics, science, history, geography, art,[7] vocal music, hygiene and of course Hebrew for the Jewish students. Hebrew and Arabic were also offered in the evening for boys and girls from the ages of 6 to 12.

It is very surprising to find that the level of teaching English was very high. In 1901 the English teacher asked the students of the fourth grade to translate from Arabic into English a certain passage. The translation, as shown, indicates that the students at that level were in structural command of the English language[8] (Pl. 2).

As early as 1903 physical punishment was not permitted at all in the Karaite Schools. (Minutes 20 July 1903 - 26 September 1903).

All the teachers, especially the teachers of Arabic, were fully qualified. They

---

5. Minutes of 30 June 1903. Minutes of 12 October 1936, in which it is stated that there were twelve students receiving financial help. They were either in secondary schools or in vocational schools. (That is just an example.)
6. Laura and Susan Suarez were the first to teach French. They were accepted after passing a test devised by Thābit Ṣāliḥ, a member of the religious council (Minutes of 20 April 1901).
7. Art included drawing and manual art (woodworking shop).
8. *Al-Tahdhīb* No. 13 (1 November 1901) and No. 14 (8 November 1901).

either had teaching diplomas or were licensed to teach. (A high school graduate could begin teaching and, after three years of supervison by a field supervisor, became a licensed teacher.) Until the 1940's the religious council had full authority to appoint and dismiss teachers, with the assistance of well educated members of the community who supervised the schools and reported to the religious council.[9] The schools must have had a good reputation, because the principal of the Ḥilwān Public School, run by the central government, applied for a similar position in the Karaite schools. His application, however, was not approved.[10]

From the 1930's on the schools were under the supervision of the Ministry of Education. Field supervisors of each subject of instruction would supervise each teacher's performance three times a year, and a copy of their report was sent to the school. Beginning in the late 1940's these reports determined whether a teacher was worthy of promotion and, if so, of a higher salary or not.

Until the 1930's the schools had summer sessions, and many Karaite children would attend. Until 1956 the schools used to close on Saturdays and on Jewish and national holidays.

In the late 1930's the Ministry of Education, in an effort to improve the quality of education in private and parochial schools, offered financial help on a voluntary basis.[11] The Karaite Schools accepted the offer, and from that time on had to follow the same curriculum offered in the public schools, with the exception of Hebrew. In 1949 the central government assumed full responsibility for teachers' salaries. This, of course, had its effect on the quality of education in all non-governmental schools, because each school began to hire only university graduates. In addition to the teachers' salaries, the government also offered an annual sum of money for each class, the amount depending on the school's facilities and the qualification of the teachers and of the quality of the education provided in general. At that time the schools were rated as first, second, or third class schools. The Karaite schools were alway rated as first class.[12]

Students of the Karaite schools enjoyed extra-curricular activities, such as gymnastics, table tennis, chorus and acting troupes. In 1955 the gymnastic team of the Karaite schools won the shield of gymnastics in competition with all primary schools of the district of North Cairo. (Silver cup for the first team, the shield for the second). The chorus and the acting troupe used to culminate their activities towards the end of the year when they presented their annual gala on one of the very well

---

9. Minutes of the religious council from 1901 until 1940.
10. Minutes of 30 June 1903.
11. The quality of education was always higher in most parochial schools. The government was attempting to use financial aid as a means to control education in all non-public schools.
12. From 1946 to 1956 the results of the primary school certificate were 100 percent (all exams were under the government control). (*Al-Kalīm,* during the period.)

known stages (Pls. 3 and 4).

There were also other activities, including publishing a "Year Book," which portrayed the students' literary production.

Final note: Establishing the schools filled a gap that was empty for a long time. It was a needed step in order that the community could follow other communities to achieve higher goals. This first and important step should have been followed by other necessary steps.

After World War I many Karaites left the Jewish neighborhood to live in other places. These members always preferred to send their children to the local public schools even if it meant at that time (1919-1940) more financial responsibilities.

In the early 1940's, when the primary and secondary schools became totally free, responsible members of the community should have examined other possibilities regarding the Karaite schools. They should have thought of building a school in 'Abbāsiyah offering English and French[13] as foreign languages, besides Hebrew for the Jewish students. In 'Abbāsiyah alone there were more than six hundred Karaite students between the ages of five and sixteen attending the different Rabbanite schools[14] and the public primary and secondary schools.

All this required money, something the rich Karaites were not willing to give. There were hundreds of rich Karaites, yet they preferred to keep the money for themselves only. It seemed enough that they pay the monthly dues — the *'Arīkhāh,* and on several occasions, they gave some money to the needy. Their attitude was "why do we need schools or a hospital if the Rabbanite community has what we need?"

Maintaining the Karaite heritage was probably not among their goals. This attitude forced members of the community to be totally dependent on the Rabbanite community in health-care and, to a lesser degree, in education. This also explains why such a community, with hundreds of young men who would not continue higher education, never tried to establish a vocational school! The Rabbanite community did have one in 'Abbāsiyah.

The Lottery

Late in the 19th century some communities in Egypt, especially non-Muslim and foreign communities, depended on a system of public lotteries as a source of revenue. With the establishment of the school in 1896, the Karaite community also established a lottery to ensure the continuity of dependable revenue to the school. This became known as the "School's Lottery," *Naṣīb al-Madrasah.*

At that time, circa 1897, the school had its own printing shop where the lot-

---

13. Teaching French was eliminated in the Karaite schools after World War I.
14. Les Ecoles Juives du Caire in 'Abbāsiyah, Mary Suarez for girls, and Mūsā, Qattāwī for boys in Sakākīnī.

tery tickets were printed (in the 1920's they were printed elsewhere), each ticket stamped with the school's official seal, without which it was considered invalid. Imprinted on the tickets were the words, "Lottery to Help the Karaite School" — "Lotterie au Profit de l'Ecole Israelite Karaim du Caire" (Pl. 5).

The drawing itself took place in the school-yard every Sunday in the late afternoon. An appointed "caller," paid thirty piasters a month, announced the winning tickets. The winner of the first prize, upon verification of his ticket, would cash it at the school. The first prize ticket was worth one hundred Egyptian pounds, then the equivalent of $500.[15]

In 1899, the community issued 9,000 tickets weekly. Two years later, in 1901, the number reached 10,000[16]; in 1903 it reached 12,000. Upon request, the community sent a report to the governor of Cairo, in which it stated that 12,000 tickets were issued, and described the system as follows: the retailer would buy one hundred tickets for eighty five piasters. He would then sell each ticket for one piaster, thus making a profit of fifteen piasters. The report put the net profit for the community at four hundred-ninety Egyptian pounds[17] (Pl. 1).

The lottery system soon became so profitable that within a short time the market was flooded with many different lotteries. It was estimated that in Cairo alone the public poured thirty thousand Egyptian pounds per month into lotteries.[18] In view of this, the Egyptian Minister of the Interior felt that prompt action was called for. An ordinance was passed, limiting the right of issuing lottery tickets to charitable organizations and, futhermore, requiring that a permit be obtained first. In the years 1904, 1905, and 1906, the community was allowed to issue twenty thousand tickets, with drawings held twice a week. But in 1907 the community went back to one drawing a week and fifteen thousand tickets.

The net profit varied yearly, depending on the economy[19] and on the total number of tickets sold. By this time the community had accepted the offer of a family-owned bank, the Fīrūz Bank, to act as the main contractor for the lottery. The Fīrūz Bank was in fact the main contractor for many lotteries. In each year, from 1921 to 1924, the contractor paid one thousand Egyptian pounds. In 1925 the community accepted the bank's offer of the reduced sum of eight hundred Egyptian pounds. In 1922 the number of tickets was raised to 20,000 then to 30,000 in 1927.[20] Yet, despite the increase in volume, the intense competition had begun a pattern of decline in the amount of profit. It was then, in 1929, that the Minister

---

15. Minutes of June 1905. (The value of dollar to the Egyptian pound increased over the years.)
16. Minutes of 11 May 1901.
17. *Al-Tahdhīb*, 19 February 1903.
18. *Al-Tahdhīb*, 12 March 1903.
19. From 1901 to 1917, one piaster was enough to provide an adult person with three meals a day.
20. Minutes of 24 December 1927.

of Interior limited permission to issue tickets to charitable organizations only.

The new ordinance notwithstanding, matters continued to get out of hand. The National Ambulance Association then proposed a new plan. According to this plan, all communities sponsoring a lottery would form a union. The National Ambulance Association would be responsible for printing and delivering the tickets, which would then carry the name, "Lottery of the Union's Ambulance." The Karaite community joined this union,[21] whose profits were divided among the various communities according to the number of tickets sold and the percentage that was agreed upon before joining the association. The Karaite community's share was always 800.00 Egyptian pounds a year, and remained almost unchanged until 1944. The Rabbanite community's share in 1934 was as follows: 444,601 Egytpian pounds for the schools, 444,601 Egyptian pounds for the welfare organizations, and 444,600 Egyptian pounds for the hospital. *(Rapport et Comptes pour L'année* 1934, page 18.) A declining trend began in 1945 when for political and religious reasons all non-Muslim associations gradually lost their share in lottery profits.[22]

The annual Report of the Karaite community, published in *al-Kalīm,* furnishes the following data:

Year	Lottery Income (Egyptian Pound)	Year	Lottery Income (Egyptian Pound)
1944	800	1950	529
1945	750	1951	277
1946	700	1952	123
1947	686	1953	109
1948	556	1954	85
1949	570	1955	77

After the Arab-Israeli War of 1956 the Karaite community lost its share in the lottery.

Places of Worship

When Ḥākhām Abrāhām Firkovitch of Russia came to Cairo in 1862, he visited the Karaite Bēt-Dīn and donated to the community two hundred English pounds to rebuild the existing synagogue at that time, that of Rab Simḥāh.[23] In return he

---

21. Minutes of 15 January 1929.
22. The National Ambulance was under the protection of the Royal Family.
23. During my visit in Cairo in July 1982, I found some papers written by Elie Bārūkh Masʿūdah, the person in charge of Karaite real estate in Jerusalem. He wrote that the Rab Simḥāh building used to belong to the Samaritans, who had a community in Egypt, and that, in 1943, he received a letter from the chief priest of the Samaritans in Israel, including a copy of the deed to the Rab Simḥāh building. I wrote to the chief priest in Ḥolōn and got the attached answer (Pl. 6).

took away four boxes full of priceless papers and documents, among them the original family tree of the al-Nāsī family, who were descendants of 'Anān.[24] The Karaite community used the money well and rebuilt the synagogue.

In 1947 the synagogue was badly in need of repairs. The religious council at that time proposed tearing it down and building in its place a new structure that would house the synagogue, the Bēt-Dīn, and a library. Many members, however, felt that it should be kept as it was without any changes. Consequently the original building was reinforced, and many items in it were renewed. The synagogue was reopened in 1949 and remained in good condition until the late 1960's. At that time, no one was using it, so all its contents were transferred to the Mosheh al-Dar'ī synagogue.

It now serves a warehouse for a plastics factory owned by Yūsuf al-Qudsī, the great-grandson of Ḥākhām Mosheh, who was the ḥākhām akbar of the community during Firkovitch's visit. The adjacent Bēt-Dīn building serves as the plastics factory.

Before the Synagogue of Rab Simḥāh, the Karaites workshipped in a small synagogue located almost underground and called the Synagogue of al-Khaznī.[25] Al Khaznī was Nissīm Kohen al-Khaznī, the head of the Karaite community at the end of the 18th century and the beginning of the 19th. The synagogue was located in "darb al-Furn," in the same street where the community had its kasher bakery until the late 1960's. The Rab Simḥāh synagogue thus had an appropriate location at the time when most of the community members lived in al-Ḥārah.

At the end of the 19th century, however, many members of the community started to move to the neighboring areas of 'Abbāsiyah, al-Ḍāhir, and Ghamrah. It was no longer easy to walk to the synagogue of Rab Simḥāh, especially on Saturdays and holidays. As a consequence, the period of time between 1906 and 1930 saw services held in various places in those neighborhoods.[26]

In 1900 the widow of a well-known Karaite donated to the community a piece of land in 'Abbāsiyah and money to build a synagogue and a school. She was Sitaytah al-Muṣaffī, the widow of Isḥaq Ṣāliḥ, the grandson of Abrāhām Maṣliyah, who came from Hīt in Iraq at the request of the Karaite community to be its ḥākhām. Other wealthy members followed suit and donated money for the same purpose. It took the community over twenty-five years to begin construction of the synagogue, and on 23 May 1926, the entire community celebrated the laying of the foundation-stone of the 'Abbāsiyah Synagogue. It was mainly through the efforts of Ibrāhīm

---

24. *Al-Ittiḥād* No. 12 (1 February 1924).
25. In the minutes of 6 January 1924 it is mentioned that some old Torahs were found under the ruins of that synagogue.
26. Among the places were the villa of Dā'ūd Isḥāq Līsha', the second story of the Karaite school when it was in 'Abbāsiyah, and the headquarters of various Karaite associations in 'Abbāsiyah.

Elīyāhū Mas'ūdah, a well known benefactor, that the project moved ahead, but when he died on February 18, 1927, construction came to a stop.

In 1928 David Zaki Līsha', at the time a relatively young and very energetic man, decided to hold Yom Kippur services at the synagogue, even though it had not been completed.[27] It was an emotional but successful day, after which enough money was collected to help complete the synagogue. It was completed in 1931,[28] and the community at the time had two respectable synagogues. When Tobiah became ḥakhām akbar of the Karaite community, he named it "Mosheh al-Dar'ī Synagogue." after a well known poet of medieval Karaism.[29]

At the time this synagogue was built, the community did not forsee the need for a cultural center or for a hall for lectures, meetings, and weddings. During the 1940's this need emerged clearly. Murād Farag donated a sum of money to build a cultural center bearing his name, and in 1947 the religious council decided to build it. It was the feeling at that time that a center should house a hall, Sunday school, offices of the Bēt-Dīn, a library, and an office for the ḥakhām. Samuel Ḥasīd, a construction engineer and professor at the University of Cairo, submitted to the religious council a blueprint for the project,[30] but, as usual, the whole community was divided between the "pros" and the "cons." Years passed, and the project was shelved. The synagogue iteslf is still in good condition but has started to deteriorate because of lack of maintenance.

Before entering the synagogue one must take off one's shoes. For this reason there is a foyer between the entrance and the sanctuary where worshippers can take their shoes off and place them on the many shelves provided for this purpose. In this foyer there are hundreds of small lockers, more like a post office box, where worshippers keep their sets of prayer books and their ṭallīts. Those who were not able to obtain a locker used to carry the prayer book and the ṭallīt in a special velvet sack.[31]

Both synagogues (Rab-Simḥāh and Mosheh al-Dar'ī) were of two levels: the main, or first, level is the sanctuary; the second level is for women only. In the Mosheh al-Dar'ī synagogue there is a hall of limited capacity that was used for many cultural and religious activities.

The sanctuary is covered with mats and rugs. There are no chairs or benches, and that gives more flexibility to the worshippers to practice all the accompanying

---

27. Karaites used rugs (not seats) in their synagogues. Many members sent clean rugs to the synagogue on that day.
28. I was unable to find in the minutes of the religious council any indication of the exact date.
29. Leon Nemoy, *Karaite Anthology*, pp. 133-146.
30. *Al-Kalīm* Nos. 63/64 (1 October 1947)
31. In both synagogues there were no extra prayer books, so each person had to have his own.

ceremonial acts of physical positions required in Karaite prayers.³²

The pulpit is few steps higher than the sanctuary. A large oak table provided a place for several scrolls. Next to the table is a high chair for the ḥākhām. The ḥākhām could be the reader and the ḥazzān too. Yet it was the custom to provide ḥazzānīm and readers in advance for Saturday and holiday services.

The scrolls are kept in the ark, where each scroll is kept in a decorative box of olive- or mahogany-wood covered with silver or gold leaves or inlaid with mother of pearl.

In a separate room, to the left of the pulpit (the same level as the sanctuary), there is room where a special scroll is kept — the scroll of the sacrifice *(Qurbān)*. Underneath the pulpit in the Mosheh al-Dar'ī synagogue there is a large room used as a *geniza*.

Above the ark there is a big Star of David with the word "YHVH" written out inside it in full.

The Karaite community of Cairo possessed valuable and rare codexes, among which is the famous Ben Asher codex,³³ which the community has preserved for over a thousand years and still preserves. The Ben Asher codex, along with others no less valuable, were kept in a safe in the Mosheh al-Dar'ī synagogue. Most of the scrolls in both synagogues were donated by members of the community to commemorate a happy occasion, especially the birth of the first baby boy born, the *beckor*.

All around the sanctuary there were silver chandeliers, most of them donated to the synagogue in memory of departed ones or for other reasons.³⁴

In a separate building there are facilities including a small kitchen. In the Mosheh al-Dar'ī syanagogue there are rooms for the beadle and his family, as well as rooms for Sunday school (Pls. 7a and b).

The possibility of a third synagogue existed for a time, when during the thirties many families moved to Heliopolis, a beautiful and very clean suburb north of Cairo. It became very difficult for members of those families to attend services that were held in any existing Karaite synagogue. Farag Ibrāhīm Levi presented to the religious council what amounted to $5,000 collected from members of that branch of the Levi family, to build a synagogue in Heliopolis.³⁵ A year earlier, the

---

32. During the 1940's some chairs at the back of the temple were provided for disabled men. See under "A Brief Discussion of the Karaite Liturgy."
33. *Firkovitch,* in his second visit to Cairo in 1864, took a codex that is as valuable and as important as the Ben-Asher codex. It is known now as the Leningrad Codex. (Lila Avrin, *The Illumination in the Mosheh ben Asher Codex of 895 C.E.,* Vol. 1, p. 75).
34. It is most unfortunate that during the 1960's responsible members of the community melted all the chandeliers in both synagogues. Many of these chandeliers had an historical value that was much more than just the value of the silver.
35. Minutes of 30 January 1945.

religious council had been able to acquire a piece of land from the 'Ayn Shams Railway Company, which owned most of the land in Heliopolis. Again, as usual, the community was divided between those who felt the need for a third synagogue and those who felt that the whole project should be carried out by the people who lived in Heliopolis. Events in the years to come decided the matter, and the synagogue was never built.

The religious council was the only body responsible for the community's establishments: schools, synagogues, bēt dīn, and for all associated expenses, such as maintenance, electricity, telephone, gardening, furniture (especially rugs) and the salary of the ḥākhām and the beadles. It was, however, the gabbāy (treasurer) who had the responsibility of looking after the synagogue's needs. He had the ultimate authority over any member, including the ḥākhām. The gabbāy, ideally, should be very well-schooled in the faith and come from a rich or at least well-to-do family. David Zaki Līsha', from the affluent branch of the Līsha' family, was the first and last gabbāy of that synagogue, serving from 1931 until he left Egypt in 1965. As for the Synagogue of Rab Simḥāh, many members held that position, among them Dā'ūd Isḥāq Līsha', Mūsā Ibrāhīm Menasha, Yūsuf Farag Hayyīnah, Yūsuf Yomtōb, and Salīm Farag Shamuel.

Cemeteries

To the south of Cairo, near the elegant suburb of al-Ma'ādi, stretches a vast arid land known as al-Basātīn.[36] That land was, and still is, the burial place for the Karaite community (Pl. 8).

The history of this piece of land, still owned by the Karaites of Cairo, is documented in the archives of the Karaite community in the Bēt-Dīn. There, an old document, in Arabic, records the donation to the Karaite community of Cairo of five hundred *faddans* (the *faddan* is somewhat larger than an acre) in the village of al-Basātīn.[37]

When I was in Egypt in July 1982, I was able to examine a document written in Arabic on the 15th of Muḥarram, 980 Higriyah (1571 C.E.). The document indicates that the community had this land in al-Wazīr in the area of al-Basātīn "since very long ago" *(min qadīm al-zaman),* and it was in their hands on the basis of older documents. The document goes on to state that Karaite Shamual (probably Samuel) had sometime earlier given the other Jews a piece of that land to bury their dead. It mentions the Rabbanites, the Maghrebites, and the Arabized Jews[38] (Pl. 9).

---

36. Al-Basātīn means "the orchards," which it possibly once was.
37. *Al-Tahdhīb* No. 38 (29 May 1902) mentioned the existence of such a document, sealed with the palm of the hand of 'Amr ibn al-'Āṣ, the Arab conqueror of Egypt (7th century).
38. The words "Arabized Jews" are mentioned twice, once quite clearly, the other time rather obscurely. There was no dot on the letter, otherwise the meaning would be "Egyptian expatriated Jews."

In the period covered here, the various religious councils were entrusted with the care of this property. This maintenance, however, usually did not extend beyond surveying the land several times. (It was not until World War II, when the British army needed a piece of the Karaite-owned land for military purposes, that running water was installed there for the first time.)

In contrast to the condition of the Karaite burial place was that of the Rabbanites' cemetery, which was located nearby. There was no comparison between the two places. The Rabbanite burial place was divided into lots, with paths running between them, and was well cared for by the Rabbanite community. It was a great source of pride for that community.

At the turn of the century, certain Karaite families purchased lots from the Karaite Bēt-Dīn. Each lot was surrounded by a stone and iron fence; and contained two or three furnished rooms with living facilities. It was the custom to visit the dead and spend one night with them during certain days (fast of Ḥameshi, for example).[39]

Members of the Karaite community built many expensive memorials for their deceased, and almost every tomb was covered wth imported Italian marble. The community assigned guards to protect the place from thieves and vandals. In the 1960's, however, when the burial places for both the Rabbanite and Karaite communities were rarely used, thieves began to steal the marble from the tombs, and eventually took away even the iron fences.

I visited al-Basātīn in July 1982. From what I saw, and from what I know to be true, I have no doubt that there will be no burial place for either community within ten years. The few remaining members of the Karaite community are trying to get a court order to protect the cemetery; they have the title to the place, and legally it is theirs.

In my judgement, this attempt on their part is a lost battle. The following diagram might help understand why:

---

39. This custom was very common among all classes of Egyptian women, including Muslim women.

CAIRO   N
                                      W   E
                                         S

al-'Imān al-Shāfi'ī

Muslim burial place, already filled with people forced "by overcrowding" to live there with the dead.

↓ . . . . ↓ . . . . ↓

The Nile   Rabbanite burial place   Hills

Karaite burial place

↑ . . . . ↑ . . . . ↑

al-Ma'ādī suburb

The arrows indicate new housing projects around al-Basātīn. It is a matter of time until takeover will occur, unless an agreement or a court order to keep these places intact is reached. This, unfortunately is unlikely.

Students of one of the classes of the third grade of the Karaite School for boys. (1947) Standing to the right is Solomon Shabbethāi Nōnō, the Hebrew teacher who became the chief rabbi of the Karaite community in Israel and kept this position until he died in 1976.

Faculty members of the Karaite School for Boys. Sitting in the middle are Murād al-Qudsī (Principal), Yūsuf Ibrāhim Yomṭōb (Hebrew teacher) to his right, and Muḥammad 'Abd al-Muṭṭalib (math teacher) to his left. Behind Murād al-Qudsī are Farag al-Qudsī (math teacher), to his left Benoit Mas'ūdah (science teacher). 1950

Moshēh al-Darʿī synagogue in ʿAbbāsiyah

The pulpit, and the ark where the scrolls are kept.

A silver candelabrum always placed on the tevah.

Inside R. Simḥāh synagogue, the pulpit and the ark.

The section assigned for women on the second floor. Notice the lattice wood in decoration.

The decorated ceiling.

The spiral stairs that lead to the second floor.

The square marble slate placed above the main door of the R. Simḥāh synagogue.

The oval slate placed on the eastern wall.

Both slates indicate that the synagogue was renovated in the year 1871, under the care of "The trusted one, Isḥāq Elīsha', son of Yūsuf, of the al-Sa'īr family."

The tomb of Ibrāhīm Elīyāhū Masʿūdah. The building next to the tomb, inside the Ḥōsh, contains three bedrooms, a living room, a kitchen and other facilities. Notice the style of the building, which is Islamic. Karaites in Egypt adopted the Islamic custom of visiting the graves of their deceased on certain days, and spending one night in the facilities in the Ḥōsh...

Some Karaites visiting the tomb of Ibrāhīm Elīyāhū Mas'ūdah.

Al-Basātin, the burial place of the Karaites, as it was in 1980. Notice the new building "x". Notice also the Ḥōsh of the Mas'ūdah family, which is still intact.

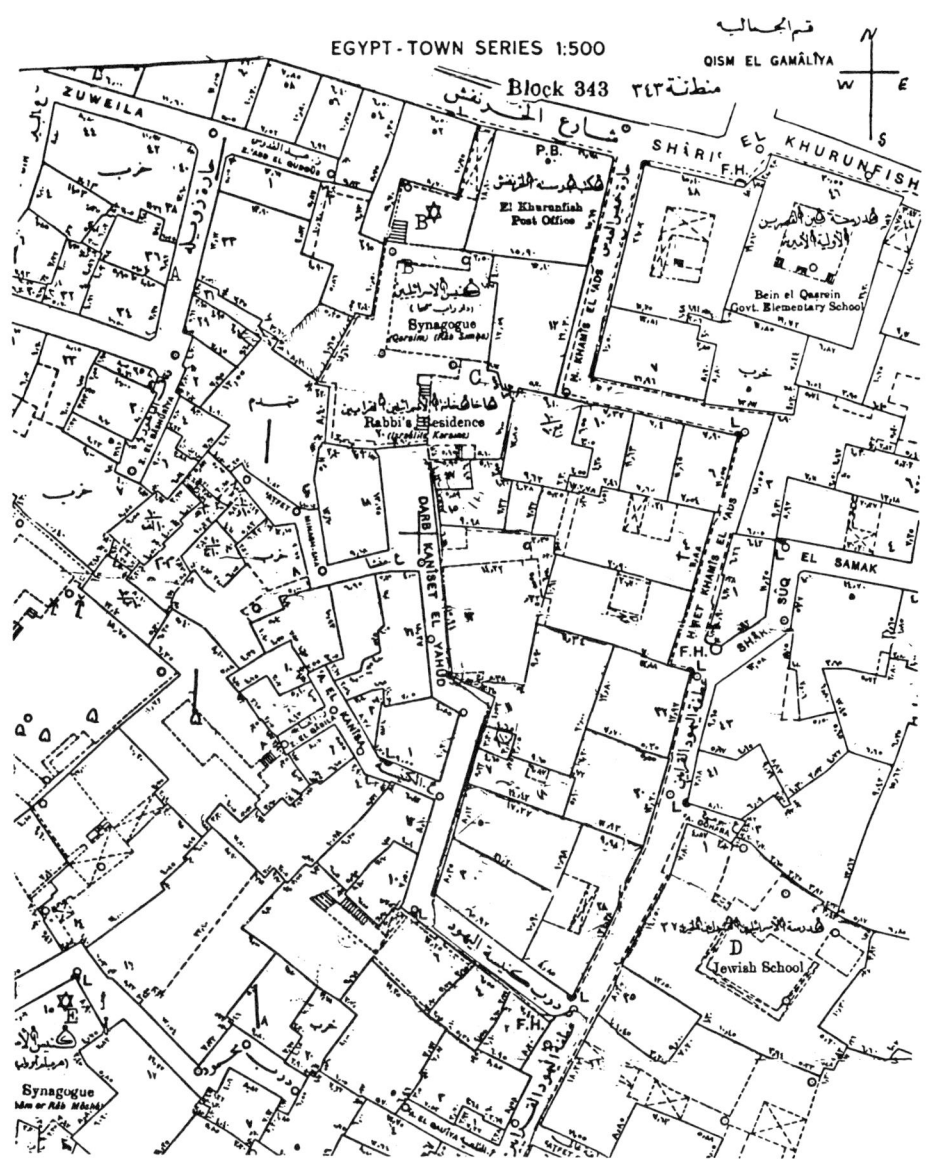

MAP: Ḥārat al-Yahūd al-Qarrā'īn: A) Ḥārat Zuwaylah. B) Synagogue Rab Simḥah. C) Karaite Bēt-Dīn. D) Karaite School. E) Synagogue Harambām which is located in Ḥārat al-Yahūd al-Rabbāniyīn.

To the north	To the east	To the South
al 'Abbāsiyah	al-Ḥusayn	old Cairo
Ghamrah	al-Azhar	al-Basātīn
al-Sakāhīnī		
al-Dāhir		

اما التقرير الذي رفعناه رفق هذا الخطاب فهو كناية° عن بيان حالة ايراد ومصرف الورق وحالة المدرسة بالتفصيل ولا بأس بتلخيص ذلك هنا فاما الورق فعدده اثنى عشر الف ورقة فے كل اسبوع توزعها المدرسة بسعر ٨٥٠ مليم المائة الى مخصوصين يتولون بيعه للناس وبحجم هو ١٥٠ مليم فى المائة قيمة الفرق بين ما يأخذون به وما يبيعون به بالثمن الاصلى وهو ١٠ مليم الورقة الواحدة فتكون قيمة الورق بالنسبة للمدرسة ١٠٠ جنيه و ٢٠٠ مليمْ يطرح من ذلك ٨ جنيه و ٥٠٠ مليم قيمة الف ورقة عبارة عن متوسط ما يكسد عادةً من الورق بغير بيع فى كل اسبوع فيكون الباقى بعد ذلك ٩٣ جنيه و ٥٠٠ مليم

وفى الورق ثلاثة وثلاثون ورقة تربح ٨١ جنيه و ٢٠٠ مليم وبطرحها من هذا الصافى يكون الفائض ١٢ جنيه و ٣٠٠ مليم ثم يكون مجموع ما يفيض فى كل شهر ٥٣ جنيه و ٢٠٠ مليمْ يطرح منه ١٣ جنيه شهريا قيمة مصارف ونفقات خاصة بالورق نفسه فيكون صافى الصافى مبلغ ٤٠ جنيه و ٢٠٠ مليم يضاف اليه مبلغ ١٩ جنيه و ٨٥٠ مليم قيمة مرتبات بعض التلاميذ والتلميذات فى الشهر فيكون مجموع الايراد مبلغ ٦٠ جنيه و ٥٠ مليم تفق المدرسة بجانبه فى الشهر ٧١ جنيه و ٧٥ مليم فيكون ما تصرفه من عند نفسها فى كل شهر مبلغ ١١ جنيه و ٧٠٠ مليم فضلاً عن صرفها بعض ادوية وكساوى مجاناً ما تبلغ قيمته فى السنة ٢٥ جنيه تقريباً

فى المدرسة ٢٣٢ تلميذاً منهم ١٣٩ من البنين ٥٥ مجاناً و٨٤ بمرتبات و٩٣ من البنات ٤٨ مجاناً و٤٥ بمرتبات فيكون المجانى ١٠٣ والذى بمرتبات ١٢٩ وقيمة هذه المرتبات ١٩ جنيه و ٨٥٠ مليم فى الشهر كما قدمنا

وفى المدرسة ناظر وخمسة عشر من المعلمين والمعلمات ولها طبيب وكاتب وصراف وعامل لطبع الورق وآخر لوضع ارقامه ثم ثلاثة فراشين

هذا وقد لاحت فے وجه سعادة المحافظ حفظه الله دلائل الارتياح والاذعان ووعد خيرا وعلى الله الاتكال والاعتماد

PLATE 1: Part of a report sent to the Governor of Cairo on 5 February 1903. The main points in the report are: number of students, their status, full tuition, reduced or free. It also mentions their religion, the staff, revenues, and expenditures. (see "Education," page 99)
al-Tahdhīb, 19 February 1903 A.D.

{ ٠ ترجمة ٠ }

يطلب جناب حبيب افندي استاذ الانجليزية بالمدرسه من تلامذة السنة الرابعة بما ترجمة النبذة الآتية الى اللغة الانجليزية ومن كانت ترجمته احسن قدم التهذيب ذكر اسمه على من دونه . اما النبذة فهى « الانسان مفتقر طبعاً في معيشته الى الاستعانة بغيره من الناس اذ هو لا يستطيع وحده ان يحصل على احتياجاته من مآكل ومشرب ومطعم وملبس وما شاكل فاذا نظرنا الى قطعة الخبز وجدنا انه ما وصل اليها الا بعد ان تعب فيها كثيرون من فلاح وحصاد ودراس ومغربل وطحان وعجان وخباز »

{ الترجمة }

قام بترجمة الجملة العربية الواردة بالتهذيب الماضي الى اللغة الانجليزية فرج ويوسف ابراهيم وفرج سليم وابراهيم فرج من تلامذة المدرسة بالسنة الرابعة وقد راعينا كما وعدنا ترتيب الاسماء بحسب درجات الاحسن فالاقل منه وعلى كل حال يشكرهم القلم والنشاط على جدهم

اما الترجمة فهي كما يأتي اوردناها بنصها اتماماً للشيء في ذاته

PLATE 2: Ḥabīb Effendi, the English teacher, asked the students of the 4th grade to translate the Arabic passage above into English. Four students were able to translate the passage into English, as shown above.
al-Tahdhīb, no. 14, 8 November 1901, p. 60.

(A person cannot dispense in his livelyhood with the help of his fellow - members of society as it is not in his power to obtain alone for himself all his requirements such as food and clothing and the like . If we examine a piece of bread , we find that it has not come into our hands until after it has passed through the hands of the farmer, the reaper, the thresher, the miller, the dough - man, and the baker)

الحفلة السنوية لمدارس الاسرائيليين القرائين

ما وافت الساعة السادسة ونصف من مساء يوم الاحد الموافق ١٣ يونية سنة ١٩٣٧ ، حتى امتلأت قاعة مسرح الحديقة بحضرات كبار الزائرين من مفتش وزارة المعارف ، وأعيان الطائفة وفى مقدمتهم سيادة الحاخام طوبيا ليفى ، والاستاذ مراد بك فرج ، وحضرة الوجيه باروخ وغيرهم . ومما زاد الحفل بهجة وسرورا تشريف سيادة الحاخام حايم ناحوم افندى .

وابتدأت الحفلة بالسلام الملكى من أور كستر جمعية الشبان الاسرائيليين القرائين ، ثم ظهر الطلبة يرددون النشيد القومى فى حماس ، ثم أعقب ذلك نشيد «فاروق» من الطالبات ثم ردد الطلبة جميعا نشيد المدارس من وضع الشاعر مراد بك فرج وتلحين الموسيقار الاستاذ داود حسنى ، فدوت القاعة بالتصفيق الحاد

ثم تلى حضرة مدير المدارس ضيف افندى كلمة ترحيب وشكر ثم كلمة من سيادة الحاخام طوبيا ليفى كان لها نعم الاثر فى النفوس . وكانت قصيدة خطيب الحفل الشاعر الكبير مراد بك فرج رنة فى السمع استعيدت أبياتها بالتصفيق الحاد

وان ما يذكر بالتقدير والفخر ، الرقص التوقيعى على نغمة الاوركستر . فقد أبدع الطالبات خصوصا فى رقصة بائعة الورد ورقصة القمر والنجوم التى أعيدت مرة أخرى بين الثناء والتقدير .

وقد مثلت جماعة التمثيل والالقاء بالمدرسة ثلاث روايات قوية الاولى ـ « مدارسنا ومدارسهم» وهى كوميدى انتقادية مبنية على فكرة نومية اجتماعية وقد أبدع الطالبات ايما ابداع .

والثانيه (الملك سليمان) وهى دراما تاريخية أحسن الطلبة فى القائها باللغة العبرية وساعد على ظهارها الاخراج القوى والمناظر التاريخية المدهشة .

والثالثة «الحلاق الفيلسوف» وكانت مسك الختام وهى كوميدى وقد شهد الزائرون نبوغ الطلبة فى تمثيل بعض المواقف القوية رغم حداثة سنهم .

وأخيرا وزعت الجوائز على المتفوقين من الطلبة والطالبات .

فالى مدارس الطائفة نزف التهاني لهذه الخطوة الجريئة وقـــ تكللت الحفلة بنجاح منقطع النظير . كما لا يفوتنا أن نثنى على همة مدرب فرقة التمثيل ابرهيم افندى حسني و ريس الاوركستر الياهو افندى أصلان .

PLATE 3: Among the school's activities was the yearly assembly held usually during the last week of the school year. It was the custom to hold it in the Azbākiyah Theater in the heart of Cairo. On June 13, 1937, the school held its assembly there. Among the dignitaries were Tobiah Babovitich (the ḥākhām akbar of the Karaite Community), Ḥākhām Ḥayyīm Nāḥūm (the ḥākhām akbar of the Rabbanite Community), Murād Farag and many members of the Religious Council, as well as members of the community.

The students introduced three acts: "Our schools and Theirs," a play comparing our schools with other schools; "King Solomon," acted in Hebrew; and "The Philosopher-Barber," a comedy in Arabic.

al-Shubbān, no. 5, 1st year, 1937.

العيد الذهبى لمدارس الطائفة

احتفلت مدارس الاسرائيليين القرائين الخيرية للبنين بالخرنفش يوم السبت الماضى بعيدها الذهبى بمناسبة مرور خمسين عام على تأسيسها . وقد بدأ الاحتفال فى تمام الساعة السابعة مساء فأتى موسى أفندى مراد رئيس لجنة المدارس كلمة سرد فيها تاريخ المدرسة منذ انشائها أيام المرحوم الطيب الذكر الحاخام شبتاى منجورى حتى الان وقد قوبلت كلمته بتصفيق حار من حضرات المستمعين خصوصا لما ذكر أن النية متجهة الى بناء مدرسة للبنين وأخرى للبنات وان المجلس الملى يسعى اشراء قطعة الأرض المجاورة لكنيس العباسية لهــذا الغرض ثم اختتم كلمته وتمنى للمدرسة كل نجاح فى ظل الفاروق وبوجود ناظرها الحالى مراد افندى موسى .

ولما انتهى من كلمته قام الاستاذ مراد فرج المحامى شاعر الاسرائيلية فألقى قصيده عصماء استعيدت ابياتها مرارا ً

ثم اعقبه مراد أفندى موسى ناظر المدرسة الحالى فشكر المدعوين ورحب بهم ثم تكلم عن مدرسة البنين ومدرسة الروضة وعن مناهج التعلم بهما وعن الروح الطيبة السائدة بين التلاميـذ بعضهم ببعض وتمنى ان تدوم هذه الروح وهذه الصداقة بين التلاميـذ فى المستقبل حتى يكون را عامـلا من عوامل الاتحـاد ثم كرر الشـكر للمدعوين واستأذنهم فى بـدأ الحفلة وقـد قام الطلبة بتمثيل تمثيلية العالم الصغير وقام الخريجون بتمثيل رواية النبل هذا عدا الاناشيد والازجال التى القاها الطلبة . وقد نجحت الحفلة نجاحا كبيرا وشهدها أكثر من ألف شخص حتى ضاقت قاعة يورت بهم

وقد كنا نود ان نرى حضرات اعضاء المجلس الملى بكامل هيئتهم ولكن الاسف تغيب الكثيرون وكان تغيبهم موضعا للحدس والتخمين وقد شهد الحفلة من الكبراء عمر بك الاسكندرى المدير المساعد للتعليم الحر كما شهدها صالح باشا حرب رئيس جمعية الشبان المسلمين وقد سرا كثيرا بمجهود التلاميذ واستمرا الى نهاية الحفل .

والـكليم تتقدم الى مدارس الاسرائيليين القرائين بهنئة راجية لها دوام التقدم والرقى؟

PLATE 4: The Golden Jubilee of the Karaite Schools: 1896-1946
On Saturday, March 9, 1946, the schools celebrated their Golden Jubilee. The festival was held in Ewart Memorial Hall of the American University in Cairo. Ḥākhām Tobiah attended the celebration, along with some members of the Religious Council and Murād Farag Līsha'. Over one thousand people attended the party. High-ranking educators were present. Sāliḥ Ḥarb Bāshā, the Chairman of the Young Men's Muslim Association, was present that night. The party was a complete success.

The students introduced a comedy "The Small World"; the graduates introduced a political play, "The Nile."

al-Kalīm, no. 27, 2nd year, 16 March 1946, p. 3

EDUCATION ILLUSTRATION

The Karaite Schools in 60 years: 1896 to 1956.
al-Tahdhīb, no. 13, 19 February 1903.

	Full tuition	Free	Total
Boys	84	55	139
Girls	45	48	93
Total	129	103	232

One principal; fifteen teachers; one visiting physician; one secretary; three custodians.

1936 From an unsigned circulation defending the deputy of the Karaite Bēt-Dīn

	Jews	Other religions	Total
Full tuition	23	59	82
Free	122	22	144
Total	145	81	226

1952 Annual Report of the Karaite Community in Egypt.
al-Kalīm, no. 180, 3 March 1953

School	Jews	Christians	Muslims	Total
Boys	25	29	175	229
Kindergarten	21	36	186	243
Total	46	65	361	472

One principal for each school; one secretary for each; one visiting physician for both; 25 teachers for both; seven custodians for both.

1955 Annual Report of the Karaite Community in Egypt
al-Kalīm, no. 244, 15 July 1956.

	Boys	Girls	Total
Karaites	12	6	18
Other religions	577	139	716
Total	589	145	734

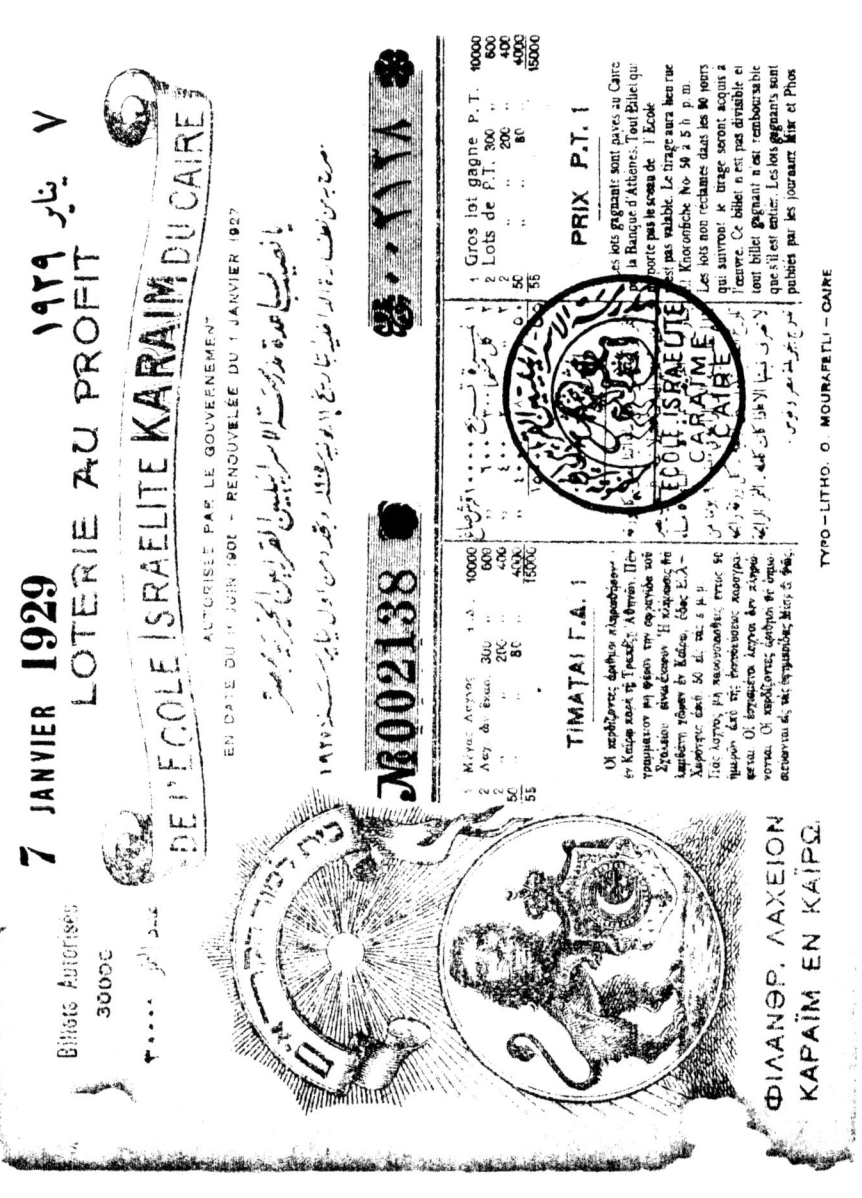

PLATE 5: A lottery ticket of January 7, 1929.

اسرائيل ارض الميعاد والاباء

١٩٨٧/١١/٢٧

حضرة الاستاذ الفاضل مراد موسى يوسف ادم الله يبقاه امين

تحية صادرة وقلب طاهر مملؤ في المحبه والاجلال والاكرام لكم ولكل من امن بشريعة النبي والكتاب موسى بن عمران عليه افضل السلام
اما بعد فهو الاجابه على سؤالكم بخصوص كنيسة سمحا في مصر وليس دمسحا لانه طائفتنا السامريين المحافظين على التراث القديم كان موجود منهم في مصر في بلد ترعه فسطاط الى غايه سنة ١٧٢٠ وكان لهم كنايس في مصر ومن جملتهم كنيسة سمحا لانه يوجد توراة على رق مكتوب في تاريخها كتبت الى كنيسة سمحا في مصر واصل هذه الكنيسه هي الى واصله تدعا سمحا بنت ابراهيم هرم الفاضل يعقوب من بني فرج
وهذا له اعمال خيريه كثيره مع المخلوقات واخذ في زمانه اسم الاب الشفوق وتوفا هذا المرحوم وورثته حرمته وبنته كنيسه في هذا المال وسميه هذه الكنيسه على اسم هذه الفاضله جدا ها الله بالاحسان امين الرجا اهدا سلامي لعائلتكم الكريمه والى الاخ السيد يوسف صباغ ولكل من يتعرف علينا والسلام من كهنين الامام بنيميم
ابراهيم بنيميم الملقب خضر في حولون

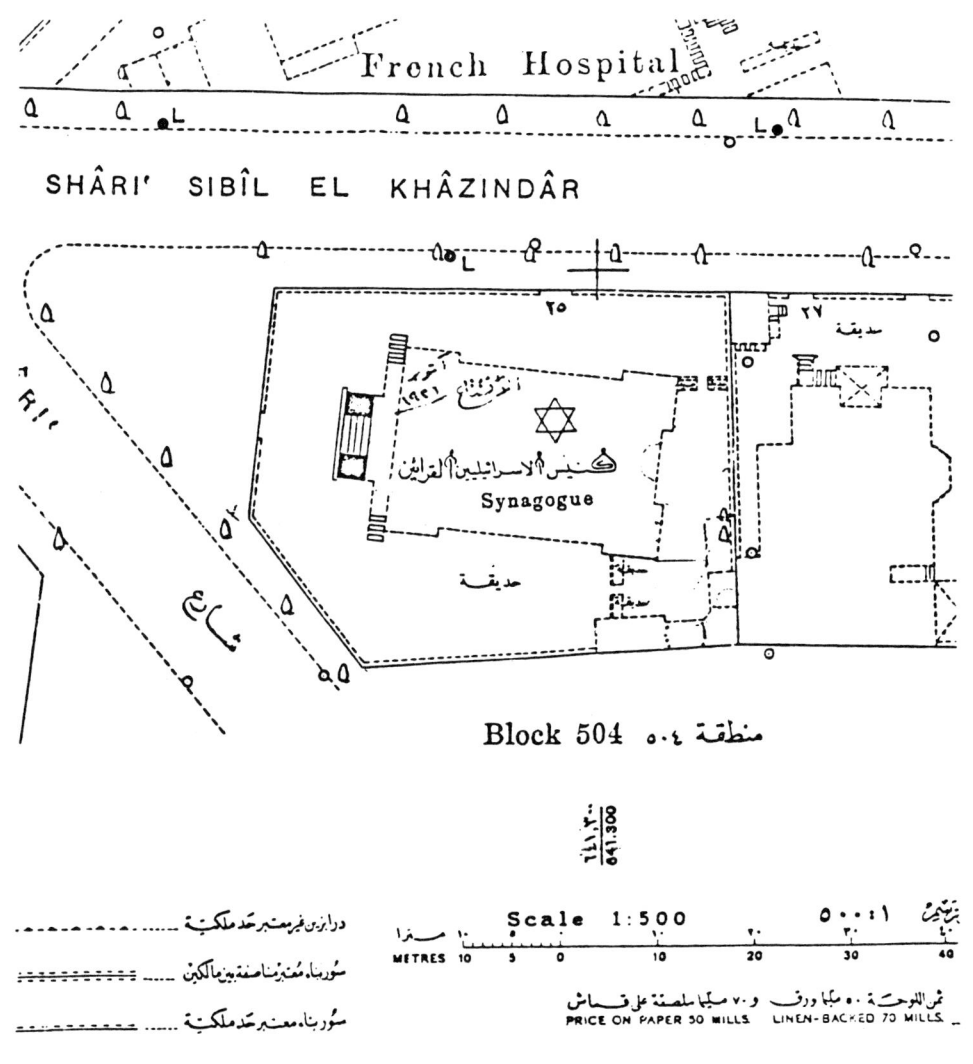

PLATE 7a: The Mosheh al-Dar'ī synagogue in al-'Abbāsiyah, Cairo.

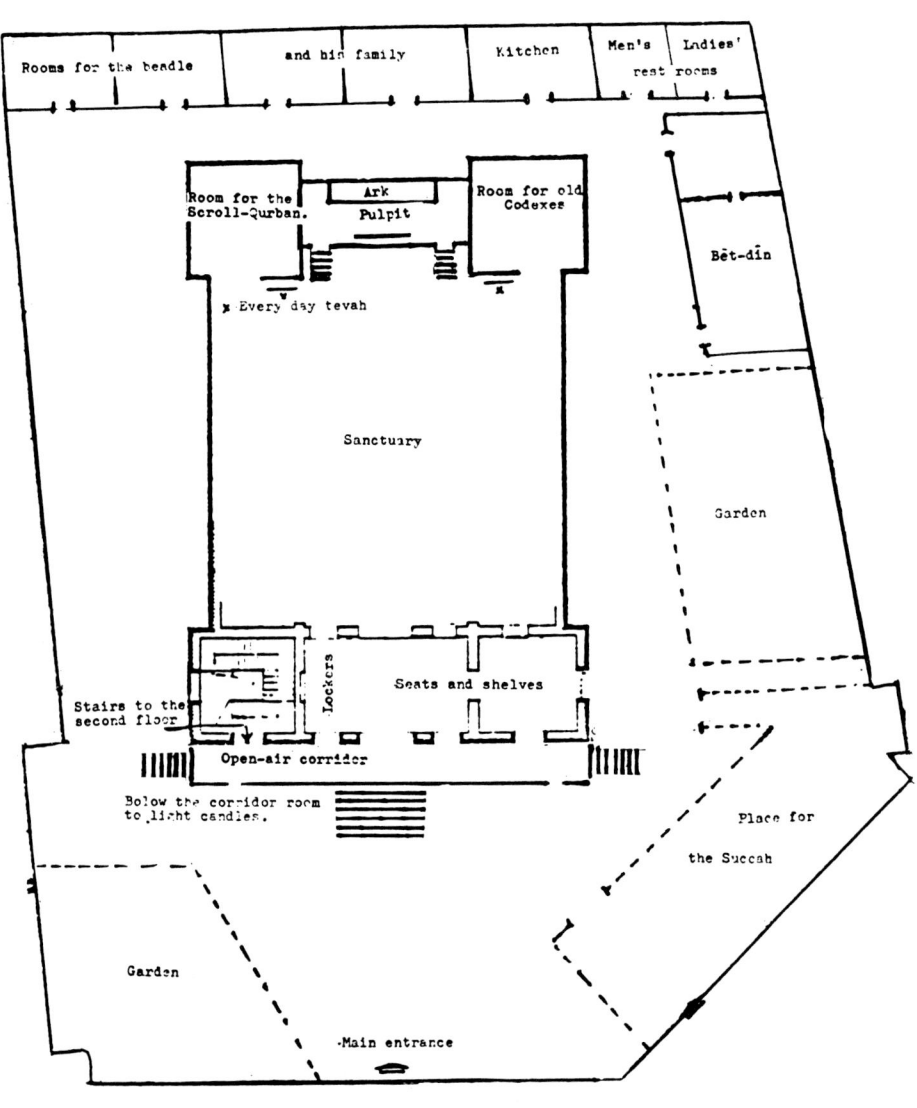

PLATE 7b: The Mosheh al-Dar'ī synagogue. Plan of the first floor and around the synagogue.

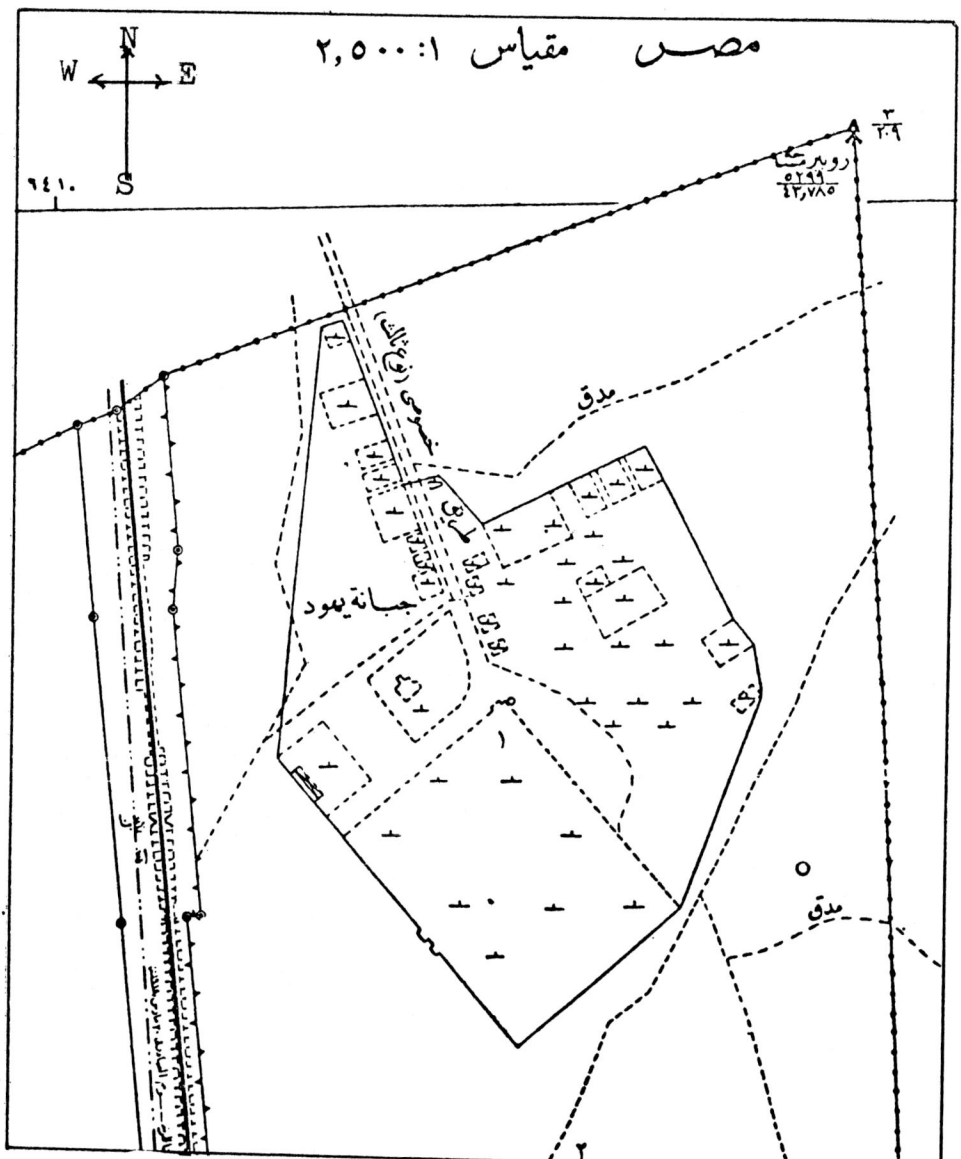

PLATE 8: Map of al-Basātīn, the burial place for both the Karaite and the Rabbanite communities. To the north is Cairo city. To the south is the elegant suburb, al-Maʿādī. The hills of al-Muqaṭṭam are to the east, and the river Nile is to the west.

بسم الله

الشريف بالباب العالي بمحضر الحروف بين يديه سببا وأو لا انفر قضاة الإسلام كالإلاه إلا الله وسيد الأنام مولانا
محرر القضايا والأحكام وسيد سلم ومستجاب الأنام عليه الصلاة والسلام والوائق بالآلاء الوفي مولانا
الحاكم لغني الذي سبح خطة آلقسم علاه دام والاستغلاء علا دفيه بدية حضر
العدل بلور ابراهيم الاسكندراني والحاخام وتجار اليهود والمتكلم على طائفة اليهود
المستخرمين والحاخام ابن يوسف اليهود الذي بالمعروف بالكبوتي والحاخام بن اليهودي اقرار
الغربي المتكلم على طائفة اليهود المذكورة وبرهوحصتهم العلم عبد الواحدين
الحكيم والمتكلم على طائفة اليهود القرائين واشهدوا على انفسهم الجماعة المذكورين وهم
طائعين مختارين من غير اكراه ولا ايجاد على ان ما هو مخصوص بالطوائف المذكورة وسعد
اموالهم بالماكين جميع المتبر الكائنة بخط البساتين المعروف بالوزير وبان...
بيد طائفة اليهود القرائين المتكلم عليهم عبد الواحد المذكور على فقرائهم واغنيائهم وقديم
بمقتضى ان ذلك في تصرف فهم من قديم الزمان كما ذلك كما بين بمكتوب شاهد بذلك ناهو
بالإنعام من الإبواب العالية باسم العلي شموال المعروف بالدستوري والمتكلم نيابة على الطائفة
وبموجب الاوامر السلطانية المورخة بتواريخ التمسكات المذكورة بتاريخ ربيع الآخر سنة اربعين
وتسعايه وان طائفة اليهود الربانيين والبلاد الخازر واليهود المصريين المستعربين اللهم جميع
القطعة الأرض الم اده لدفن اموائهم بالتمليك الشرعي من العلم شموال المذكور اعلاه
من قديم الزمان والى تاريخه كما ذلك مبين بالتمسكات الشرعية الحمله تحت ايديهم
وان الفاصل بين المتبر المعده لدفن اموات اليهود القرائين وبين المتبر المعد لدفن
اليهود الربانيين الإيدهم بالتمليك الشرعي من شموال المذكور اعلاه وقدرذلك مايذرع
وخمسة وستة ن ذراع على الدا وتدرالارض وذراع عماخشاء ذراع وثلاثة راع

PLATE 9: Part of a document written in Arabic on the 15th of Muḥarram, 980 Higriyah (1571 C.E.). The document states "that the Karaite Community of Egypt had this land in al-Wazīr in the area of al-Basāṭīn 'since very long ago,' and it was in their hands on the basis of an older document." The document goes on to state that the Karaite Shamwal had sometimes earlier given the other Jews a piece of that land to bury their dead. The document mentions the Rabbanite Jews, the Maghrebites, and the Arabized Jews.

Chapter IV

Caring for the Needy

The Role of the Religious Councils

The Role of the Various Organizations

The Role of the Religious Council.

Knowing the situation of the Karaite community during the period covered in this book, no one can argue that there was a kind of caring shown by members of the community towards their unfortunate brothers, even if that care was not managed properly.

The Karaite community in Egypt, being an eastern community in an Islamic one, was much affected by the customs that prevailed in the country, among which was charity to the poor, and so the Karaites gave.

There are no records about the situation during the last quarter of the nineteenth century, but it can be safely assumed, as most of the Karaites — rich and poor — were living in the Jewish neighborhood, that the rich took care of the poor members of their own family.

The number of persons who needed help at the turn of the century was less than one hundred, while in the 1950's it grew to over 150.

During the first quarter of the twentieth century, the Karaite religious council, several organizations, and many members of the community provided a kind of help for the poor, but that was not enough.

From the beginning, the religious council provided monthly payments and medical care for certain families. Some Karaite residents of the Jewish neighborhood used to receive that sort of help, besides free or almost free housing. A committee from the religious council used to decide who should receive assistance, but the preliminary and principal work used to be done by the clerk of the Karaite Bēt-Dīn, who also resided in the Karaite neighborhood. The financial help in education was also decided by members of the religious council, but starting in the 1950's, that task was delegated to two members who examined every case and gave their recommendations.

During the holidays, winter, and on other occasions (such as birth of the first born, marriage, memorial, etc.) some members used to donate food, money and clothing to the poor residents of the Karaite neighborhood. They used to give these donations by themselves or ask the clerk of the Karaite Bēt-Dīn to do it for them.

This situation prevailed until the late 1940's, when, at the request of a certain member of the religious council, a committee was formed to be responsible, among other things, for all donations.

The religious council provided health care for everyone who needed it, and once again written permission from the clerk of the Bēt-Dīn was enough to have that person admitted to the Jewish hospital free of charge or at reduced charges. The Karaite doctors, and there were many, had their own share of help in that regard and they used to render their services free or for minimal charges.

From the turn of the century onward, the religious council provided financial help in education. Students in primary and secondary schools, or even in the universities, upon request, could receive partial or full coverage of their tuition or whatever was needed. That was aside from helping each year more than two hundred students in the Rabbanite schools. The religious council used to pay a flat rate to the Rabbanite community, but after 1950 it was decided that the Karaite community should cover the difference between what the students actually paid and the full tuition.

On 6 January 1946, the community celebrated the opening of a home for the elderly in the Karaite neighborhood. That home was of three levels and included 17 rooms, 4 kitchens, and other facilities.

The Role of the Various Organizations.

Besides the help of the religious council, there were other organizations that provided similar or different kinds of help to the needy. The first one on record was the "Association to Help the Sick."[1]

The "'Ezrāt ha-Betulōt" provided financial help for poor girls to get married. In the annual report of 1939, it recorded offering to help 7 girls in getting married, and to 26 girls having their education in primary, secondary, and vocational schools. The association started in 1908 and terminated its activities in 1942. Another similar organization carried out the same kind of activity until 1965.[2]

1, 2 and 3. See Cultural and Social Activities, Chapter 7.

Mourad El-Kodsi

The "Karaite Brothers," for almost seven years (1945-1952), provided hot meals and food for the needy residents of the Karaite neighborhood.[3]

Yet, in my judgement, most of that help was more giving than caring, since it did not provide a permanent solution to the problem.

The monthly payment for the needy was limited; the distribution of donations was the voluntary responsibility of the clerk of the Karaite Bēt-Dīn, according to a list he himself had prepared. Needy members who resided in other neighborhoods, members who felt that asking hurts a great deal — and in many cases they never did — were deprived of almost any donations.

As for statistics, the first budget of the community published in 1903 mentions $11 for charitable purposes. The next budget records I was able to find, were those of 1927, in which $2,300 was spent on the needy.

In 1956, the community published the last budget, in which it is stated that the religious council spent $2,780 helping the needy and $500 to run the home for the elderly; $4,550 was sepnt on medical care, including donations to the Jewish Hospital. Financial help in education was $1,262.[4]

Although good intentions for giving and, to a certain extent, for caring existed, and although there was great improvement throughout the years in the type and amount of help, yet the proper way of accomplishing this was lacking.

---

4. For all financial matters see "Financing the Community" in Chapter 2.

Chapter V

A Brief Discussion of the Karaite Liturgy*

Creed

According to Samuel ben Moses al-Maghribī (15th century), Karaite beliefs can be summed up in the following:[1]
1. The belief in His Lordship.
2. The belief in the Apostleship of Moses.
3. The belief in the Prophets and the Emissaries who came before, with and after him.
4. The belief in the Revealed Book, The Torah.
5. The belief in Qiblah. (The place which is prescribed for the Jews to face in prayer — Jerusalem.)
6. The belief in the day of judgement.

Prayer

Karaites consider prayers a substitute for the continual offering in the temple. For this reason, Karaites practice prayer twice a day: in the morning at sunrise and

---

*. This chapter is intended only to give the reader a very brief idea about Karaite Liturgy.

1. A.S. Halkin, *Studies in Judaica, Karaitica and Islamica,* Bar-Ilan Universtiy Press, pp 145-153. Mr. Halkin wrote about Karaite Creed. His source of information was the code of Karaite law compiled by Rabbi Israel ben Samuel the Maghribī (13th and 14th centuries). The article is a perfect English translation of a similar article translated from the Hebrew into Arabic and published in Cairo in 1904 by Mattatiah Mūsā al-Sirgānī, who mentioned Rabbi Samuel al-Maghribī (15th century) as the author.

in the evening at sunset.

Prayer is an ordinance for everyone, females included, over the age of ten. Prayer is accompanied by definite ceremonial acts of position which may be summarized as follows:

1. Standing upright, feet balanced.
2. Raising the eyes.
3. Stretching out the hands.
4. Supplication.
5. Laudatory and silent prayer.
6. Raising the voice.
7. Bowing the head.
8. Kneeling, heels folded.
9. Bending down with the face touching the ground. (Full prostration, *Sagdah.*)

These ceremonial acts of positions are almost identical to those practiced by Muslims and it is the belief of some Rabbanite scholars that the Karaites were affected by the surrounding Islamic environment, yet Karaites strongly deny this theory, insisting that in early Judaism this practice was common. As Selvin Goldberg puts it, "There seems to be no doubt that in pre-Talmudic times, prayer was accompanied by definite acts of position."[2]

Prayer Books

The Karaites have four prayer books:
1. Vol. 1: Daily prayers including Saturday.
2. Vol. 2: Holy day eves and Holy days, including Saturdays that fall during the Holy day.
3. Vol. 3: Eve and day of Yom Kippur, ten days of penitence, some *piyyutim* by Karaite rabbis.
4. Vol. 4: All blessings for regular days, for Saturdays and holidays, and all other occasions such as circumcision, marriage, death, and others (Pls. 1 and 2).

All four volumes are written in Hebrew and no other language is used. However, when the prayer books were reprinted in Cairo in the 1940's, some pages in Arabic were added at the end.

Most of the Karaite prayers are taken from the Old Testament. Additional parts were written by Karaite sages and rabbis throughout the ages until the 19th century. Karaites and Rabbanites borrowed from each other. For example the Karaites borrowed the psalms written by Yehudah ha-Levi (12th century). The Rabbanites borrowed the two well known songs, "Ki eshmerah Shabbat," and " 'it dodīm

---

2. P. Selvin Goldberg, *Karaite Liturgy*, (Manchester University Press: 1957), p. 8.

Kallah," as well as "Adon 'Olām."[3]

Elements of Prayer

While there are some similarities between the elements of Rabbanite and Karaite prayer, there are some differences.

Here are the elements found in Karaite prayers:

נפילת אפים. חדו. הודאה. תפלה בלחש. קדושה. שבח. יחוד. בקשה, תחנה
ברכה . פרשת שיר .

Karaites read the law on the basis of one cycle each year, starting at the beginning of the month of Tishri. As to the Haftarah, Karaites follow a pattern similar to that of the Rabbanites in some parts and differ in others (see Appendix D).

Place of worship, synagogue

The synagogue is the place where both Rabbanites and Karaites perform their prayers. Regulations applied to its usage are completely different among both sects.

Because Karaites consider the synagogue as typifying the Temple, they have always maintained that rules and observances prescribed for the Temple apply in a lesser degree and with minor differences to the synagogue.

Ritual cleanliness for prayer is required. Karaites consider personal hygiene as a ritual requirement for prayer, and one must go to the synagogue with the cleanest garment possible and must wear the ṭallīt during both services, sunrise and sunset.

Ritually unclean women are not permitted at all in the sanctuary.[4]

The Ṭallīt and the Ṣiṣit.

The ṭallīit is a garment of cloth which contains four corners, each of which has a fringe. Jews in general wear them in compliance with Num. 15:38, 39.[5]

Karaite use silk or cotton or any other material for the ṭallīt as long as it is white or blue. As for the fringes, they must be made of one kind of material, preferably cotton or silk but never a mixture of both; the color must be white and blue. The fringes must be braided in a certain way so that the number of knots would be eight as the number of letters in the Shemā', to affirm the oneness of God. The material of the ṭallīt could be made by any person, but the material of the ṣiṣit must be made by a Jew. While making the ṣiṣit, the person must be ritually clean and has to read

---

3. Ankori Zvi, *Karaites in Byzantium*, p. 354.
4. Prayers are accepted from everyone, but the synagogue has its regulations.
5. "Speak unto the children of Israel and bid them that they make them fringes in the border of their garments throughout their generations, and they put upon the fringe of the border a ribband of blue." "And it shall be unto you for a fringe, that ye may look upon it, and remember all the commands of the Lord, and do them."

the Shemāʻ, certain prayers and some psalms.

Before wearing the ṭallīt one must recite a special blessing. Karaites wear the ṭallīt during prayer, during the marriage ceremony, and during circumcision (the person who is holding the baby); the face of the dead is covered with it when buried.[6]

The Tefillin

Karaites interpret Deut. 11:18 differently from the Rabbanites. Karaites feel that those scriptural ordinances must always be kept in mind, not just during the prayer, and must always be observed. Thus the literal interpretation is not acceptable to them. They refer to similar passages in the Scripture, viz. "Circumcise therefore the foreskin of your heart" (Deut. 10:16) and "My son, keep thy father's commandment, and forsake not the law of your mother; bind them continually upon thine heart, and tie them about the neck" (Prov. 6:20,21).

Karaites interpret these passages as metaphorical admonitions which cannot be taken literally. For this reason, Karaites do not use the tefillin.

The Mezuzah

"And ye shall teach them to your children, speak of them when thou sittest in thine house, and when thou walkest by the way, when thou liest down, and when thou risest up" (Deut. 11:19). "And thou shalt write them upon the door posts of thine house, and upon thy gates" (Deut. 11:20). Again Karaites feel that they cannot take these admonitions literally and so they do not put any mezuzah upon the doors of their houses.[7]

The Shofar

Karaites do not blow the shofar on Yom Terūʻāh. They consider it as part of the sacrificial service which is not carried out anymore because of the destruction of the Temple.

---

6. During the last quarter of the 19th century, there was a dispute between the Rabbanites and the Karaites of Cairo regarding the burial places, where one ends and the other begins. It was decided to open some graves where bodies were found covered by ṭallīts, that sufficed to settle the dispute.
7. Many Karaites in Israel put the Mezuzah upon the doors of their homes.

THE FOUR VOLUMES OF THE KARAITE PRAYER BOOKS

PLATE 1: The first page of Vols. 1 and 2.

PLATE 2: The first page of Vols. 3 and 4.

סדור התפלות
כמנהג
הקראים
חלק שלישי
כולל תפלות
יום הכפורים וסדר עשרת ימי רחמים
ועוד הוספנו בסוף הסדור עקידות חבור חכמינו הראשונים והאחרונים.
ותרגום קצת פתורים ופיוטים של תפלת ערב ובקר יום הכפורים.
הסדורים האלו נדפסו על הוצאותי
יעקב בכ"ר (יוסף הגבאי הזקן ז"ל)
ובניו שישמן יצ"ו.
ИЗДАНІЕ
КУПЦА
Я. І. ШИШМАНА.
בק"ק ווילנא יע"א
בדפוס ר' יהודה ליב נ"י, ב'המחוקק מהור"ר אליעזר ליפמאן כ"ץ ז"ל.
שנת ה'ת'ר'ן לפ"ק
סדור התפלות
כמנהג
הקראים
חלק רביעי
כולל סדר הברכות
לכל ימי חול שבתות השנה
חגים ומועדים ולכל קרות העתים
ובהוצאה זו הוספנו שירים וזמירות חבורי חכמינו ז"ל
אשר חיו בכ"י ויצאו לאור פ"א.
הסדורים האלו נדפסו על הוצאותי
יעקב בכ"ר (יוסף הגבאי הזקן ז"ל)
ובניו שישמן יצ"ו.
ИЗДАНІЕ
КУПЦА
Я. І. ШИШМАНА.
בק"ק ווילנא יע"א
בדפוס ר' יהודה ליב נ"י, ב'המחוקק מהור"ר אליעזר ליפמאן כ"ץ ז"ל.
שנת ה'ת'ר'ן לפ"ק

Chapter VI

Customs and Traditions

Saturdays

Holy Days

Rites of Passage

Food

Customs and Traditions

*Customs are a product of many factors, among which are faith, beliefs and environment. Jews everywhere have similar customs, yet Western Jews and Eastern Jews also maintain their own distinctive customs.

In Egypt the Karaites had customs which differed from those of the Rabbanites, although some were similar.

In Cairo, more members of both communities lived in certain neighborhoods, in 'Abbāsiyah, Ghamrah, Sakākīnī and al-Ḍāhir. The well-to-do lived in Ḥīlwān, Ma'ādī, or Heliopolis. The wealthy had villas in Garden City or Zamalek. That, of course, does not include many among the poor, the middle class and even a few well-to-do members who preferred to stay in the Karaite neighborhood in Khurunfish where they felt more secure and were very near to Rab Simḥāh synagogue.

---

* My deep gratitude to Rab Yūsuf al-Gamīl of Ramlah, Rab Ḥayyīm Levi of Ashdod, Ovadiah al-Gamīl, and Simon Shamuel of Ashdod for their help and contribution in parts of this chapter.

In general, both Karaites and Rabbanites liked, and even preferred, to live near their synagogues.

Because most of the Karaites were of Egyptian origin, they acquired certain Egyptian customs. The men dressed like natives. Until early in the 20th century, most of the goldsmiths used to wear the *gibbah* and *quftān*.[1] Lower class men wore the *galabiyah* with a coat over it, especially in winter.

Most women wore a two-piece dress, usually black. The bottom part was almost like a skirt, the top a plain piece of material that covered the head and shoulders to the waist. It could also be used to veil the face. This is the same kind of clothing that the middle class Muslim women in Egypt and in Turkey used to wear during the first quarter of the 20th century; it is called *habarah*. Upper middle class and wealthy women wore European dress. In the period covered, there were no restrictions on the kind of material or the style of clothes, as was the case in earlier centuries.[2] It was not easy, therefore, to distinguish Jews, Christians, or Muslims by their style of dress.

Karaites tended to be more conservative than Rabbanites. While the latter quickly adopted European customs, the Karaites held on longer to the Oriental ways, especially with regard to women's activities. Rabbanite girls occupied many different jobs, while Karaite girls were more interested in getting married.

During the 1920's and the 1930's, while it was common for Rabbanite girls to attend social gatherings and dance with young men, this was unthinkable for Karaite girls. Until the early 1930's it was not acceptable for young Karaites of different sex to meet with each other.

Karaites in general mingled more freely with non-Jewish Egyptians. They did not have a noticeable accent, as did the Rabbanites. They did, however, use some Arabic words in a manner different from the non-Jews.[3]

Some Karaite women, especially the poor, were affected by their Muslim neighbors and wore amulets to keep away the evil eye and evil spirits.[4]

Until the first quarter of the 20th century, the poor among the Karaites depended a great deal on folk medicine.

---

1. The material from which the *gibbah* and *quftān* were made, as well as their style, depended upon the person's status in the community.
2. N. Stillman, *Jews in Arab Lands,* pp. 70, 167, 204.
3. They used to pronounce the "sh" in "Shams" as a soft "s" ("Sams") and some even used to pronounce the "k" as "t," "akalt — atalt." This was common mostly among uneducated members and especially women. What is surprising here is that many Egyptian Karaites used to say: "Dah 'mā qalb" ("This is a blindness of heart") to express their dissatisfaction, an expression used by al-Qirqisānī about one thousand years ago. *Ya'qūb al-Qirqisānī Kitāb al-Anwār wal-Marāqib,* edited by Leon Nemoy, Vol. 1, p. 18, line 8.
4. Sura XCII. al-Falaq: The Dawn. 1) Say: I seek refuge with the Lord of the Dawn... 4) From the mischief of those who practice secret Arts. 5) And from the mischief of the envious one as he practiced envy. Sura CXIV: al-Nās or Mankind verses 4, 5 and 6.

Egyptian men were more attracted to fat women. Karaites were no different. It was not difficult for women to put on more weight. In the neighborhood of al-Azhar there was and still is a market called "Sūq al-'Attārīn" spice market, where one can find all kinds of spices, herbs and the like. Women used to visit the market and buy what was usually offered as a sure formula to put on more weight. The spice market is a short distance from al-Ṣāghah, where most of the Karaite men carried on their businesses as silver or goldsmiths. It was no trouble to get what their women wanted.

Karaites were well known for their cleanliness. Even the poor among them kept a clean house and especially a clean kitchen. Until they left Egypt, Karaites used to clean their utensils with soft sand and yellow clay. It was common to see two copper containers next to the kitchen sink, one for the soft sand and the other for the yellow clay *(Tafl)*.

Social activities among the Karaites were limited to visits among relatives and friends. Sunday was the preferred day for this. Late in the 1930's dance parties were held at homes to encourage young people to get together. Gambling with cards was very common among rich and poor members. Rich people used to get together in their villas, while the poor used to play in the cafes owned by Jews.

Karaite synagogues did not carry on any social activities, but there were some educational activities such as teaching Hebrew and the faith. From time to time, there were lectures in the synagogue or in the center of any existing association.

The Sabbath:

Contrary to what many believed and have said, Karaites have always considered the Sabbath the most joyous day of the week and among the most holy days in the Jewish calendar.

According to the faith, the Sabbath is holy and hence sexual intercourse is not permitted during that day. It is a day of joy, so no mourning or fasting is permitted during this day unless Yom Kippur falls on the Sabbath. It is the day when every head of the family, even the poorest, takes pains to provide the best affordable meal for his family.

In the Karaite neighborhood at lunch time on any Saturday there was an aroma of good food mixed with the distinctive odor of thyme and that of the preferred liqueur among the Karaites of Cairo, ouzo.

Along with Purim and Rosh ha-Shanah, the Sabbath is the day chosen by most young men and women for becoming engaged. Everything, however, must be prepared before the Sabbath.

To prolong the Sabbath the Karaites start sunset prayers earlier than usual. At home, before and after dinner, they recite prayers fit for the occasion (Pl. 1). They also sing songs to welcome the Sabbath (Pl. 2). Saturday morning, before and after breakfast, other prayers are recited (Pl. 3). Saturday evening prayers, however, are said shortly after the sun sets. Prayers end when the ḥazzan reads the *habdalah*, a blessing to thank the Lord that the Sabbath has ended safely and the days of labor have arrived (Pl. 4). Because it is not permitted to have wine inside the synagogue, the ḥazzan reads the blessing outside the sanctuary. Worshippers then exchange greetings in Arabic, *gom'itkum khaḍrah* ("May your week be green") or in Hebrew, *Shebuwa' Ṭōb* ("May you have a good week").

At home the reading of the habdalah continues and this time the blessing is also read over a cup of wine, along with a myrtle or rue branch, followed by chanting special songs (Pl. 5).

It was common to see worshippers going very early in the morning to the synagogue of Mosheh al-Dar'ī in 'Abbāsiyah. A little before noon many returned home carrying the velvet bag that contains the ṭallīt and the prayer books. They were all well dressed, looking happy and content. In al-Ḥārah, the Karaite neighborhood, a joyous feeling filled the air: it is the Sabbath.

Holy Days

Karaites base their calendar on the actual observance of the moon. Therefore, the holy days could fall on any day. They also observe one day for all the holy days except Passover.

The Rabbanites adopted a system of a fixed calendar, and thus certain holy days must fall on certain days, for example Passover must fall on Saturday, Sunday, Tuesday or Thursday. Shabu'ot must fall on the same day of the week as the second day of Passover; Rosh Hashanah must fall on the same day of the week as the third day of Passover; Yom Simḥat Torah, on the same day of the week as the fourth day of Passover; Yom Kippur on the same day of the week as the fifth day; and Purim on the same day as the sixth day.

Karaites believe that this kind of calculation has no basis in the scripture and is the invention of the early sages of the Rabbanites.

Passover

This is the feast of freedom, liberty, and the end of bondage that the Jews in Egypt suffered for centuries. "And this day shall be unto you for a memorial; and ye shall keep it a feast to the Lord throughout your generations; ye shall keep it a feast by an ordinance for ever" (Exodus 12:14). "Seven days shall ye eat unleavened bread" (Exodus 12:15).

Among the Karaites of Egypt, the preparations for this holiday began as early as January. It was the responsibility of the chairman of the Maṣṣōt Committee to take all the necessary steps: to buy wheat, grind it, and bag the flour in ritually clean bags. It was his responsibility to get the kasher bakery ready and to start baking the maṣṣōt seven weeks before Passover.

Those who used to make the maṣaōt were Egyptians. They came from a village north of Cairo. Once they arrived at the Karaite Bēt-Dīn, they were under the strictest possible regulations. They were all sent to the public bath house, after which each member received a set of clean white clothes. During the making of the maṣṣōt, no bread or non-kasher food was allowed inside the bakery. The workers all slept in a special place in the bakery building. In all, they were 11 persons: a dough maker and his helper; a person to cut the dough and weigh each piece to almost a half a pound; and two groups of four each, who sat at two long oak tables spreading the dough to a certain size. The last one spread it until it was almost transparent (18 inches in diameter) and then threw it to the baker, who then baked it to a golden color and afterwards let it cool. When ready, it was wrapped in a special paper, usually 5 or 10 pieces per package. They were then put in a crate made of palm branches. The maṣṣōt were stored in a special room for future delivery. The person who used to wrap the maṣṣōt was responsible for the daily production count as well as for the total production.

Another responsibility of the Bēt-Dīn was to prepare the list of those who would need help. Because of the unusual expenses needed for this holiday, those members of the community who could afford it were often more generous during Passover. They would donate meat, rice, eggs, potatoes, cooking oil, vegetables, and clothes. Af first some members would deliver personally what they donated. But beginning with the year 1950, the welfare committee assumed this responsibility and organized the delivery system so that needy persons received a fair share of the donated goods.[5]

The most difficult responsibility fell on the shoulders of the women. Karaites are extremely fussy about cleanliness, and about making their houses ritually clean for Passover. Beginning right after Purim, each woman would start to purify her house room by room. Once a room was purified, no ḥameṣ[6] was allowed in. A room is considered ritually cleaned if its walls, windows and doors are cleaned with soap and water and if the furniture in it is thoroughly cleaned inside and out. The kitchen was the last room to be purified; that would generally be done the day before the eve of Passover. From that time on, no bread was allowed in the house.[7]

During the seven days of Passover, Karaites refrain from eating any grains that have to be soaked before cooking, including all kinds of beans.[8] Karaite women also sifted all rice and wheat to remove all broken grains, leaving only the perfect ones.[9] Until the first decade of the 20th century each family used to grind its own wheat at home, or send it to a stone mill in al-Ḥārah. It then became the respon-

---

5. A few days before Passover, donated steers and lambs were slaughtered in the courtyard of the Bēt Dīn, skinned, cut into portions of one, two, or three pounds, and wrapped ready for delivery.
6. *Ḥameṣ*: all kinds of leavened materials, whatever is fermented, including all liquors and, of course cheese.
7. The idea of selling the ḥameṣ to non-Jews is not accepted by Karaites.
8. Elijah Bashyatci, *Adderet Elīyāhū*. (Ramlah: 1966), p. 134.
9. It was felt at the time that broken grain was likely to be fermented.

sibility of the Karaite Bēt-Dīn to prepare the flour and the maṣṣōt needed for the holiday. At first there were many complaints about the quality and the quantity of the maṣṣōt. That encouraged some individuals to offer to take responsibility for the whole operation, but more problems occurred.[10] Beginning in the third decade of the 20th century, the Karaite religious council decided once again to give more time and effort to the operation, and yet until the 1950's there were many complaints.

In the early days of the sect, Karaites used to make the maṣṣōt from barley, but later they made it from wheat. ʿAnān considered the barley the food of the poor, as were the Jews when they left Egypt.[11]

Aside from fruits and fresh vegetables, Karaites used to refrain from eating anything not made at home: candies, chocolate, and jams, for example; they used to make their jams preferably from morello cherry and coconut. To be sure that it was completely ritually clean, they used to buy the whole coconut, peel it, and then grate it themselves.

During the week before Passover, teams of four men each, upon request, used to go to Karaite homes with their ritually cleaned utensils and make a special cake for Passover. It was a pleasure to watch these men arrive in their clean white aprons, working together, and within less than one hour many sheets were ready to be sent to the bakery. In addition, another well known cookie, "the lozato" macaroon was made as well (it was common not to find stoves in homes in Egypt).

The bakery, too, had to be purified at least ten days before the holy days. Many bakers where Karaite lived welcomed the season and agreed to have their bakeries ritually cleaned.

Passover in Egypt used to have a very joyous atmosphere. This was partly due to the beautiful spring weather which usually prevailed in Egypt, as well as to the new look of the house after having been cleaned and, in many cases, repainted.

One sure sign of Passover among the Karaites was a new tablecloth that had to be ritually clean. Each family brought out all the kasher utensils used only for Passover: pots, pans, silverware, plates, glasses, etc.

A few days before the holiday, the man of the house would buy a variety of nuts and dry dates. In preparation for the holy day all shops closed early.

A rich table was always ready to welcome the holy day: barbecued lamb,[12] bitter herbs *(merorim),* as mentioned in the Torah,[13] a special maṣṣah for the blessing,[14] rice, various kinds of vegetables, especially stuffed grape leaves, and, of

---

10. Minutes of 24 October 1912.
11. Elijah Basyatchi, *Adderet Elīyāhū,* (Ramlah: 1966), p. 133.
12. It was once the custom to burn whatever was left over from this barbecued lamb, but later this custom was no longer followed.
13. Numbers 9:11.
14. That maṣṣah was made of flour, water, and oil. No salt was added, so that the Karaites would feel the poverty of the Children of Israel when they left Egypt. Karaites depended heavily on this maṣṣah.

course, wine made especially for Passover.[15]

In Egypt, Karaites were very strict about any food or drink that did not fall into the "kasher for Passover" category. Despite this, many (especially those who lived in al-Ḥārah) used to drink ouzo during this feast. Ḥākhām Tobiah tried in vain to put an end to this illegal practice.

The Haggadah was read on the first night only, and not again on the second night.[16]

Karaites consider the first and the last days of Passover holy days, and so no work was permitted. Both days are called "Holy Convocation." The last day is also called "Yōm Shebe'i 'Aṣeret."[17] At the synagogue there were special prayers for the first and the last day of Passover.[18]

Ḥag ha-Shabu'ot

According to the Karaite interpretation of Leviticus 23:15 this feast must fall on Sunday.[19] It is also known by other names, among them are *Yom Ḥamishīm Lisfīrat Hanfat ha-'Omer,* that is the fiftieth day from the day of offering the spikes of crops, and *Ḥag ha-Bikkurīm,* that is the feast of harvesting.

During this feast, a pilgrimage to Jerusalem is required. As usual, the Karaites had a special menu for the holiday. The recipes featured milk and honey, signifying hope for a good year. It was also the custom to eat the new crops — *bikkurīm.* There was another custom among the Karaites of Egypt, one whose origin I have been unable to trace. A husband must offer his wife a goose which is to be cooked and eaten to avoid any misunderstanding in the future. It was not surprising then that in Cairo another name was added to this feast: the feast of the goose, *'Id al-Wizzah.*

---

15. The Karaites would soak red seedless raisins less than 24 hours before reading the Haggadah, in order to make sure that they would not ferment. The raisins were then squeezed and drained to produce a brownish juice that replaced wine for the blessing and the service.
16. The Haggadah was taken mostly from Psalms, Genesis, Exodus, Ezekiel, Deuteronomy, and Leviticus. See Appendix E.
17. al-Murshid al-Amīn (Cairo: 1948), pp. 75-79.
18. On the first day, the lesson *Perashah* read is from Exodus 12:14 to 13:10. The *haftarah* is from 2 Kings 23:21 to 30. On the seventh day the lesson is from Exodus 13:17 to 15:26. Before reading the sixth part, the reader reads an introduction from the Karaite Prayer Book (Vol. II, p. 225). The *haftarah* read is from Judges (all of chapter 5). Before the sunset prayers, the Song of Songs and an introduction to it from the Karaite Prayer Book (Vol. II, pp. 223-235, are read, followed by a psalm. It should be noted here that on each Saturday after the first Saturday of Passover until Saturday night before Shabu'ot, which were called "The Seven Saturdays," Karaites read before the sunset prayers Psalms 119 to 134 which are also found in the Karaite Prayer Book (Vol. I, pp. 422-426).
19. And "Ye shall count unto you from the morrow after the Sabbath, from the day that ye brought the sheaf on the wave offering, seven Sabbaths shall be complete."

As always, special services were held in the synagogue on this day.[20]

Yom Terū'āh

More commonly known as Rosh ha-Shanah, this festival is celebrated on the first day of the month in Tishri, as mentioned in the Torah.[21] Karaites do not blow the shofar, because neither the temple nor the altar exist in Jerusalem.

Everyone comes to the synagogue wearing his best clothes, and in most cases these are new.

Karaites allow no work on that day except what is needed to prepare food (Leviticus 23:23, 24). The central government allowed its Jewish employees to take this day off, as was the case with Yom ha-Kippurim. It is a joyous holy day and Karaites took full advantage of that. It was the day to pay parents and grandparents a visit, a day to have parties and celebrations. Yet is was considered a day of prayer and rest.[22]

The Ten Days of Penitence

These start from the evening of Yom Terū'āh and end on Yom ha-Kippurim. On those days Karaites used to go to the synagogue before dawn and recite *Seliḥōt* (penitential prayers). The Seliḥōt used to last until sunrise, when the morning prayers began. Although the period is named the "Ten Days of Penitence," the Seliḥōt are read only on seven and sometimes even on six days, as they were read neither on the Saturday (the Sabbath) nor on Yom Terū'āh, nor on Yom Kippur. During these ten days sexual intercourse is completely forbidden.

Yom Kippur

Karaites refrain from eating or drinking for 26 or 27 hours, from sometime before sunset on the eve of the fast until the evening prayer of the following day, Yom Kippur, is completed. Both synagogues were crowded on that day. Those who lived within walking distance used to walk, while residents of the suburbs, such as

---

20. On this day the lesson is read from Exodus 19:1 to 20:26. Before the sixth part of the lesson, the reader reads the 10 commandments and an introduction to it from the Karaite Prayer Book (Vol. II, pp. 234-225). The *hafṭarah* read is from Habbakuk (all of chapter 3). Before the sunset prayers an introduction is read from the Karaite Prayer Vook (Vol. II, p. 245), then the Story of Ruth is read from the *Tanakh*. The prayer is concluded with a psalm read from the Karaite Prayer Book (Vol. II, pp. 245-246).
21. Leviticus 23:23, 24. "And the Lord spoke unto Moses saying Speak unto the Children of Israel, in the seventh month, in the first day of the month shall ye have a sabbath," etc. That is why Karaites consider this feast one day only.
22. On that day, the lesson is read from Leviticus — all of Chapter 19 and 20. The *Hafṭarah* is read from Joel, Chapter 2:14 to the end.

Ḥilwān and Heliopolis would spend the fast day with their relatives who lived near the synagogues.

Everyone wore his cleanest clothes. Because the fast falls during the warm season, many men used to don a new white *galabiyah*. This might also have had something to do with Ecclesiastes 9:9, "Let thy garment be always white." Women were not permitted to wear makeup.

According to Karaite belief, prayers are a substitute for offerings and sacrifices. On that day, therefore, prayers were extended up to the time of the afternoon orison.

Then all the Torah scrolls were taken out and passed from hand to hand for the blessing involved in carrying them. The worshippers circled the synagogue many times, while prayers of penitence and for mercy were recited (compassion, forgiveness). When the prayers were completed the scrolls were returned to their place amidst loud rejoicing and exultation. At that point, it was time for a short rest followed by the evening prayer. At the end of the prayer the ḥākhām takes out a scroll and blesses the worshippers and asks the Lord to accept their fast and prayers. (Karaite Prayer Book, Vol. 3, p. 192, "El-Elohim")[23] (Pl. 6). He ends his blessing when he reads line A; the worshippers reply with line B.

Karaites had a bad way of breaking their fast; they would drink very cold homemade lemonade. That never helped; on the contrary, it caused more trouble. And sometimes the rich table prepared for the occasion was never touched.

Yom Sukkot

This is a holiday commemorating the Exodus and the gathering of the harvest.

A beautiful *sukkah* was built each year in both synagogues. Each one was covered with four kinds of plants: palm and willow branches, thick branches, and citrus fruits, especially etrog.

To give the sukkah a more beautiful look, it was filled with olive branches, pomegranates, and myrtle branches.

Sukkot is one of the three holidays when pilgrimage to Jerusalem is required of all Jews. Karaites would often make this pilgrimage. Because Jews were not permmitted to pray at the Wailing Wall, Karaites would pray at their old synagogue, which is within walking distance of the Wall.[24]

Sukkot provided a good opportunity for the children who had finished their Hebrew education to attend the prayers in the sukkah and join with everyone in

---

23. On Yom Kippur, the lesson read is from Leviticus (16:29 until the end of the chapter). Two *Hafṭarahs* are read: The first one from Isaiah, all of Chapter 58; the second one all of Jonah. When the *Minḥah* approaches, the compassion and the forgiveness are read until the last circle of the *Sefarīm* is completed.
24. The lesson is Emor from the book of Vayyiqra, Leviticus 22:26 until the end of Chapter 23. The *hafṭarah* is from Zachariah, all of Chapter 14.

singing (Pl. 7). From time to time the beadle of the synagogue would pass around grapes and dates taken from the sukkah. The sukkah itself was kept until the eve of Yom Simḥat Torah; then it was dismantled. On the Sabbath between Sukkot and Simḥat Torah, after the *Hafṭarah,* the Karaites read a special lamentation in memory of Moses which starts with "al-Mibbikhī" (*Karaite Prayer Book,* Vol. I, p. 341) (Pl. 8).

Yom Simḥat Torah

This most joyous of all holy days is known also as Yom Shemini 'Aṣeret. It is the day when the Torah was completed.

According to Karaite belief, Simḥat Torah marks the 22nd day of the 7th month, and is the last of the 18 days that the Torah designates as "holy convocation".

Karaites do not work on this day.

On Yom Simḥat Torah, both associations that offered instruction in Hebrew used the occasion to celebrate a kind of graduation. In the morning, all the boys and girls who had completed their Hebrew schooling would gather in the headquarters of both associations. Each boy and girl would cover his or her head with a new ṭallīt; the girls would wear white and hold candles and flowers. Each group walked in procession to the synagogue, following a brass band. The celebration included the singing of the *Shemā', Adonāi Mēlēkh,* and *Anna Adonāi Hoshī'a Na.*[25]

In the synagogue the day used to start early as usual. The service is long, rich with songs, the reading of psalms, and many rituals.

As is the case with all Jews, the service started with prayers. From Volume 2 of the Karaite Prayer Book, worshippers read parts of pages 58 until 216.

When this part was completed the treasurer, *gabbāy,* and beadle, *shammās,* of the synagogue would sell the pomegranates which were taken from the sukkah. Each one would be sold for $25, whereupon the buyer would donate it to the synagogue to be sold again and so on. Some preferred to keep it as a blessing. The money collected was donated to the Jewish Hospital run by the Rabbanite Community.

Prayers for taking the scrolls out were recited. On Yōm Simḥat Torah two lessons were read; the first one, *Zot ha-Berakhah,* marks the completion of reading the Torah. The second one, *Bereshit* marks the beginning of reading the Torah. Each lesson was read from a different scroll. When the reading was ended all the scrolls were taken out to start a joyous procession in the sanctuary. That usually coincided with the arrival of all the children at the synagogue, who were welcomed

---

25. After the Arab-Israeli War of 1956, it was felt that for the safety of the children this custom should be stopped.

by the worshippers with singing and rejoicing.

A special table, *tevah,* was placed in the center of the sanctuary of the synagogue and a special scroll was placed on it.

Each child in turn read a portion of certain songs for Simḥat Torah while the worshippers circled the sanctuary carrying the scrolls. Before each portion was read all the worshippers would recite the *Shemā'* three times, and when each portion was completed, *Adonai Mēlēkh* was recited three times (Pl. 9).

When all the portions were read, all the scrolls were returned except two; one of them was the *Sefer Qurbān,* the other was the *Sefer Bereshit.*[28]

Once again special prayers and blessings were recited, after which the *hafṭarah* was read, followed by other prayers and blessings, and thus the service for Yom Simḥat Torah ended.[27]

Purim

This is a holiday and a memorial day dedicated to the miracle of saving all the Jews. Both communities used to celebrate it in the gayest way. It was almost a tradition among the youth of both communities to spend the eve of Yom Purim in Ḥārat al-Yahud. For this reason the whole area was cleaned and some parts were decorated.

A wide variety of legal and illegal entertainment was offered, most of which consisted of gambling games. Belly dancers were everywhere. Stands sold shish-kabab, pasta, pickles, and salads.

Both Jewish neighborhoods were closed, so that no outsider could get in unless accompanied by a Jew. Even then, a non-Jew very likely would feel out of place. Celebrations often started a few days before Purim, and on the eve of Purim itself they lasted the entire night until early next morning.

It was the custom among the youth of both communities to dress in fancy clothing and move freely in the neighborhood where they lived. The natives for this reason called the feast *'Id al-Maskharah,* the feast of masquerade.

In almost every Karaite home one can find two kinds of light dessert: *wedān hāmān,* "haman's ears," which are very thin and light cookies shaped like big ears. The second dessert is a kind of rectangular strudel filled with cream; it is called *bughāshah.*

Purim was the day for exchanging gifts. The head of the family would give each member a generous monetary gift.

In the synagogues, it was an occasion to light candles. All candles were made out of beeswax in a special room in the Karaite Bēt-Dīn, under the supervision of

---

26. According to Karaite traditions, the scroll is returned after reading the *hafṭarah.*
27. The *hafṭarah* read is from 1 Kings 8:4 to the end of the chapter.

a member of the community.[28]

Most, if not all, Karaites used to close their shops that day. In addition, Purim was by tradition among the favorite holidays when engagements were announced.

Days of Fasting and Mourning

The Karaites have fast days which are also considered days of mourning: The 24th of Tishri, the 10th of Tevet, the 9th of Tammuz, the 7th and the 10th of Av. Karaites consider the period from the first of Tammuz until the 10th of Av a period of mourning for the destruction of the Temple. They refrain from eating meat, and weddings and all kinds of entertainment are not permitted.[29]

On the Saturdays from the 9th of Tammuz until the 10th of Av, four or five special prayers are read in the morning (Pl. 10).

On the 7th of Av, after the service, Karaites read special prayers.[30]

Their mourning reaches its peak on the 10th of Av. On this day, following the service, Karaites read Lamentation, *Qinnōt,* followed by a reading of the entire book of Job. When they finish reading it, some of the worshippers leave the synagogue for the cemetery to read a memorial, after which they return to the synagogue and join with the other worshippers in reading the "Consolation," *Neḥamōt,* and thus the services for that day are concluded. Ritual slaughterers are then permitted to slaughter. Because the time then would be after twelve noon, special arrangements were made to keep the slaughter house open until that hour.

It was also common among older people to fast on Mondays and on Thursdays on a voluntary basis.

The Karaites always welcome the first of the new months, which is also the day of the new moon.

The Rites of Passage

Circumcision

When a child was born, it was the responsibility of the head of the house to inform the Bēt-Dīn of the birth. The message was sent as quickly as possible when the newborn was a boy, but many neglected this responsibility when the child was a girl.

The circumcision of a boy, according to Jewish law, must take place on the

---

28. On Purim eve, as well as on Yom Purim, special prayers are read from the Karaite Prayer Book (Vol. 1, pp. 30 to 33). An introduction to the story of Esther as well as the story itself is read on both days.
29. From the 9th of Tammuz until the 10th of Av, Karaites do not bring out the scrolls nor do they open the Ark. All prayers have a mourning tone. Lessons are read from the *Ḥomāsh.*
30. *Karaite Prayer Book,* Vol. 1, pp. 121 to 127.

8th day of life. Nothing can be permitted to delay it, unless the baby is sick.[31] The Karaite community had at least five ritual circumcisers at all times. They performed this service free of charge; it was considered a pious deed (a *mizvah*). There was a schedule to be followed, so that each circumciser, *mohel,* would have his chance, yet it was always understood that the father of the newborn reserved the right to choose any *mohel* he preferred.

Two days before the assigned date, a special chair was sent to the house of the newborn,[32] along with a handbag containing all the needed equipment (a formality, since each *mohel* had his own private tools). The father, or grandfather if living, would sit in the chair and hold the baby in his lap. The mohel recites a special blessing, then he performs the circumcision. The blessing is also a reminder of the ordinance that an eight days old boy must be circumcised.

בָּרוּךְ אַתָּה יְיָ אֱלֹהֵינוּ מֶלֶךְ הָעוֹלָם אֲשֶׁר קִדְּשָׁנוּ בְּמִצְוֹתָיו וְצִוָּנוּ לְהִמּוֹל בַּיּוֹם הַשְּׁמִינִי: כַּכָּתוּב וּבַיּוֹם הַשְּׁמִינִי | יִמּוֹל בְּשַׂר עָרְלָתוֹ :

The operation itself is similar to that of the Rabbanites, except that the Karaites never followed the old Rabbanite custom of sucking the blood (no longer practiced at all).[33] After circumcision the rsponsibility of the *mohel* included one or more visits to the baby, if needed.

The Karaites had a beautiful custom associated with the circumcision. Before the operation, the baby was put on a velvet pillow decorated with lace. The older sister of the baby (if she was of marriageable age), or any other relative, would carry the baby, while the mother stood a short distance in front. As the guests sang and recited prayers, the baby was introduced several times to the mother. After that, another song was chanted, then the operation took place, followed by a third song (P. 11).

It was a tradition to serve special cookies called *lozato,* made from almond paste (known elsewhere as "macaroons").

Engagement

Until the 1930's, the matchmaker played a major part, although not an exclusive one, in engagements. Even then, not all engagements were arranged by matchmakers. By the early 1930's, when the various associations began to engage in mixed social activities, the role of the matchmaker diminished. Another factor was the freedom that women were beginning to enjoy.

All engagements were recorded in the Bēt-Dīn. All necessary information was

---

31. Genesis 17:12
32. It was a kind of high armchair, with four poles, a velvet canopy, and *"romanīm"* (ornately carved silver ornaments) at the top.
33. See Appendix A.

noted: names of the fiancé and the fiancée, family names, wedding date, the responsibility of each family, and the penalty to be paid should the engagement be broken.

An engagement party was held with members of both families present, usually on a Saturday or a holiday (Purim was especially popular for engagement parties). It was the custom that the prospective groom would offer his fiancée a gold ring engraved on the inner side with his name, while he put on his own finger a similar ring engraved on its inner side with her name.

The ring would be wrapped in a white silk handkerchief, with a branch of rue (herb of grace).[34] The ring would be accompanied by two things: a gift of jewelry, its value dependent on the status of the fiancé, and a covered candy dish made of crystal, silver, or gold and filled with special candy and chocolate.[35]

The engagement period was meant to give both parties a chance to become acquainted. As was often the case, the fiancé used to visit his fiancée on Saturdays, to have lunch with her and her family, stay there all the afternoon, then go out with his fiancée for the evening. It was not common to break an engagement, but it did happen, and in many cases it was mostly over financial matters.

Wedding

Announcement for the engagement meant that the wedding preparations had begun. The two families met and decided together on the amount of money to be spent and the details of the wedding. One thing always agreed upon was that the trousseau must include an Oriental rug, copper pots and pans, and above all, a heavy brass mortar.

One month before the wedding, the invitations to the ceremony were sent out. There was no rule as to what language was to be used; invitations were usually in Arabic and French, Arabic alone, or French alone. Hebrew was very rarely used. Invitations to the dinner party were separate and it was assumed that every person invited would attend. Members of both families were also able to invite someone at the last moment, even during or after the wedding ceremony. The dinner party itself would take place at the bride's house,[36] with the bride's family usually doing all the cooking and baking. Only on occasion was a caterer called in to cater the party. Like all Karaite parties, wedding dinners were well known for their delicious and generous menu (see below, under "Food").

A week or two before the wedding, the bride's family would hold an exhibi-

---

34. White was the symbol of virginity and green indicates the hope for good years to come. If rue was not available, it was replaced by myrtle, *ḥadās*.
35. The candy, as well as the wedding candy, was a thin almond, sugarcoated in white or pink (sometimes known locally as "Jordan almond").
36. Until 1948 it was the custom to erect four flagpoles in front of both houses, two Jewish and two Egyptian.

tion party, at which the entire trousseau was displayed. It was the custom at this party to serve fried fish with hard rolls. On the day following the party, the trousseau was taken to the groom's house, or to the couple's new apartment. Until the 1940's, most of the trousseau was handmade, each girl beginning in her teens to collect tablecloths, sheets, pillow cases, etc.

Here again we find a custom that could have been taken from the Egyptians: the bride's party would rent two or three carts, cover them with a special cloth, and then with a brass band of six or more members in front, carry the trousseau to the groom's house (or the couple's new house) where relatives would be waiting. On that day, everything was put in order for the long awaited moment. Again, rue or myrtle must be the first thing to go into the groom's house.

The community never had its own wedding hall, so in most cases a hall would be rented,[37] or a luxurious Oriental tent would be erected in the synagogue court or in any other suitable space.[38]

On the day of the wedding, the groom would be the first to arrive. At the appointed hour or a little later, the bride would arrive with members of her family, the bridesmaids and ushers.

It was the custom that they all rode in landau cars, and would tour the neighborhood before heading for the wedding place.

On the morning of the wedding, the custom was for the mother of the bride to send chicken and soup to the newlyweds.

The Wedding Ceremony

The ceremony itself was simple, conducted entirely by the ḥakhām. (The Karaites in Egypt had no official cantors to assist him.) Its basic steps were as follows:

The ḥakhām, the groom, the bride, her father or guardian stand together along with some relatives. The ḥakhām asks the groom to take the vow that he is taking his wife with a dowry *(mohār)*, writ of marriage *(kitāb),* and a consummation of the union *(bi'āh).*

בִּבְרִית הַר סִינַי וּבְחֻקֵּי הַר חֹרֵב וּבְעֵדוּת יָיֽ צְבָאוֹת וּבְעֵדוּת זְקֵנֵינוּ וַחֲשׁוּבֵנוּ
אֲנִי פְלֹנִי בֶּן פְלֹנִי מְאָרֵשׂ וּמְקַדֵּשׁ אֶת פְּלָנִית בַּת פְּלֹנִי הֱיוֹת לִי
לְאִשָּׁה עַל טָהֳרָה וּקְדֻשָּׁה בְּמֹהַר בִּכְתָב וּבְבִיאָה כְּדַת מֹשֶׁה וְיִשְׂרָאֵל:

---

37. Either Ewart Memorial Hall (of the American University of Cairo) or the hall of the American School for Girls.
38. In most cases, the roof of either the bride's or the groom's house was the best place. In this case the tent could hold at least 300 guests.

According to the covenant of Mount Sinai, and according to the statues of Mount Horeb, and by the testimony of the Lord of Hosts, and by the testimony of our elders and notables, I, So-and-so, son of So-and-so, do betroth and sanctify unto myself So-and-so, daughter of So-and-so, to be my wife, in purity and holiness, by way of bridal gift, writ of marriage, and marital intercourse, according to the law of Moses and Israel.

Usually the ḥākhām says the vow and the groom repeats word for word after him, as he does when the ḥākhām affirms that the groom has taken the vow to marry his wife in purity and holiness.

וְאֵרַשְׂתִּיךְ לִי לְעוֹלָם ׀ וְאֵרַשְׂתִּיךְ לִי בְּצֶדֶק וּבְמִשְׁפָּט וּבְחֶסֶד וּבְרַחֲמִים ׃
וְאֵרַשְׂתִּיךְ לִי בֶּאֱמוּנָה ׀ וְיָדַעַתְּ אֶת־יְהוָה ׃

And I will betroth thee unto me for ever;
And I will betroth thee unto me in righteousness and in
    justice, and in lovingkindness, and in compassion;
And I will betroth thee unto me in faithfulness;
And thou shalt know the lord.

The ḥākhām then reads the first lines and the last ones of the next part which is a reminder to the groom of the importance of the wife for her husband, her family and her house. After each line those who are around the bride and groom repeat the underlined words.

מָצָא אִשָּׁה מָצָא טוֹב ׀ וַיָּפֶק רָצוֹן מֵיְהוָה ׃ וַיָּפֶק רָצוֹן מֵיְהוָה
אֵשֶׁת־חַיִל מִי יִמְצָא ׀ וְרָחֹק מִפְּנִינִים מִכְרָהּ ׃ א
בָּטַח בָּהּ לֵב בַּעְלָהּ ׀ וְשָׁלָל לֹא יֶחְסָר ׃ א
גְּמָלַתְהוּ טוֹב וְלֹא־רָע ׀ כֹּל יְמֵי חַיֶּיהָ ׃ א
דָּרְשָׁה צֶמֶר וּפִשְׁתִּים ׀ וַתַּעַשׂ בְּחֵפֶץ כַּפֶּיהָ ׃ א
הָיְתָה כָּאֳנִיּוֹת סוֹחֵר ׀ מִמֶּרְחָק תָּבִיא לַחְמָהּ ׃ א
וַתָּקָם בְּעוֹד לַיְלָה וַתִּתֵּן טֶרֶף לְבֵיתָהּ ׀ וְחֹק לְנַעֲרֹתֶיהָ ׃ א
זָמְמָה שָׂדֶה וַתִּקָּחֵהוּ ׀ מִפְּרִי כַפֶּיהָ נָטְעָה כָּרֶם ׃ א
חָגְרָה בְעוֹז מָתְנֶיהָ ׀ וַתְּאַמֵּץ זְרוֹעֹתֶיהָ ׃ א
טָעֲמָה כִּי־טוֹב סַחְרָהּ ׀ לֹא־יִכְבֶּה בַלַּיְלָה נֵרָהּ ׃ א
יָדֶיהָ שִׁלְּחָה בַכִּישׁוֹר ׀ וְכַפֶּיהָ תָּמְכוּ פָלֶךְ ׃ א

כַּפָּהּ פָּרְשָׂה לֶעָנִי ׀ וְיָדֶיהָ שִׁלְּחָה לָאֶבְיוֹן׃
לֹא־תִירָא לְבֵיתָהּ מִשָּׁלֶג ׀ כִּי כָל־בֵּיתָהּ לָבֻשׁ שָׁנִים׃
מַרְבַדִּים עָשְׂתָה־לָּהּ ׀ שֵׁשׁ וְאַרְגָּמָן לְבוּשָׁהּ׃
נוֹדָע בַּשְּׁעָרִים בַּעְלָהּ ׀ בְּשִׁבְתּוֹ עִם־זִקְנֵי־אָרֶץ׃
סָדִין עָשְׂתָה וַתִּמְכֹּר ׀ וַחֲגוֹר נָתְנָה לַכְּנַעֲנִי׃
עֹז־וְהָדָר לְבוּשָׁהּ ׀ וַתִּשְׂחַק לְיוֹם אַחֲרוֹן׃
פִּיהָ פָּתְחָה בְחָכְמָה ׀ וְתוֹרַת־חֶסֶד עַל־לְשׁוֹנָהּ׃
צוֹפִיָּה הֲלִיכוֹת בֵּיתָהּ ׀ וְלֶחֶם עַצְלוּת לֹא תֹאכֵל׃
קָמוּ בָנֶיהָ וַיְאַשְּׁרוּהָ ׀ בַּעְלָהּ וַיְהַלְלָהּ׃
רַבּוֹת בָּנוֹת עָשׂוּ חָיִל ׀ וְאַתְּ עָלִית עַל־כֻּלָּנָה׃
שֶׁקֶר הַחֵן וְהֶבֶל הַיֹּפִי ׀ אִשָּׁה יִרְאַת־יְהוָה הִיא תִתְהַלָּל׃
תְּנוּ־לָהּ מִפְּרִי יָדֶיהָ ׀ וִיהַלְלוּהָ בַשְּׁעָרִים מַעֲשֶׂיהָ׃
וּמָצָא־חֵן וְשֵׂכֶל טוֹב ׀ בְּעֵינֵי אֱלֹהִים וְאָדָם׃

Whoso finds a wife, finds a great good, and obtains favor from the Lord.
A valiant woman, who can find?
For her price is far above rubies.
The heart of her husband does safely trust in her,
And he has no lack of gain.
She does him good, and not evil,
All the days of her life.
She seeks wool and flax,
And works willingly with her hands.
She is like the merchant ships,
She brings her food from afar.
She rises while it is yet night,
And gives food to her household,
And a portion to her maidens.
She considers a field, and buys it,
With the fruits of her hand she plants a vineyard.
She girds her loins with strength,
And makes strong her arms.
She perceives that her merchandise is good;
Her lamp goes not out by night.
She lays her hands to the distaff,
And her hands hold the spindle.

She stretches out her hand to the poor
And reaches forth her hands to the needy.
She fears not the snow for her household,
For all her household are clothed in scarlet.
She makes for herself coverlets;
Her clothing is fine linen and purple.
Her husband is known in the gates,
Where he sits among the elders of the land.
She makes linen garments and sells them,
And delivers girdles to the merchant.
Strength and dignity are her clothing,
And she laughs at the time to come.
She opens her mouth with wisdom,
And the law of kindess is upon her tongue.
She looks well to the ways of her household,
And eats not the bread of idleness.
Her children rise up and call her blessed;
Her husband also, and he praises her:
Many daughters have acted valiantly,
But thou has excelled them all.
Grace is deceitful, and vain is beauty;
But a woman that feareth the Lord, she shall be praised
Give ye her of the fruit of her hands,
And let her works praise her in the gates.
So shall thou find grace and good favor in the sight of God
and Man (Prov. 3:4).

A member of the bride's or the groom's family or even a friend of either one reads the contract of marriage in Hebrew *(ketubbah)*, then in Arabic or French after which the couple signs the contract.

The ḥākhām then repeats part 2 and asks the groom to wear his ring and to put the bride's ring on her finger.

One of the relatives of the bride covers the couple's heads with a new ṭallīt while the ḥākhām reads the blessing for wearing the ṭallīt.[39]

He then asks the Lord to bless the groom and the bride and their house and to bless them with children as he did with Perez

---

39. The ṭallīt, along with silk pajamas, was a gift from the bride to the groom. The ṭallīt is presented in a velvet sack that would be used also for the prayer books, and the *Homāsh*.

בִּרְכַּת־יְהֹוָה אֲלֵיכֶם ׀ בֵּרַכְנוּ אֶתְכֶם בְּשֵׁם יְהֹוָה: בָּרוּךְ הַבָּא בְּשֵׁם יְהֹוָה:
וְיִתֶּן־לְךָ הָאֱלֹהִים מִטַּל הַשָּׁמַיִם וּמִשְׁמַנֵּי הָאָרֶץ ׀ וְרֹב דָּגָן וְתִירֹשׁ:
וַיֹּאמְרוּ כָּל־הָעָם אֲשֶׁר־בַּשַּׁעַר וְהַזְּקֵנִים עֵדִים ׀ יִתֵּן יְהֹוָה אֶת־הָאִשָּׁה הַבָּאָה
אֶל־בֵּיתֶךָ כְּרָחֵל וּכְלֵאָה אֲשֶׁר בָּנוּ שְׁתֵּיהֶם אֶת־בֵּית יִשְׂרָאֵל וַעֲשֵׂה־חַיִל
בְּאֶפְרָתָה וּקְרָא־שֵׁם בְּבֵית לָחֶם: וִיהִי בֵיתְךָ כְּבֵית פֶּרֶץ אֲשֶׁר־יָלְדָה תָמָר
לִיהוּדָה ׀ מִן־הַזֶּרַע אֲשֶׁר יִתֵּן יְהֹוָה לְךָ <u>מִן־הַנַּעֲרָה הַזֹּאת</u>:

The blessing of the Lord be upon you;
We bless you in the Name of the Lord (Ps. 129:8).
Blessed be he who comes in the name of the Lord
  (Ps. 118:26).
So God give thee of the dew of heaven and of the fat of the
  earth, and plenty of corn and wine (Gen. 27:28).
And all the peole who were in the gate, and the elders, said,
  We are witnesses; the Lord make the woman who is com-
  ing into my house like Rachel and like Leah, which two
  did build the House of Israel. And do thou worthily in
  Ephrath, and be famous in Beth-lehem.
And may the house be like the house of Perez, whom Tamar
  bore unto Judah, from the seed which the Lord shall give
  thee <u>out of this young woman</u> (Ruth 4:11).

It is the custom that the Karaite guests repeat the underlined part with the ḥakhām.

It is time then to give the couple the seven benedictions. After giving the first one the ḥakhām sips from the cup of wine, then he continues on with the blessings.

ויקח המברך כוס יין בידו ויאמר שבע ברכות : ברכה ראשונה

הוֹדוּ לַיהֹוָה כִּי־טוֹב ׀ כִּי לְעוֹלָם חַסְדּוֹ: הוֹדוּ לֵאלֹהֵי הָאֱלֹהִים ׀ כִּי לְעוֹלָם
חַסְדּוֹ: הוֹדוּ לַאֲדֹנֵי הָאֲדֹנִים ׀ כִּי לְעוֹלָם חַסְדּוֹ : כּוֹס־יְשׁוּעוֹת אֶשָּׂא ׀
וּבְשֵׁם יְהֹוָה אֶקְרָא: כִּי שֵׁם יְהֹוָה אֶקְרָא ׀ הָבוּ גֹדֶל לֵאלֹהֵינוּ: בָּרוּךְ יְהֹוָה אֱלֹהֵי
יִשְׂרָאֵל מֵהָעוֹלָם וְעַד־הָעוֹלָם אָמֵן ׀ וְאָמֵן: נָתַתָּה שִׂמְחָה בְלִבִּי ׀ מֵעֵת דְּגָנָם
וְתִירוֹשָׁם רָבּוּ: בָּרוּךְ אַתָּה יְהֹוָה אֱלֹהֵינוּ מֶלֶךְ הָעוֹלָם הַמַּצְמִיחַ גֶּפֶן מִן הָאָרֶץ
וּמֵיַיִן מְשַׂמֵּחַ לְבַב בְּנֵי הָאָדָם : כַּכָּתוּב וְיַיִן יְשַׂמַּח לְבַב־אֱנוֹשׁ לְהַצְהִיל
פָּנִים מִשָּׁמֶן ׀ וְלֶחֶם לְבַב־אֱנוֹשׁ יִסְעָד : בָּרוּךְ אַתָּה יְהֹוָה אֱלֹהֵינוּ מֶלֶךְ הָעוֹלָם
הַנּוֹתֵן לָנוּ שָׂשׂוֹן וְשִׂמְחָה ובוֹרֵא פְּרִי הַגֶּפֶן אמן

Mourad El-Kodsi

The First Benediction
Give ye thanks unto the Lord, for He is good,
For His mercy endureth for ever.
Give ye thanks unto the God of gods,
For His mercy endureth for ever.
Give ye thanks unto the Lord of lords,
For His mercy endureth for ever (Ps. 136:1-3).
I will lift up the cup of salvation,
And call upon the Name of the Lord (Ps. 116:13).
I will proclaim the Name of the Lord—
Ascribe ye greatness to our God (Deut. 32:3)
Blessed be the Lord, the God of Israel, from everlasting and
  to everlasting. Amen, and again amen! (Ps. 41:14).
Thou has put gladness into my heart,
More than when their corn and their wine increase (Ps. 4:8).
Blessed art Thou, O Lord, our God, King of the Universe,
  who growest the vine from the earth, and with its wine
  makest glad the heart of the children of man;
As it is written; And wine which gladdens the heart of man,
  causing his face to shine more than with oil, and bread
  which sustains man's heart (Ps. 104:15).
Blessed art Thou, O Lord, our God, King of the universe, who
  givest us joy and gladness, and dost create the fruit of the
  vine. Amen!

ברכה שנית בָּרוּךְ יְהוָה אֱלֹהִים
אֱלֹהֵי יִשְׂרָאֵל עֹשֵׂה נִפְלָאוֹת לְבַדּוֹ : וּבָרוּךְ שֵׁם כְּבוֹדוֹ לְעוֹלָם וְיִמָּלֵא כְבוֹדוֹ
אֶת־כָּל־הָאָרֶץ אָמֵן וְאָמֵן : אָנֹכִי עָשִׂיתִי אֶרֶץ וְאָדָם עָלֶיהָ בָרָאתִי אֲנִי יָדַי
נָטוּ שָׁמַיִם וְכָל־צְבָאָם צִוֵּיתִי : אַף־יָדִי יָסְדָה אֶרֶץ וִימִינִי טִפְּחָה שָׁמָיִם קֹרֵא
אֲנִי אֲלֵיהֶם יַעַמְדוּ יַחְדָּו : כֹּה־אָמַר יְהוָה גֹּאֲלֶךָ וְיֹצֶרְךָ מִבָּטֶן אָנֹכִי יְהוָה עֹשֶׂה
כֹּל נֹטֶה שָׁמַיִם לְבַדִּי רֹקַע הָאָרֶץ מֵאִתִּי : בָּרוּךְ אַתָּה יְיָ אֱלֹהֵינוּ מֶלֶךְ
הָעוֹלָם שֶׁהַכֹּל בָּרָאתָ לִכְבוֹדֶךָ אָמֵן

The Second Benediction:
Blessed be the Lord God, God of Israel, who alone does won-
  drous things;
And blessed be His glorious name forever; and let the whole
  earth be filled with his glory. Amen, and again amen!
  (Ps. 72:18-19).
I, even I, have made the earth, and have created man upon it;

> I, Mine own hands, have stretched out the heavens, and all
> their host I have commanded (Isa. 45:12).
> Yea, My hand has laid the foundation of the earth,
> And My right hand has spread out the heavens,
> When I call unto them, they stand up together (Isa. 48:13).
> Thus said the Lord, thy Redeemer, and he who formed thee
> from the womb,
> I am the Lord who makes all things, who alone stretches forth
> the heavens, who spreads out the earth, by Myself
> (Isa. 44:24).
> Blessed art Thou, O Lord, our God, King of the universe, who
> has created all things for the sake of Thy majesty. Amen!

3 ברכה שלישית בָּרוּךְ יְהוָה אֱלֹהֵי יִשְׂרָאֵל
מִן־הָעוֹלָם וְעַד הָעוֹלָם וְאָמַר כָּל־הָעָם אָמֵן הַלְלוּיָהּ: כִּי־כֹה אָמַר־יְהוָה בּוֹרֵא
הַשָּׁמַיִם הוּא הָאֱלֹהִים יֹצֵר הָאָרֶץ וְעֹשָׂהּ הוּא כוֹנְנָהּ לֹא־תֹהוּ בְרָאָהּ לָשֶׁבֶת
יְצָרָהּ ׀ אֲנִי יְהוָה וְאֵין עוֹד: כֹּה־אָמַר הָאֵל יְהוָה בּוֹרֵא הַשָּׁמַיִם וְנוֹטֵיהֶם רֹקַע
הָאָרֶץ וְצֶאֱצָאֶיהָ ׀ נֹתֵן נְשָׁמָה לָעָם עָלֶיהָ וְרוּחַ לַהֹלְכִים בָּהּ: וַיִּיצֶר יְהוָה אֱלֹהִים
אֶת־הָאָדָם עָפָר מִן־הָאֲדָמָה וַיִּפַּח בְּאַפָּיו נִשְׁמַת חַיִּים ׀ וַיְהִי הָאָדָם לְנֶפֶשׁ
חַיָּה: בָּרוּךְ אַתָּה יְיָ אֱלֹהֵינוּ מֶלֶךְ הָעוֹלָם יוֹצֵר הָאָדָם אָמֵן

> *The Third Benediction:*
> Blessed be the Lord, God of Israel, from the everlasting even
> to everlasting; and let all the people say, Amen, praise ye
> the Lord! (Ps. 106:48).
> For thus said the Lord, Creator of the heavens, He is God
> who formed the earth and made it; He established it, He
> created it not a waste, He formed it to be inhabited—I am
> the Lord, and there is none else (Isa. 45:18).
> Thus said God, the Lord, who created the heavens and stretched them forth, who spread forth the earth and its produce, who gives breath unto the people upon it, and spirit
> to those who walk therin (Isa. 42:5).
> And the Lord God formed man of the dust of the ground, and
> He breathed into his nostrils the breath of life, and man
> became a living soul (Gen. 2:7).
> Blessed art Thou, O Lord, our God, King of the universe, who
> hast formed man. Amen!

ברכה רביעית

בָּרוּךְ אֱלֹהִים ׀ אֲשֶׁר לֹא־הֵסִיר תְּפִלָּתִי וְחַסְדּוֹ מֵאִתִּי : וְעַתָּה כֹּה־אָמַר יְהוָה בֹּרַאֲךָ יַעֲקֹב וְיֹצֶרְךָ יִשְׂרָאֵל ׀ אַל־תִּירָא כִּי גְאַלְתִּיךָ קָרָאתִי בְשִׁמְךָ לִי־אָתָּה : וַיֹּאמֶר אֱלֹהִים נַעֲשֶׂה אָדָם בְּצַלְמֵנוּ כִּדְמוּתֵנוּ ׀ וְיִרְדּוּ בִדְגַת הַיָּם וּבְעוֹף הַשָּׁמַיִם וּבַבְּהֵמָה וּבְכָל־הָאָרֶץ וּבְכָל־הָרֶמֶשׂ הָרֹמֵשׂ עַל־הָאָרֶץ : וַיִּבְרָא אֱלֹהִים אֶת־הָאָדָם בְּצַלְמוֹ בְּצֶלֶם אֱלֹהִים בָּרָא אֹתוֹ ׀ זָכָר וּנְקֵבָה בָּרָא אֹתָם : וַיְבָרֶךְ אֹתָם אֱלֹהִים וַיֹּאמֶר לָהֶם אֱלֹהִים פְּרוּ וּרְבוּ וּמִלְאוּ אֶת־הָאָרֶץ וְכִבְשֻׁהָ ׀ וּרְדוּ בִּדְגַת הַיָּם וּבְעוֹף הַשָּׁמַיִם וּבְכָל־חַיָּה הָרֹמֶשֶׂת עַל־הָאָרֶץ : זָכָר וּנְקֵבָה בְּרָאָם ׀ וַיְבָרֶךְ אֹתָם וַיִּקְרָא אֶת־שְׁמָם אָדָם בְּיוֹם הִבָּרְאָם : טוֹבִים הַשְּׁנַיִם מִן־הָאֶחָד ׀ אֲשֶׁר יֵשׁ־לָהֶם שָׂכָר טוֹב בַּעֲמָלָם : וַיֹּאמֶר יְהוָה אֱלֹהִים לֹא־טוֹב הֱיוֹת הָאָדָם לְבַדּוֹ ׀ אֶעֱשֶׂה־לּוֹ עֵזֶר כְּנֶגְדּוֹ : וַיַּפֵּל יְהוָה אֱלֹהִים תַּרְדֵּמָה עַל־הָאָדָם וַיִּישָׁן ׀ וַיִּקַּח אַחַת מִצַּלְעֹתָיו וַיִּסְגֹּר בָּשָׂר תַּחְתֶּנָּה : וַיִּבֶן יְהוָה אֱלֹהִים אֶת־הַצֵּלָע אֲשֶׁר־לָקַח מִן־הָאָדָם לְאִשָּׁה ׀ וַיְבִאֶהָ אֶל־הָאָדָם : וַיֹּאמֶר הָאָדָם זֹאת הַפַּעַם עֶצֶם מֵעֲצָמַי וּבָשָׂר מִבְּשָׂרִי ׀ לְזֹאת יִקָּרֵא אִשָּׁה כִּי מֵאִישׁ לֻקֳחָה־זֹּאת : עַל־כֵּן יַעֲזָב־אִישׁ אֶת־אָבִיו וְאֶת־אִמּוֹ ׀ וְדָבַק בְּאִשְׁתּוֹ וְהָיוּ לְבָשָׂר אֶחָד : בָּרוּךְ אַתָּה יְיָ אֱלֹהֵינוּ מֶלֶךְ הָעוֹלָם יוֹצֵר הָאָדָם אָמֵן

The Fourth Benediction:

Blessed be God who has not turned away my prayer, nor His mercy from me (Ps. 66:20).

And now thus says the Lord who has created thee, O Jacob, and who has formed thee, O Israel, Fear not, for I have redeemed thee, I have called thee by thy name, thou art Mine (Isa. 43:1).

And God said, Let Us make man in Our Image, after Our Likeness, and let them have dominion over the fish of the sea, and over the fowl of the air, and over the cattle, and over all the earth, and over every creeping thing that creeps upon the earth.

And God created man in His image, in the image of God did He create him, male and female created He them.

And God blessed them, and God said to them, Be fruitful and multiply, and replenish the earth and subdue it, and have dominion over the fish of the sea, and over the fowl of the air, and over every living thing that creeps upon the earth (Gen. 1:26-28).

Male and female created He them, and He blessed them, and
   called their name Man, on the day when they were created
   (Gen. 5:2).
Two are better than one, because they have a good reward for
   their labor (Eccles. 4:9).
And the Lord God said, It is not good that the man should be
   alone; I will make him a help meet for him (Gen. 2:18).
And the Lord God caused a deep sleep to fall upon the man,
   and he slept; and He took one of his ribs, and closed up
   flesh in its place.
And the rib, which the Lord God had taken from the man,
   made He a woman, and He brought her to the man.
And the man said, This now is a bone of my bones, and flesh
   of my flesh; she shall be called Woman, because she was
   taken out of man.
Therefore shall a man leave his father and his mother, and
   shall cleave unto his wife, and they shall be one flesh
   (Gen. 2:21-24).
Blessed art Thou, O Lord, our God, King of the universe, who
   hast formed man. Amen!

5: ברכה הסישית בָּרוּךְ
יְהֹוָה מִצִיּוֹן שֹׁכֵן יְרוּשָׁלָם הַלְלוּיָהּ: רָנִּי עֲקָרָה לֹא יָלָדָה | פִּצְחִי רִנָּה וְצַהֲלִי לֹא־
חָלָה כִּי־רַבִּים בְּנֵי־שׁוֹמֵמָה מִבְּנֵי בְעוּלָה אָמַר יְהֹוָה: רָנִּי בַת־צִיּוֹן הָרִיעוּ
יִשְׂרָאֵל | שִׂמְחִי וְעָלְזִי בְּכָל־לֵב בַּת יְרוּשָׁלָם: רָנִּי וְשִׂמְחִי בַּת־צִיּוֹן | כִּי הִנְנִי־בָא
וְשָׁכַנְתִּי בְתוֹכֵךְ נְאֻם־יְהֹוָה: כֹּה אָמַר יְהֹוָה שַׁבְתִּי אֶל־צִיּוֹן וְשָׁכַנְתִּי בְּתוֹךְ
יְרוּשָׁלָם | וְנִקְרְאָה יְרוּשָׁלַם עִיר הָאֱמֶת וְהַר־יְהֹוָה צְבָאוֹת הַר הַקֹּדֶשׁ: עוֹד
יֹאמְרוּ בְאָזְנַיִךְ בְּנֵי שִׁכֻּלָיִךְ | צַר־לִי הַמָּקוֹם גְּשָׁה־לִּי וְאֵשֵׁבָה: וְאָמַרְתְּ בִּלְבָבֵךְ
מִי יָלַד־לִי אֶת־אֵלֶּה וַאֲנִי שְׁכוּלָה | וְגַלְמוּדָה | גֹּלָה וְסוּרָה וְאֵלֶּה מִי גִדֵּל הֵן
אֲנִי נִשְׁאַרְתִּי לְבַדִּי אֵלֶּה אֵיפֹה הֵם: יִשְׂמַח יִשְׂרָאֵל בְּעוֹשָׂיו | בְּנֵי־צִיּוֹן יָגִילוּ
בְמַלְכָּם: בָּרוּךְ אַתָּה יְיָ אֱלֹהֵינוּ מֶלֶךְ הָעוֹלָם מְשַׂמֵּחַ צִיּוֹן בְּבָנֶיהָ אָמֵן:

The Fifth Benediction
Blessed be the Lord out of Zion, who dwells in Jerusalem.
   Praise ye the Lord! (Ps. 135:21).
Sing, O barren one, thou who didst not bear,
Break forth into song and shout, thou who didst not travail,
For more are the children of the desolate than the children of
   the married wife, says the Lord (Isa. 54:1).

Sing, O daughter of Zion, shout, O Israel,
Rejoice and be glad wholeheartedly, O daughter of Jerusalem! (Zeph. 3:14).
Sing and rejoice, O daughter of Zion, for behold, I am coming and I will dwell in the midst of thee, said the Lord (Zech. 2:14).
Thus says the Lord, I am returning to Zion, and I will dwell within Jerusalem,
And Jerusalem shall be called the city of truth, and the mountain of the Lord of Hosts shall be called the holy mountain (Zech. 8:3).
They shall say in thine ears, the children of thy bereavement,
The place is too strait for me; give place to me that I may dwell.
And thou shalt say in thy heart, Who has begotten me these, seeing that I am bereaved and lonely, exiled and wandering; and who has brought these up? Behold I was left alone; these, where had they been? (Isa. 49:20-21).
Let Israel rejoice in their Maker,
Let the children of Zion be joyful in their King (Ps. 149:2).
Blessed art Thou, O Lord, our God, King of the universe who causest Zion to rejoice in her children. Amen!

6 בְּרָכָה שִׁשִּׁית בָּרוּךְ אֲדֹנָי יוֹם יוֹם יַעֲמָס־לָנוּ הָאֵל יְשׁוּעָתֵנוּ סֶלָה: שִׂמְחוּ צַדִּיקִים בַּיהוָה וְהוֹדוּ לְזֵכֶר קָדְשׁוֹ: שִׂמְחוּ בַיהוָה וְגִילוּ צַדִּיקִים וְהַרְנִינוּ כָּל־יִשְׁרֵי־לֵב: שִׂמְחוּ אֶת־יְרוּשָׁלַםִ וְגִילוּ בָהּ כָּל־אֹהֲבֶיהָ: שִׂישׂוּ אִתָּהּ מָשׂוֹשׂ כָּל־הַמִּתְאַבְּלִים עָלֶיהָ: לְמַעַן תִּינְקוּ וּשְׂבַעְתֶּם מִשֹּׁד תַּנְחֻמֶיהָ: לְמַעַן תָּמֹצּוּ וְהִתְעַנַּגְתֶּם מִזִּיז כְּבוֹדָהּ: אָז תִּשְׂמַח בְּתוּלָה בְּמָחוֹל וּבַחֻרִים וּזְקֵנִים יַחְדָּו: וְהָפַכְתִּי אֶבְלָם לְשָׂשׂוֹן וְנִחַמְתִּים וְשִׂמַּחְתִּים מִיגוֹנָם: וְרִוֵּיתִי נֶפֶשׁ הַכֹּהֲנִים דָּשֶׁן וְעַמִּי אֶת־טוּבִי יִשְׂבָּעוּ נְאֻם־יְהוָה: וְצַדִּיקִים יִשְׂמְחוּ יַעַלְצוּ לִפְנֵי אֱלֹהִים וְיָשִׂישׂוּ בְשִׂמְחָה:

The Sixth Benediction
Blessed be the Lord;
Day by day He bears our burden, the God who is our salvation. Selah! (Ps. 68:20).
Rejoice in the Lord, O ye righteous ones,
And give thanks to his holy Name (Ps. 97:12).
Rejoice in the Lord and be joyful, O ye righteous ones,

And shout for joy, all ye upright of heart (Ps. 32:11).
Rejoice with Jerusalem, and be joyful with her, all ye who love her;
Rejoice with her in joy, all ye who mourn for her;
In order that ye may suck and be satisfied with the breast of her consolations,
That ye may drink deeply with delight of the abundance of her glory (Isa. 66:10-11).
Then shall the virgin rejoice in dancing,
And young men and old men together;
For I will turn their mourning into joy,
And I will console them and make them rejoice from their sorrow.
And I will satiate the soul of the priests with fat,
And My people shall be satisfied with My goodness, says the Lord (Jer. 31:12-13).
And let the righteous rejoice, let them be joyful before God,
And let them be glad with joy (Ps. 68:4).
Blessed art Thou, O Lord, our God, King of the universe, who causest bridegroom and bride to rejoice. Amen!

בָּרוּךְ אַתָּה יְיָ אֱלֹהֵינוּ מֶלֶךְ הָעוֹלָם מְשַׂמֵּחַ חָתָן וְכַלָּה אָמֵן ; 7 ברכה שביעית
בָּרוּךְ אַתָּה יְהֹוָה לַמְדֵנִי חֻקֶּיךָ : שׂוֹשׂ אָשִׂישׂ בַּיהֹוָה תָּגֵל נַפְשִׁי בֵּאלֹהַי כִּי
הִלְבִּישַׁנִי בִּגְדֵי־יֶשַׁע מְעִיל צְדָקָה יְעָטָנִי | כֶּחָתָן יְכַהֵן פְּאֵר וְכַכַּלָּה
תַּעְדֶּה כֵלֶיהָ : כִּי־אִם־יָשִׂישׂוּ וְגִילוּ עֲדֵי־עַד אֲשֶׁר אֲנִי בוֹרֵא | כִּי הִנְנִי בוֹרֵא
אֶת־יְרוּשָׁלַם גִּילָה וְעַמָּהּ מָשׂוֹשׂ : וְגַלְתִּי בִירוּשָׁלַם וְשַׂשְׂתִּי בְעַמִּי | וְלֹא־יִשָּׁמַע
בָּהּ עוֹד קוֹל בְּכִי וְקוֹל זְעָקָה : שְׂאִי־סָבִיב עֵינַיִךְ וּרְאִי כֻּלָּם נִקְבְּצוּ בָאוּ־לָךְ |
חַי־אָנִי נְאֻם־יְהֹוָה כִּי כֻלָּם כַּעֲדִי תִלְבָּשִׁי וּתְקַשְּׁרִים כַּכַּלָּה : כִּי־יִבְעַל בָּחוּר
בְּתוּלָה יִבְעָלוּךְ בָּנָיִךְ | וּמְשׂוֹשׂ חָתָן עַל־כַּלָּה יָשִׂישׂ עָלַיִךְ אֱלֹהָיִךְ :
בָּרוּךְ אַתָּה יְיָ אֱלֹהֵינוּ מֶלֶךְ הָעוֹלָם מְשַׂמֵּחַ הֶחָתָן עִם הַכַּלָּה מַצְלִיחַ וּמְשַׂמֵּחַ
הֶחָתָן עִם הַכַּלָּה אָמֵן : הוֹדוּ לַיהֹוָה כִּי־טוֹב | כִּי לְעוֹלָם חַסְדּוֹ :
תִּרְבֶּינָה שְׂמָחוֹת בְּיִשְׂרָאֵל : תִּרְבֶּינָה נֶחָמוֹת בְּיִשְׂרָאֵל : תִּרְבֶּינָה יְשׁוּעוֹת
בְּיִשְׂרָאֵל : תִּרְבֶּינָה בְּשׂוֹרוֹת טוֹבוֹת בְּיִשְׂרָאֵל : תִּרְבֶּה אַהֲבָה בְּיִשְׂרָאֵל : תִּרְבֶּה
בְּרָכָה בְּיִשְׂרָאֵל : תִּרְבֶּה גִילָה בְּיִשְׂרָאֵל : תִּרְבֶּה דִיצָה בְּיִשְׂרָאֵל : יִרְבֶּה הוֹד
בְּיִשְׂרָאֵל : יִרְבֶּה וַעַד בְּיִשְׂרָאֵל : יִרְבֶּה זְכוּת בְּיִשְׂרָאֵל : יִרְבּוּ חֲתָנִים בְּיִשְׂרָאֵל :
תִּרְבֶּינָה כַּלּוֹת בְּיִשְׂרָאֵל : כְּהַיּוֹם הַזֶּה וּבִירוּשָׁלַם שָׂשִׂים וְגַם שְׂמֵחִים בְּבִנְיַן

Mourad El-Kodsi

בֵּית הַמִּקְדָּשׁ אֵלִיָה הַנָּבִיא מְהֵרָה יָבֹא אֵלֵינוּ הַמֶּלֶךְ הַמָּשִׁיחַ יִצְמַח בְּיָמֵינוּ :
וְיִשְׂמְחוּ שְׁנֵיהֶם זֶה עִם זֹאת : וְיָשִׂישׂוּ שְׁנֵיהֶם זֹאת עִם זֶה : וְיַאֲרִיכוּ יָמִים
זֶה עִם זֹאת : וְיִזְכּוּ לְבָנִים הֲגוּנִים זֹאת עִם זֶה : וְיִבְנוּ וְיַצְלִיחוּ זֶה עִם זֹאת :
כְּשֵׁבְנוּ כְּשֶׁהִצְלִיחוּ : וְשָׁבֵי יְהוּדָיֵא בְּנַיָן וּמַצְלְחִין : יִשְׂמַח חָתָן עִם כַּלָּה
כַּלָּה תִּשְׂמַח בְּחָתָן : בַּבָּנִים וּבַבָּנוֹת בָּעֹשֶׁר וּבַנְכָסִים : בְּבָנִים עוֹסְקֵי תּוֹרָה
וּמְקַיְּמֵי מִצְוֹת בְּיִשְׂרָאֵל : הוֹדוּ לַיהוָה כִּי־טוֹב | כִּי לְעוֹלָם חַסְדּוֹ :

וישתה החתן והכלה מהכום ובשתות החתן תאמר לו זה

The Seventh Benediction
Blessed art Thou, O Lord, teach me Thy statues (Ps. 119:12).
I will greatly rejoice in the Lord,
My soul will be joyful in my God,
For He has clothed me with the garments of salvation,
He has covered me with the robe of righteousness,
As a bridegroom puts on a priestly diadem,
And as a bride adorns herself with jewels (Isa. 61:10).
But be ye glad and rejoice for ever in that which I create,
For behold, I create Jerusalem a rejoicing, and her people a
  joy;
And I will rejoice in Jerusalem,
And joy in My people,
And no more shall there be heard within her the sound of
  weeping and the voice of crying (Isa. 65:18-19).
Lift up thine eyes round about and behold,
All these gather themselves together and come to thee;
As I live, says the Lord, thou shalt surely clothe thyself with
  them all, as with an ornament,
And gird thyself with them, like a bride (Isa. 49:18).
For as a young man espouses a virgin, so shall thy sons
  espouse thee,
And as the bridegroom rejoices over the bride,
So shall thy God rejoice over thee (Isa. 62:5).
Blessed are Thou, O Lord, our God, King of the universe,
  who givest joy to the bridegroom with the bride, who
  givest happiness and joy to the bridegroom with the bride.
  Amen!
Give thanks to the Lord, for He is good, for His mercy en-
  dureth for ever (Ps. 136:1).
May joys be many in Israel!

May consolations be many in Israel!
May salvations be many in Israel!
May good tidings be many in Israel!
May love multiply in Israel!
May blessing multiply in Israel!
May rejoicing multiply in Israel!
May joy multiply in Israel!
May splendor multiply in Israel!
May council multiply in Israel!
May merit multiply in Israel!
May bridegrooms be many in Israel!
May brides be many in Israel!
As of this day, and in Jerusalem, may they rejoice and be glad in the rebuilding of the Temple. May Elijah the Prophet come to us soon.
May the King Messiah spring up in our days.
May they both be glad, this one with that one!
May they both rejoice that one with this one!
May they both prolong their days, this one with that one!
May they be vouchsafed proper sons, that one with this one!
May they build their household and prosper, this one with that one!
As they build, so may they prosper, as it is written: And the elders of the Jews builded and prospered (Ezra 6:14).
May the bridegroom rejoice with the bride,
May the bride rejoice with the bridegroom,
In sons and in daughters, in wealth and in possessions;
In sons who engage in the study of the Law
And fulfill the commandments in Israel.
Give thanks to the Lord, for He is good, for His mercy endureth for ever (Ps. 136:1).

The English translation is taken from Leon Nemoy, *Karaite Anthology,* pp. 274-305

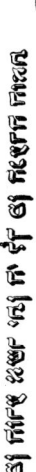

When this part is completed the ḥakhām asks the groom to drink from the cup of wine while he blesses him and prays that his house be blessed.

שְׁתֵה־מַיִם מִבּוֹרֶךָ ׀ וְנוֹזְלִים מִתּוֹךְ בְּאֵרֶךָ ׃ יָפוּצוּ מַעְיְנֹתֶיךָ חוּצָה ׀ בָּרְחֹבוֹת פַּלְגֵי־מָיִם ׃ יִהְיוּ־לְךָ לְבַדֶּךָ ׀ וְאֵין לְזָרִים אִתָּךְ ׃ יְהִי־מְקוֹרְךָ בָרוּךְ ׀ וּשְׂמַח מֵאֵשֶׁת נְעוּרֶיךָ ׃

> Drink water out of thine own cistern
> And running water out of thine own well.
> Let thy fountains be dispersed abroad
> In the streets, as streams of water.
> Let them be for thee alone,
> And not for strangers with thee.
> Let they spring be blessed,
> And have joy of the wife of thy youth (Prov. 5:15-18).

Then he asks the bride to drink from the cup of wine while he blesses her.

אַיֶּלֶת אֲהָבִים וְיַעֲלַת־חֵן דַּדֶּיהָ יְרַוֻּךָ בְכָל־עֵת ׀ בְּאַהֲבָתָהּ תִּשְׁגֶּה תָמִיד ׃ מָצָא אִשָּׁה מָצָא טוֹב ׀ וַיָּפֶק רָצוֹן מֵיְהוָה ׃ אֵשֶׁת־חַיִל מִי יִמְצָא ׀ וְרָחֹק מִפְּנִינִים מִכְרָהּ ׃ שֶׁקֶר הַחֵן וְהֶבֶל הַיֹּפִי ׀ אִשָּׁה יִרְאַת־יְהוָה הִיא תִתְהַלָּל ׃ בַּיִת וָהוֹן נַחֲלַת אָבוֹת ׀ וּמֵיְהוָה אִשָּׁה מַשְׂכָּלֶת ׃ וּמְצָא־חֵן וְשֵׂכֶל טוֹב ׀ בְּעֵינֵי אֱלֹהִים וְאָדָם ׃

> A lovely hind and a graceful doe,
> Let her breasts satisfy thee at all times,
> In her love take thou delight always (Prov. 5:19).
> Whoso finds a wife, finds a great good,
> And obtains a favor from the Lord (Prov. 18:22).
> A valiant woman who can find?
> For her price is far above rubies (Prov. 31:10).
> Grace is deceitful, and vain is beauty;
> But a woman that feareth the Lord, she shall be praised (Prov. 31:30).
> House and riches are the inheritance of fathers,
> But a prudent wife is from the Lord (Prov. 19:14).
> So shalt thou find grace and good favor in the sight of God and man (Prov. 3:4).

The ṭallīt then is lowered to the shoulders and the ḥakhām reminds the couple of the sad state of Jerusalem.

פְּלֵטִים מֵחֶרֶב הִלְכוּ אַל־תַּעֲמֹדוּ ׀ זִכְרוּ מֵרָחוֹק אֶת־יְהוָֹה וִירוּשָׁלַםִ תַּעֲלֶה עַל־לְבַבְכֶם : אִם־אֶשְׁכָּחֵךְ יְרוּשָׁלָםִ תִּשְׁכַּח יְמִינִי : תִּדְבַּק לְשׁוֹנִי לְחִכִּי אִם־לֹא אֶזְכְּרֵכִי ׀

> Ye who have escaped the sword, go ye, stand not still;
> Remember the Lord from afar,
> And let Jerusalem come to your mind (Jer. 51:50).
> If I forget thee, O Jerusalem,
> Let my right hand forget her cunning;
> Let my tongue cleave to the roof of my mouth,
> If I remember thee not (Ps. 137:5-6).

He continues on with the next part and when he reaches the words: *Shuv meharon apekha,* the ṭallīt once again covers the couple's head and the ḥakhām completes the part.

אִם לֹא אַעֲלֶה אֶיְרַ"שָׁ : שָׁבַת מְשׂוֹשׂ לִבֵּנוּ נֶלִי"מָ : נָפְלָה עֲטֶרֶת רֹאשֵׁנוּ אֲנַלְבִּ"חָ : עַל זֶה הָיָה דָוֶה לַעֲאַחָ"עֵ . עַל הַר צִיּוֹן שֶׁשָּׁמֵם שֶׁהָ"ב : וְאַחֲרֵי כָּל הַבָּא עָלֵינוּ בְּמַעֲשֵׂינוּ הָרָעִים וּהַכִּ"א אֶחֱלָ"ימַ וְלָפִ"כָּ : יְיָ אֱלֹהֵי יִשְׂרָאֵל צַדִּיק אַתָּה כִּנְפִכִּ"הַ הִלִ"ב כָּאֵ"ל לְעַוּ"לַ רַמְלִ"חָ : וְאַתָּה צַדִּיק עַל כָּל הַבָּא עָכִ"א עָוִיהַ ׀ שׁוּב מֵחֲרוֹן אַפֶּךָ וְעַי"הַ לְעַמֶּךָ : שׁוּב לְמַעַן עֲבָדֶיךָ שִׁבְטֵי נַחֲלָתֶךָ : הֲשִׁיבֵנוּ יְיָ אֵלֶיךָ וְחַיִּ"בְּ : וְסָלַחְתָּ לַעֲוֹנֵנוּ וּלְחַטֹּאתֵנוּ וּנְחַלְתָּנוּ : בָּרוּךְ יְהוָה לְעוֹלָם ׀ אָמֵן ׀ וְאָמֵן :

> If I set not Jerusalem above my chief joy (Ps. 137:6).
> The joy of our hearts has ceased,
> Our dance has been turned into mourning,
> The crown is fallen from our head;
> Woe unto us, for we have sinned.
> For this our heart is faint,
> For these things are our eyes dim;
> For the mountain of Zion which is desolate,
> And foxes walk upon it (Lam. 5:15-18).
> And after all that has come upon us for our evil deeds, and
>> our great guilt, seeing that Thou, our God, hast punished
>> us less than our iniquities deserve, and hast given us such
>> a remnant (Ezra 9:13).
> O Lord, God of Israel, Thou are righteous, for we are left a
>> remnant that is escaped, as it is this day. Behold, we are

> before Thee in our guilt, for none can stand before Thee,
> because of this (Ezra 9:15).
> Howbeit Thou are just in all that is come upon us,
> For Thou hast dealt truly,
> But we have done wickedly (Neh. 9:33).
> Turn from Thy fierce wrath,
> And repent of this evil against Thy people (Expd 32:12).
> Turn back for the sake of Thy servants,
> The tribes of Thine inheritance (Isa. 63:17).
> Turn Thou us to Thee, O Lord, and we shall be turned,
> Renew our days as of old (Lam. 5:21).
> And forgive our sin and our transgression,
> And take us for Thine inheritance (Exod. 34:9).
> Blessed be the Lord into eternity. Amen, and again amen!

The couple are now officially married, so it is once again time to bless the groom (part A), then the bride (part B), then all the guests (part C).

The ḥakhām then asks the couple to kiss the Torah, which is placed on a table near the ḥakhām. And when this is done, the ḥakhām and the Karaite guests start to sing "Amen Yehi Raṣon" (Pl. 11).

A — ותברך לחתן

וְאַתָּה אָחִינוּ יַקִּירֵנוּ הֶחָתָן יְיָ אֱלֹהֵי יִשְׂרָאֵל יִתֵּן לְךָ מִשְׁאֲלוֹת לִבְּךָ לְטוֹבָה: וְתִכְלֶה יָמֶיךָ וּשְׁנוֹתֶיךָ בַּנְּעִימִים: וְהָיָה רֵאשִׁיתְךָ מִצְעָר וְאַחֲרִיתְךָ יִשְׂגֶּה מְאֹד: וְיִתֵּן לְךָ בָּנִים וּבְנֵי בָנִים הֹגִים בַּתּוֹרָה: בָּרוּךְ אַתָּה בְּבֹאֶךָ וּבָרוּךְ אַתָּה בְּצֵאתֶךָ: בָּרוּךְ תִּהְיֶה מִכָּל־הָעַמִּים| לֹא־יִהְיֶה בְךָ עָקָר וַעֲקָרָה וּבִכְהֶמְתֶּךָ: יְהוָה יִשְׁמָרְךָ מִכָּל־רָע| יִשְׁמֹר אֶת־נַפְשֶׁךָ: יְהוָה יִשְׁמָר־צֵאתְךָ וּבוֹאֶךָ| מֵעַתָּה וְעַד־עוֹלָם: בְּלֶכְתְּךָ לֹא־יֵצַר צַעֲדֶךָ| וְאִם־תָּרוּץ לֹא תִכָּשֵׁל:

B — ותברך גם לכלה ותאמר

וְאַתְּ אֲחוֹתֵנוּ הַכַּלָּה אַתְּ הֲיִי לְאַלְפֵי רְבָבָה וְיִירַשׁ זַרְעֵךְ אֵת שַׁעַר שֹׂנְאָיו: בְּרוּכָה אַתְּ לַיְיָ בְּרוּכָה אַתְּ וּבָרוּךְ טַעְמֵךְ: בְּרוּכִים אַתֶּם לַיהוָה| עֹשֵׂה שָׁמַיִם וָאָרֶץ: אֱלֹהֵינוּ וֵאלֹהֵי אֲבוֹתֵינוּ הָקֵם לָנוּ אֶת דְּבָרְךָ הַטּוֹב אֲשֶׁר דִּבַּרְתָּ: כֹּה אָמַר יְהוָה עוֹד יִשָּׁמַע בַּמָּקוֹם־הַזֶּה אֲשֶׁר אַתֶּם אֹמְרִים חָרֵב הוּא מֵאֵין אָדָם וּמֵאֵין בְּהֵמָה| בְּעָרֵי יְהוּדָה וּבְחֻצוֹת יְרוּשָׁלַיִם הַנְשַׁמּוֹת מֵאֵין אָדָם וּמֵאֵין יוֹשֵׁב וּמֵאֵין בְּהֵמָה: קוֹל שָׂשׂוֹן וְקוֹל שִׂמְחָה קוֹל חָתָן וְקוֹל כַּלָּה קוֹל אֹמְרִים הוֹדוּ אֶת־יְהוָה צְבָאוֹת כִּי־טוֹב יְהוָה כִּי־לְעוֹלָם חַסְדּוֹ מְבִאִים תּוֹדָה בֵּית יְהוָה| כִּי־אָשִׁיב אֶת־שְׁבוּת־הָאָרֶץ כְּבָרִאשֹׁנָה אָמַר יְהוָה:

Mourad El-Kodsi

וְאַתֶּם קָהָל הַקֹּדֶשׁ עַם יְיָ מְיֻחֲדֵי אֵל סְגֻלַּת אֱלֹהִים חַיִּים | אֲשֶׁר נִקְבַּצְתֶּם בִּלְוָיַת הֶחָתָן וְהַכַּלָּה וּגְמַלְתֶּם הַחֶסֶד הַזֶּה עֲלֵיהֶם | אֱלֹהֵי יִשְׂרָאֵל יְבָרֵךְ אֶתְכֶם וְיִשְׁמֹר אֶתְכֶם וְיִנְצֹר אֶתְכֶם וְיָעֹז אֶתְכֶם וִיקַיֵּם עֲלֵיכֶם מִקְרָא שֶׁכָּתוּב : יְהוָה אֱלֹהֵי אֲבוֹתֵכֶם יֹסֵף עֲלֵיכֶם כָּכֶם אֶלֶף פְּעָמִים | וִיבָרֵךְ אֶתְכֶם כַּאֲשֶׁר דִּבֶּר לָכֶם : הַקָּטֹן יִהְיֶה לָאֶלֶף וְהַצָּעִיר לְגוֹי עָצוּם | אֲנִי יְהוָה בְּעִתָּהּ אֲחִישֶׁנָּה : בּוֹנֵה יְרוּשָׁלַיִם יְהוָה | נִדְחֵי יִשְׂרָאֵל יְכַנֵּס : בּוֹרֵא נִיב שְׂפָתָיִם | שָׁלוֹם שָׁלוֹם לָרָחוֹק וְלַקָּרוֹב אָמַר יְהוָה וּרְפָאתִיו : הַמֹּשֵׁל וָפַחַד עִמּוֹ | עֹשֶׂה שָׁלוֹם בִּמְרוֹמָיו : יְהוָה עֹז לְעַמּוֹ יִתֵּן | יְהוָה יְבָרֵךְ אֶת־עַמּוֹ בַשָּׁלוֹם :

c- בָּרוּךְ יְהוָה לְעוֹלָם | אָמֵן | וְאָמֵן :

a- And thou, our dear brother, the bridegroom, may the Lord, God of Israel, give thee thy heart's desire in the way of good things.

Mayest thou spend thy days and thy years in pleasantness.

While thy beginning is small, may thy ending be very great (Job. 8:7).

May He grant thee sons, and sons' sons, studying the Law.

Blessed be thou in thy coming, and blessing be thou in thy going (Deut. 28:6).

Blessed be thou more than all nations, and may there be no childless man or woman with thee, nor any unfruitful animal with thy cattle.

The Lord guard thee from all evil; may He guard thy soul.

The Lord guard thy going and thy coming, from now and into eternity (Ps. 121:6f.).

When thou goest, may they footstep not be narrow, and if thou runnest, mayest thou not stumble (Prov. 4:12).

b- And thou, our sister, the bride, mayest thou become a thousand times ten thousand descendants, and may thy seed inherit the gate of their enemies (Gen. 24:60).

Blessed be thou unto the Lord, blessed be thou, and blessed be thy reputation.

Blessed be ye both unto the Lord, the Maker of heaven and earth.

Our God and God of our fathers, fulfill for us Thy good word which Thou hast spoken, to wit:

Thus says the Lord: There shall yet be heard in this place, of which ye say that it is desolate, devoid of man, and devoid of beast, even in the cities of Judah and in the streets of Jerusalem, which are abandoned, devoid of man, and devoid of inhabitant, and devoid of beast—

The voice of joy, and the voice of gladness, the voice of the bridegroom and the voice of the bride, the voice fo them that say, Give thanks to the Lord of Hosts, for the Lord is good, for His mercy endureth for ever, eve of them that bring offerings of thanksgiving into the House of the Lord. For I will cause the captivity of the Land to return, as at the first, says the Lord (Jer. 33:10-11).

And you, O holy congregation, people of the Lord, who proclaim the oneness of God, precious possession of the living God, who have gathered together to accompany the bridegroom and the bride, and have done this kindness unto them;

May the God of Israel bless you, and guard you, and watch over you, and help you, and fulfill upon you the written blessing, to wit:

May the Lord, God of your fathers, add unto you as many as ye are, a thousand times, and may He bless you, as He has spoken to you (Deut. 1:11).

The smallest shall become a thousand,
And the least a mighty nation;
I, the Lord, will hasten it in its time (Isa. 60:22).
The Lord does build up Jerusalem,
He gathers together the dispersed of Israel (Ps. 147:2).
Peace, peace, to him that is far off and to him that is near,
Says the Lord that creates the fruit of the lips,
And I will heal him (Isa. 57:19).
Dominion and awe are with Him,
He makes peace in His high places (Job 25:2).
The Lord will give strength to His people,
The Lord will bless His people with peace (Ps. 29:11).
Blessed be the Lord in eternity. Amen, and again amen!

The custom of breaking a glass to signal the end of the ceremony was not known to the Karaites in Egypt, but now it is followed in Israel.

Other pertinent Karaite wedding traditions in Egypt:

— Sundays and Tuesdays were reserved for virgins who were to be married for the first time.

— Thursday and Saturday night were reserved for those divorced or widowed.

— To make a marriage complete, there must be: 1. a contract *(ketubbah)*; 2.

a dowry *(mohār)*; and 3. consummation of the union *(bi'āh)*.[40]
— The *ketubbah* was executed at the Bēt-Dīn and was signed by ten witnesses.[41]
— The *ketubbah* was written in Hebrew (not in Aramaic, as is the Rabbanite *ketubbah*).
— The groom, and not the ḥākhām, was responsible for the ring.

One final note: it was assumed that a girl never married before was a virgin. If this was not the case, the groom dissolved the contract and returned the bride to her family.

To encourage young men to get married it was the custom that the father of the bride would offer a large sum of money to the prospective groom. This money was considered as a loan to the groom which he should pay back. If, however, he died before paying it back, it used to be returned to his wife before any partition of the inheritance takes place.

Divorce

The legal source for divorce among Rabbanites and Karaites is Deuteronomy 24-1: "When a man taketh a wife, and marrieth her, then it cometh to pass, if she finds no favour in his eyes, because he hath found some unseemly thing in her, that he writeth her a bill of divorcement."

The difference in the interpretation of this part constituted the difference in the law of divorce among both sects.

Karaites legal authorities throughout the centuries wrote many books to deal with what is legal and illegal in that matter, as well as in all matters of daily life.

One among the many books that the Karaites of Egypt depended upon is *Adderet Elīyāhū* by Elijah Bashyatchi.

Murād Farag, a prominent poet, writer, and attorney-at-law, published in April 1917, an abbreviated translation into Arabic of that book entitled *Shi'ār al-Khiḍr,* in which he devoted a complete chapter to divorce.

At the request of the Egyptian Government and the religious council of the Karaite community in Egypt, Murād Farag compiled a manual in 1935 entitled "Legal Rules Affecting Personal Status, as Current Among Karaite Israelites, Based on the Torah, Authoritative Legal Manuals, General Independent Opinions and the Principles of Common Equity."

Professor Leon Nemoy examined the manual and wrote about it and gave a complete translation with comments on the part of the manual about divorce.[42]

---

40. Bashyatchi, *Adderet El-yāhū* (Ramlah, Israel: 1966).
41. According to Karaite tradition, the witnesses must sign the *ketubah* after reading it during the wedding ceremony, but it has become the custom to sign it earlier.
42. *Henoch.:* studi storicofilogici sull'ebraismo redatti presso la Biblioteca PAUL KAHLE dell'Istituto di Orientalistica dell' Università di Torino.

I felt it very appropriate to choose and to record some parts of this work about divorce.

The manual consists of numbered articles — from 1 to 438 — covering many legal matters, including divorce.

The articles about divorce are those from 286 to 354. Here are some:

General Rules:

286. The marital bond may be dissolved only by divorce.
287. There is no divorce except at the hand of the Karaite court of law.
288. Any divorce-executed-at the hand of -an authority-other than the-court of- law is null and void.
289. Divorce may be legally granted when consented to by both parties.
290. Husband and wife have an equal legal right to seek divorce when-they think that- it is needed.
291. The law must not proceed hastily-in-case of-divorce; oftentimes conciliation may be hoped for.

Application of Divorce:-323

323. Divorce applies equally to a fiancée-a woman under bond of acquisition, *qinyān*, and to a wedded wife, even if she is a co-wife.[43]

Grounds for a Divorce: 324 to 346

324. No divorce without the wife's consent may be executed, except when there is a-legal- ground.
325. The ground must be acceptable, both in law and in custom.[44]
326. If the husband himself is the cause of the ground, even if only unintentionally, it has no standing in law, so long as he does not induce the wife to consent-to the divorce-.
346. If divorce is-legally-due (to one of the parties), waiver of it constitutes an act of compassion and generosity.

Implementation and Certification of the Divorce: 347 to 354

347. Divorce is implemented by being committed to writing,

---

43. Murād Farag used here the word *darrah* which indicates a second wife while the wife is still on bond with the husband.
44. He also used the word (*'urf*) custom because Karaites of Egypt — rich and poor alike — were able to have a second wife on legal grounds. During the time of Hākhām Abrāhām Kohen (1920-1933), he and Murād Farag were able to put an end to this unpleasant practice as no longer acceptable to custom.

and is certified by the legal writ thereof.
348. The form of the writ is the well-known one, in the Hebrew language, as regularly used.
351. The writ may not specify that the divorce was granted on the ground of a certain defect, but if the ground is adultery, it must be so stated.

Obviously Farag's book was meant to serve as a practical manual for Karaite parties and for their secular legal advisers, and not as a guide for the ḥākhām (the Karaite counterpart of the Rabbanite rabbi) sitting as judge of the Karaite court, and certainly not for the members of the Karaite Religious Council *(al-majlis al-Millī),* to whom the court's decisions could be appealed. These no doubt did not need instruction from a lay attorney-at-law, and whenever necessary went for their own guidance to the classical Karaite codes written in Arabic or Hebrew.

We might conclude this paper with a few observations on the practical influence of the Cairene divorce law upon the social and economic position of the two parties in general, and of the wife in particular, as reflected in Farag's digest.

While the husband's initiative in dismissing his wife, being of Scriptural formulation, had to be maintained in Karaite law, steps are taken to surround it with certain limitations. The husband may initiate divorce proceedings, but he must take his case to court, and only the court can formally disssolve the marriage (Articles 286-288). If both parties agree to the divorce, the court grants it automatically (Art. 289). The wife, too, may apply for a divorce (Art. 290), although it is for the court to determine whether her grounds for it are valid. If they are, the divorce is granted in disregard of the husband's protest (Art. 311). The same limitation applies to the husband, and if the wife contests the divorce, he must convince the court that his grounds are valid, both in law and in custom (Arts. 324-325); any ground caused by the husband himself is not valid (Art. 326). The divorcée is entitled to maintenance during the obligatory three months' waiting period after the divorce, and if she is found to be pregnant, until she is delivered (Art. 321).

And yet the list of admissible grounds is rather long and liberal, and includes not only barrenness, insanity, and mental deficiency, but also prolonged and incurable illness, physical defects such as loss of sight, speech, or hearing, and even halitosis, as well as unseemly and offensive conduct and of course downright adultery (Arts. 335-336). In respect to the wife, additional grounds are fraudulent wedlock without her consent, inability to provide proper maintenance, and imcompatability (Art. 337). Absence, voluntary (by way of emigration, or for other reasons) or involuntary (due to imprisonment), for a period of longer than one year, is also a valid ground, and so is renunciation of the Karaite faith (Arts. 341-344).

In order not to blight the wife's prospects of remarriage, the writ of divorcement may not specify the ground upon which the divorce was granted to her former husband, unless it was adultery (Art. 351). The court must maintain a record of all divorce proceedings, stating all the pertinent particualrs of each case (Arts. 352-354), thus ensuring that the loss of the writ of divorcement will not cause either party — particularly the wife, who is normally the recipient and holder of the writ — any serious difficulty or damage in the future.

It would take an expert in modern Western family law (which I certainly am not) to determine whether Farag's digest shows any traces of Western influence. My own guess woudl be that it does, at least in his evident concern for the wife's welfare and the protection of both her good name and her sources of livelihood. This concern appears clearly in at least one other work of Farag's, his comparative study of Karaite and Rabbanite law referred to earlier in this paper.

During the 19th century the ḥākhām was the person responsible for looking into divorce cases. From 1901 until 1940 the Karaite Religious Council was the responsible body, and when the religious courts were formed in 1940, it was their responsibility to look into all legal matters including divorce.

Karaites in general do not encourage divorce. The various ḥākhāmīn, religious councils, and religious courts always preferred conciliation, if it was at all possible. This explains, in part, the very few cases of divorce recorded form 1901 until 1956. In 1902 the Karaite Religious Council looked into two cases and agreed on divorce as requested. Between 1946 and 1956 there were 20 cases of divorce in this community of 5,000.

Death

The moment the Bēt-Dīn received the notice of a death, the clerk would take the following steps: 1) Inform the ḥākhām; 2) Inform the grave digger; 3) Prepare the coffin; 4) Send a special group (men or women) *Ḥebrāt Qaddisha* to the residence of the deceased.[45]

The coffin was left in the house of the deceased, facing Jerusalem, until the time of the funeral. If it was to be left overnight, two large candles in holders were placed there, one at the deceased's head and one at his feet.

For the residents of the suburbs, arrangements were made to bring the coffin to the synagogue court, and the funeral would start from there.

When everything is ready, the ḥakhām and the mourners read from Job "The Lord gave, and the Lord hath taken away, blessed be the name of the Lord." They all continue with part 1, and when it is completed the ḥakhām alone repeats the underlined words.

יְהוָה נָתַן וַיהוָה לָקָח יְהִי שֵׁם יְהוָה מְבֹרָךְ:

בָּרוּךְ שַׁדַּי דַּיָּן אֱמֶת וּמִשְׁפָּטוֹ מִשְׁפָּט אֱמֶת מְחַיֶּה בְּחֶסֶד וּמֵמִית בְּצֶדֶק: הַצּוּר תָּמִים פָּעֳלוֹ כִּי כָל־דְּרָכָיו מִשְׁפָּט‎‎ אֵל אֱמוּנָה וְאֵין עָוֶל צַדִּיק וְיָשָׁר הוּא: צַדִּיק יְהוָה בְּכָל־דְּרָכָיו וְחָסִיד בְּכָל־מַעֲשָׂיו: צַדִּיק אַתָּה יְהוָה וְיָשָׁר מִשְׁפָּטֶיךָ: כִּי־צַדִּיק יְהוָה צְדָקוֹת אָהֵב וְיָשָׁר יֶחֱזוּ פָנֵימוֹ: כִּי־צַדִּיק יְהוָה אֱלֹהֵינוּ עַל־כָּל־מַעֲשָׂיו אֲשֶׁר עָשָׂה וְלֹא שְׁמַעֲנוּ בְּקֹלוֹ: לְהַגִּיד כִּי־יָשָׁר יְהוָה צוּרִי וְלֹא־עַוְלָתָה בּוֹ: וְאַתָּה צַדִּיק עַל כָּל־הַבָּא עָלֵינוּ | כִּי־אֱמֶת עָשִׂיתָ וַאֲנַחְנוּ הִרְשָׁעְנוּ: אֶשָּׂא דֵעִי לְמֵרָחוֹק וּלְפֹעֲלִי אֶתֵּן־צֶדֶק: לָכֵן אַנְשֵׁי לֵבָב שִׁמְעוּ לִי חָלִלָה לָאֵל מֵרֶשַׁע וְשַׁדַּי מֵעָוֶל: אַף־אָמְנָם אֵל לֹא־יַרְשִׁיעַ וְשַׁדַּי לֹא־יְעַוֵּת מִשְׁפָּט: הָאֵל יְשׁוּעַת מִשְׁפָּט | וְאִם־שַׁדַּי יְעַוֵּת־צֶדֶק: צֶדֶק וּמִשְׁפָּט מְכוֹן כִּסְאֶךָ | חֶסֶד וֶאֱמֶת יְקַדְּמוּ פָנֶיךָ: צִדְקָתְךָ כְּהַרְרֵי־אֵל מִשְׁפָּטֶיךָ תְּהוֹם רַבָּה אָדָם וּבְהֵמָה תּוֹשִׁיעַ יְהוָה: אָבוֹא בִּגְבֻרוֹת אֲדֹנָי יְהוִה אַזְכִּיר צִדְקָתְךָ לְבַדֶּךָ: וְצִדְקָתְךָ אֱלֹהִים עַד־מָרוֹם אֲשֶׁר־עָשִׂיתָ גְדֹלוֹת | אֱלֹהִים מִי כָמוֹךָ: צִדְקָתְךָ לֹא־כִסִּיתִי בְּתוֹךְ לִבִּי | אֱמוּנָתְךָ וּתְשׁוּעָתְךָ אָמָרְתִּי | לֹא־כִחַדְתִּי חַסְדְּךָ וַאֲמִתְּךָ לְקָהָל רָב: צִדְקָתְךָ צֶדֶק לְעוֹלָם | וְתוֹרָתְךָ אֱמֶת:

1-

The ḥakhām continues on with parts 2 and 3.

---

45. This was a four-member group whose main responsibility was to wash the corpse according to Jewish traditions and dress it in a white or off-white shroud. The shroud was shaped like a bag with two openings that would be tied with ribbons after inserting the corpse, which is placed in the coffin. The Karaite community in Egypt owned many coffins of different grades, which were used again and again as the Karaites in Egypt did not bury the dead in coffins.

וַיהוָה אֱלֹהִים אֱמֶת הוּא־אֱלֹהִים חַיִּים וּמֶלֶךְ עוֹלָם ׀ מִקִּצְפּוֹ תִּרְעַשׁ הָאָרֶץ
וְלֹא־יָכִלוּ גוֹיִם זַעְמוֹ ׃ לְפָנָיו וַעְמוֹ מִי יַעֲמֹד וּמִי יָקוּם בַּחֲרוֹן
אַפּוֹ ׀ חֲמָתוֹ נִתְּכָה כָאֵשׁ וְהַצֻּרִים נִתְּצוּ מִמֶּנּוּ ׃ אַתָּה נוֹרָא אַתָּה וּמִי־יַעֲמֹד
לְפָנֶיךָ מֵאָז אַפֶּךָ ׃
2-

כִּי יְהוָה אֱלֹהֵיכֶם הוּא אֱלֹהֵי הָאֱלֹהִים וַאֲדֹנֵי הָאֲדֹנִים ׀ הָאֵל הַגָּדֹל הַגִּבֹּר
וְהַנּוֹרָא אֲשֶׁר לֹא־יִשָּׂא פָנִים וְלֹא יִקַּח שֹׁחַד ׃ וְעַתָּה יְהִי פַחַד־יְהוָה עֲלֵיכֶם ׀
שִׁמְרוּ וַעֲשׂוּ כִּי־אֵין עִם־יְהוָה אֱלֹהֵינוּ עַוְלָה וּמַשֹּׂא פָנִים וּמִקַּח־שֹׁחַד ׃ כִּי
מוֹת נָמוּת וְכַמַּיִם הַנִּגָּרִים אַרְצָה אֲשֶׁר לֹא יֵאָסֵפוּ ׀ וְלֹא־יִשָּׂא אֱלֹהִים נֶפֶשׁ
וְחָשַׁב מַחֲשָׁבוֹת לְבִלְתִּי יִדַּח מִמֶּנּוּ נִדָּח ׃
3-

Depending on the identity of the deceased, the ḥākhām then reads a special prayer (4 for a ḥakhām, 5 for a young man, etc.).

ואם הוא חכם תוסיף זה

אַשְׁרֵי אָדָם מָצָא חָכְמָה ׀ וְאָדָם יָפִיק תְּבוּנָה ׃ הַחָכְמָה תָּעֹז לֶחָכָם ׀
מֵעֲשָׂרָה שַׁלִּיטִים אֲשֶׁר הָיוּ בָּעִיר ׃ תּוֹרַת אֱמֶת הָיְתָה בְּפִיהוּ וְעַוְלָה
לֹא־נִמְצָא בִשְׂפָתָיו ׀ בְּשָׁלוֹם וּבְמִישׁוֹר הָלַךְ אִתִּי וְרַבִּים הֵשִׁיב מֵעָוֹן ׃ מִי
כְּהֶחָכָם וּמִי יוֹדֵעַ פֵּשֶׁר דָּבָר ׀ חָכְמַת אָדָם תָּאִיר פָּנָיו וְעֹז פָּנָיו יְשֻׁנֶּא ׃ כִּי
בְּצֵל הַחָכְמָה בְּצֵל הַכָּסֶף ׀ וְיִתְרוֹן דַּעַת הַחָכְמָה תְּחַיֶּה בְעָלֶיהָ ׃
4-

ואם יהיה בחור תאמר

גַּם־הַיּוֹם מְרִי שִׂחִי ׀ יָדִי כָּבְדָה עַל־אַנְחָתִי ׃ כְּבוֹדִי מֵעַל הַפְּשָׁטִים ׀ וַיָּסַר עֲטֶרֶת
רֹאשִׁי ׃ וַיְהִי לְאֵבֶל כִּנֹּרִי ׀ וְעֻגָבִי לְקוֹל בֹּכִים ׃ יִתְּנֵנִי סָבִיב וְאֶזְעָק ׀
וַיֵּסַע כָּעֵץ תִּקְוָתִי ׃ כִּי טוֹב קִוִּיתִי וַיָּבֹא רָע ׀ וַאֲיַחֲלָה לְאוֹר וַיָּבֹא אֹפֶל ׃ כִּי
פַחַד פָּחַדְתִּי וַיֶּאֱתָיֵנוּ ׀ וַאֲשֶׁר יָגֹרְתִּי יָבֹא לִי ׃ לֹא שָׁלַוְתִּי וְלֹא־שָׁקַטְתִּי וְלֹא־
נַחְתִּי וַיָּבֹא רֹגֶז ׃ שָׁלֵו הָיִיתִי וַיְפַרְפְּרֵנִי ׀ וְאָחַז בְּעָרְפִּי וַיְפַצְפְּצֵנִי ׀ וַיְקִימֵנִי לוֹ
לְמַטָּרָה ׃ יִפְרְצֵנִי פֶרֶץ עַל־פְּנֵי־פָרֶץ ׀ יָרֻץ עָלַי כְּגִבּוֹר ׃ פָּנַי חֳמַרְמְרוּ מִנִּי־בֶכִי ׀
וְעַל עַפְעַפַּי צַלְמָוֶת ׃ לֹא־יִתְּנֵנִי הָשֵׁב רוּחִי ׀ כִּי יַשְׂבִּעַנִי מַמְּרֹרִים ׃ הֲדָפַנִי עָלַי
בַּלָּהוֹת תִּרְדֹּף כָּרוּחַ נְדִבָתִי ׀ וּכְעָב עָבְרָה יְשֻׁעָתִי ׃ כִּי־עָלָה מָוֶת בְּחַלּוֹנֵינוּ בָּא
בְּאַרְמְנוֹתֵינוּ ׀ לְהַכְרִית עוֹלָל מִחוּץ בַּחוּרִים מֵרְחֹבוֹת ׃
5-

The ḥakhām then asks the nearest relatives of the deceased to repeat after him, word for word, part 6. It is read in a very moving tone and it indicates that the Lord is always right in whatever he does, and everyone has to meet death one day.

דִּין אֱמֶת שֹׁפֵט צֶדֶק וֶאֱמֶת דַּיָּן הָאֱמֶת כִּי כָל מִשְׁפָּטָיו צֶדֶק וֶאֱמֶת: וּמָה אֶעֱשֶׂה כִּי־יָקוּם אֵל וְכִי־יִפְקֹד מָה אֲשִׁיבֶנּוּ: עַל־כֵּן מִפָּנָיו אֶבָּהֵל אֶתְבּוֹנֵן וְאֶפְחַד מִמֶּנּוּ: מֶלֶךְ יוֹשֵׁב עַל־כִּסֵּא־דִין: מְזֹרָה בְּעֵינֵי כָל־רָע: מִי יֹאמַר זִכִּיתִי לִבִּי טָהַרְתִּי מֵחַטָּאתִי:

6-

While the coffin is being placed inside the hearse the ḥakhām reads 7 and 8. The mourners respond to him with the underlined part in 8. He then reads Psalm No. 90 which is a "Prayer to Moses the man of God."9

אָנָה אֵלֵךְ מֵרוּחֶךָ וְאָנָה מִפָּנֶיךָ אֶבְרָח: אִם־אֶסַּק שָׁמַיִם שָׁם אָתָּה וְאַצִּיעָה שְּׁאוֹל הִנֶּךָ: אֶשָּׂא כַנְפֵי־שָׁחַר אֶשְׁכְּנָה בְּאַחֲרִית יָם: גַּם־שָׁם יָדְךָ תַנְחֵנִי וְתֹאחֲזֵנִי יְמִינֶךָ: וָאֹמַר אַךְ־חֹשֶׁךְ יְשׁוּפֵנִי וְלַיְלָה אוֹר בַּעֲדֵנִי: גַּם־חֹשֶׁךְ לֹא־יַחְשִׁיךְ מִמֶּךָ וְלַיְלָה כַּיּוֹם יָאִיר כַּחֲשֵׁיכָה כָּאוֹרָה: סָמַר מִפַּחְדְּךָ בְשָׂרִי וּמִמִּשְׁפָּטֶיךָ יָרֵאתִי: וְאַל־תָּבוֹא בְמִשְׁפָּט אֶת־עַבְדֶּךָ כִּי לֹא־יִצְדַּק לְפָנֶיךָ כָל־חָי:

7-

וְהוּא רַחוּם יְכַפֵּר עָוֹן וְלֹא יַשְׁחִית וְהִרְבָּה לְהָשִׁיב אַפּוֹ וְלֹא יָעִיר כָּל־חֲמָתוֹ: וַיִּזְכֹּר כִּי־בָשָׂר הֵמָּה רוּחַ הוֹלֵךְ וְלֹא יָשׁוּב: רַחוּם וְחַנּוּן יְהוָה אֶרֶךְ אַפַּיִם וְרַב־חָסֶד: לֹא־לָנֶצַח יָרִיב וְלֹא לְעוֹלָם יִטּוֹר: לֹא כַחֲטָאֵינוּ עָשָׂה לָנוּ וְלֹא כַעֲוֺנֹתֵינוּ גָּמַל עָלֵינוּ: כִּי כִגְבֹהַּ שָׁמַיִם עַל־הָאָרֶץ גָּבַר חַסְדּוֹ עַל־יְרֵאָיו: כִּרְחֹק מִזְרָח מִמַּעֲרָב הִרְחִיק מִמֶּנּוּ אֶת־פְּשָׁעֵינוּ: כְּרַחֵם אָב עַל־בָּנִים רִחַם יְהוָה עַל־יְרֵאָיו: כִּי־הוּא יָדַע יִצְרֵנוּ זָכוּר כִּי־עָפָר אֲנָחְנוּ: זְכֹר רַחֲמֶיךָ יְהוָה וַחֲסָדֶיךָ כִּי מֵעוֹלָם הֵמָּה: רַחֲמֶיךָ רַבִּים יְהוָה כְּמִשְׁפָּטֶיךָ חַיֵּנִי: אַתָּה יְהוָה לֹא־תִכְלָא רַחֲמֶיךָ מִמֶּנִּי חַסְדְּךָ וַאֲמִתְּךָ תָּמִיד יִצְּרוּנִי: וְאַתָּה אֱלוֹהַּ סְלִיחוֹת חַנּוּן וְרַחוּם אֶרֶךְ־אַפַּיִם וְרַב־חֶסֶד וְלֹא עֲזַבְתָּם: כִּי אֵל רַחוּם יְהוָה אֱלֹהֶיךָ

לֹא יְרַפְּךָ וְלֹא יַשְׁחִיתֶךָ | וְלֹא יִשְׁכַּח אֶת־בְּרִית אֲבֹתֶיךָ אֲשֶׁר נִשְׁבַּע לָהֶם :
וַיָּחָן יְהֹוָה אֹתָם וַיְרַחֲמֵם וַיִּפֶן אֲלֵיהֶם לְמַעַן בְּרִיתוֹ אֶת־אַבְרָהָם יִצְחָק וְיַעֲקֹב |
וְלֹא אָבָה הַשְׁחִיתָם וְלֹא־הִשְׁלִיכָם מֵעַל־פָּנָיו עַד־עָתָּה : וְעַתָּה יְהֹוָה אָבִינוּ
אָתָּה | אֲנַחְנוּ הַחֹמֶר וְאַתָּה יֹצְרֵנוּ וּמַעֲשֵׂה יָדְךָ כֻּלָּנוּ : וַיִּיצֶר יְהֹוָה אֱלֹהִים אֶת־
הָאָדָם עָפָר מִן־הָאֲדָמָה וַיִּפַּח בְּאַפָּיו נִשְׁמַת חַיִּים | וַיְהִי הָאָדָם לְנֶפֶשׁ חַיָּה :
בְּזֵעַת אַפֶּיךָ תֹּאכַל לֶחֶם עַד שׁוּבְךָ אֶל־הָאֲדָמָה כִּי מִמֶּנָּה לֻקָּחְתָּ | כִּי־עָפָר
אַתָּה וְאֶל־עָפָר תָּשׁוּב : הַכֹּל הוֹלֵךְ אֶל־מָקוֹם אֶחָד | הַכֹּל הָיָה מִן־הֶעָפָר
וְהַכֹּל שָׁב אֶל־הֶעָפָר : וַיָּשָׁב הֶעָפָר עַל־הָאָרֶץ כְּשֶׁהָיָה | וְהָרוּחַ תָּשׁוּב אֶל־
הָאֱלֹהִים אֲשֶׁר נְתָנָהּ :

8-

תְּפִלָּה לְמֹשֶׁה אִישׁ־הָאֱלֹהִים

9-

The procession then starts and the coffin is carried in a horse-drawn hearse, followed by the ḥakhām, the relatives of the deceased and the friends for almost a quarter of a mile. On the way the ḥakhām and the mourners read Psalm No. 81. When they reach the verse: "For He will give His angels charge over you, To guard you in all your ways," they repeat it three times (part No. 10). In fact, the whole Psalm may be repeated until the procession reaches the designated place. The relatives of the deceased would then stand in line to accept condolences, after which taxis or private cars take them and who ever wants to the burial place.

כִּי מַלְאָכָיו יְצַוֶּה־לָּךְ   לִשְׁמָרְךָ בְּכָל־דְּרָכֶיךָ :

10-

The coffin is then transferred to another hearse that carried it to the burial place *(al-Basātīn).*[46]

Usually the ḥakhām and the mourners arrive at the burial place a few minutes before the hearse carrying the coffin. In most cases, however, all other arrangements at the burial place were taken care of.

When the body was being lowered to its final rest, the ḥakhām would read part 11. The mourners repeat after him the last few words. He would be then the first

---

46. The grave would be six feet or more long, six feet deep and three feet wide. At the bottom of one side was a hole two feet deep where the body would be placed. The hole would then be covered with limestone slates and cemented with sand and water. The ground in al-Basātīn is solid and dry.

one to throw a stone or some earth after the body had been completely tombed. Other mourners and friends would do the same until the hole was covered.

וכשיורידו המת בקברו תאמר :

קָטֹן וְגָדוֹל שָׁם הוּא וְעֶבֶד חָפְשִׁי מֵאֲדֹנָיו: דּוֹר הֹלֵךְ וְדוֹר בָּא וְהָאָרֶץ לְעוֹלָם עֹמָדֶת: מַה-יִּתְרוֹן לָאָדָם בְּכָל-עֲמָלוֹ שֶׁיַּעֲמֹל תַּחַת הַשָּׁמֶשׁ: כִּי מִקְרֶה בְנֵי-הָאָדָם וּמִקְרֶה הַבְּהֵמָה וּמִקְרֶה אֶחָד לָהֶם כְּמוֹת זֶה כֵּן מוֹת זֶה וְרוּחַ אֶחָד לַכֹּל וּמוֹתַר הָאָדָם מִן-הַבְּהֵמָה אָיִן כִּי הַכֹּל הָבֶל: הַכֹּל כַּאֲשֶׁר לַכֹּל מִקְרֶה אֶחָד לַצַּדִּיק וְלָרָשָׁע לַטּוֹב וְלַטָּהוֹר וְלַטָּמֵא וְלַזֹּבֵחַ וְלַאֲשֶׁר אֵינֶנּוּ זֹבֵחַ כַּטּוֹב כַּחֹטֶא הַנִּשְׁבָּע כַּאֲשֶׁר שְׁבוּעָה יָרֵא: אַל-תְּבַהֵל עַל-פִּיךָ וְלִבְּךָ אַל-יְמַהֵר לְהוֹצִיא דָבָר לִפְנֵי הָאֱלֹהִים כִּי הָאֱלֹהִים בַּשָּׁמַיִם וְאַתָּה עַל-הָאָרֶץ עַל-כֵּן יִהְיוּ דְבָרֶיךָ מְעַטִּים: כֹּל אֲשֶׁר תִּמְצָא יָדְךָ לַעֲשׂוֹת בְּכֹחֲךָ עֲשֵׂה כִּי אֵין מַעֲשֶׂה וְחֶשְׁבּוֹן וְדַעַת וְחָכְמָה בִּשְׁאוֹל אֲשֶׁר אַתָּה הֹלֵךְ שָׁמָּה: שַׁבְתִּי וְרָאֹה תַחַת-הַשֶּׁמֶשׁ כִּי לֹא לַקַּלִּים הַמֵּרוֹץ וְלֹא לַגִּבּוֹרִים הַמִּלְחָמָה וְגַם לֹא לַחֲכָמִים לֶחֶם וְגַם לֹא לַנְּבֹנִים עֹשֶׁר וְגַם לֹא לַיֹּדְעִים חֵן כִּי-עֵת וָפֶגַע יִקְרֶה אֶת-כֻּלָּם: כִּי גַּם לֹא-יֵדַע הָאָדָם אֶת-עִתּוֹ כַּדָּגִים שֶׁנֶּאֱחָזִים בִּמְצוֹדָה רָעָה וְכַצִּפֳּרִים הָאֲחֻזוֹת בַּפָּח כָּהֵם יוּקָשִׁים בְּנֵי הָאָדָם לְעֵת רָעָה כְּשֶׁתִּפּוֹל עֲלֵיהֶם פִּתְאֹם: כֹּל אֲשֶׁר תִּמְצָא יָדְךָ לַעֲשׂוֹת בְּכֹחֲךָ עֲשֵׂה כִּי אֵין מַעֲשֶׂה וְחֶשְׁבּוֹן וְדַעַת וְחָכְמָה בִּשְׁאוֹל אֲשֶׁר אַתָּה הֹלֵךְ שָׁמָּה: סוֹף דָּבָר הַכֹּל נִשְׁמָע אֶת-הָאֱלֹהִים יְרָא וְאֶת-מִצְוֹתָיו שְׁמוֹר כִּי-זֶה כָּל-הָאָדָם: כִּי אֶת-כָּל-מַעֲשֶׂה הָאֱלֹהִים יָבִא בְמִשְׁפָּט עַל כָּל-נֶעְלָם אִם-טוֹב וְאִם-רָע: <u>סוֹף דָּבָר הַכֹּל נִשְׁמָע אֶת-הָאֱלֹהִים יְרָא וְאֶת-מִצְוֹתָיו שְׁמוֹר כִּי-זֶה כָּל-הָאָדָם</u> :

11-

The ḥākhām would then read part 12. This part is for males only. However there is another similar one for females. For a child the ḥakhām would read the parts in brackets instead of the underlined. The mourners respond to the ḥakhām with the parts between the quotation marks.

אֲסִיפַת שָׁלוֹם תְּהֵא אֲסִיפָתוֹ: רְבִיצַת שָׁלוֹם תְּהֵא רְבִיצָתוֹ: אָמְרוּ לוֹ
כָּל קְהַל עֲדָתוֹ: יָבוֹא שָׁלוֹם יָנוּחַ עַל מְנָחָתוֹ: אסיפת מתהלך
הָיָה בְּתֻמָּתוֹ: בְּשֵׁם טוֹב פָּנָה אֶל‎ על הילד תמור מתהלך היה תאמר כך
קְבוּרָתוֹ: הִכְבִּידוּ אַנְחָתוֹ: אָמְרוּ לוֹ‎ כְּצִיץ יָצָא בְּיַלְדוּתוֹ: בְּקֹצֶר יָמִים פָּנָה
כָּל קְהַל עֲדָתוֹ: יָבוֹא שָׁלוֹם יָנוּחַ‎ אֶל קְבוּרָתוֹ: הִכְבִּידוּ אַנְחָתוֹ:
עַל מְנָחָתוֹ: אסיפת אוי כי פתאום‎ אמרו וכו':
נִשְׁלְלָה נִשְׁמָתוֹ: סָפְדוּ לוֹ אַנְשֵׁי
בֵיתוֹ: אָמְרוּ לוֹ כָּל קְהַל עֲדָתוֹ: יָבוֹא שָׁלוֹם יָנוּחַ עַל מְנָחָתוֹ: כַּכָּתוּב
וְהַמַּשְׂכִּילִים יַזְהִירוּ וכו'

12-

Finally the ḥakhām would read a memorial, part 13, which is the same for everyone except if the deceased has no children, then the underlined words would be changed accordingly. Here the mourners repeat the last 3 words.

זכר

13-

זכרון טוב וחן וחסד ורחמים וחמלה וחנינה. ורצון.
וכפרה מלפני אלוהי הרוחות לכל־בשר שהוא צור
עולמים על נפש כבוד מעלת‎ שעבר
מן העולם הזה במאמר אלהי ישראל בחפצו וברצונו
והלך לבית עולמו בשם טוב וזכר טוב וכמעשים טובים
אלהי ישראל יזכרהו ברצון עמו ויפקדהו בישועתו ככתוב
זכרני יהוה ברצון עמך פקדני בישועתך לראות בטובת
בחיריך לשמח בשמחת גויך להתהלל עם נחלתך ויתן
חלקו עם הצדיקים ועם המשכילים ככתוב: והמשכילים
יזהרו כזהר הרקיע ומצדיקי הרבים ככוכבים לעולם ועד:
נפשו בטוב תלין וזרעו יירש ארץ יבוא שלום ינוח על
משכבו הולך נכוחו ויקים עליו מקרא שפתוב אז יבקע
כשחר אורך וארוכתך מהרה תצמח והלך לפניך צדקך
כבור יהוה יאספך. מנוחתו בגן עדן.

The Karaites of Egypt picked up a custom from the Muslim natives. After the burial each person would get a loaf of bread, an egg, and a cucumber (if it was the season). Everyone should eat them.

It was a must for those who attended the burial to wash themselves completely for the purpose of purification.

The funeral was followed by a mourning period of 30 days, although Karaites, like other Egyptians, extended to it to 40 days.

According to Karaite tradition, people in mourning must refrain from rejoicing of any kind, sexual intercourse, and eating meat. Until the 1940's it was the custom for mourners to sleep on mattresses spread on the floor. Everything in the house would be covered with black cloth, and some mourners would stay home for seven days if this was possible. Others, however, for reasons beyond their control, were unable to follow this tradition.

It was the custom that prayers would be recited for seven days, either at the synagogue or at the residence of the deceased. This was a regular prayer followed by a memorial prayer over a cup of wine, if the prayers were held at home, from which the relatives would then drink. On the seventh day the relatives, accompanied by the ḥakhām or his deputy, would visit the grave to recite a special blessing and memorial prayer. Upon returning home, each person would wash for purification. On the seventh day the special prayers ended.

During the 30 days of mourning, life for the family would gradually return to normal.

It was the custom to execute the tombstone during these 30 days, after which special prayers would be said. At that point men were allowed to shave, while women continued to wear black for a year. They were not allowed to join in any rejoicing.

If Passover or Sukkot fell during the period of mourning, the mourning period came to an early end.

Food

When the word Karaite was mentioned, the word good food was always associated with it. Jews in general and Karaites in particular were well known for their rich menu and cuisine.

Some of the best known Karaite dishes included:

1. *Reshtath and Tagarīnes:* Almost like noodles, but soft and made by hand with ingredients that gave them a delicious taste, *reshtah* was always added to chicken soup; *tagarīnes* was served cold with two spices, cardamom and thyme.

2. *Matfūnah:* A special kind of omelet. The main ingredients are: ground meat, eggs, coriander, salt, black pepper, and onion. It is always served cold.

3. *Stuffed turkey:* A unique recipe. The wings and the legs are cut. The turkey is carefully skinned. The breast is carefully deboned. Two or three bags are made of the skin and then stuffed with the breast of the turkey and ground meat. Finally

it is either cooked or baked in the oven. Usually when it is cooked or baked, a good, delicious gravy is provided. After being cooked the turkey is left to cool, then it is sliced. It is served with or without gravy. The legs, the wings, the neck and the meatless chest make an excellent soup.

The *tagarīnes,* the *matfūnah,* the stuffed turkey, along with sauteed vegetables and crisp home-made potato chips, formed the main dishes of most Karaite parties. The regular daily meals were also delicious, and they included meat, vegetables, chicken, and rice.

The ability of Karaite women to make several different dishes from one item was unmatched. For example from chicken they can make at least four different dishes.

1. *Stuffed chicken:* The legs and wings are cut; the chicken is thoroughly cleaned and made ritually clean.[47] The main body is stuffed with ground meat, rice and pine nuts, then the skin is sewed together to lock in everything. When it is cooked along with the wings and the legs, it provides the soup and the ingredients for two other dishes. The cooked chicken must be fried before it is served. Part of the soup can be made *ḥāmiḍ,* or *gōz we tōm.* Both have the same basic ingredients: chicken soup and pureed rice.

2. *Ḥāmiḍ:* Tumeric and lime juice are added during cooking; it is an amber color with a tart taste. It solidifies quickly after being poured into bowls. It is considered a light summer side-dish.

3. *Gōz we tōm:* It is a dark green color and has a zesty taste, the result of adding sauteed Egyptian chard and garlic. This also solidifies and is a winter side-dish.

4. *Meʿaliyah:* The legs and the wings are sauteed with chopped onion and oil. They make a very delicious dish which was always served with rice.

Karaite women made many kinds of rice dishes: plain rice, rice with tomatoes and potatoes, rice with broad green beans, and fried rice.

Stuffed vegetables: Karaite women used rice, ground meat and pine nuts to stuff grape leaves, lettuce, cabbage, artichokes, tomatoes, potatoes, zucchini, and small eggplants. Salt and specially prepared black pepper gave an excellent aroma to that dish.

Stuffed pureed potatoes: Potatoes are boiled until they are soft. The skin is peeled off. From the potatoes a soft dough is made. The dough is spread on a flat surface and cut into round pieces using a cup. Each piece was stuffed with presauteed ground meat and chopped onion, sprinkled with flour and then fried gently to a golden color.

The most important point here is that almost every Karaite woman was an expert cook. Her cuisine had a special taste and a distinctive irresistible aroma. The

---

47. According to Karaite tradition certain veins and sinews, especially the sciatica from the legs and the wings must be removed.

two important meals in the weekly menu were those of Friday evening and Saturday noon. On Friday evening a soup must be served. Besides the soup there were more than one kind of vegetable dish and that, of course, depended on the season of the year. Rice was there and also cooked apricots, which was not considered a dessert.

On Saturday noon the menu differed. For those who maintained strict tradition, all dishes were served cold. In fact most recipes were meant to be served cold in order to keep the tradition. At that meal we find the stuffed turkey, the *matfūnah,* the *gōz we tōm* or the *ḥāmiḍ.* Those who were more liberal served stuffed chicken which had to be fried before serving, which obviously meant using fire on the Sabbath. The rest of the meal was the same as above.

During winter there was a variety of soups: chicken soup, beef soup with tomatoes, vegetable soup, green soup, whose main ingredients were broad green beans, dill, chard and spices.

During the summer, yogurt, especially for supper, with home-made cheese and home-pickled black olives, was the favorite. Most Karaites used to prepare the yogurt at home. It was eaten plain or mixed with chopped sweet onions, chopped cucumbers, salt, hot pepper and a drop of oil. Until the first quarter of the 20th century, Jews in general used sesame oil for all their cooking. When cooking oil taken from cotton seeds was introduced at that time (1920) under the name "French Oil," *al-zayt al-faransāwī,* almost everyone switched to it. That marked the quick decline of the sesame oil mills, which before could be found everywhere. The Karaites used farm butter as well. They would buy large quantities of butter during the months of February and March. They would then clarify the butter and store it in special jars for the whole year. The clarified butter, called *samn balady,* thus became a ready-made cooking base for many Karaite dishes and for baking.

Until the 1950's many Karaites used to bake their own bread. They were well known for their white bread dotted with sesame seeds. Another well-known kind of bread was the egg roll. These were either plain or covered with sesame seeds. They were crispy and very delicious, almost like the French baguette. These rolls were the only bread served at parties.

For the processing of meat the Karaite community had its own ritual slaughtereres *(shohetīm).* During the 1940's there were at least 6 butcher shops selling ritually slaughtered meat in Cairo and Heliopolis. Under an agreement with the Karaite Bēt-Dīn, these stores sold only ritually slaughtered meat.

Cows, steers, calves, and lambs used to be slaughtered daily (except Saturdays and holy days) by special Karaite *shohetīm* licensed by the Karaite Bēt-Dīn. They were skilled men, respected by the community for their skill and compassion for animals. According to Karaite tradition the animal must be healthy with no bruises anywhere. It is completely forbidden to slaughter a pregnant animal. If this should happen, then the animal is not ritually clean. There are rules to be followed regarding how to slaughter an animal. They are all meant to ensure mercy and not to let the animal suffer unnecessarily. "Moreover, the Karaite and Rabbanite rules dealing with the slaughter of animals for food differ enough so that devout Karaites consider meat processed by Rabbanites unclean and unfit to be eaten."[48] The butcher shops made a good profit from selling meat. During World War II meat was officially priced. A kasher butcher had the right to raise the price of meat a few piasters. Each shop had to pay monthly dues to the Karaite Bēt-Dīn, and was required to display a sign reading "kasher meat." Many Egyptians, especially Muslims, preferred buying kasher meat, even if it meant paying a higher price. They were sure of the quality of the meat.

---

48. Leon Nemoy, *Karaite Anthology*, Introduction, p. 24.

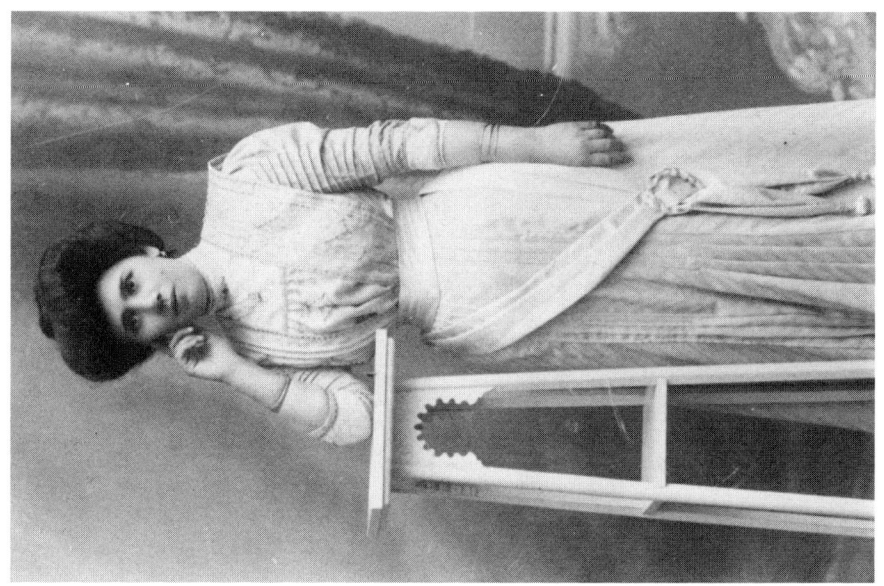

The mode of dress of well-to-do Egyptian Karaite women at the turn of the century.

Farag Yaʻqūb Aṣlān Kohen

Yūsuf Mūsā al-Qudsī
Men's clothing of the goldsmith and jewelers trades, until the 1930's.

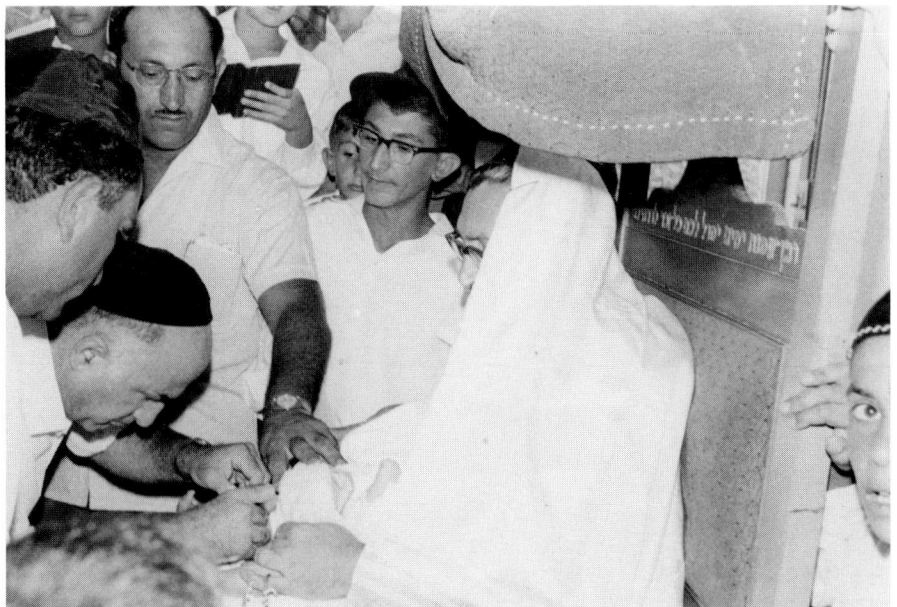

The grandfather, covered with a ṭaillīt, is holding the baby while the mohel performs the circumcision.

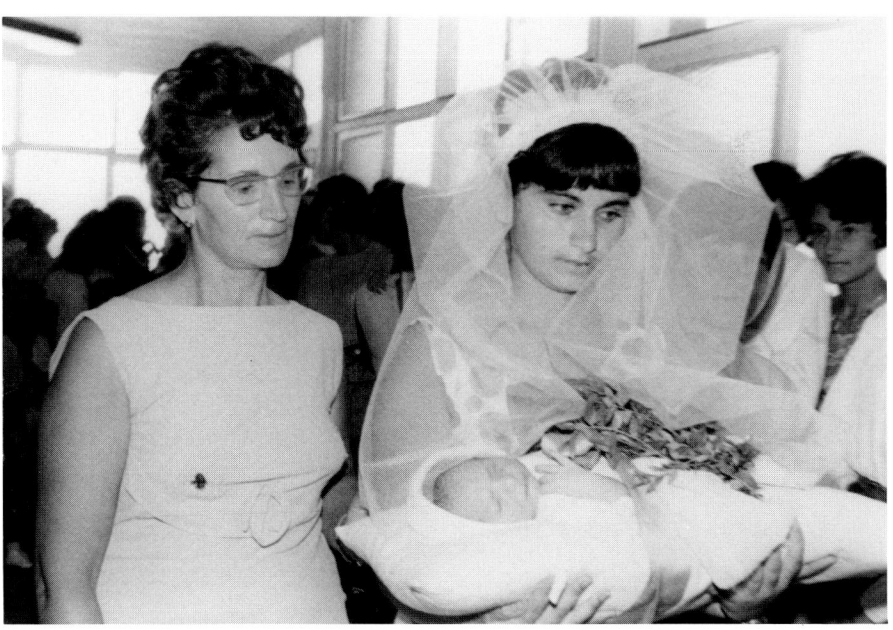

Before the circumcision, the baby is placed on a velvet pillow. While the guests chant a special prayer, the baby is introduced seven times to the mother.

Over a cup of wine, Ḥākhām Tobiah blesses the groom. Both the groom and the bride are covered with a ṭallīt.

Ḥabīb Lieto B. Masʿūdah and his wife, Regine Yūsuf Līshaʿ (after the wedding). The picture was taken during the last quarter of the 19th century.

Girls of the Ahavāt ha-Torāh *association on* Yōm Simḥāt Torāh.

The acting ḥākhām, Murād Hārūm, *performing the marriage of Denise 'Abd al-Waḥid to Fawzī Līsha'*.

קדוש על היין בערב שבת

עֵת לְהַקְדִּישׁ ׀ וַיְכֻלּוּ הַשָּׁמַיִם וְהָאָרֶץ וְכָל־צְבָאָם : וַיְכַל אֱלֹהִים בַּיּוֹם הַשְּׁבִיעִי מְלַאכְתּוֹ אֲשֶׁר עָשָׂה ׀ וַיִּשְׁבֹּת בַּיּוֹם הַשְּׁבִיעִי מִכָּל־מְלַאכְתּוֹ אֲשֶׁר עָשָׂה : וַיְבָרֶךְ אֱלֹהִים אֶת־יוֹם הַשְּׁבִיעִי וַיְקַדֵּשׁ אֹתוֹ ׀ כִּי בוֹ שָׁבַת מִכָּל־מְלַאכְתּוֹ אֲשֶׁר־בָּרָא אֱלֹהִים לַעֲשׂוֹת : וּבָרוּךְ אֱלֹהֵינוּ מֶלֶךְ הָעוֹלָם אֲשֶׁר בָּרָא עֵץ הַגֶּפֶן וּמֵיינוּ מְשַׂמֵּחַ לְבַב בְּנֵי הָאָדָם : כַּכָּתוּב וְיַיִן יְשַׂמַּח לְבַב־אֱנוֹשׁ לְהַצְהִיל פָּנִים מִשָּׁמֶן ׀ וְלֶחֶם לְבַב־אֱנוֹשׁ יִסְעָד : בָּרוּךְ אַתָּה יְיָ אֱלֹהֵינוּ מֶלֶךְ הָעוֹלָם הַמְבֹרַךְ וְהַמְקַדֵּשׁ אֶת יוֹם הַשַּׁבָּת לְעַמּוֹ יִשְׂרָאֵל אָמֵן : וּבָרוּךְ אֱלֹהֵינוּ מֶלֶךְ הָעוֹלָם הַנֹּתֵן לָנוּ שָׂשׂוֹן וְשִׂמְחָה וּבוֹרֵא פְּרִי הַגֶּפֶן אָמֵן :

ותעשה המוציא

בָּרוּךְ אַתָּה יְיָ אֱלֹהֵינוּ מֶלֶךְ הָעוֹלָם הַמּוֹצִיא לֶחֶם מִן הָאָרֶץ אָמֵן :

ברכת המזון

וְשָׁמְרוּ בְנֵי־יִשְׂרָאֵל אֶת־הַשַּׁבָּת ׀ לַעֲשׂוֹת אֶת־הַשַּׁבָּת לְדֹרֹתָם בְּרִית עוֹלָם : בֵּינִי וּבֵין בְּנֵי יִשְׂרָאֵל אוֹת הִיא לְעֹלָם ׀ כִּי־שֵׁשֶׁת יָמִים עָשָׂה יְהוָה אֶת־הַשָּׁמַיִם וְאֶת־הָאָרֶץ וּבַיּוֹם הַשְּׁבִיעִי שָׁבַת וַיִּנָּפַשׁ : וַיַּקְהֵל מֹשֶׁה אֶת־כָּל־עֲדַת בְּנֵי יִשְׂרָאֵל וַיֹּאמֶר אֲלֵהֶם ׀ אֵלֶּה הַדְּבָרִים אֲשֶׁר־צִוָּה יְהוָה לַעֲשֹׂת אֹתָם : שֵׁשֶׁת יָמִים תֵּעָשֶׂה מְלָאכָה וּבַיּוֹם הַשְּׁבִיעִי יִהְיֶה לָכֶם קֹדֶשׁ שַׁבַּת שַׁבָּתוֹן לַיהוָה ׀ כָּל־הָעֹשֶׂה בוֹ מְלָאכָה יוּמָת : לֹא־תְבַעֲרוּ אֵשׁ בְּכֹל מֹשְׁבֹתֵיכֶם ׀ בְּיוֹם הַשַּׁבָּת : אֶת־שַׁבְּתֹתַי תִּשְׁמֹרוּ וּמִקְדָּשִׁי תִּירָאוּ ׀ אֲנִי יְהוָה : אִישׁ אִמּוֹ וְאָבִיו תִּירָאוּ וְאֶת־שַׁבְּתֹתַי תִּשְׁמֹרוּ ׀ אֲנִי יְהוָה אֱלֹהֵיכֶם : וַעֲבַדְתֶּם אֵת יְהוָה אֱלֹהֵיכֶם וּבֵרַךְ אֶת־לַחְמְךָ וְאֶת־מֵימֶיךָ ׀ וַהֲסִרֹתִי מַחֲלָה מִקִּרְבֶּךָ : וּבָתִּים מְלֵאִים כָּל־טוּב אֲשֶׁר לֹא־מִלֵּאתָ וּבֹרֹת חֲצוּבִים אֲשֶׁר לֹא־חָצַבְתָּ כְּרָמִים וְזֵיתִים אֲשֶׁר לֹא־נָטָעְתָּ ׀ וְאָכַלְתָּ וְשָׂבָעְתָּ : וְאָכַלְתָּ וְשָׂבָעְתָּ ׀ וּבֵרַכְתָּ אֶת־יְהוָה אֱלֹהֶיךָ עַל־הָאָרֶץ הַטֹּבָה אֲשֶׁר נָתַן־לָךְ : בֵּית יִשְׂרָאֵל בָּרֲכוּ אֶת־יְהוָה ׀ בֵּית אַהֲרֹן בָּרֲכוּ אֶת־יְהוָה : בֵּית הַלֵּוִי בָּרֲכוּ אֶת־יְהוָה ׀ יִרְאֵי יְהוָה בָּרֲכוּ אֶת־יְהוָה : בָּרוּךְ יְהוָה מִצִּיּוֹן שֹׁכֵן יְרוּשָׁלָ͏ִם הַלְלוּיָהּ : יְהוָה עֹז לְעַמּוֹ יִתֵּן ׀ יְהוָה יְבָרֵךְ אֶת־עַמּוֹ בַשָּׁלוֹם : בָּרוּךְ יְהוָה לְעוֹלָם ׀ אָמֵן ׀ וְאָמֵן :

PLATE 1: Kiddush on Friday Night. 1) Before dinner. 2) After dinner. *Karaite Prayer Book,* Vol. 4, pp. 8-9.

זמר לשבת בנגון נאה

כִּי אֶשְׁמְרָה שַׁבָּת : אֵל יִשְׁמְרֵנִי :
אוֹת הִיא. אוֹת הִיא לְעוֹלְמֵי עַד בֵּינוֹ וּבֵינִי :

אָסוּר מְצֹא חֵפֶץ : לַעֲשׂוֹת דְּרָכִים :
גַּם מִלְּדַבֵּר בּוֹ. דִּבְרֵי צְרָכִים : דִּבְרֵי סְחוֹרָה. אוֹ דִבְרֵי מְלָכִים :
אֶהְגֶּה בְּתוֹרַת אֵל : וּתְחַכְּמֵנִי :
אוֹת הִיא אוֹת הִיא לְעוֹלְמֵי עַד בֵּינוֹ וּבֵינִי : כי

בּוֹ אֶמְצְאָה תָּמִיד : נֹפֶשׁ לְנַפְשִׁי :
הִנֵּה לְדוֹר רִאשׁוֹן . נָתַן קְדוֹשִׁי : מוֹפֵת בְּתֵת לֶחֶם. מִשְׁנֶה בְּשִׁשִּׁי :
כָּכָה בְּכָל שִׁשִּׁי : יַכְפִּיל מְזוֹנִי :
אוֹת הִיא אוֹת הִיא לְעוֹלְמֵי עַד בֵּינוֹ וּבֵינִי : כי

רָשׁוּם בְּדַת הַיּוֹם. חֹק אֶל סְגָנָיו : בּוֹ לַעֲרֹךְ לֶחֶם. פָּנִים בְּפָנָיו :
עַל כֵּן לְהִתְעַנּוֹת : עַל פִּי נְבוֹנָיו :
אָסוּר לְבַד מִיּוֹם : כִּפּוּר עֲוֹנִי :
אוֹת הִיא לְעוֹלְמֵי עַד בֵּינוֹ וּבֵינִי : כי

הַיּוֹם מְכֻבָּד הוּא : יוֹם תַּעֲנוּגִים :
לֶחֶם וְיַיִן טוֹב. בָּשָׂר וְדָגִים : מִשְׁתַּמְּשִׁים הֵם בּוֹ. אָחוֹר נְסוֹגִים :
כִּי יוֹם שְׂמָחוֹת הוּא : וִישַׂמְּחֵנִי :
אוֹת הִיא אוֹת הִיא לְעוֹלְמֵי עַד בֵּינוֹ וּבֵינִי : כי

מֵחֵל מְלָאכָה בּוֹ. סוֹפוֹ לְהַכְרִית : עַל כֵּן אֲכַבֵּס בּוֹ . לִבִּי כְּבוֹרִית :
אֶתְפַּלְלָה אֶל אֵל : עַרְבִית וְשַׁחֲרִית :
אֶקְרָא לָאֵל עֶלְיוֹן : כִּי יַעֲנֵנִי :
אוֹת הִיא אוֹת הִיא לְעוֹלְמֵי עַד בֵּינוֹ וּבֵינִי : כי

בכתוב ביני ובין בני ישראל אות היא לעולם :

PLATE 2: One of the many songs which are chanted on Friday night after dinner to welcome the Sabbath.
Karaite Prayer Book, Vol. 4, pp. 103-106.

קדוש על היין ביום השבת בבקר

הוֹדוּ לַיהוָה כִּי־טוֹב ׀ כִּי לְעוֹלָם חַסְדּוֹ : הוֹדוּ לֵאלֹהֵי הָאֱלֹהִים ׀ כִּי לְעוֹלָם חַסְדּוֹ : הוֹדוּ לַאֲדֹנֵי הָאֲדֹנִים ׀ כִּי לְעוֹלָם חַסְדּוֹ : וּבָרוּךְ אֱלֹהֵינוּ מֶלֶךְ הָעוֹלָם אֲשֶׁר בֵּרַךְ וְקִדֵּשׁ אֶת יוֹם הַשְּׁבִיעִי מִכָּל הַיָּמִים : כַּכָּתוּב וַיְבָרֶךְ אֱלֹהִים אֶת־יוֹם הַשְּׁבִיעִי וַיְקַדֵּשׁ אֹתוֹ ׀ כִּי בוֹ שָׁבַת מִכָּל־מְלַאכְתּוֹ אֲשֶׁר־בָּרָא אֱלֹהִים לַעֲשׂוֹת : וּבָרוּךְ אֱלֹהֵינוּ מֶלֶךְ הָעוֹלָם אֲשֶׁר בָּרָא עֵץ הַגֶּפֶן וּמִיֵּינוֹ מְשַׂמֵּחַ לְבַב בְּנֵי הָאָדָם כַּכָּתוּב וְיַיִן יְשַׂמַּח לְבַב־אֱנוֹשׁ לְהַצְהִיל פָּנִים מִשָּׁמֶן ׀ וְלֶחֶם לְבַב־אֱנוֹשׁ יִסְעָד : בָּרוּךְ אַתָּה יְיָ אֱלֹהֵינוּ מֶלֶךְ הָעוֹלָם הַמְבָרֵךְ וְהַמְקַדֵּשׁ אֶת יוֹם הַשַּׁבָּת לְעַמּוֹ יִשְׂרָאֵל אָמֵן : וּבָרוּךְ אֱלֹהֵינוּ מֶלֶךְ הָעוֹלָם הַנֹּתֵן לָנוּ שָׂשׂוֹן וְשִׂמְחָה וּבוֹרֵא פְּרִי הַגֶּפֶן אָמֵן :

ברכת המזון

טוֹב יְהוָה לַכֹּל ׀ וְרַחֲמָיו עַל־כָּל־מַעֲשָׂיו : שֶׁבְּשִׁפְלֵנוּ זָכַר לָנוּ ׀ כִּי לְעוֹלָם חַסְדּוֹ : וַיִּפְרְקֵנוּ מִצָּרֵינוּ ׀ כִּי לְעוֹלָם חַסְדּוֹ : בָּרוּךְ הַנֹּתֵן לֶחֶם לְכָל־בָּשָׂר ׀ כִּי לְעוֹלָם חַסְדּוֹ : הוֹדוּ לְאֵל הַשָּׁמָיִם ׀ כִּי לְעוֹלָם חַסְדּוֹ : יְהִי־חַסְדְּךָ יְהוָה עָלֵינוּ ׀ כַּאֲשֶׁר יִחַלְנוּ לָךְ : בָּרוּךְ יְהוָה : בָּרוּךְ אַתָּה יְהוָה אֱלֹהֵי יִשְׂרָאֵל אָבִינוּ מֵעוֹלָם וְעַד־עוֹלָם : לְךָ יְהוָה הַגְּדֻלָּה וְהַגְּבוּרָה וְהַתִּפְאֶרֶת וְהַנֵּצַח וְהַהוֹד כִּי־כֹל בַּשָּׁמַיִם וּבָאָרֶץ ׀ לְךָ יְהוָה הַמַּמְלָכָה וְהַמִּתְנַשֵּׂא לְכֹל ׀ לְרֹאשׁ : וְהָעֹשֶׁר וְהַכָּבוֹד מִלְּפָנֶיךָ וְאַתָּה מוֹשֵׁל בַּכֹּל ׀ וּבְיָדְךָ כֹּחַ וּגְבוּרָה ׀ וּבְיָדְךָ לְגַדֵּל וּלְחַזֵּק לַכֹּל : וְעַתָּה אֱלֹהֵינוּ מוֹדִים אֲנַחְנוּ לָךְ ׀ וּמְהַלְלִים לְשֵׁם תִּפְאַרְתֶּךָ : וַאֲנַחְנוּ נְבָרֵךְ יָהּ מֵעַתָּה וְעַד־עוֹלָם הַלְלוּיָהּ : עֵינֵי כֹל אֵלֶיךָ יְשַׂבֵּרוּ ׀ וְאַתָּה נוֹתֵן־לָהֶם אֶת־אָכְלָם בְּעִתּוֹ : פּוֹתֵחַ אֶת־יָדֶךָ ׀ וּמַשְׂבִּיעַ לְכָל־חַי רָצוֹן : רָצוֹן תְּשַׂבְּעֵנוּ וְרָזוֹן הַעֲבֵר מִמֶּנּוּ וְהַטְרִיפֵנוּ לֶחֶם חֻקֵּנוּ וְשֻׁלְחָנְךָ עָרוּךְ לַכֹּל : בְּאֶרֶךְ אַפֶּךָ וּבְגְמִילוּת חֲסָדֶיךָ אָנוּ חַיִּים וְקַיָּמִים וּמִפְּתִיחַת יָדֶךָ : כִּי אַתָּה הוּא זָן וּמְפַרְנֵס וּמְכַלְכֵּל לַכֹּל וּמֵכִין מָזוֹן וּמִחְיָה לְכָל בְּרִיּוֹתֶיךָ אֲשֶׁר בָּרָאתָ : בָּרוּךְ אַתָּה יְהוָה הַזָּן אֶת הַכֹּל :

וכל הישכים בשלחן מחיבים לענות אמן

PLATE 3: 1) Kiddush before breakfast on Saturday. 2) Part of a blessing on Saturday.

Karaite Prayer Book, Vol. 4, pp. 9-12.

כּוֹס־יְשׁוּעוֹת אֶשָּׂא ׀ וּבְשֵׁם יְהוָה אֶקְרָא: אָנָּא יְהוָה הוֹשִׁיעָה נָּא אָנָּא יְהוָה הַצְלִיחָה
נָּא: בָּרוּךְ הַבָּא בְּשֵׁם יְהוָה ׀ בֵּרַכְנוּכֶם מִבֵּית יְהוָה: אֵל יְהוָה וַיָּאֶר לָנוּ אִסְרוּ־
חַג בַּעֲבֹתִים ׀ עַד־קַרְנוֹת הַמִּזְבֵּחַ: אֱלֹהִים יְחָנֵּנוּ וִיבָרְכֵנוּ ׀ יָאֵר פָּנָיו אִתָּנוּ סֶלָה:
הָבָה־לָּנוּ עֶזְרָת מִצָּר ׀ וְשָׁוְא תְּשׁוּעַת אָדָם: בֵּאלֹהִים נַעֲשֶׂה־חָיִל וְהוּא יָבוּס צָרֵינוּ:
בֵּאלֹהִים נַעֲשֶׂה־חָיִל ׀ וְהוּא יָבוּס אֹיְבֵינוּ: בֵּאלֹהִים הִלַּלְנוּ כָל־הַיּוֹם ׀ וְשִׁמְךָ לְעוֹלָם
נוֹדֶה סֶלָה: בֵּאלֹהִים אֲהַלֵּל דָּבָר ׀ בַּיהוָה אֲהַלֵּל דָּבָר: בֵּאלֹהִים אֲהַלֵּל דְּבָרוֹ בֵּאלֹהִים
בָּטַחְתִּי לֹא אִירָא ׀ מַה־יַּעֲשֶׂה בָשָׂר לִי: בֵּאלֹהִים בָּטַחְתִּי לֹא אִירָא מַה־יַּעֲשֶׂה אָדָם
לִי: יְהוָה לִי לֹא אִירָא ׀ מַה־יַּעֲשֶׂה לִי אָדָם: יְהוָה לִי בְּעֹזְרָי ׀ וַאֲנִי אֶרְאֶה בְשֹׂנְאָי: טוֹב
לַחֲסוֹת בַּיהוָה ׀ מִבְּטֹחַ בָּאָדָם: טוֹב לַחֲסוֹת בַּיהוָה ׀ מִבְּטֹחַ בִּנְדִיבִים: אַל־תִּבְטְחוּ
בִנְדִיבִים ׀ בְּבֶן־אָדָם שֶׁאֵין לוֹ תְשׁוּעָה: בָּרוּךְ אַתָּה יְהוָה אֱלֹהֵינוּ מֶלֶךְ הָעוֹלָם
הַמַּבְדִּיל בֵּין קֹדֶשׁ לְחֹל בֵּין אוֹר לְחֹשֶׁךְ בֵּין יִשְׂרָאֵל לָעַמִּים הַקַּדְמוֹנִים בֵּין
טָמֵא לְטָהוֹר בֵּין שֵׁשֶׁת יְמֵי הַמַּעֲשֶׂה לַיּוֹם הַשְּׁבִיעִי: כַּכָּתוּב וִהְיִיתֶם לִי
קְדֹשִׁים כִּי קָדוֹשׁ אֲנִי יְהוָה ׀ וָאַבְדִּל אֶתְכֶם מִן־הָעַמִּים לִהְיוֹת לִי: וְכָתוּב
וּלְהַבְדִּיל בֵּין הַקֹּדֶשׁ וּבֵין הַחֹל ׀ וּבֵין הַטָּמֵא וּבֵין הַטָּהוֹר: וּלְהוֹרֹת אֶת־בְּנֵי
יִשְׂרָאֵל ׀ אֵת כָּל־הַחֻקִּים אֲשֶׁר דִּבֶּר יְהוָה אֲלֵיהֶם בְּיַד־מֹשֶׁה: אֱלֹהֵינוּ וֵאלֹהֵי
אֲבוֹתֵינוּ הָחֵל עָלֵינוּ שֵׁשֶׁת יְמֵי הַמַּעֲשֶׂה הַבָּאִים לִקְרָאתֵנוּ לְשָׁלוֹם וּלְשַׁלְוָה
לְשָׂשׂוֹן וּלְשִׂמְחָה לִישׁוּעָה וּלְנֶחָמָה לְפַרְנָסָה וּלְכַלְכָּלָה: חֲשׂוּכִים מִכָּל דָּבָר
רַע וּמֻצָּלִים מִכָּל חֵטְא וְעָוֹן. וַעֲבֵירָה: וּמְדֻבָּקִים בְּלִמּוּד וְהִגְיוֹן תּוֹרָתְךָ וַחֲנוּנִים
מֵאִתְּךָ חָכְמָה דֵעָה וְהַשְׂכֵּל וּבִינָה: וְלֹא קִנְאָתֵנוּ וְשִׂנְאָתֵנוּ תַּעֲלֶה עַל לֵב
אָדָם: וְלֹא קִנְאַת וְשִׂנְאַת אָדָם תַּעֲלֶה־עַל לִבֵּנוּ: וְכָל הָיֹעֵץ עָלֵינוּ עֵצָה
טוֹבָה וּמַחֲשָׁבָה טוֹבָה קַיְּמֵהוּ וְקַיֵּם עֲצָתוֹ: כָּאָמוּר וְחַנֹּתִי אֶת־אֲשֶׁר אָחֹן
וְרִחַמְתִּי אֶת־אֲשֶׁר אֲרַחֵם: וְכָל הָיֹעֵץ עָלֵינוּ עֵצָה רָעָה וּמַחֲשָׁבָה רָעָה קַלְקֵל
מַחֲשַׁבְתּוֹ הָפֵר עֲצָתוֹ: כָּאָמוּר עֻצוּ עֵצָה וְתֻפָר ׀ דַּבְּרוּ דָבָר וְלֹא יָקוּם כִּי עִמָּנוּ
אֵל: רַבּוֹת מַחֲשָׁבוֹת בְּלֶב־אִישׁ ׀ וַעֲצַת יְהוָה הִיא תָקוּם: כִּי־יְהוָה צְבָאוֹת יָעָץ
וּמִי יָפֵר ׀ וְיָדוֹ הַנְּטוּיָה וּמִי יְשִׁיבֶנָּה:

בָּרוּךְ אַתָּה יְהוָה אֱלֹהֵינוּ מֶלֶךְ הָעוֹלָם הַמֵּפֵר עֲצוֹת הָרָעוֹת הַמִּתְרַגְּשׁוֹת
הַמִּתְחַלְּחֲשׁוֹת מֵעָלֵינוּ וּמֵעַל בָּתֵּינוּ וּמֵעַל כָּל בָּתֵּי כְּלָל עַמְּךָ בֵּית
יִשְׂרָאֵל אָמֵן: וּבָרוּךְ אֱלֹהֵינוּ מֶלֶךְ הָעוֹלָם הַמַּבְדִּיל בֵּין קֹדֶשׁ לְחֹל וְהַנֹּתֵן לָנוּ
שָׂשׂוֹן וְשִׂמְחָה וּבוֹרֵא פְּרִי הַגָּפֶן אָמֵן:

PLATE 4: After Saturday evening prayers, the ḥazzan and the worshippers read the *habdalah*. The *habdalah* is read outside the synagogue because wine is not permitted in the sanctuary.

Karaite Prayer Book, Vol. 4, pp. 12-13.

וגם זה להבדלה וכננונו לרב מרדכי ז"ל

מָלֵא עוֹלָם בִּכְבוֹד יָפְיִ: גְּדֻלַּת אֵל יְזַמֵּר פִּי: יֹצְאֵי שַׁבָּת עֹרְכִים תְּפִלָּה: גַּם בֹּקֶר וְגַם עֶרֶב: מלא

רִאשׁוֹן שֹׁפְכִים תְּפִלָּתָם: לְאֵל עֶלְיוֹן עֲתִירָתָם: הוּא יְקַבֵּל תְּחִנָּתָם: לְמַן בֹּקֶר וְגַם עֶרֶב: מלא

דִּבֶּר יְיָ אֲלֵיהֶם: בְּיַד מֹשֶׁה אֲדֹנֵיהֶם: לְהַבְדִּיל לְבֵין קָדְשֵׁיהֶם: לְבֵין הַחֹל הוּא בָּעֶרֶב: מלא

כּוֹס יְשׁוּעוֹת בְּשֵׁם אֶשָּׂא: נָא יְיָ הוֹשִׁיעָה נָּא: וְהַצְלִיחָה רֹאשׁ אוֹיְבַי שָׂא: מַהֵר נָטוּ צִלְלֵי עֶרֶב: מלא

יַיִן הַטּוֹב יַצְהִיל פָּנִים: יְשַׂמַּח גַּם לֵב מִיגוֹנִים: לִכְבוֹד שַׁבָּת עָבַר בָּנִים: מַבְדִּילִים בּוֹ הֵם בָּעֶרֶב: מלא

חָקֹר נַפְשִׁי וְגַם תֵּדַע: רֵיחַ בְּשָׂם הוּא בָּעֵדָה: סָבְתוֹ מְאֹד חֲמוּדָה: מְנוּחָה חָלְפָה בָּעֶרֶב: מלא

זָעַמְנוּ מִתְרַגְּשִׁים: עֵצוֹת רָעוֹת מְאֹד דּוֹרְשִׁים: קַלְקֵל מַחֲשַׁבְתָּם תָּשִׂים: עֲלֵיהֶם נְוֵה בָּעֶרֶב: מלא

קִנְאָתֵנוּ לֹא תַעֲלֶה: עַל לֵב אָדָם אֲשֶׁר עוֹלֶה: וְלֹא קִנְאַת שִׂנְאַת אֵלֶּה: תַּעֲלֶה עַל לֵב בָּעֶרֶב: מלא

כַּכָּתוּב כּוֹס יְשׁוּעוֹת אֶשָּׂא וּבְשֵׁם יְיָ אֶקְרָא:

אחר להבדלה בננון נאה של הרב אליקים

אֶת כּוֹס יְשׁוּעוֹת: אֶשָּׂא בְּזִמְרָה: וּבְשֵׁם יְיָ: אוֹדֶה וְאֶקְרָא: את

לַיְלָה וְיוֹמָם: עֻזּוֹ אֲמַלֵּל: וּלְשֵׁם כְּבוֹדוֹ: תָּמִיד אֲהַלֵּל: כִּי הוּא לְבַדּוֹ: יוֹצֵר מְחוֹלֵל: מַעְלָה וּמַטָּה: יָצַר וּבָרָא: את

יָרוּם וְיִגְדַּל: עַל כָּל יְצוּרִים: זִכְרוֹ מְבוֹרָךְ: נֶצַח לְדוֹרִים: מוֹרִישׁ וּמַעֲשִׁיר: מַשְׁפִּיל וּמֵרִים: לוֹ הַגְּדֻלָּה: לוֹ הַגְּבוּרָה: את

קָרוֹב יְיָ: תָּמִיד לְקוֹרְאָיו: רַבּוּ וְעָצְמוּ: נִסֵּי פְּלָאָיו: טוּבוֹ וְרַחֲמָיו: עַל כָּל בְּרוּאָיו: לָכֵן בְּצָרוֹת: נִמְצָא לְעֶזְרָה: את

יְקָרוּ דְרָכָיו: עַל כָּל דְּרָכִים: מַנְהִיג וּמוֹשֵׁל: עַל כָּל פְּלָכִים: נוֹרָא וְעֶלְיוֹן: מֶלֶךְ מְלָכִים: אַדִּיר וְנִגְדָּל: גִּבּוֹר וְנוֹרָא: את

מָעוֹז וּמַחֲסֶה: אֶל דַּל וְאֶבְיוֹן: יִשְׁלַח לְעַמּוֹ: יֵשַׁע וּפִדְיוֹן: מֶלֶךְ וְכֹהֵן: יָבִיא לְצִיּוֹן: יִבְנֶה מְהֵרָה: בֵּית הַבְּחִירָה: את

PLATE 5: Two of many songs that are chanted at home after the *habdalah* on Saturday night.

Karaite Prayer Book, Vol. 4, pp. 120-121.

אֵל אֱלֹהִים | יַאֲזִין שַׁוְעַתְכֶם : בּוֹרֵא עוֹלָם | יְבָרֵךְ אֶתְכֶם :
גְּדוֹל הָעֵצָה | יַגְדִּיל לָכֶם : דּוֹבֵר צֶדֶק | יְדַבֵּר שָׁלוֹם עַל לְבַבְכֶם :
הָאֵל הַנּוֹרָא | יִהְיֶה בְּעֶזְרַתְכֶם | וְהַמּוֹשִׁיעַ עֲשׁוּקִים | יוֹשִׁיעַ אֶתְכֶם :
זֵכֶר הַבְּרִית | יִזְכּוֹר לָעַד בְּרִית אֲבוֹתֵיכֶם : חַנּוּן וְרַחוּם יָחוֹן עַל פְּלֵיטַתְכֶם :
טוֹב וּמֵטִיב | יֵיטִיב אֶתְכֶם : יָשָׁר וְנֶאֱמָן | יְיַשֵּׁר אֹרְחוֹתֵיכֶם :
כֹּתֵב חֻקִּים | יִכְתּוֹב לָעַד זִכְרוֹנְכֶם : לוֹבֵשׁ גֵּאוּת | יְרַחֵם אֶתְכֶם :
מֶלֶךְ עוֹלָם | יִמְלוֹךְ עֲלֵיכֶם : נָאוֹר וְאַדִּיר | יְנַחֶמְכֶם בְּבִנְיַן הֵיכַלְכֶם :
סָלַח וָטוֹב | יִסְלַח לְכָל עֲוֹנוֹתֵיכֶם : עוֹנֶה קְרִיאוֹת | יַעֲנֶה קְרִיאַתְכֶם :
פֹּדֶה נְפָשׁוֹת | יִפְדֶּה אֶת נַפְשְׁכֶם : צוּר עוֹלָמִים | יְצַוֶּה יְשׁוּעַתְכֶם :
קָרוֹב לְכָל קוֹרְאָיו | יְקָרֵב גְּאֻלַּתְכֶם : רֹצֶה יְרֵאָיו | יִרְצֶה אֶתְכֶם :
שֹׁמֵעַ שַׁוְעָה | יִשְׁמַע שַׁוְעַתְכֶם : תַּעֲלֶה לְפָנָיו | תְּפִלַּתְכֶם :
תְּהִי אָזְנוֹ | קַשֶּׁבֶת לְרִנַּתְכֶם : תִּדְרְשׁוּהוּ | וְיִמָּצֵא לָכֶם :
תִּקְרָאוּהוּ | וְיַעֲנֶה קְרִיאַתְכֶם : כַּכָּתוּב | וְהָיָה טֶרֶם יִקְרָאוּ וַאֲנִי אֶעֱנֶה
עוֹד הֵם מְדַבְּרִים וַאֲנִי אֶשְׁמָע : וִיקַיֵּם עֲלֵיכֶם מִקְרָא שֶׁכָּתוּב
יְהֹוָה אֱלֹהֵי אֲבוֹתֵכֶם יוֹסֵף עֲלֵיכֶם כָּכֶם אֶלֶף פְּעָמִים | וִיבָרֵךְ אֶתְכֶם כַּאֲשֶׁר
דִּבֶּר לָכֶם : הַקָּטֹן יִהְיֶה לָאֶלֶף | וְהַצָּעִיר לְגוֹי עָצוּם | אֲנִי יְהֹוָה בְּעִתָּהּ
אֲחִישֶׁנָּה : בּוֹנֵה יְרוּשָׁלַיִם יְהֹוָה | נִדְחֵי יִשְׂרָאֵל יְכַנֵּס : בּוֹרֵא נִיב שְׂפָתָיִם |
שָׁלוֹם שָׁלוֹם לָרָחוֹק וְלַקָּרוֹב אָמַר יְהֹוָה | וּרְפָאתִיו : הַמְשֵׁל וָפַחַד עִמּוֹ | עֹשֶׂה
שָׁלוֹם בִּמְרוֹמָיו : יְהֹוָה עֹז לְעַמּוֹ יִתֵּן | יְהֹוָה יְבָרֵךְ אֶת־עַמּוֹ בַשָּׁלוֹם :
בָּרוּךְ יְהֹוָה לְעוֹלָם | אָמֵן | וְאָמֵן :

ואחרי כן יקום החזן וילך לטקימו ויאמר לקהל

a _____ תַּעֲלֶה תֵּרָצֶה תְּקֻבַּל תְּפִלַּתְכֶם :

והקהל יענו לו

b _____ תֵּעָנֶה וְתֵרָצֶה :

———◆◇◈◉◈◇◆———

PLATE 6: *El-Elohīm: Karaite Prayer Book*, Vol. 3, pp. 192-193.

: הישב בסכה סברך

בָּרוּךְ אַתָּה יְיָ אֱלֹהֵינוּ מֶלֶךְ הָעוֹלָם אֲשֶׁר קִדְּשָׁנוּ בְּמִצְוֹתָיו וְצִוָּנוּ לַעֲשׂוֹת סֻכָּה וְלָשֶׁבֶת בַּתּוֹכָה : כַּכָּתוּב בַּסֻּכֹּת תֵּשְׁבוּ שִׁבְעַת יָמִים | כָּל־הָאֶזְרָח בְּיִשְׂרָאֵל יֵשְׁבוּ בַּסֻּכֹּת : לְמַעַן יֵדְעוּ דֹרֹתֵיכֶם כִּי בַסֻּכּוֹת הוֹשַׁבְתִּי אֶת־בְּנֵי יִשְׂרָאֵל בְּהוֹצִיאִי אוֹתָם מֵאֶרֶץ מִצְרָיִם | אֲנִי יְהוָה אֱלֹהֵיכֶם : וַיְדַבֵּר מֹשֶׁה אֶת־מֹעֲדֵי יְהוָה | אֶל־בְּנֵי יִשְׂרָאֵל : כַּאֲשֶׁר סַכַּכְתָּ אֶת אֲבוֹתֵינוּ בַּמִּדְבָּר כֵּן תָּסֵךְ אוֹתָנוּ אֶת בָּנֵיהֶם : וְיִשְׂמְחוּ כָל־חוֹסֵי בָךְ לְעוֹלָם יְרַנֵּנוּ וְתָסֵךְ עָלֵימוֹ וְיַעְלְצוּ בְךָ אֹהֲבֵי שְׁמֶךָ :

וְכֵן יָקִים הַשֵּׁם יִתְעַלֶּה בְּיָמֵינוּ יְעוּדָיו הַטּוֹבִים כָּאָמוּר וּבָרָא יְהוָה עַל־כָּל־מְכוֹן הַר־צִיּוֹן וְעַל־מִקְרָאֶהָ עָנָן יוֹמָם וְעָשָׁן וְנֹגַהּ אֵשׁ לֶהָבָה לָיְלָה | כִּי עַל־כָּל־כָּבוֹד חֻפָּה : וְסֻכָּה תִּהְיֶה לְצֵל־יוֹמָם מֵחֹרֶב | וּלְמַחְסֶה וּלְמִסְתּוֹר מִזֶּרֶם וּמִמָּטָר : וְכָתוּב בַּיּוֹם הַהוּא אָקִים אֶת־סֻכַּת דָּוִיד הַנֹּפֶלֶת | וְגָדַרְתִּי אֶת־פִּרְצֵיהֶן וַהֲרִסֹתָיו אָקִים וּבְנִיתִיהָ כִּימֵי עוֹלָם : כִּימֵי צֵאתְךָ מֵאֶרֶץ מִצְרָיִם | אַרְאֶנּוּ נִפְלָאוֹת : בּוֹנֵה יְרוּשָׁלַיִם יְהוָה | נִדְחֵי יִשְׂרָאֵל יְכַנֵּס : בִּמְהֵרָה בְּיָמֵינוּ וּבִזְמַן קָרוֹב וְנֹאמַר אָמֵן :

PLATE 7: 1) Blessing read inside the booth of Sukkot.
Karaite Prayer Book, Vol. 4, pp. 68-69

זמר לזמר בסכה

חברו אמו"ר הרב המפורסם כמה"ר יוסף שלמה הסלסד הגדול נ"ע לוצקי :

חַג הַסֻּכּוֹת הַזֶּה לָכֶם .	בַּעֲלֵי מִקְרָא מוֹעֲדֵיכֶם .
זִכְרוֹן לִימֵי תְּשׁוּעַתְכֶם .	גַּנָּן הִצִּיל אֲבוֹתֵיכֶם .
פָּרַשׂ עָנָן אֱלֹהֵיכֶם .	וּבוֹ סְכָךְ מוֹשִׁיעֲכֶם .
לָכֵן צִוָּה בְּתוֹרַתְכֶם .	לַעֲשׂוֹת סֻכּוֹת בְּבָתֵּיכֶם .
לְמַעַן יֵדְעוּ דוֹרוֹתֵיכֶם .	כִּי הוֹשִׁיבָם צוּר בַּסֻּכּוֹת:
חָגֵּי יְהוּדָה חַגֵּךְ .	שַׁלְּמִי אֶת נְדָרַיִךְ .
כִּימֵי עוֹלֵי רְגָלַיִךְ .	בַּשְּׁבִיעִי בְּחַג סֻכּוֹת:
גַּם חַג הָאָסִיף מִקְרָא .	כִּי יוֹבִילוּ שַׁי לַמּוֹרָא .
בְּאָסְפָּם בְּשֵׁם אֵל נוֹרָא .	כָּל־מַעֲשֵׂיהֶם עֲדֵי גָמְרָא .
וְיִשְׂמְחוּ שִׂמְחָה יְתֵרָה .	בְּחַג סֻכּוֹת בִּקְרוֹא מִקְרָא .
נוֹדָע בִּיהוּדָה תְּדִירָה .	הָאֵל בְּצִיּוֹן הַבִּירָה .

הגי	גָּדוֹל שְׁמוֹ בְּחַג סֻכּוֹת :		בְּיִשְׂרָאֵל אֻמָּה בָרָה .
	קוֹנֵנוּ לוֹ הוֹשִׁיעֵנוּ .		הִנֵּה זֶה הוּא אֱלֹהֵינוּ .
	נָגִילָה־בּוֹ כָּל יָמֵינוּ .		זֶה יְהוָה לוֹ קִוִּינוּ .
	בִּקְדוֹשׁ יִשְׂרָאֵל מַלְכֵּנוּ .		כִּי בֵאלֹהִים מָעֻזֵּנוּ .
	זִכְרוֹן שָׁלֹשׁ רְגָלֵינוּ .		מִקְרָא קֹדֶשׁ מוֹעֲדֵינוּ .
הגי	תֵּשְׁבוּ לָכֶם בַּסֻּכּוֹת :		שִׁבְעָה יָמִים צִוָּה לָנוּ .
	הוֹדִיעָנוּ בְּתוֹרָתוֹ .		סוֹד יְהוָה גַּם בְּרִיתוֹ .
	יוֹשֵׁב בְּחַג בְּסֻכָּתוֹ .		לִהְיוֹת כָּל־אִישׁ שׁוֹרֵר בֵּיתוֹ .
	בְּנֵי בֵיתוֹ הִיא דִירָתוֹ .		שִׁבְעַת יָמִים וּבְחֶבְרָתוֹ .
	מִמִּצְרַיִם בַּהֲלִיכָתוֹ .		כַּאֲשֶׁר יִשְׂרָאֵל בְּצֵאתוֹ .
חגי	סֻכַּת עָנָן כְּבַסֻּכּוֹת :		בַּמִּדְבָּר יוֹשְׁבֵי סֻכָּתוֹ .
	לָשֶׁבֶת בְּאֶרֶץ חַיִּים .		כֹּה לֶחַי נִזְכֶּה בַחַיִּים .
	כִּימֵי קֶדֶם הָרְאוּיִם .		בַּסֻּכּוֹת כָּל־הַפְּדוּיִים .
	כָּל יְהוּדָה וְאֶפְרַיִם .		צוּר יְקַבֵּץ מִכָּל־אַיִים .
	לְצִיּוֹן לִירוּשָׁלַם .		מִכָּל פֵּאָה הַשְּׁבוּיִים .
חגי	יָחֹגּוּ שָׁם חַג הַסֻּכּוֹת :		כָּל הָאֶזְרָח הָרְצוּיִים .
	סֻכָּה זֹאת מִבְחַר מְעוֹנִי .		תְּהִי בְעֵינֵי יְהוָה .
	מְקַבֶּלֶת כְּיוֹם סִינַי .		בְּחַצְרוֹת בֵּית אֵל יְהוָה .
	מַמְלֶכֶת כֹּהֲנִים נְבוֹנַי .		כְּסֻכּוֹת מִבְחַר כֹּהֲנֵי .
	יָחִישׁ יָקִים צוּר בִּרְצוֹנִי .		מִקְרָא מָלֵא אוֹר לְעֵינַי .
הגי	וְלָחֹג אֶת חַג הַסֻּכּוֹת :		לְהִשְׁתַּחֲווֹת לַיהוָה .
	עַל אֲסִיפַת כָּל־תְּנוּבָה .		הֵן בְּסֻכּוֹת טוֹב לְהוֹדוֹת .
	בַּעֲבוּר גִּשְׁמֵי נְדָבָה .		גַּם שְׁאֵלוֹת בּוֹ חֲמוּדוֹת .
	לַנְּשָׁמָה גַּם לְגֵוָה .		נוֹעֲדוֹת בּוֹ עוֹד תְּעוּדוֹת .
	כַּהֲלָכָה הַכְּתוּבָה .		עֵת לְבָרֵךְ צוּר בְּתוֹדוֹת .
הגי	עַל הָאָרֶץ הַטֹּבָה :		וּבֵרַכְתָּ אֶת אֱלֹהֶיךָ .

2) Whenever the worshippers are inside the booth of ḥag ha-Sukkot and after reciting the blessing (1), they sing this song.

Karaite Prayer Book, Vol. 4, pp. 123-124.

וזאת הקינה על אדנינו משה רבינו ע"ה לאמרו בתשלום התורה אחר הפרשה וההפטרה:

כִּי נֶאֱסַף	אַל מִבְּכִי תֶחְדְּשָׁה זֶרַע אֱמוּנִי . כִּי נֶאֱסַף מֹשֶׁה עֶבֶד יְיָ .
	אָדוֹן אֲשֶׁר עָלָה אֶל הָאֱלֹהִים . עַד שֹׁכְנֵי אֶרֶץ שָׁבוּ תְמִיחָם .
כִּי נֶאֱסַף	וּבְעֵת אֲשֶׁר יָרַד מָן הַגְּבָדִים . קָרַן מְאוֹר פָּנָיו בִּכְבוֹד יְיָ .
	פָּנִים אֱלֵי פָנִים הִבִּיט וְרָאָה . לֹא בַחֲלוֹם נִבָּא גַם לֹא בְמַרְאָה .
כִּי נֶאֱסַף	וּבְעֵת אֲשֶׁר יָדַע סוֹד הַנְּבוּאָה . וַיַּעֲנֵהוּ יִגְדַּל כֹּחַ אֲדֹנָי .
	רַחוּם קְרָאָהוּ מִשְּׁמֵי מְעוֹנִים . עָלָה וְדִבֶּר בּוֹ פָּנִים בְּפָנִים .
כִּי נֶאֱסַף	הוֹרִיד עֲלֵי יָדָיו לֻחוֹת אֲבָנִים . מַעֲשֵׂה אֱלֹהִים הֵם מִצְוֹת יְיָ .
	יִבְכּוּ בְּמוֹת מֹשֶׁה כָּל הַבְּרוּאִים . כִּי מַעֲשָׂיו הֵמָּה רַבִּים וְנָאִים .
כִּי נֶאֱסַף	לֹא קָם כְּמוֹ מֹשֶׁה עוֹד בַּנְּבִיאִים . עָלָיו יָקָר תּוֹרָה מֵאֵת יְיָ .
	מִי קָם כְּמוֹ מֹשֶׁה אוֹ מִי כְמוֹתוֹ . נָבִיא וְלֹא תוּכַל עַיִן רְאוֹתוֹ .
כִּי נֶאֱסַף	נֶאֱמָן מְאֹד צַדִּיק תָּמִים בְּבֵיתוֹ . מִי זֶה אֲשֶׁר עָלָה אֶל הַר יְיָ .

יַעְלְזוּ חֲסִידִים בְּכָבוֹד וִירַנְּנוּ עַל-מִשְׁכְּבוֹתָם: יָבוֹא שָׁלוֹם יָנוּחוּ עַל-מִשְׁכְּבוֹתָם ׀ הוֹלֵךְ נְכֹחוֹ: וְהַמַּשְׂכִּילִים יַזְהִירוּ כְּזֹהַר הָרָקִיעַ ׀ וּמַצְדִּיקֵי הָרַבִּים כַּכּוֹכָבִים לְעוֹלָם וָעֶד: בָּרוּךְ יְהוָה לְעוֹלָם ׀ אָמֵן ׀ וְאָמֵן:

PLATE 8: On the Sabbath between Sukkōt and Simḥāt Torah, the Karaites read a special prayer after the *hafṭarah* in memory of Moses (al-Mibbēkhī). *Karaite Prayer Book*, Vol. 1, p 341.

אַשְׁרֵיכֶם יִשְׂרָאֵל : שֶׁבָּכֶם בָּחַר אֵל : וְהִנְחִילְכֶם הַתּוֹרָה : מִסִּינַי מַתָּנָה :
אַשְׁרֵיכֶם אֲהוּבֵי אֵל : אַשְׁרֵיכֶם בְּרוּכֵי אֵל : אַשְׁרֵיכֶם גְּאוּלֵי אֵל :
שֶׁבָּכֶם בָּחַר אֵל : וְהִנְחִילְכֶם הַתּוֹרָה : מִסִּינַי מַתָּנָה :
אַשְׁרֵיכֶם דְּגוּלֵי אֵל : אַשְׁרֵיכֶם הַדּוּרֵי אֵל : אַשְׁרֵיכֶם וְתִיקֵי אֵל : שֶׁבָּכֶם בָּחַר אֵל : וְהִנְחִילְכֶם הַתּוֹרָה : מִסִּינַי מַתָּנָה :
אַשְׁרֵיכֶם זַכָּאֵי אֵל : אַשְׁרֵיכֶם חֲסִידֵי אֵל : אַשְׁרֵיכֶם טְהוֹרֵי אֵל : שֶׁבָּכֶם בָּחַר אֵל : וְהִנְחִילְכֶם הַתּוֹרָה : מִסִּינַי מַתָּנָה :
אַשְׁרֵיכֶם יִשְׁרֵי אֵל : אַשְׁרֵיכֶם כַּבִּירֵי אֵל : אַשְׁרֵיכֶם לְהֵגִי דַת אֵל : שֶׁבָּכֶם בָּחַר אֵל : וְהִנְחִילְכֶם הַתּוֹרָה : מִסִּינַי מַתָּנָה :
אַשְׁרֵיכֶם מְהַלְלֵי אֵל : אַשְׁרֵיכֶם נֶאֱמָנֵי אֵל : אַשְׁרֵיכֶם סְגֻלּוֹת אֵל : שֶׁבָּכֶם בָּחַר אֵל : וְהִנְחִילְכֶם הַתּוֹרָה : מִסִּינַי מַתָּנָה :
אַשְׁרֵיכֶם עֲנָוֵי אֵל : אַשְׁרֵיכֶם פְּדוּיֵי אֵל : אַשְׁרֵיכֶם צַדִּיקֵי אֵל : שֶׁבָּכֶם בָּחַר אֵל : וְהִנְחִילְכֶם הַתּוֹרָה : מִסִּינַי מַתָּנָה :
אַשְׁרֵיכֶם קְדוֹשֵׁי אֵל : אַשְׁרֵיכֶם רוֹמְמֵי אֵל : אַשְׁרֵיכֶם רְצוּיֵי אֵל : שֶׁבָּכֶם בָּחַר אֵל : וְהִנְחִילְכֶם הַתּוֹרָה : מִסִּינַי מַתָּנָה :
אַשְׁרֵיכֶם תְּמִימֵי אֵל : שֶׁבָּכֶם בָּחַר אֵל : וְהִנְחִילְכֶם הַתּוֹרָה מִסִּינַי מַתָּנָה :

וְעֵד תִּזְמֹר

שִׂמְחוּ יְדִידִים בְּשִׂמְחַת תּוֹרָה : שִׂמְחוּ אֲהוּבִים בְּשִׂמְחַת תּוֹרָה : כִּי הִיא אוֹרָה : כִּי מִצִּיּוֹן תֵּצֵא תוֹרָה :
שִׂמְחוּ בְּרוּכִים בְּשִׂמְחַת תּוֹרָה : שִׂמְחוּ גְּאוּלִים בְּשִׂמְחַת תּוֹרָה : שִׂמְחוּ דְּגוּלִים בְּשִׂמְחַת תּוֹרָה : שִׂמְחוּ הֲדוּרִים בְּשִׂמְחַת תּוֹרָה : כִּי הִיא

יָרוּם אֱלֹהִים חַי וְיִתְגַּדַּל : בּוֹרֵא לְכָל דָּבָר בְּאֶמְרָתוֹ :
מִי יַעֲרֹךְ אֵלָיו בְּכָל נִמְצָא : אֵין לוֹ כְּלָל עֶרֶךְ לִדְמוּתוֹ :
שָׁלַח לָכֵן עַמְרָם בְּזִיו הוֹדוֹ : מֹשֶׁה נְבִיאוֹ נֶאֱמַן בֵּיתוֹ :
הָיְתָה נְבוּאָתוֹ אֱלֵי פָנִים : מַבִּיט בְּהָקִיץ אֶת תְּמוּנָתוֹ :

יִגְדַּל אֱלֹהִים חַי וְיִשְׁתַּבַּח : נִמְצָא וְאֵין עֵת אֶל מְצִיאוּתוֹ :
אֶחָד וְאֵין יָחִיד כְּיִחוּדוֹ : נֶעְלָם וְאֵין סוֹף לְאַחְדוּתוֹ :
אֵין לוֹ יְסוֹד הַגּוּף וְאֵינוֹ גוּף : לֹא נַעֲרֹךְ אֵלָיו קְדֻשָּׁתוֹ :
קַדְמוֹן לְכָל דָּבָר אֲשֶׁר נִבְרָא : רִאשׁוֹן וְאֵין רֵאשִׁית לְרֵאשִׁיתוֹ :

אֶקְרָא בְּשִׁיר וְזִמְרָה : לָאֵל פּוֹעֵל בִּגְבוּרָה :
כִּי הוּא גָּדוֹל וְנוֹרָא : נָתַן אֶת זֹאת הַתּוֹרָה : אקרא
הֲדַר עֹז מְעִידִים : קוֹרְאֵי תוֹרָה חֲסִידִים :
וּמְאֹד הֵמָּה חֲרֵדִים : נַעֲשָׂה עַל פִּי הַתּוֹרָה : אקרא

PLATE 9: On Yom Simḥat Torah a joyous procession circles the sanctuary while the children chant portions of Yom Simḥat Torāh songs. These songs are: *Ashreikhem Yisrael, Simḥu Yedidim, Yarūm Elohim, Yighdāl Elohim, Eqrā Beshīr Vezimrāh*. Plate 14 shows the full words of *Ashreikhem* and portions of the other songs.

Karaite Prayer Book, Vol. 2, pp. 250-253.

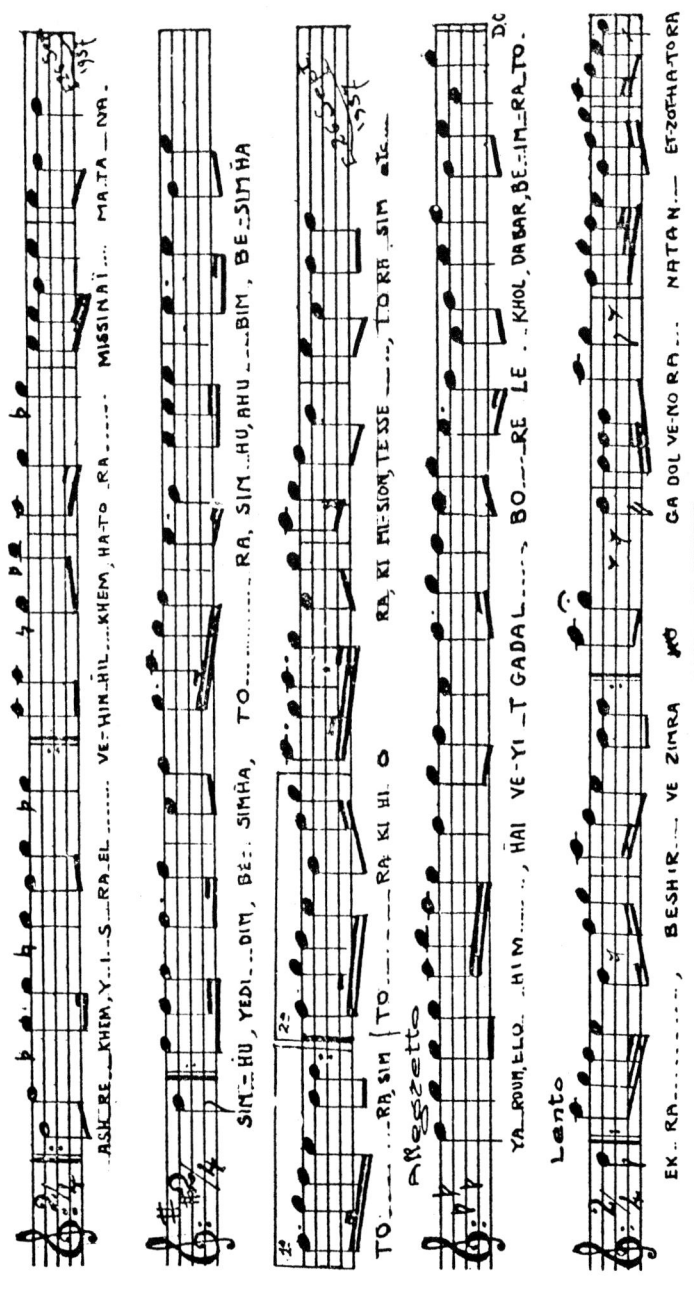

Songs of yom Simḥāt Torah.

I וַיֹּאמֶר יְהֹוָה אֶל־מֹשֶׁה | הִנְּךָ שֹׁכֵב עִם־אֲבֹתֶיךָ | וְקָם הָעָם הַזֶּה | וְזָנָה | אַחֲרֵי | אֱלֹהֵי | נֵכַר־הָאָרֶץ | אֲשֶׁר הוּא בָא־שָׁמָּה | בְּקִרְבּוֹ | וַעֲזָבַנִי | וְהֵפֵר אֶת־בְּרִיתִי | אֲשֶׁר כָּרַתִּי אִתּוֹ | וְחָרָה אַפִּי בוֹ בַיּוֹם־הַהוּא | וַעֲזַבְתִּים וְהִסְתַּרְתִּי פָנַי מֵהֶם וְהָיָה לֶאֱכֹל | וּמְצָאֻהוּ רָעוֹת רַבּוֹת וְצָרוֹת | וְאָמַר בַּיּוֹם הַהוּא | הֲלֹא עַל כִּי־אֵין אֱלֹהַי בְּקִרְבִּי | מְצָאוּנִי הָרָעוֹת הָאֵלֶּה | וְאָנֹכִי הַסְתֵּר אַסְתִּיר פָּנַי בַּיּוֹם הַהוּא | עַל כָּל־הָרָעָה אֲשֶׁר עָשָׂה | כִּי פָנָה אֶל־אֱלֹהִים אֲחֵרִים: וְעַתָּה כִּתְבוּ לָכֶם אֶת־הַשִּׁירָה הַזֹּאת | וְלַמְּדָהּ אֶת־בְּנֵי־יִשְׂרָאֵל שִׂימָהּ בְּפִיהֶם | לְמַעַן תִּהְיֶה־לִּי הַשִּׁירָה הַזֹּאת לְעֵד בִּבְנֵי יִשְׂרָאֵל: כִּי־אֲבִיאֶנּוּ אֶל־הָאֲדָמָה | אֲשֶׁר

1 שׁוֹטְטוּ בְּחוּצוֹת יְרוּשָׁלַםִ | וּרְאוּ־נָא וּדְעוּ וּבַקְשׁוּ בִרְחוֹבוֹתֶיהָ | אִם־תִּמְצְאוּ אִישׁ אִם־יֵשׁ עֹשֶׂה מִשְׁפָּט מְבַקֵּשׁ אֱמוּנָה | וְאֶסְלַח לָהּ: וְאִם חַי־יְהֹוָה יֹאמֵרוּ | לָכֵן לַשֶּׁקֶר יִשָּׁבֵעוּ: יְהֹוָה עֵינֶיךָ הֲלוֹא לֶאֱמוּנָה | הִכִּיתָה אֹתָם וְלֹא־חָלוּ כִּלִּיתָם מֵאֲנוּ קַחַת מוּסָר | חִזְּקוּ פְנֵיהֶם מִסֶּלַע מֵאֲנוּ לָשׁוּב: וַאֲנִי אָמַרְתִּי אַךְ דַּלִּים הֵם | נוֹאֲלוּ כִּי לֹא יָדְעוּ דֶּרֶךְ יְהֹוָה | מִשְׁפַּט אֱלֹהֵיהֶם:

קינות לשבת השנית

2 ובשבת השנית גם כן תדרך הדרך אשר הודעתיך ר״ל שתתחיל מן וַיֹּאמֶר יְיָ אֶל מֹשֶׁה הִנְּךָ שֹׁכֵב עִם אֲבֹתֶיךָ : יחד עם השירה . ואחרי כן תאמר זו הקרסה והתימסת .

בֶּן־אָדָם אֲמָר־לָהּ אַתְּ אֶרֶץ לֹא מְטֹהָרָה הִיא | לֹא גֻשְׁמָהּ בְּיוֹם זָעַם : קֶשֶׁר נְבִיאֶיהָ בְּתוֹכָהּ כַּאֲרִי שׁוֹאֵג טֹרֵף טָרֶף | נֶפֶשׁ אָכָלוּ חֹסֶן וִיקָר יִקָּחוּ | אַלְמְנוֹתֶיהָ הִרְבּוּ בְתוֹכָהּ: כֹּהֲנֶיהָ חָמְסוּ תוֹרָתִי | וַיְחַלְּלוּ קָדָשַׁי | בֵּין־קֹדֶשׁ לְחֹל

קינות לשבת השלישית

וכן בשבת השלישית תדרך בדרך אשר הודעתיך לעיל . ואחרי כן תאמר זאת הקרסה :

וְאַתָּה בֶן־אָדָם | הֲתִשְׁפֹּט הֲתִשְׁפֹּט אֶת־עִיר הַדָּמִים | וְהוֹדַעְתָּהּ אֵת כָּל תּוֹעֲבוֹתֶיהָ : וְאָמַרְתָּ כֹּה אָמַר אֲדֹנָי יְהֹוִה | עִיר שֹׁפֶכֶת דָּם בְּתוֹכָהּ לָבוֹא עִתָּהּ | וְעָשְׂתָה גִלּוּלִים עָלֶיהָ לְטָמְאָה : בְּדָמֵךְ אֲשֶׁר־שָׁפַכְתְּ אָשַׁמְתְּ וּבְגִלּוּלַיִךְ אֲשֶׁר־עָשִׂית טָמֵאת | וַתַּקְרִיבִי יָמַיִךְ וַתָּבוֹא עַד־שְׁנוֹתָיִךְ | עַל־כֵּן נְתַתִּיךְ חֶרְפָּה לַגּוֹיִם | וְקַלָּסָה לְכָל־הָאֲרָצוֹת : הַקְּרֹבוֹת וְהָרְחֹקוֹת מִמֵּךְ

קינות לשבת הרביעית

4 ובשבת הרביעית תדרך גם כן הדרך ואחר תאמר ההקדמה לקינה חו היא :

שִׁמְעוּ־זֹאת הַזְּקֵנִים | וְהַאֲזִינוּ כֹּל יוֹשְׁבֵי הָאָרֶץ | הֶהָיְתָה זֹּאת בִּימֵיכֶם | וְאִם בִּימֵי אֲבֹתֵיכֶם : עָלֶיהָ לִבְנֵיכֶם סַפֵּרוּ | וּבְנֵיכֶם לִבְנֵיהֶם | וּבְנֵיהֶם לְדוֹר אַחֵר : יֶתֶר הַגָּזָם אָכַל הָאַרְבֶּה | וְיֶתֶר הָאַרְבֶּה אָכַל הַיָּלֶק | וְיֶתֶר הַיֶּלֶק אָכַל הֶחָסִיל : הָקִיצוּ שִׁכּוֹרִים וּבְכוּ | וְהֵילִלוּ כָּל־שֹׁתֵי יָיִן | עַל־עָסִיס כִּי נִכְרַת מִפִּיכֶם :

5 ואולם אם יקרה שבת חמישית מאל השבתות תדרך כדרך שהודעתיך בשבת הראשונה או בשבת השניה ובמסקס האיכה תאמר זה :

זְכֹר יְהֹוָה מֶה־הָיָה לָנוּ | הַבִּיטָה וּרְאֵה אֶת־חֶרְפָּתֵנוּ : נַחֲלָתֵנוּ נֶהֶפְכָה לְזָרִים | בָּתֵּינוּ לְנָכְרִים : יְתוֹמִים הָיִינוּ וְאֵין אָב | אִמֹּתֵינוּ כְּאַלְמָנוֹת : מֵימֵינוּ בְּכֶסֶף שָׁתִינוּ | עֵצֵינוּ בִּמְחִיר יָבֹאוּ : עַל צַוָּארֵנוּ נִרְדָּפְנוּ | יָגַעְנוּ וְלֹא הוּנַח־לָנוּ :

PLATE 10: Parts of special prayers during the months of Tammuz and Av.

During the Saturdays from the 9th of Tammuz until the 10th of Av, Karaites read special prayers from the *Karaite Prayer Book,* Vol. 1, pp. 107-121.

On each Saturday they read an introduction (I), followed by part one on the first Saturday, part two on the second, and so on.

Plate 10 shows the first lines of the introduction and the prayers for each of the five Saturdays.

צד

1

נם זה לנמול כנגון ישראל נושע של הרב יהושע ז"ל

יְהִי שָׁלוֹם בְּחֵילֵנוּ . וְשַׁלְוָה בְּקִקְהָלֵנוּ . בְּסִימָן טוֹב בֵּן בָּא לָנוּ . יָבוֹא לְצִיּוֹן גּוֹאֵל :
יהי

הַיֶּלֶד יְהִי רַעֲנָן . בְּצֵל שַׁדַּי יִתְלוֹנָן . וּבַתּוֹרָה יִתְבּוֹנָן . יָאֱלֶף דַּת לְכָל שׁוֹאֵל .
יהי

וּמְקוֹרוֹ יְהִי בָּרוּךְ . זְמַן חַיָּיו יְהִי אָרוּךְ . וְשֻׁלְחָנוֹ יְהִי עָרוּךְ . וְזַכַּאי לֹא יִתְגָּאֵל :
יהי

שְׁמוֹ יִגְדַּל לְכָל עֵבֶר . עֲדֵי יִצְלַח לְכָל גֶּבֶר . לִירֵאֵי אֵל יְהִי חָבֵר . יְהִי בְּדוֹרוֹ כִּשְׁמוּאֵל :
יהי

עֲדֵי זִקְנָה וְגַם שֵׂיבָה . יְהִי דָשֵׁן בְּרוֹב טוֹבָה . וְשָׁלוֹם לוֹ וְגַם אַהֲבָה . כִּי כֵן יֹאמַר הָאֵל :
יהי

חַי זַכַּאי קָדוֹשׁ שְׁמָךְ . לְיַד יָמִין יְהִי נִסְמָךְ . לְבַקֵּר וְלַחֲזוֹת נֹעֲמָךְ . בְּקֶרֶב כָּל יִשְׂרָאֵל :
יהי

כַּכָּתוּב יְהִי שָׁלוֹם בְּחֵילֵךְ שַׁלְוָה בְּאַרְמְנוֹתָיִךְ :

צה

2

נם זה לנמול כנגון יחיד אל מרומם של הרב יהושע ז"ל

יְרֻשַּׁת נַחֲלָה . לְשֵׁם טוֹב וּתְהִלָּה . בְּבִרְכַּת הַמִּילָה . אָמֵן עוֹנִים : ירשת

הַנִּמּוֹל לִשְׁמוֹנָה . יִזְכֶּה לִתְבוּנָה . וּלְעֵדוּת נֶאֱמָנָה . וּלְשִׂמְחַת שׁוֹשְׁבִינִים :
ירשת

וּלְשִׁמוֹנַת יָמִים . בִּבְרִית אֵל נְכוֹנִים . בְּבָנִים נֶאֱמָנִים . חֲכָמִים וּנְבוֹנִים : ירשת

שָׁלוֹם וְשַׁלְוָה . אַחֲרִית וְתִקְוָה . וְתוֹרָה וּמִצְוָה . וּבְרִית רִאשׁוֹנִים : ירשת

עִנְיָנוֹ עָנָה טוֹב . סִימָנוֹ סִימָן טוֹב . הֶגְיוֹנוֹ הִגָּיוֹן טוֹב . בְּמוֹשַׁב זְקֵנִים : ירשת

כַּכָּתוּב וִירוֹמְמוּהוּ בִּקְהַל עָם וּבְמוֹשַׁב זְקֵנִים יְהַלְלוּהוּ :

PLATE 11: Song #1 is read before the circumcision. Song #2 is read after the circumcision.

Karaite Prayer Book, Vol. 4, pp. 151-153.

זמר נאה לחתן של הרב אהרן ז"ל

אָמֵן יְהִי רָצוֹן לְקוֹנְךָ: יַגְדִּיל וְגַם יַרְבֶּה שְׂשׂוֹנְךָ: אמן
הַתּוֹם וְהַחָכְמָה לְבוּשֶׁךָ: הַחֵן וְהַמִּשְׂרָה אֲשִׁישֶׁךָ: אַשְׁרֵי אֲנָשֶׁיךָ מְשָׁרְתֶיךָ:
שׁוֹקְדִים וְגַם עוֹמְדִים לְפָנֶיךָ: אמן
רֶכֶם בְּדוֹלָחַי לְשָׁמֶיךָ: רָפוּד בְּמֶרְקָחַי בְּשָׂמֶיךָ: יָדְךָ הֲלֹא תִמְצָא לְקָמֶיךָ:
צָרִים הֲכִי תִמְשׁוֹל יְמִינֶךָ: אמן
נַפְשִׁי בְּנוֹזְלֵי חֵן חֲסָדֶיךָ: תַּשְׂבִּיעַ נִדְבוֹת חֵן אֲפוּדֶךָ: חָשְׁקָה לְהִתְלוֹנֵן בְּסוֹדֶךָ:
תִּשְׁכֹּן בְּצֵל תַּחַת שְׁרוֹנֶךָ: אמן
חַי אֵל אֲשֶׁר תִּכֵּן יְסוֹד כֻּלָּם: יָבִיא בְיָמֶיךָ גְּבִיר נֶעְלָם: כִּסְאוֹ תְּהֵא תָמִיד עֲדֵי
עוֹלָם: תִּזְכֶּה רְאוֹת בָּנִים לְבָנֶיךָ: אמן
כַּכָּתוּב וּרְאֵה בָנִים לְבָנֶיךָ שָׁלוֹם עַל יִשְׂרָאֵל:

PLATE 12: Song after the wedding ceremony.
Karaite Prayer Book, Vol. 4, p. 141

Wedding invitation in Arabic (1962)

Nous serons heureux de vous recevoir à la bénédiction nuptiale de

Mourad Kodsy & Rose Tawil

qui sera donnée le Dimanche 13 Juin 1948 à 7 h. 30 p.m. à leur domicile, sis rue Saïd No. 7 Héliopolis

Mr. Liéto Y. Kodsy
Dr. Youssef Tawil

Adr. Télég. Kodsy - Tawil

نتشرف بدعوة حضرتكم لحضور الاحتفال بزفاف

مراد موسى قدسى و روز يوسف طويل

وذلك فى الساعة السابعة والنصف تماماً، مساء الأحد الموافق ١٣ يونيه سنة ١٩٤٨ بالمنزل رقم ٧ بشارع سعيد بمصر الجديدة
ليتو يوسف القدسى
الدكتور يوسف الطويل

العنوان التلغرافى : قدسى - طويل

Wedding invitation in Arabic and French (1948)

Chapter VII

Cultural and Social Activities

The Various Organizations and
Their Achievements

Literary Output

Leading Men

Murād Farag

Dā'ūd Ḥusnī

The Various Organizations and Their Achievements

The community was rich in its activities. There was a wide range of organizations, including those devoted to charity, helping poor girls get married, providing health care, and teaching Hebrew and Arabic. Other organizations dealt with sports, excursions, and social activities, such as dancing and acting. Lectures on various topics were given on a regular basis by members of both the Karaite and the Rabbanite communities.

Often, there was more than one organization with similar goals and activities. During the 1920's and 1930's it was not easy to become a member of the religious council, which many felt was the best way to serve the community. The alternative, especially for younger members, was to form or be a member of an organization with goals oriented to community service.

Most of the organizations were centered in 'Abbāsiyah, the district in which most of the Karaites lived at the time. On several occasions, active members of the Ḥārat al-Yahūd community formed new organizations for various purposes, only to have their activities terminated for lack of membership or a decent center. Thus, we find many organizations that started strongly, but within a few years faded away.

The Karaite community, then, certainly lacked nothing in the number of organizations which it maintained. What the community did lack, and what became a long-term factor in lessening their effect, was coordination of their activities. Each organization worked alone, following its own guidelines. The religious council, in part, failed to unify their efforts by failing to take a strong stand towards members of the various organizations to direct their efforts in the best possible way.[1]

Another important point was that the officers of these organizations often remained the same from the beginning until the end. There were almost no new officers, who would have brought in new ideas and new blood. What happened was that when the founding officers' interest diminished, the organization came to an end.

Just as it was not easy to become a member of the religious council, so was it also not easy to become an acting member of an organization. To reiterate, this accounted for the founding of many new, and similarly oriented, organizations. Each organization, before becoming active, was required to ask the religious council for recognition. The only explanation for this that I can offer is that the Karaites are, by nature, law-abiding persons. The founders of the various organizations must have felt that such a recognition gave them a kind of legality.

It must be understood here that no organization depended on the religious council for financial help. The support came from interested members of the Karaite community, even though there is no record of any wealthy Karaite ever donating a substantial sum of money to any organization.

As for the organizations themselves, we have no records of their existence before 1897. The first record of note was of "The Association for Helping the Sick," which, in January 1902, published its budget from October 1897 until December 1901[2] (Pl. 1). The organization's support came from monthly membership dues. The only help from the religious council came in the form of providing a meeting place. Within the organization, Dr. Marco Sinānī, a Karaite who came from Istanbūl in 1901, offered to treat the poor without charge.

On 12 August 1901, the first issue of *al-Tahdhīb* was published, a four-page paper issue printed in the community school's printing shop. Murād Farag, a member of the religious council, served as chief editor; the religious council itself was the responsible owner. It appeared weekly, then every ten days. A yearly

---

1. The minutes of the religious council from 1923 to 1946.
2. *al-Tahdhīb* No. 24. (December 1902).

subscription cost 10 piasters (the equivalent of 50 cents),[3] and it offered news of interest to members of the community: legal matters, such as those of inheritance, consanguinity, circumcision, kashrut (kasher slaughtering), and others.[4] It was mainly the product of one person, Murād Farag. *Al-Tahdhīb* remained in print until 1904 (Pl. 2).

Thereafter, the community was without a magazine until 1908, when *al-Irshād* was first published on 15 May 1908. It appeared twice a month, at 8 pages an issue. Printed also in the school's printing shop, its theme was, "A reformed scientific and literary magazine." Its publisher was Farag Salīm Līshaʿ. By November of 1908, it was published three times a month. On 21 March 1909, it published its last issue (Pl. 2).

On 10 October 1916, the religious council gave its permission to a group of young men to form an organization under the name of "The Association for Reforms," and to begin activities under the full supervision of the religious council. The association was concentrated mainly in Ḥārat al-Yahūd. It remained active until 1921.

Another short-lived organization was the "Brotherhood Association," *Mugtamaʿ al-Akhāʾ*, formed on 19 December 1916, with three goals in mind: to promote educational lectures, to establish a library and to establish a sports club. Yet little by little, members of the association engaged themselves in other activities and by 1919 they called for new elections and for complete administrative reforms in the community.

The "Association for Guidance," *Gamʿiyat al-Irshād*, appeared in May 1921, to fight illiteracy in Hebrew and Arabic. The religious council agreed to provide the association with classroom space in the school building, as long as they would pay for its maintenance.[5]

In the years 1919 and 1920, many young members of the community graduated from the University of Cairo and from European universities. Many of these young people got together and formed one of the strongest associations of all, under the name, "The Society of Israelite Union," *Gamʿiyat al-Ittiḥād al-Isrāʾīlī*. The group applied to the religious council for recognition,[6] and their application was accepted on condition that the religious council had the right to supervise revenues and expenditures.

After approval by the religious council, the association published its constitution, recording its goals as follows:

---

3. Minutes of 11 August 1901.
4. See *al-Tahdhīb*, first and second year.
5. Minutes of May 1921.
6. The application was sent on 4 November 1921. The religious council gave its consent on 3 December 1921. The first chairman was Murād Yūsuf al-Qudsī, an engineer in the central government.

1. To promote awareness of the faith, and greater understanding of its principles.
2. To be a "watchdog" of the activities of the religious council.
3. To publish a magazine to speak on behalf of the community.

On 21 March 1924, the association published "The Israelite Union," *al-Ittiḥād al-Isrā'īlī*. It was published twice a month, with eight pages of articles written by members of the Karaite community (Pl. 2). The articles dealt, for the most part, with matters of faith, the relationship between the community and the religious council, legal issues, and news about Jews in general all over the world. Each issue had an editorial that treated a problem of concern to the community.

In almost every issue there was an article about the Zionist movement all over the world, especially in Palestine.[7] Most important, however, were the articles about the relationship between the Karaite and the Rabbanite communities. One of several highly educated members of the Rabbanite community who wrote often in *al-Ittiḥād al-Isrā'īlī* was Dr. Hillel Farḥī. He discussed the history of the Jews, and the ever increasing problems that faced them. *Al-Ittiḥād al-Isrā'īlī* had representatives in many countries in the Middle East.[8]

Unfortunately, in 1930 the paper was forced to cease publication for lack of funds. The association did, however, continue all other activities: teaching the Hebrew language, giving weekly lectures, and promoting excursions to different places all over the country. The association also carried on such activities as sporting events, music and acting (Pl. 3).

The headquarters of the association was at 5 'Abbāsiyah Street, in a large apartment in an affluent neighborhood where many Jews lived. As early as 1924, Sabbath and holiday services were conducted in the headquarters for members of the community who lived in the neighboring areas.

In 1935, another group of well-educated young men formed yet another organization, "The Association for Protecting the Community's Interest," *Gam'iyat al-Difā' 'an Maṣāliḥ al-Ṭā'ifah*.

It had three main goals:
1. To hold new elections for the religious council;
2. To rewrite the Internal Code;
3. To codify Personal Status.

The Israelite Union remained relatively strong until 1936. In that year, other community members formed a new group under the name "Young Men's Karaite Association," *Gam'iyat al-Shubbān al-Qarrā'īn*. It was, as the Arabic expression goes, "a carbon copy" of *al-Ittiḥād al-Isrā'īlī*.

---

7. At that time (1924-1930), the Egyptian government had not yet outlawed Zionist activities.
8. Ḥassan 'Abdul-Ṣamaḍ, director of the Bureau of the Egyptian Arabic Press, was the representative of *al-Ittiḥād* in Iraq, Syria and Lebanon.

The new organization, likewise run by well-educated young men, carried out many of the same activities as the Israelite Union and received much encouragement from members of the community. Officers of the Israelite Union had no choice but to join hands with the new association, and so they merged into one association under the name of "Young Men's Israelite Karaite Association," *Gam'iyat al-Shubbān al-Isrā'īlīyīn al-Qarrā'īn.*[9]

The unification brought into the open the need for a magazine that would speak on behalf of the community, especially at a time when every organization in the country was striving for some kind of recognition. It was also the beginning of a new era: It was the beginning of the reign of King Fārūq.

On 17 April 1937, the first issue appeared with a portrait of King Fārūq on its front page. It was a very well organized magazine. The first two issues were of 12 pages each, pages 10 through 12 in French. The third issue was 16 pages, with pages 14 and 15 in French. After that it was again 12 pages, but all in Arabic. Unfortunately, again for lack of funds and other reasons, the last issue was published on 17 November 1937[10] (Pl. 4).

It is worthwhile to examine for a moment the reasons why such an organized effort was forced to stop publishing such a magazine. Undoubtedly, it is not an easy task to publish a magazine. It needs continuous efforts, new ideas, new materials of interest to the reader; but most of all, it requires the commitment of a full-time job. One person working on a voluntary basis cannot carry the responsibility for long. It must be shared by other members. When that does not happen, sooner or later the publication of the magazine will come to an end.

Again, the association continued all its other activities. The community badly needed such an association, for it filled the gap in the situation in which many young Karaite men found themselves. In Egypt at that time there was the Y.M.C.A.*, as well as the newly formed Y.M.M.A.** Neither of these filled the needs of the young Karaites. In addition, the Rabbanite community had many sports and social clubs. Yet is was not easy for many young Karaites to join any of these groups. Their education was mostly Egyptian, while that of the Rabbanite young men was mostly French. Not knowing the French language was a major obstacle for many Karaites to joining Rabbanite clubs or associations. Nevertheless those who knew French found it more rewarding to join those clubs, especially the Maccabi and the ha-Kowah. Among many others Benoit 'Abd al-Wāḥid, a Karaite, was the captain of the Maccabi basketball team that was internationally known during the 1940's.

---

9. *Magazine of the Young Men's Israelite Karaite Association* No. 1 (17 April 1937). The new association took over some officers from the old one.
10. Tawfīq Ibrāhīm was the chief editor. Yūsuf Kamāl and his brother Ibrāhīm Ḥusnī worked with him.
*. Y.M.C.A. Young Men's Christian Association.
**. Y.M.M.A. Young Men's Muslim Association.

The new organization was thus able to attract many young men. Many activities were carried out successfully. There was a weightlifting team;[11] the table tennis team won the second place title in Egypt in 1937.[12] There was an excellent orchestra that gained a widespread reputation among the Jewish community at large.[13] The association had an acting group, also with an excellent reputation, that put on four shows yearly.[14]

The association put great effort into promoting religious awareness among members of the community. Hebrew classes were opened in Ḥārat al-Yahūd and in 'Abbāsiyah. In the late 1940's new classes were begun in Heliopolis, the suburb to which many of the Jews had moved.[15] Although the association collected membership dues, usually this was not enough. Donations from rich members were minimal. One of the main sources of revenue until 1950 was excursions to the Pyramids, especially when the moon was full, to the Suez Canal, and to many parts of the country. Besides providing a source of revenue, these excursions were also excellent opportunities for the youth to get together.

On 16 February 1945, the first issue of *al-Kalīm* was in the hands of almost all Karaite families. *Al-Kalīm* was a bimonthly magazine of 16 pages. It, too, treated many topics of interest to members of the community: religion, short stories, relations with authorities and with the Jewish mainstream, news of Jews all over; there was no mention, however, of Zionism, or any Zionist movement.[16] Everyone was welcome to contribute to *al-Kalīm;* no article was refused as long as it met the requirements of a worthwhile contribution (Pl. 5).

Al-Kalīm was the product of the efforts of a group of educated people, and not just one person. For this reason it endured for 12 years, and would have continued had there been enough Karaites in Egypt. After the second Arab-Israeli war, many members of the community left the country, and there was no more sense in publishing *al-Kalīm*. In fact, the association stopped all its activities. The history of the Karaite community from 1945 to 1957 is recorded in the pages of *al-Kalīm*.

Had it not been for *al-Kalīm,* the Young Men's Israelite Karaite Association would have stopped all its activities after the Israeli War of Independence in 1948. As it was, the Boy Scouts and the Explorers of the association maintained their activities until 1959, although under a new name, it declared complete independence

---

11. Jacques Aṣlān got the bronze medal in 1937.
12. *Al-Shubbān al-Qarrā'īn* No. 10 (2 October 1937).
13. Elīyāhū Aṣlān was the first violinist and conductor of the orchestra. The orchestra members wore beautiful uniforms of white and blue.
14. Ibrāhīm Ḥusnī and his brother were responsible for the group.
15. The Rabbanite community willingly allowed the use of the Abraham Beteish School for evening classes.
16. By that time all Zionist activities were outlawed in the Arab countries.

from any other association. The older one was recognized by the National Boy Scout Association and participated in many national and local events. The new one was registered on 17 May 1954, under the name of "Boy Scout and Explorers of the Young Men (of) the Israelite Karaite (Community)."[17]

In 1939, a member of the community started a project, all by himself, to provide poor members of the Karaite community with fresh bread three times a week. This project continued to serve the community until its founder left for Israel in the late 1950's.[18]

On 26 January 1945, the "Kitchen for the Poor" offered its first hot meal. It was located in the facilities of the Karaite Primary School in al-Ḥārah. The idea of offering hot meals to the poor was so successful that it prompted those responsible to take a larger step: to form an association to ensure the continuity of this and other humanitarian projects. Thus in January 1946, the "Karaite Brothers Association" was registered with the ministry of Social Affairs as number 55.[19] Its goals were summarized in three words: "Religion, Education, Health."

A vigorous competition developed between the Karaite Brothers and the Young Men's Israelite Karaite Association. Efforts to reconcile them were unsuccessful. The Karaite Brothers were better organized, and had limited and defined goals. Its members were more dedicated, yet none of them had any previous experience in any association. In short, they knew nothing of organizational politics.

The Karaite Brothers had in mind to build a new public dining hall where they could serve meals to the poor of Ḥārat al-Yahūd. They also wanted to build a new and modern kasher bakery.

The religious council gave them a piece of land suitable for the project, and donations were collected for the two projects. When the first Arab-Israeli war broke out, the Karaite Brothers, all in their twenties, were afraid to take any action, even if legal. Hence, in 1952 the association terminated its activities and turned all of its assets over to the religious council.[20]

Women, it must be noted, also took part in the already mentioned activities. In addition, they had activities of their own.

On Sunday, 7 February 1937, many women and celebrities gathered in the headquarters of the Y.M.I.K.A., and formed a new organization: "The Benovolent Workshop for Girls."[21] It had one goal: to teach girls of Ḥārat al-Yahūd, regardless

---

17. Murād al-Qudsī assumed full responsibility for the troop. Clement Līsha' provided in his house (villa) a place for the troop to conduct its activities.
18. He was Farag Ṣāliḥ.
19. In the early 1940's, a law was passed requiring each association to register with the Secretary of Social Affairs, indicating its goals, methods of achieving its goals, and its sources of revenue.
20. Minutes of 16 December 1952.
21. Those who gathered on that day considered themselves a "General Assembly," and thus all the officers were elected the same evening.

of religion, the art of sewing. Classes were held each Monday afternoon in the art room of the Karaite School in Khurunfish. It was a very successful project and served the community until January of 1949.[22]

As early as 1908, a group of concerned members of the community formed the *"Ezrāt ha-Betulōt,"* an organization to help poor girls get married and provide financial assistance during the first year of marriage. This association served the community for over 30 years. On 24 January 1942, it handed over all its assets to the religious council.[23] The organization could have functioned longer had it not been for a similar one that appeared in 1940 under the name, "Benevolent Association for the Marriage of the Poor Israelite Karaite Girls"[24] (Pl. 6).

The association was very well organized; its officers, in fact, functioned like a family. It had a policy to follow and a plan to execute. Its revenues came 10% from membership, 85% from donations. One of the main sources of donations was the memorial gifts for the deceased. It worked as follows: the association, upon request and free of charge, used to send chairs, clean Oriental rugs, plates, cups, silverware, practically everything needed by the family to conduct Kaddish (memorial) prayers at home followed by a light meal. Prayerbooks were always available. It was the custom that prayers were said at the house of the deceased for seven days, and on Saturday morning. Psalm readers would arrive an hour earlier, and read psalms until it was time for the evening prayers. After the prayers, donations in memory of the deceased were collected.

Usually, if the deceased was old, a light meal was offered. On Saturday following the service, a lavish breakfast was served. Each year the association published its budget, with a complete list of donations. This association helped hundreds of girls get married, and provided the new households with financial help. It maintained its activities until 1965, at which time there was no longer any need for its services, as there were no more young girls to get married.

Another well-organized association was the *Ahavāt Torah (Gamʻiyat Shubbān Ḥubb al-Tawrāh)*. It, too, started in Ḥārat al-Yahūd, where most of its members lived. The association started in 1940 with one specific goal: teaching the Hebrew language and promoting better understanding of the faith.[25] At that time, the Y.M.I.K.A. had similar classes in ʻAbbāsiyah, then later in Heliopolis.

Gradually, owing to better organization, the new group started to take over.

---

22. Minutes of 11 January 1949.
23. Minutes of 24 January 1942.
24. The most active member was Farag Aṣlān, who was responsible for all activities and organization of the group. Mattātiah Marzūq was treasurer for 13 years; chairmen included Clement Līshāʻ, Ibrāhīm Farag Masʻūdah, and Yūsuf Farag Hayyīnah.
25. Barakāt ʻAbdū Farag was its first chairman. Murād al-Qudsī took over from 1949 until 1959 (*al-Kalīm* No. 163).

Because of its success in Ḥārat al-Yahūd, classes were opened in 'Abbāsiyah. A few years later, when the first Arab-Israeli war broke out, and many Karaites planned to leave for Israel, there was a greater need to learn Hebrew. A group of dedicated university students, with some other volunteers, carried out efficiently the responsibility, and within a short time adult classes for beginners were filled to capacity.[26]

It was also a golden opportunity for the association to train interested members of the community to become ritual slaughterers, circumcisers, and cantors.[27]

At that time there was a great need for prayerbooks. The association was able to reprint hundreds of copies of all four volumes of the Karaite prayerbook.[28]

In 1959 the association, under pressure from the authorities, had to stop all its activities, and returned all its assets to the religious council.[29]

One Final Note

There is no doubt that members of the Karaite community were involved in many activities, yet the community could have profited more if members of the different organizations had examined carefully what the community needed and had worked together so that each organization could have taken care of one of the community's problems or needs. At times there was more than one group with similar activities and goals, while, for example, there was no organization that provided vocational training for the poor youth of the community. The presence of the Rabbanite Jewish hospital in Ghamrah and the many dispensaries in "Ḥārat al-Yahūd al-Rabbāniyyīn" left no need for any Karaite organization or even the Karaite religious council to put any effort into health care. All of the activities were centered in 'Abbāsiyah while there was a large number of Karaites in Heliopolis and in "Ḥārat al-Yahūd al-Qarrā'īn."

Literary Output

The Karaites in Egypt had a common bond in that they were mainly of Egyptian descent and Egyptian cultural background.[30] They spoke Arabic and used Arabic as their language both orally and in writing. This explains why all periodicals and other publications that appeared from 1897 until 1956 were in Arabic. On the other hand the Rabbanite community, in that regard, was completely different. Members of the Rabbanite community came from all over the world. Some were British or

---

26. In 1956, the number of students reached 350 (*al-Kalīm* No. 227).
27. In the minutes of 20 February 1955 it is stated that 8 ritual slaughterers graduated in 1955.
28. The last set of prayerbooks had come from Russia in 1901.
29. Minutes of 11 October 1960.
30. Families like Fīrūz, al-Tawīl, al-Gamīl, Shamuel and many others were in the country for centuries. While others like al-Qudsī, Marzūq and 'abd-Allah, though of non-Egyptian origin, had been living in Egypt for decades.

French or Italian or Austrian or Greek or Spanish or Turkish. That explains why there were different congregations for the Rabbanite community in Cairo and in Alexandria. It also explains why that community had periodicals in English, French, Italian, Hebrew, Arabic, Spanish and Yiddish. Among Karaites English and French were also common. Some spoke Hebrew, Spanish, Italian, Greek, Russian and Turkish. A good number knew Hebrew well, although few knew it well enough to be considered an authority in the language.

Since the time of the British occupation in 1882, Jews, and minorities in general, enjoyed more safety and more equality, which served as a good basis for prosperity. It was expected then that this new prosperity would lead to productivity in art and science. That did not happen. Popular interest lay more in material matters, which would bring about a better life-style.

"Scholarly works of any importance are rare and many of them are of a didactic nature."[31] That was the situation among Rabbanites. Among the Karaites, the situation was basically the same, with two important exceptions: Murād Farag and Dā'ūd Ḥusnī, who will be discussed later.

Among the chief rabbis of this period, three are worth mentioning. Ḥakhām Shlomoh Kohen (1873-1876) was a poet, philosopher, and Hebrew scholar. In his lifetime he wrote four books, the most important of which is *Yerī'ōt Shlomoh*. The book is in two parts — each part has 20 articles. Both parts discuss Judaism in general and Karaism in particular. Efforts are under way to publish this book in English. In 1985 the Hebrew one was published in Israel.

He also wrote *Asfé Kayez,* in which he recorded what had happened to the Karaite community in Istanbūl in 1847.

Another book was *Safah Berōrah,* in which he explains the correct way to write Hebrew.

The fourth book, entitled *Gefen ha-Adderet,* is a summary of chosen parts of *Adderet Elīyāhū.*

Ḥakhām Abrāhām Kohen (1920-1933), another poet, philosopher, and Hebrew scholar, wrote a number of books; none of them has been published. They were kept in the library of the Karaite community in Cairo until the late 1960's. In the middle of the 1970's, when most members of the community had left, an unscrupulous member of the community was able to sell many of the priceless community treasures. Many opportunists came to Egypt, paid the price and returned with the booty. In 1979 I went to San Francisco, where I visited the Magnes Museum and found a handwritten book by Ḥakhām Abrāhām Kohen.

During his service in Cairo, Ḥakhām Tobiah Babovitch (1934-1956) wrote many articles in *al-Kalīm* about the faith and about its history. He also managed to publish a book in Hebrew — *Rōsh Penah* — translated into Arabic by Mūsā Farag al-

---

31. Jacob Landaū, *Jews in 19th Century Egypt* (pp. 100-101).

Sirgānī. In it Tobiah writes about three great scholars of the faith: 'Anān ha-Nāsī, Benjamin al-Nahāwandī, and Daniel al-Qumīsī.

Ḥākhām Tobiah also wrote a book while he was still in Russia. The book contains three treatises: in the first he wrote about the history of the Karaites in the Crimea; in the second he gave in detail the history of the city of Kalé (Chufūt-Kalé) and proved that it was a Karaite city. In the third he defended Abrāhām Firkovitch regarding his discoveries in the Crimea. The three treatises were published in *al-Ittiḥād* in 1928.

In 1948, David Līsha', the gabbāy of the synagogue Mosheh al-Dar'ī, along with Ḥākhām Yūsuf Ibrāhīm Yomtōb, published a booklet in Arabic: *al-Murshid al-Amīn, Moreh Ṣedq,* a short manual of the Karaite faith.

There were quite a number of poets fluent in iambic poetry: "Zagal" Zakī Menashah, Amīn al-Gamīl, Zakī Ḥayyīm Ṣāliḥ and many others. The pages of *al-Ittiḥād, al-Shubbān,* and *al-Kalīm* are full of their work (Pls. 7 and 8).

The community was also fortunate to have three artists and one cartoonist who were nationally known.[32]

At the Art Exhibition in Cairo in 1925 and in Rome in 1926, Ibrāhīm Dā'ūd Ṣāliḥ was awarded the first prize and the gold medal respectively for his oil paintings. They were not the same in both exhibitions[33] (Pl. 9).

Ibrahim Yūsuf Levi graduated from the "Académie des Beaux Arts" with honour, and was among those honoured by King Fārūq in a special reception at the Royal Palace in Ra's al-Tīn, in Alexandria, in August 1945.[34] His painting "Laylat al-Ḥinnah," the project for his degree, was rated among the best.[35]

Ibrāhīm Elīyāhū Mas'ūdah, another graduate of the Académie des Beaux Arts, exhibited some of his painting at the Art Exhibition in Rome in 1947. The Egyptian Ministry of Education bought his painting "The Crucified," while two of his paintings, "The Young Shepherd" and "Welcoming the Virgin," earned him high recognition.

Zakī Amīn was a well-known cartoonist. Many Egyptian magazines in the 1940's and the 50's used his work. He volunteered to work for *al-Kalīm,* and among others he created the character of "Abū-Ya'qūb" ("The Father of Jacob"), a symbol of the Karaite Jew (Pls. 5 and 10).

Nevertheless, one cannot claim that the community was rich in men of art and science.

---

32. *Al-Kalīm* No. 86 (16 October 1948).
33. *Al-Ittiḥād* No. 24 (26 March 1926).
34. *Al-Kalīm* No. 14 (1 September 1945).
35. *Al-Kalīm* No. 86 (16 October 1948).

Leading Men:

In such a community, how are we to define a leading man? Rich? Well educated in the faith? Holding a high government position? A well known professional man or businessman?

It is impossible to mention all of them and even difficult to try to choose some of them. However I felt it would be appropriate if I mentioned a few from various families.

The Līshaʿ Family:

Dāʾūd Isḥāq Līshaʿ (1844-1919): head of the community in the last quarter of the 19th century. A very well known businessman, one of the early gabbāys of the synagogue Rab-Simḥāh, and a member of the first religious council in 1901.

Murād Farag Līshaʿ: will be mentioned in a separate part.

David Zakī Līshaʿ (1900-): served in many organizations in his youth, and was one of the owners of one of the best known and finest jewelry shops. One of the few who helped build the synagogues of Mosheh al-Darʿī, and its only gabbāy. Co-author of *al-Murshid al-Amīn*.

Dr. Elie Bārūkh Līshaʿ (1901-1973): a noted eye specialist, often sought out by the Arab aristocracy. An expert in tropical eye diseases.

The Masʿūdah Family:

Ibrāhīm Elīyāhū Masʿūdah (1862-1927): a successful businessman, benefactor to both communities, the Karaite and the Rabbanite. It was mainly due to his effort that the synagogue al-Darʿī was built.

Yūsuf Bārūkh Masʿūdah (1876-1941): a well known lawyer, served his community as a member of the religious council. He was the executive chairman of the Rabbanite "Bēt Yisrael," and was known for his support to the Zionist movement.

Khiḍre Yefet Masʿūdah (1885-1965): Chairman of the religious council more than once. A benevolent man, he and his brother ʿAbbās had a well-known law firm in Cairo.

Dr. Farīd Masʿūdah (1890-1985): among the early physicians in Egypt and in the community. He also earned a higher medical degree from England. Served the community for more than 50 years.

The Levi Family:

Raḥmīn Farag Levi (1892-1947): a successful and philanthropic businessman. Headed several organizations and helped many of them financially.

Dr. Salīm Ibrāhīm Levi (1884-1941): was in the first graduating class of the new School of Medicine. Was considered among the leading general practitioners. Served his community as a physician and as a member of the Temporary Committee in 1936.

Victor Levi (1909-): active since his youth in many organizations. A member of the religious council for many years, he was the first to call for a set policy in regard to the needed projects. He was a high-ranking engineer in the central government, when he was forced to retire. When he came to the U.S.A. he worked as an engineer in the R.C.A. Company.

Ibrāhīm Ḥusnī (1908-), and his brother Kamāl Ḥusnī (1910-1984): both were very active in most of the community organizations. *Al-Shubbān al-Qarrā'īn* and *al-Kalīm* depended on their efforts. In the 1930's they helped acting groups of the Rabbanite Schools with their end-of-the-year activities.

The Menashah Family:

Mūsā Ibrāhīm Menashah (1878-1956): among the members of the first Karaite religious council of 1901. A well known *ḥazzān, gabbāy* and *mohel.* Helped in the rebuilding of the synagogue of Rab Simḥah in 1948. Was its *gabbāy* for many years.

Dr. Ibrāhīm Mūsā Menashah (1900-): among the early physicians of the community, he graduated from a medical school in Germany. During the 1950's he was the private physician of the royal family of Libya.

Zakī Menashah (1900-1957): a dedicated member of the religious council for many years. Organized and saved the docuementary treasures of the community. Served as a secretary of the religious council for many years, during which time he was responsible for preparing the yearly budget.

Various branches of the Marzūq Family:

Yūsuf Mūsā Marzūq (1884-1968): an authority on the faith and the Hebrew language. A successful businessman. His patience and understanding helped to narrow the gap among members of the community whose opinion differed. Refused to be the chief ḥākhām of the Karaite community in Israel but accepted the post of its religious consultant.

Yūsuf Ibrāhīm Marzūq (1882-1952): a member of the religious council, then the deputy of the community for many years. At times, especially in the 1930's, he was the only authority. At times he served the community well, but used funds illegally and had to resign.

Mattātiah Nissīn Marzūq (1894-1952): a very active member, treasurer, and head of *Hebrāt 'Ezrāt,* and in this capacity he served his community well. A very successful businessman.

Dr. Mosheh Marzūq (1925-1955): graduated young as a physician (1947), worked in the Jewish Hospital as a surgeon and became well known. A dedicated Zionist, he lost his life in 1955 defending his cause (the Levon affair).

The Mangūbī Family:

Ḥākhām Shabbethāi Mangūbī (1836-1906): see Chief Rabbis.

Jacques Lieto Mangūbī (1898-1977): grandson of Ḥākhām Mangūbī, was one of the founders and officers of the Bank Miṣr. A member of many organizations since 1917, served his community as member, secretary and chairman of the religious council for many years. Came to the United States in 1966. A short time before his death he was able to establish a Karaite community in Chicago.

The al-Qudsī Family:

Ḥākhām Mosheh al-Qudsī (1810-1905): see Chief Rabbis.

Yūsuf Mūsā al-Qudsī (1850-1931): son of Ḥākhām Mosheh. A very successful and benevolent man. Helped the community with its real estate in Jerusalem, as he himself once lived there. Was a leader in the community but never tried to be a member of any organization or even the religious council.

Murād Mūsā al-Qudsī (1919-): Principal of the Karaite Schools for twelve years (1944-1956), and "Les Alliances Juives" for two years (1957-1959). A member and chairman of many Karaite organizations from 1944 to 1959. Member and secretary of the Karaite religious council for 10 years. Chaired the real estate, the welfare, the maṣṣōt, and the *'Arīkhāh* committees where his efforts were most successful.

The 'Abd-Allah Family:

Farag 'Abd-Allah (1841-1922): the head of the 'Abd-Allah family. Was the chairman of the Egyptian hallmark of gold and silver for over 20 years, until his death. Was among the leading circumcisers and cantors in the community, a talent shared by members of the 'Abd-Allah family.

Ya'qūb Farag 'Abd-Allah (1881-1943): chaired the Karaite religious council from 1941 until he died. A very successful businessman, known for his outstanding ability as a cantor and a circumciser. In fact he was known as *'Abd-Allah al-mohel.*

From the Aṣlān-Kohen-family:

Elīyāhū Ya'qūb Aṣlān (1809-1967): served his community from his youth as a member of the different organizations. Excellent violinist, headed the very well known orchestra of *al-Ittiḥād* and the Young Men's Karaite Associations during the 1930's and early 1940's. Was a high-ranking engineer in the central government, and an active member of the Karaite religious council.

Farag Ya'qūb Aṣlān (1813-1982): A dynamic person. Served in many organizations, but was known for his activities and innovations in the "Benevolent Association for the Marriage of the Poor Israelite Karaite Girls." Member of the Karaite council where he cooperated with Murād al-Kodsī to reform the internal system of governing the community.

From various families:

Mūsā Murād Mūsā (1905-): served his community from his early youth. Was member and chairman of *al-Shubbān al-Isrā'īliyīn al-Qarrā'īn*. A zealous advocate of reforms, he often paid for projects out of his own pocket. Advocated mass *'Aliyah* to Israel.

Yūsuf Murād (1911-1981): completed his primary education in the Karaite Schools. Finished his higher education in the Egyptian University and graduated with high honours. Obtained his Ph.D. in 1947. In 1951 was sent for post-doctoral study to King's College in New Castle, England. In 1962 was promoted to professor of solid state physics. He initiated and supervised the semiconductor division in the National Research Center in Cairo. Wrote over 35 technical papers which were published in recognized international journals.

'Abd-al-'Azīz 'Abd-al-Wāḥid (1895-1973): was the chairman of the religious council during the 1950's. He and his brother Murād were called the "Gold Kings."

Nagīb and Thābit Khiḍr brothers (1902-1975), (1906-1961): both owned the largest factory of silver and silverplated wares. For some time supplied the mosques of Saudi Arabia with ornamental items.

Yūsuf Farag Hayyīnah (1898-1954): a successful businessman. Was one of the leading cantors and ritual slaughterers. His father and grandfather were the leading *shoḥetīm* in the public slaughterhouse. He himself was an authority on the faith. He was a self-educated person. He liked to read and widen his knowledge, but more importantly he liked to share his knowledge with others. For this reason he always wrote in *al-Kalīm* and always lectured in the synagogues or in other places.

Yūsuf Ibrāhīm Yomtōb (1878-1953): a walking encyclopedia on the faith, he was a *ḥazzān* and a *shoḥet*. In the late 1950's he helped *"Ahavāt Torah"* conduct classes for those who were interested in becoming *hazzānīm, shoḥetīm,* or *mohelīm*. Besides Arabic he spoke Hebrew, French, English, Italian and Greek. He taught Hebrew in the Karaite Schools, and was the head teacher in *"Ahavāt Torah"* classes.

Farag Mūsā al-Sirgānī (1850-1920): was a *ḥākhām, ḥazzān,* and very well educated in the faith. One of the twelve who formed the first religious council in 1901.

Mūsā Farag al-Sirgānī (1874-1949): learned much from his father, but was also well-educated in his own way. For almost ten years he was the principal of the Karaite Schools. During the 1940's he published in *al-Kalīm* the translation of Jacob Mann's book, *Texts and Studies*. Besides Arabic and Hebrew, he spoke French, English, German, Spanish and Greek.

Salīm Farag Shamuel (1889-1948): he and his brother formed the "Shamuel Chemical Company," a well-known company that conducted business throughout Europe and the United States. A benevolent leader in the community, he served as a member of the religious council and as a gabbāy of Rab-Simḥāh synagogue.

Amīn Barakāt al-Gamīl (1897-1961): a high-ranking employee in the central government. Was truly productive in the field of literature. The pages of *al-Ittiḥād, al-Shubbān* and *al-Kalīm* are full of his *zagal,* poetry, and short stories.

Mūsā Pessaḥ (1916-1987): a successful businessman. Had the means to live in a fashionable neighborhood, but preferred to live in al-Khurunfish near al-Ḥārah to be near the residents of al-Ḥārah who needed his help. Used to give financial help and moral support to poor Karaite students to continue their higher education.

Yūsuf Farag al-Ṭanānī (1900-1955): was the clerk of the Karaite Bēt-Dīn for over 20 years. Served his community in this capacity with dedication. He was the backbone of its activities, be they circumcision, engagement, marriage, death or delivering the donations by himself to the needy. An authority on family names and their genealogy. An excellent Hebrew teacher and a master in the Karaite way of chanting the Torah.

Undoubtedly there are many others who should have been mentioned here, but the pages of this book could not possibly accommodate the names of everyone.

Members of the 'Ezrāt ha-Betulōt Association (1931). From right to left, sitting: Lieto Farag Masʿūdah, ʿAbd al-ʿAzīz ʿAbd al-Wāḥid, Mattatiah Rāṣōn al-Sirgānī, Murād Farag, Yaʿqūb Farag ʿAbd-Allah. David Zaki Līshaʿ, Jaques Lieto Mangūbī. Second row: Yūsuf Mūsā Marzūq, Yūsuf ʿAbd al-Wāḥid, Raḥmīn Farag Levi, Amīn Barkāt al-Gamīl, Ḥabīb Farag Ṣāliḥ, Yūsuf Dāʾūd Ṣāliḥ, Lieto Yūsuf al-Qudsī. Third row: Mattatiah Nissīm Marzūq, Yūsuf Farag Līshaʿ, Mūsā Mūrad Mūsā, Mūsā Masʿūdah, Zakī Mūsā Darwīsh.

Some members of the Israelite Karaite Union Association at a gathering in the home of one of the members. (1934)

Some members of the Israelite Karaite Union Association at a summer camp in Ra's al-Barr, a summer resort near the city of Dumiāṭ. (1935)

Some members of the Young Men's Israelite Karaite Association in a trip to al-Qanāṭir al-Khayriyah (a park north of Cairo) 1937

Volunteer teachers and girls of the "Benevolent Workshop for Girls" (1945)

Some members of the Young Men's Israelite Karaite Association in a trip to Ḥilwān (a suburb south of Cairo) 1955.

Some members of the Young Men's Israelite Karaite Association in a trip to al-Qanāṭir al-Khayriyah. (1955)

A family gathering of members of the Young Men's Israelite Karaite Association, 1948, in the house of Bārūkh Masʿūdah (in white shirt). Sitting in the middle are Mūsā Murād Mūsā (chairman), Zakī Menashah to his left (vice-chairman), and Kamāl Ḥusnī to his right (editor of al-Kalīm). Standing from right to left are: Elie Masʿūdah, Murād al-Qudsī, Elie ʿAbd allah, Elie Amīn Līshaʿ, Benoit Masʿūdah, Farag al-Qudsī, Badīʿ Ḥusnī and Ibrāhīm Ḥusnī.

Thābit Ṣāliḥ

Farag 'Abd-Allah

Ibrāhīm Elīyāhū Mas'ūdah

Ya'qūb Farag 'Abd-Allah

Yūsuf Ibrāhīm Marzūq

Mūsā Ibrāhīm Menashah

Yūsuf Farag al-Ṭanānī

Dr. Mosheh Marzūq

Yūsuf Mūsā Marzūq

Yūsuf Murād

Thābit Khiḍr

Zakī Menashah

Dr. Elie B. Līsha'

Victor Levi

David Zakī Līsha'

Dr. Marco Sinānī

{حساب الجمعية الخيرية للمرضى}

تقدم هذا الحساب الآتي من الجمعية الخيرية للمرضى بالطائفة الى اللجنة الملية بالحاخاخانة للعلم به
وندرجه بالتهذيب فنحن لهذا ندرجه وهو كما يأتي

كشف

بيان حساب صندوق الجمعية الخيرية للمرضى بالطائفة من شهر اكتوبر سنة ١٨٩٧ الى آخر سنة ١٩٠١

اصله

مليم	جنيه	
١٦٨	٣١٠	محصل من المشتركين لغاية سنة ١٩٠١
٠٢٨	٦٤٢ —	تبرعاً لغاية السنة المذكورة
٠١٩	٨٦٥ —	توفيرات من الاطباء لغاية السنة المذكورة
٠٠٩	٨١٧ —	فوائد وارباحات لغاية السنة المذكورة

مليم	جنيه
٢٢٦	٦٣٥ —

منصرف

	مليم	جنيه	
	٠٠٦	١١٧ —	من اكتوبر الى ديسمبر سنة ١٨٩٧
٨٩٨	٠٣٠	٠٤٦	سنة
٨٩٩	٠٣٦	٨٠٠	سنة
٩٠٠	٠٣٦	٢٥٦	سنة
٩٠١	٠٥٢	٠٩٦ —	سنة

| ١٦١ | ٣١٦ |

بــــاقي

مليم	جنيه	
٠٦٥	٣١٩	باقي بصندوق الجمعية لغاية ديسمبر سنة ١٩٠١

تحريراً في ٣٣ يناير سنة ٩٠٢

امضا
سكرتير الجمعية
فرج يوسف صالح

PLATE 1: Al-Gamʿiyah al-Khayriyah lil-Marḍā. The Benevolent Association for the Sick. The first recorded activities by any association in the community. The budget for the period from October 1897 until December 1901.

Revenues: 226 Egyptian pounds.
Expenditures: 161 Egyptian pounds. The Egyptian pound equaled $5.00 at the time.
al-Tahdhīb, no. 24, 1st year, 12 January 1902, p. 102.

PLATE 2:

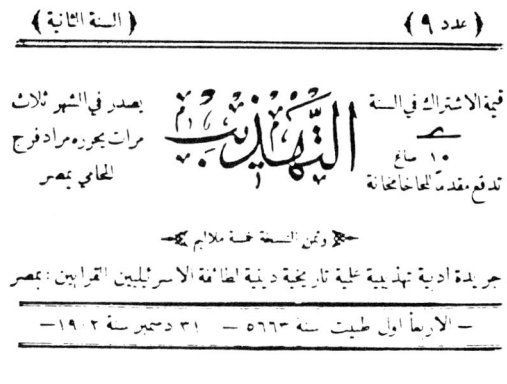

al-Tahdhīb: 12 August 1901 to 1904.

al-Irshād: 15 May 1908 to 21 March 1909.

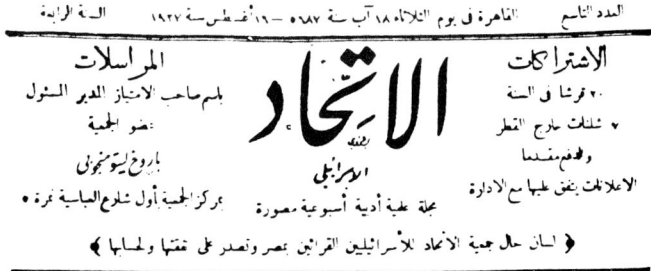

al-Ittiḥād: 20 April 1924 to 1930.

Page 2 of the printed program.

PLATE 3: The cover of the printed program of the festival celebrating Yom Purim, 8 March 1936.

PLATE 4: *Al-Shubbān al-Qarrā'īn*, no. 8, 1st year, 2 August 1937. The poem is written by Murād Farag congratulating King Fārūq of Egypt on becoming a king.

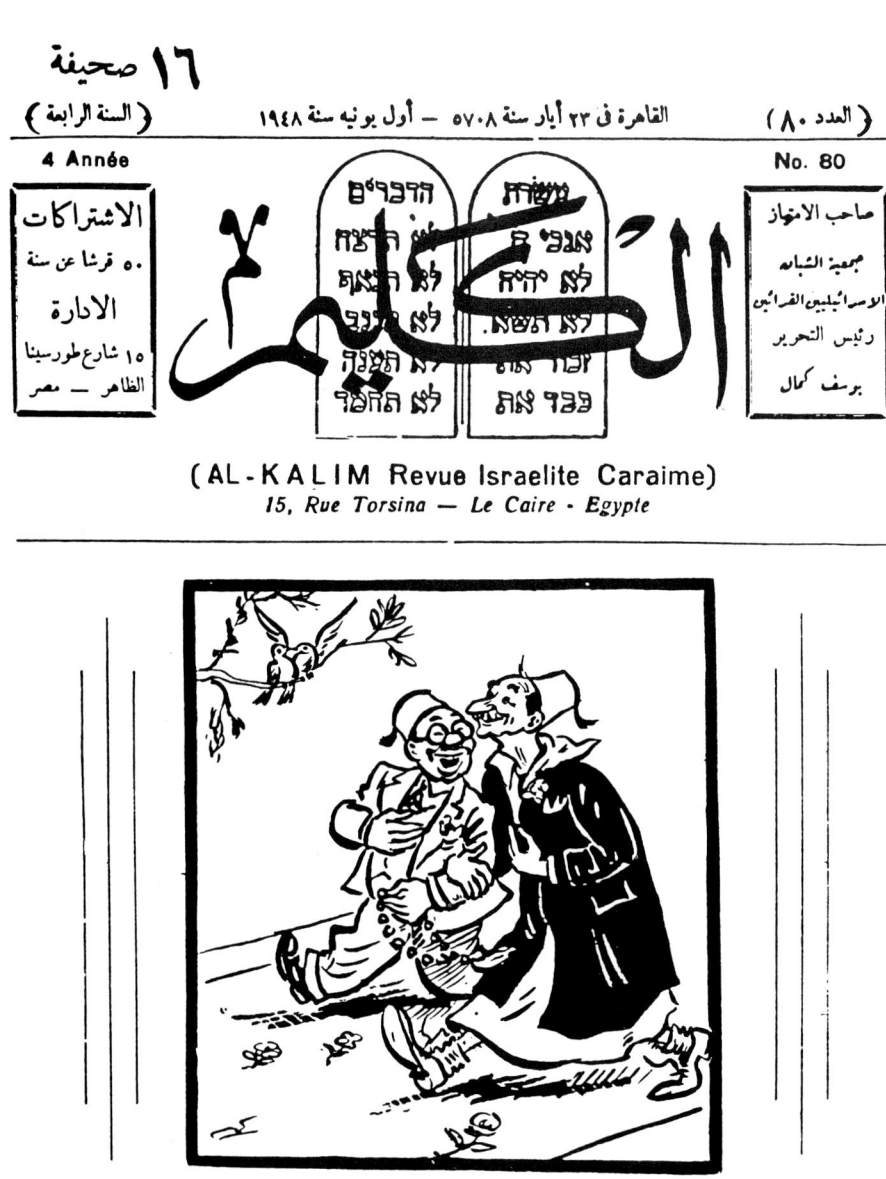

PLATE 5: During the Arab-Israeli War of 1948 anti-Jewish feeling was at its peak. A good number of newspapers and magazines wrote about the subject calling for understanding. A few weeks before bombarding the Jewish neighborhood (Rabbanite and Karaite), *al-Kalīm* cartoonist, Zakī Amīn, drew this cartoon of al-Miṣrī effendi, symbol of the Egyptian, walking hand in hand with abū-Yaʿqūb, symbol of the Karaite. The title is "Two persons but one heart."

جمعية مساعدة الفقيرات على الزواج
الاسرائيليين القرائين بمصر
شارع العباسية رقم ٨ بالقاهرة

הברת עזרת זווג העניית
לישראלים הקראים במצרים

Ass. de Bienfaissance pour le Mariage des
Pauvres Jaunes Filles Israélite Caraïme du Caire

مسجلة بوزارة الشئون الاجتماعية برقم ٢١٠ القاهرة

קחו נשים והולידו בנים ובנות וקחו לבניכם נשים ואת
בנותיכם תנו לאנשים ותלדנה בנים ובנות
ורבו שם ואל תמעטו

خذوا نساء وأولدوا بنين وبنات وخذوا لبنيكم نساء واعطوا بناتكم لرجال
يملكون بنين وبنات واكثروا هناك ولا تقلوا

(أربا ٢٩:٦)

נותן לרש אין מחסור ומעלים עיניו רב־מארות

من يعطى الفقير لا يحتاج ومن يحجب عنه عينيه لعنات كثيرة

(أمثال ٢٨:٢٧)

تقرير

مجلس الادارة عن العام الثامن للجمعية

ومعه حسابات الإيرادات والمصروفات والميزانية العمومية

حضرات الكرام

الشكر والحمد لله وحده واجب على الجمعية ، فبإرادته وقوته عاشت الجمعية ثمان سنوات جاهدة مكافحة فى سبيل مساعدة الفقيرات على الزواج . فباسمه نعمل وننجح راجين مبتهلين من أعماق قلوبنا إلى الله سبحانه وتعالى ونضرع اليه أن يديم علينا رضاه راجين دوام توفيقه فيما نحن بسبيله من خدمة طائفتنا العزيزة فى ظل العرش المفدى .

مقدمة

حـبنا من هذه المقدمة أن نذكر أن نسبة الفقيرات فى الطائفة كبير جداً بالقياس إلى غيرها من الطوائف . وهذه النسبة إن أوحت بشئ ، فبأن يكون جهادنا فى علاج هذه الناحية أضعاف نظيره فى الطوائف الأخرى

لقد نهضت الطائفة ـ محمد الله ـ نهضة مباركة وألقى إليها الزمن كثيراً من أسباب الطموح والرقى والتقدم . وهذا هو المجتمع الذى نشق لاـمداه ونعمل لرفع يحمل بين جوانبه الكثير من الفقيرات يحن إلى مساكن ومعــال الأغنياء. تسائلنهم عن مساعدة لزواجن مستعطفات لمن لستر أعراضهن . فهذه الشائبة التى أصبت الطائفة جدير بأن تكون الهدف الأول للمصلحين والعاملين على النهوض بها ـ يعملون على مساعدتهن وتعضيدهن ليخلقوا منهن عائلات صالحة .

PLATE 6: The first page of the Annual Report of the Association for Helping Poor Girls Get Married.

al-Kalīm, no. 229, 11th year, 16 June 1955.

PLATE 7: A needed project. Why was it forgotten?

The whole *Zagal* consists of 37 verses. I chose here to show 12 verses only. The first two are considered an introduction. In the next five, the writer talks about the need for a school and a synagogue. The last five urged members of the community to unite and work together.

The *Zagal* was published in *al-Ittiḥād,* Vol. 1, no. 3, on 18 May 1924. At that time the community was in need of a new building for the schools and of a new synagogue to be built in 'Abbāsiyah.

The *Zagal* is written by Zakī Ḥayyīm Ṣaliḥ.

مشروع مفيد ـ ليه اتنسى؟
بقلم حضرة الاديب الفاضل زكي افندي حييم صالح

عندي كلام شرحه يطول   بس اللي يسمع مني مين
أنا بدي ازعـق واقـول   ع اللي ف ضميري ياقرايين

نا الكنيس والمدرسه   ده شيء ضروري وعتم
مشروع مفيد ـ ليه اتنسى؟   دائماً عليـه بنتوحم
هي رجالنا مفاسه ؟   ولا الكنيس أمر محرم ؟
هي القهـاوى مقـدسـه؟   شي عجيب موش قادر اقهم
في الهاس بنضيع تاول   والجـد دايـع؟ فيـه خايبين
عندي كلام شرحه يطول   . . . . . .

ياقرايين شـدوا حيلكم   وهيا بينا للعمل
مش ممكن الحظ يجيلكم   وانتم كدهف راحو كسل
للاتحاد اظهروا ميلكم   وانتم تنولوا الامـل
ليلي نهاري بدعيلكم   يمكن دعاي يتقبـل
يارب خلينـا ننول   اللي ف بالنا نقي هايصين
عندي كلامي شرحه يطول   . . . . . .

240

PLATE 8: "Let's Work"

This *Zagal* was published in *al-Kalīm*, no. 58, 3rd year, on 1 July 1947.

The writer urges all members of the community to work together and to give generously so that the responsible members will be able to build a center for cultural and social activities, to build a synagogue in Heliopolis, to build a kindergarten, and finally to take care of the elderly who need care, for children who need much attention and for the poor who need help.

The *Zagal* was written by Amīn Bārūkh al-Gamīl

هيــــا الى العمل

يا طايفة قوى صحى النوم   بزياده همــز وكز ولوم
آدى المشاريع صارت كــوم   عاوزه الهمم والجهود م اليوم
قوى قلوبنا يا رحمن
الحالة خفت عقدتها   آن الأوان جت فرصتها
خطوة كان نخلص منها   ونشوف ضياما وفايدتها
هلت علينا يا اخوان
وف هليوبوليس أعطتنا   الشركة أرض لمعبدنا
وآدى كرم ابى جالا   مبلغ سخى فيه تشجيعنا
يا ربت قوام يجى الفرمان
بعدين ولازم نجمـع   وف حفلة كبرى تبرع
زى الأساس بعده ونشرع   فى رفع معبد فيه نسمع
ترتيل رسالة آل عمران (١)
عاوزين كمان روضة أطفال   وعبادة كبرى عال العال
ومؤسسات ألوان واشكال   تحيى النفوس تحيى الآمال
تحيى كان جسم الحرمان
ياما شيوخ عاوزه عنايه   ياما نفوس عاوزه هدايه
ياما عيال عاوزه رعايه   ياما نساء عاوزه جرايه
يا الله ابذلوا شىء م الاحسان
نفسى أشاهد ف البستان   الورد فتح ع الاغصان
نعنش وفرش النعمان   منا وخلاء فاق مفتان
طالب يماون ف البنيان
يا بخت من وكل جوعان   ولا ستر جسم العريان
ولا تبرع للعميان   ولا تعطف ع الظمآن
كله طريق جنة رضوان

أمين باروخ الجميل

(١) عمران والد موسى وهارون عليهما السلام

(فنانونا في معرض التصوير والزخارف)

ان من زار معرض هذا العام الذي نظمته جمعية محبي الفنون الجميلة تحت رعاية حضرة صاحب الجلالة الملك أثناء الشهر الماضي لا بد انه شاهد ثلاث صور استلفت نظر الزائرين بدقتها عرضها حضرة زميلنا ابراهيم افندي داود صالح أحد أفراد طائفتنا الحائزين على دبلوم في الفنون الجميلة وقد حازت صورته الاولى التي تمثل (الحب الامومي) في شخص امرأة وطنية فقيرة تحنو إلى طفلها وهو يرضع اعجاب الزائرين واشترتها حكومتنا المصرية بالثمن المحدد لها وقدره اثنا عشر جنيها بناء على توصية لجنة تحكيم مكونة من كبار رجال الفنون الجميلة في مصر وثانية معروضاته صورة (الشيخ المقرئ) والثالثة صورة (البواب)

فنهنئ زميلنا القدير بمجهوده الفني الذي لاق تشجيعا وتعضيدا من لجنة المعرض

PLATE 9: Our Artists in the Art Exhibition
Those who visited the art exhibition must have noticed the good work of Ibrāhīm Dā'ūd Ṣāliḥ. The artist had won first prize for his painting "Motherly Love." The Egyptian government bought the painting at the judges' request.
al-Ittiḥād, no. 26, 1st year, 5 April 1925.

PLATE 10: In the middle of the 1940's the Religious Council was in need of money to carry out new projects.

This cartoon shows a caricature of a well known rich member of the Community saying: "Take out my soul but take no money out of my pocket," The cartoon is by Zakī Amīn.

al-Kalīm no. 68, 3rd year, 1 September 1947, p. 13.

Some comic cartoons by Zaki Amin that *al-Kalim* used to publish.

The Karaite Jews of Egypt

Murād Farag Līsha' (1867-1956)

Murād Farag Līsha' was a writer and a poet who stood as a leader and a legal authority in the Karaite community.

The Līsha' family was a prominent Karaite family, and as his surname suggests, he was a member of this large family. The son of a goldsmith, at the time a trade common among Karaites, Murād Farag refused to follow that line of work, and instead educated himself in Arabic, Hebrew, and jurisprudence.

In 1901, at the age of 34, he was elected a charter member of the first Karaite religious council in Cairo. He served his community as a member and as a chairman of the religious council for more than 30 years, until he chose not to run for re-election. Until he died, however, he remained the consultant for the Karaite Bēt-Dīn.

During that long period many legal questions were raised, such as the question of changing the faith from Karaism to Rabbanism and vice-versa, the definition of the word *mamzer,* the law of incest and others. Many members of the community, as well as its religious leaders, entered into a lengthy discussion to reach a solution to such problems. Murād Farag himself had many discussions with Ḥākhām Abrāhām Kohen (1920-1933) and Ḥākhām Tobiah Babovitch (1934-1956). They used to write to each other, and sometimes their opinion was published in the community periodicals, *al-Ittiḥād* and *al-Kalīm*. He felt that these discussions would lead to better understanding and he always asked his "opponents" to base their findings on well established opinions, as well as on well known facts, as he himself used to do so. In a few cases the discussion reached a point that presented a threat to the community, and in such cases the Karaite religious council intervened. In the late 1920's the whole community got involved in a legal issue which involved whether a baby born should be related to his Karaite mother or to his non-Karaite father. Based on facts taken from the Torah and the consensus among the sages of the faith, Murād Farag gave his opinion that the child should be related to his Karaite mother. At about the same time, another issue was raised when a certain Karaite wanted to marry the sister of the husband of his sister (which related to the law of incest). The religious council, led by Murād Farag, supported Ḥākhām Kohen when he advised on the legality of the matter according to the rules of the

Eupatoria convention of 1910,[36] with which many members of the community disagree.

In all his arguments Murād Farag never resorted to demagogy. He was known for his clear-cut documentation. He had the knowledge and the courage to discuss his views in the open although they were not that of the majority. Because of his views on these legal matters, he was always at odds with some members of the community, and often with members of the strong organization, al-Ittiḥād al-Isrā'īlī.

For almost three years, from 1924 until 1927, members of this group lashed out at him publicly on the pages of al-Ittiḥād. However, when in time an understanding was reached, Murād Farag was noble and generous enough to forgive and not to deprive the magazine, al-Ittiḥād, of his articles and poetry.

Murād Farag was a writer and a poet. During his lifetime he wrote more than 30 books. His first one was *A Treatise on Lawful Money.* That was in 1898, and he continued writing until 1950, when he wrote his last book, *The Book of Job* (Pls. 1-4).

In his writing Murād Farag advocated kindness, love, understanding and cooperation between individuals, as well as between communities.

Among the books he wrote, three of them were to defend Jews and Judaism: al-Nahlist, al-Yuhūdī Ma'nā wa 'Aqīdah and al-Qudsiyāt. Al-Qudsiyāt in Arabic and in its translation into Hebrew, ha-Qudsiyot, contains verses and articles dedicated to defend the Jews in Palestine. In the preface to al-Qudsiyāt he wrote: "These verses and articles reflect the love of peace in my heart for Palestine-bilād al-Quds-. It is a gift to literature, to justice, and to fairness. I hope that those who oppose the Jews [in Palestine] will not reject the book, will think about it and reconsider, will work for brotherhood and forsake hostility. May God grant us success."

He wrote al-Yahūdiyah to defend Karaism against the false accusations of Ephraim Deinard, a Rabbanite from the Crimea. Murād Farag wrote the book in such a tactful way that a well known Rabbanite rabbi, Ḥayyim Qīqī, sent him a letter of praise.

Murād Farag produced "a long series of scholarly works all in Arabic. Some dealt with modern Egyptian law,[37] but most of them were devoted to Biblical exegesis, Karaite law, Hebrew grammar, comparative Arabic-Hebrew philology, and kindred subjects."[38]

In 1937 Murād Farag published his third volume of *Multaqā al-Lughatayn.* Dr. I. A. Edham Litt. D. Hon., Ph.D., Sc.D. (Moscow), Vice-President of the Rus-

---

36. Minutes of 8 April 1926.
37. The Egyptian Government ordered the use of *Da'āwī Waḍ' al-Yad,* "Claim to Possession," in the School of Law. *Al-Tahdhīb* No. 38, 29 May 1902.
38. *Revue des études juives,* "Leon Nemoy" Publication subventionnée par le Centre national de la Recherche scientifique et le Fond social juif unifié, tome CXXXV, Janvier-septembre 1976, fascicule 1-3.

sian Soviet Institute for Islamic Studies, wrote its introduction. From it I quote:

"These examples give a real knowledge of the analysis of the author concerning the origin of roots in the Hebrew and Arabic languages. I refer scholars, specially linguistics and Orientalists, to p. 125, in which the author deals with the word יוֹדֵעַ, to p. 42, in which he deals with the word גּוּלְשִׁים; and to p. 282, in which he deals with the word לְהֵם, since they will find important views, analysis and illuminating suggestions.

I have selected these examples from the third volume in order to show the author's masterly faculty in comparative language study.

Finally, I would candidly emphasize without the least bias that this standard work has never been preceded in its originality by any other author let alone excelled, and that it is destined to rank as one of the classical productions of the Arabic language in the field of comparative etymology."

—I.A. **Edham**

As early as 1900 Murād Farag started to write poetry which he published a year later in *al-Tahdhīb*. In 1902 he published his first *dīwān*, followed by his second one in 1924, and a third one in 1929. In 1935 he published his fourth and last one. Yet, until a few months before he died he never stopped writing. He wrote in *al-Shubbān*, *al-Kalīm*, and in *al-Shams*, which was published by a Rabbanite. In fact he prepared a fifth *dīwān* for publication, along with the fourth volume of *Multaqā al-Lughatayn al-'Arabiyah wal-'Ibriyah*. But for reasons beyond his control they never saw the light.[39]

About his poetry, Leon Nemoy wrote: "It is, therefore, very much worthwhile to find one Karaite Arabic poet, albeit a quite modern one, whose output is voluminous enough and whose command of prosody and style is solid enough to stand comparison with the *dīwān* of Muslim poets"[40] (Pl. 5a, b, and c).

Murād Farag was an exceptional person. The fact is that he never had any schooling; nevertheless, he reached a degree of education and knowledge that was the envy of many.

In 1902, while working as a legal counsel to the reigning Khudaywī, a certain Hayyīm Kahānah, a Rabbanite Jew from Port Said, was indicted on the charge of ritual murder. At the request of a Rabbanite official, Murād Farag defended Kahānah and proved his innocence[41] (Pl. 6).

---

39. In 1952 Murād Farag gave Dr. Ibrāhīm Menashah, a Karaite physician, well informed in Arabic and Hebrew, two manuscripts: *Dīwān Murād*, volume 5, and *Multaqā al-Lughatayn*, volume 4. For reasons beyond his control, Dr. Menashah left the country unexpectedly. Dr. Menashah's library, including the two manuscripts, was stored in the second floor of Mosheh al-Dar'ī synagogue. Until today no one has been able to find *Dīwān Murād*, volume 5.
40. *Revue de études juives*. (see note 38).
41. *Al-Tahdīb* No. 8, 21 December 1902, No. 9, 31 December 1902. Jacob Landau, *Jews in 19th Century Egypt*, pp. 294-295.

During his youth, in the 1920's, Murād Farag was well known and active in both the Rabbanite and the Karaite communities. At that time, too, there was mutual rapprochement between the Egyptian government and the Zionist movement, and in that regard Murād Farag was very active.[42]

In 1922, when Egypt became an independent state, King Fu'ād nominated Murād Farag as a member of the committee to draft the new constitution, which was completed in April 1923.

On 18 June 1956, Murād Farag died at the age of 89. In characteristic fashion, he requested in his will that his funeral be as simple as possible. His only son, Tawfīq, fulfilled his father's last wish.

---

42. Jaques Mangūbī, the chairman of the Karaite religious council for fifteen years reported that Murād Farag was among those who were chosen to mediate between the Arabs and the Zionists.

PLATE 1: Books written by Murād Farag. All except two have been published.

﴾- المؤلفــات ﴿-

Risālah fī al-Amwāl al-Qānūniyah: "A Treatise on Lawful Money."

رسالة فى الاموال القانونية

Al-Magmūʿ fī Sharḥ al-Shurūʿ: "The Complete in Interpreting the Laws.

المجموع فى شرح الشروع

Al-Tahdhīb: An Arabic magazine published weekly from 1901 to 1904.

التهذيب

Al-Nahlist: A novel defending Judaism.

رواية النهلست

Maqālāt Murād: Articles written by Murād Farag.

مقالات مراد

Dīwān Murād: Volumes 1,2,3,4. Arabic poems.

ديوان مراد جزء ١ و ٢ و ٣ و ٤

Daʿāwī Waḍʿ al-Yad: "Claims to Possessions."

دعاوى وضع اليد طبعة أولى وثانية

Al-Furūq al-Qānūniyah: "Distinctions and Differences."

الفروق القانونية

Shiʿār al-Khiḍr: A summarized Arabic translation of *Adderet Elīyāyhū.*

شعار الخضر

Al-Quarrāʿūn wal-Rabbānūn: [History and Differences between] The Karaites and the Rabbanites.

القراؤن

Al-Yahūdiyah: A novel in which Murād Farag defended Karaism.

اليهودية

Al-Qudsiyāt: Hebrew and Arabic poems and verses addressed to the Palestinians asking for their understanding and calling for peace with the Jews.

القدسيات عربية وعبرية

Ustādh al-ʿIbriyah: "Hebrew Grammar."

استاذ العبرية

248

Intiqād al-Kanz: "Commentary on al-Kanz."[1]   انتقاد كتاب الكنز العبرى العربى

Kalimah fī Mīrāth al-Bint: "The Daughter as Heir."   كلمة فى ميراث البنت

Tafsīr al-Tawrāh: "Commentary on the Torah." Volume 1.   تفسير التوراة الجزء الاول

Al-Shuʿarāʾ al-Yahūd al-ʿArab: "The Jewish Arab Poets."   الشعراء اليهود العرب

Multaqā al-Lughatayn al-ʿArabiyah wal-ʿIbriyah: "Comparative Arabic-Hebrew Philology" in 3 volumes. (The 4th is still in manuscript.)   ملتقى اللغتين الجزء الاول والثانى والثالث

Al-Aḥkām al-Sharʿiyah lil-Isrāʾīliyīn al-Qarrāʾīn: "Karaite Personal Status Code."   الاحكام الشرعية للاسرائليين القرائين

Rad Iʿtirāḍ: "Responsa and Brief Explanation of the Book al-Aḥkām."   رد اعتراض وشرح وجيز لكتابى الاحكام

Amthāl Sulaymān: "The Book of Proverbs."   امثال سليمن

Al-Yahūdī Maʿnā wa ʿaqīdah: "The Jew: Meaning and Belief." In this book Murād Farag defended Judaism.   اليهودى معنى وعقيدة

Ayyūb: "The Book of Job."   أيوب

Multaqā al-Lughatayn al-ʿarabiyah wal-ʿIbriyah, Volume 4 (to be published).   ملتقى اللغتين الجزء الرابع معد للطبع

Dīwān Murād, 5th volume (to be published).   ديوان مراد الجزء الخامس معد للطبع

---

1. In September 1927 the Egyptian Ministry of Education approved *Kitāb al-Kanz* as a Hebrew text book to be used by the students of the Higher Institute of Learning Arabic, *Kolliyat Dār al'Ulūm.* Murād Farag examined the book and found 124 linguistic errors. For this reason he wrote this commentary.

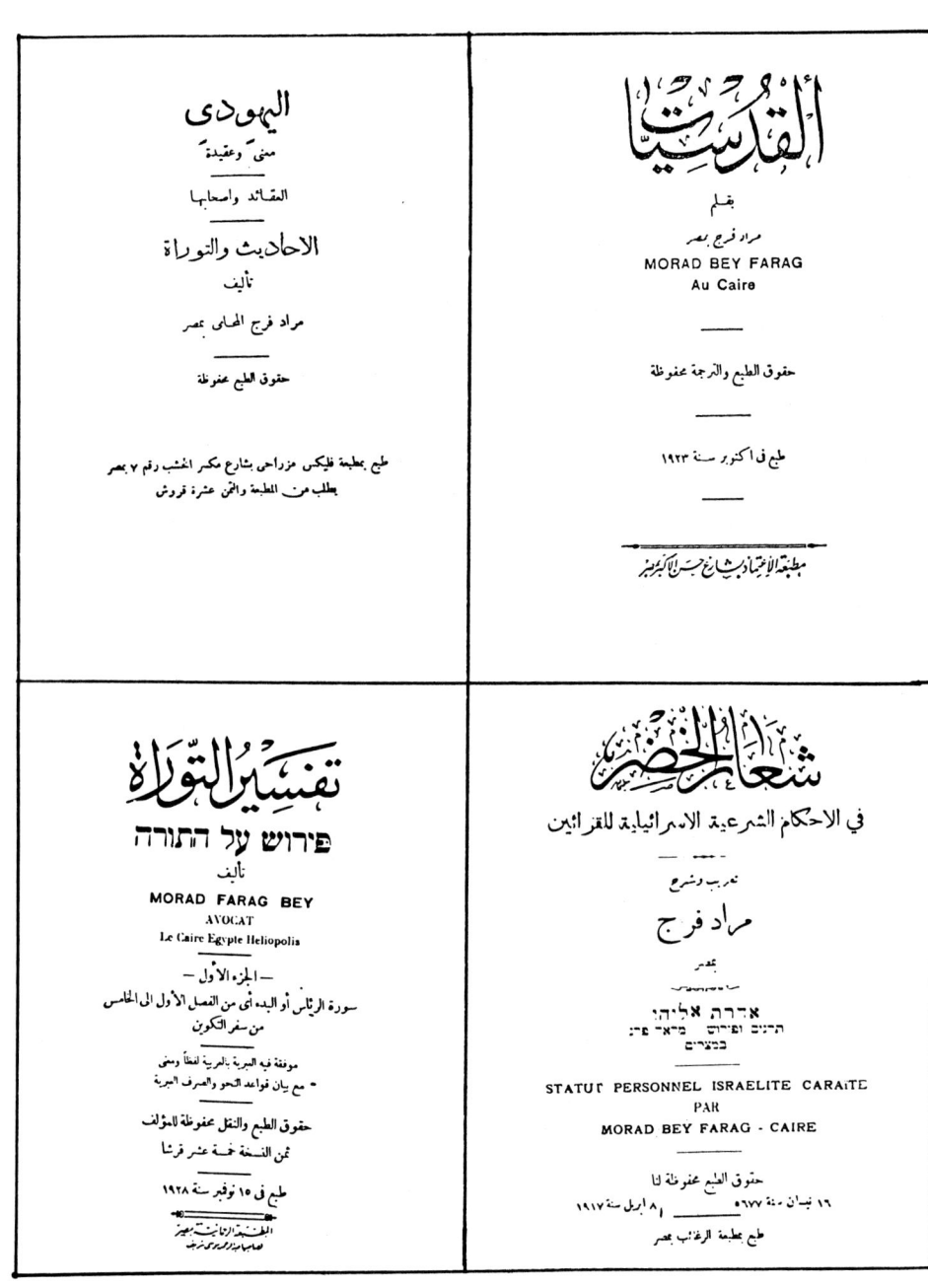

PLATE 2: Some of the books written by Murād Farag.

اليهودى
معنىً وعقيدةً
العقائد واصحابها
الاحاديث والتوراة
تأليف
مراد فرج المحامى بمصر
حقوق الطبع محفوظة
طبع بمطبعة فليكس مزراحى بشارع مكسر الخشب رقم ٧ بمصر
يطلب من المطبعة والثمن عشرة قروش
القدسيات
بقلم
مراد فرج بمصر
MORAD BEY FARAG
Au Caire
حقوق الطبع والترجمة محفوظة
طبع فى اكتوبر سنة ١٩٢٣
مطبعة الاعتماد بشارع حسن الاكبر بمصر
تفسير التوراة
פירוש על התורה
تأليف
MORAD FARAG BEY
AVOCAT
Le Caire Egypte Heliopolis
— الجزء الأول —
سورة الرئاس أو البدء أى من الفصل الأول الى الخامس
من سفر التكوين
موفقة فيه العبرية بالعربية لفظاً ومعنى
مع بيان قواعد النحو والصرف العبرية
حقوق الطبع والنقل محفوظة للمؤلف
ثمن النسخة خمسة عشر قرشا
طبع فى ١٥ نوفمبر سنة ١٩٢٨
المطبعة الرحمانية بمصر
لصاحبها محمد رمزى فرج
شعار الخضر
في الاحكام الشرعية الاسرائيلية للقرائين
تعريب وشرح
مراد فرج
بمصر
אדרת אליהו
תרגום ופירוש מראד פרג:
במצרים
STATUT PERSONNEL ISRAELITE CARAITE
PAR
MORAD BEY FARAG - CAIRE
حقوق الطبع محفوظة لنا
١٦ نيسان سنة ٥٦٧٧ ـــــ ٨ ابريل سنة ١٩١٧
طبع بمطبعة الرغائب بمصر

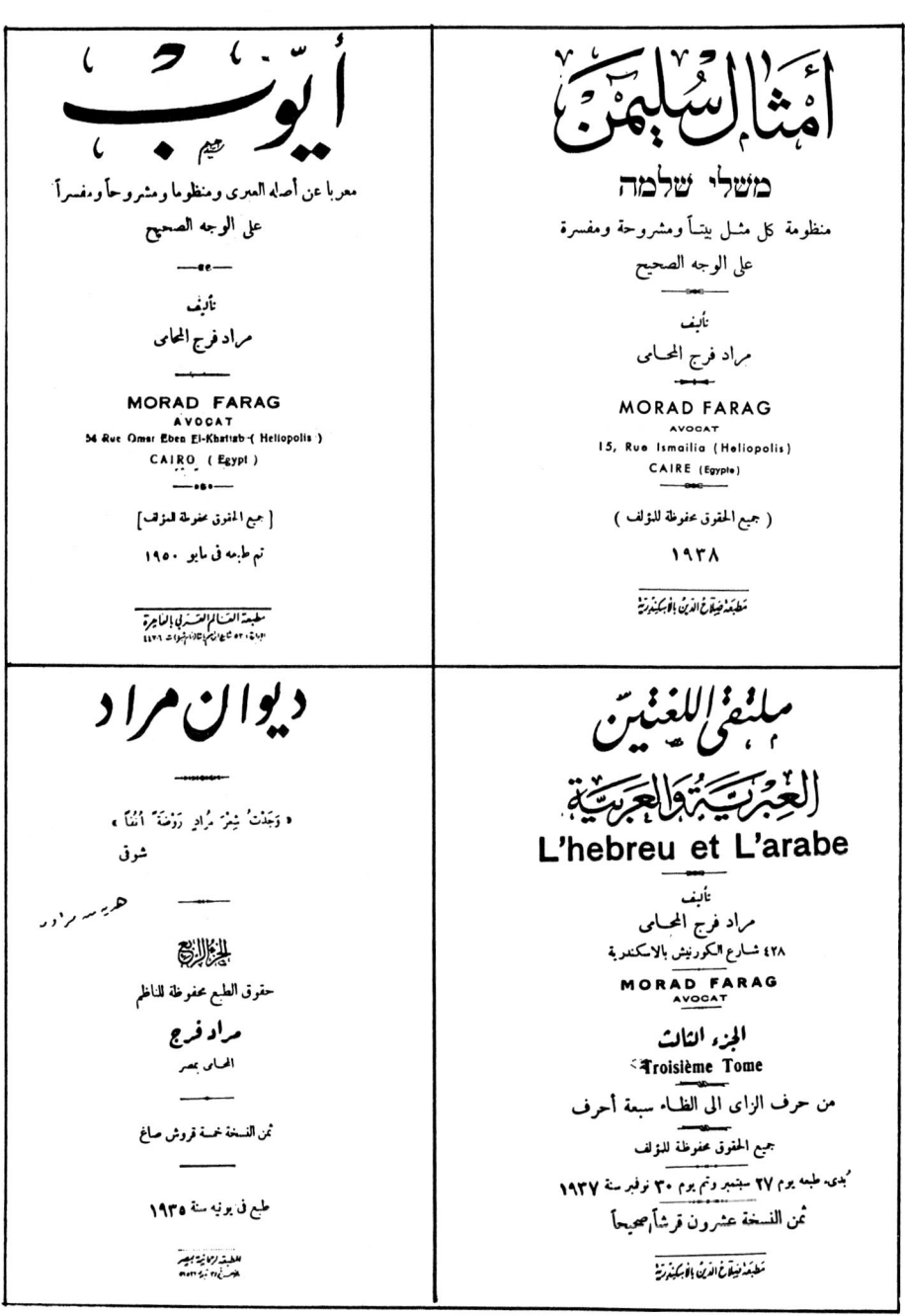

PLATE 3: Some of the books written by Murād Farag.

أيوب
معربا عن أصله العبرى ومنظوما ومشروحاً ومفسراً
على الوجه الصحيح
تأليف
مراد فرج المحامى
MORAD FARAG
AVOCAT
54 Rue Omar Eben El-Khattab (Heliopolis)
CAIRO (Egypt)
[جميع الحقوق محفوظة للمؤلف]
تم طبعه فى مايو ١٩٥٠
مطبعة العالم العربي بالقاهرة
أمثال سليمن
משלי שלמה
منظومة كل مثل بيتاً ومشروحة ومفسرة
على الوجه الصحيح
تأليف
مراد فرج المحامى
MORAD FARAG
AVOCAT
15, Rue Ismailia (Heliopolis)
CAIRE (Egypte)
(جميع الحقوق محفوظة للمؤلف)
١٩٣٨
مطبعة صلاح الدين بالاسكندرية
ديوان مراد
« وَجَدْتُ شِعْرَ مُرادٍ رَوْضَةً أُنُفاً »
شوقى
الجزء الرابع
حقوق الطبع محفوظة للناظم
مراد فرج
المحامى بمصر
ثمن النسخة خمسة قروش صاغ
طبع فى يونيه سنة ١٩٣٥
المطبعة الرحمانية بمصر
ملتقى اللغتين
العبرية والعربية
L’hebreu et L’arabe
تأليف
مراد فرج المحامى
٤٢٨ شارع الكورنيش بالاسكندرية
MORAD FARAG
AVOCAT
الجزء الثالث
Troisième Tome
من حرف الزاى الى الظاء سبعة أحرف
جميع الحقوق محفوظة للمؤلف
بُدئ طبعه يوم ٢٧ سبتمبر وتم يوم ٣٠ نوفبر سنة ١٩٣٧
ثمن النسخة عشرون قرشاً صحيحاً
مطبعة صلاح الدين بالاسكندرية

مؤلفات مراد بك فرج

من العلماء من يعملون فى صمت، وينجون فى صمت، عا كفين فى محاريبهم . لا يستهويهم جلبة الثناء ولا ضجيج المدح ، ولا يأبهون لزخرف المناصب وأبهة السلطان . وإنما مهم كل مهم أن يفيدوا وينفعوا بعمارة ما في مهم من جهد، وبمقدار ما لديهم من قوة، وبما ذخروا فى عقولهم الكبيرة من معرفة وفن . وهم إن أنكروا ذواتهم فقد تعوضوا من متـ ـع الحياة ما أقدروا وأمتعوا ، ورأوا من ثمرات باقية على الأحقاب .

من هؤلاء العلماء العاملين صديقى الأستاذ مراد بك فرج المحامى ، ذلك الرجل الذى ملأ حياته بالعمل والتأليف فى مختلف الميادين التشريعية واللغوية والتاريخية ـ وله من زهاء ثلاثين مجلداً ـ وأكثر ما يكون عملا فى فقه اللغة واشتقاقها واستمدادها من أصولها .

وقد انصرف فى معظم حياته الحافلة إلى تحقيق ما فى المفردات العربية من شبه أو صلة بالعبرية : تلك الصلة التى قد تكون قريبة ، وقد تكون بعيدة وقد تكون واشجة النسب ، حتى ليتطابق اللفظان أحياناً أو يتحدان .

ومما درسته من تآليفه المقارنة كتاب (ملتقى اللغتين) . وهو كتاب عائل ضخم ، وكتاب (الشعراء اليهود) ، وكتاب (أيوب) .

ولو أنى تعرضت بالتحليل والنقد التعليق لهذه الكتب الثلاثة لطال فى القول . وإنما يكفى أن أقول : إننا فى عصرنا هذا ونحن مقبلون على نهضة واسعة النطاق فى اللغة وفلسفتها وخصائصها ، لفى حاجة ماسة إلى من يهدينا إلى أسرارها وتطورها ، ومن غير خاف أن معاجم اللغة العربية قديمها وحديثها ، كثيراً ما نتقف حائزة أمام معانى كثير من الألفاظ فنقف نحن أيضاً حائرين لا نهتدى .

ولا شك فى أن هذه الحيرة إنما ترجع غالباً إلى أن مؤلفى هذه المعجمات لم يكونوا على دراية باللغات التى ترجع هى والعربية إلى أرومة واحدة أو التى افترضت العربية منها فهضمت ما اقترضت ، ومثله فى ذات نفسها .

ولهذا ضل كثير من قدامى المؤلفين فى شروحهم وتفسيراتهم لبعض النصوص القديمة . ثم اتضح المعنى الحق

على ضوء البحوث اسوية الحديثه المقارنه . فإذا المعنى يتفايرما كان مفهوما من قبل أئمة المقارنة ، أو يضاده، أو لا تجمعه به جامعة مطلقاً .

سام مراد بك إذا فى هذه النهضة اللغوية الحديثة ، وعمل فى زمرة العاملين المتعمقين الذين يريدون أن تفهم اللغة فهما صحيحا ، خاليا من الفروض الواهية . والاستظهارات الغامضة .

وبحوث مراد بك اللغوية عميقة ، وتحقيقاته من الدقة بحيث لا ينتفع بها إلا الخاصة من الباحثين . فأجدر بها أن تكون فى متناولهم وبين أيديهم ، يهتدون بهديها ، ويعملون على نورها فى تحقيق معانى المفردات والتراكيب

وقد تلجلج فى صدرى منذ عرفت مراد بك . وفطنت إلى مواهبه وقرأت كتبه ، أن أكتب إليه منوها بمجهوده العلمى الغزير الذى ملأ حياته كلها ، لا يزدهيه عجب ، ولا تلويه شواغل المحاماة ، ولا تثنيه قضاياها ومشاكلها ـ حتى وجدت بين يدى كتابه الجديد (أيوب) ويقع فى أربع وأربعمائة صفحة . فقلت يا سبحان الله ! أفى مثل هذه السن العالية يضطلع الرجل بهذا الجهد الشاق : ينظم (سفر أيوب) من العهد القديم ، ثم يكر عليه بالتحقيق اللغوى . والبحث التاريخى ، حتى يكشف عن كل نواحيه ، ويتقصى أبعد مراميه .

فلما عبرت بادى ، ذى بدء. أدركت مكانته وبعد غوره بين كتب التاريخ الدينى ، والتمحيص اللغوى . فلم أتمالك أمام هذا العمل الباذخ والجهد الكبير ، أن أمسك بالقلم ، وكتبت هذه الكلمة التى لا شك فى أنها تقصر كل التقصير عن تبيان فضل الرجل ، وسعة أفقه وغزارة مواهبه .

ولعله قد يتاح لى يوما أن أعود بالدراسة على كتبه الثلاثة منه ، فأقف من صديقى مراد بك موقف المناقش أو المحاور أو المساجل . والله ولى التوفيق .

أحمد العوامرى
عضو بجمع فؤاد الأول للغة العربية

PLATE 4: Many appreciated the scholarly work of Murād Farag. Aḥmad al-'Awāmrī, a member of the "Fu'ād I Academy of the Arabic Language," wrote the above comment.

A few summary remarks on Farag's Arabic poetry will be sufficient here. In general he has remained faithful to the canons of the classical Arabic *ars poetica* and has not succumbed, as did more recent Arab poets, to the lure of Western free verse. His meters are all classical, his language is relatively free of modernisms, and even his themes are mostly those of classical poetry: the mutual intolerance of religious faiths, the virtue of patience and steadfastness against despair, the viciousness of envy and the malice of hypocrites, the tragedy of youth overtaken by untimely death, the perfidy of women, the inevitability and finality of death. Where a Muslim poet would sing the praises of the Arab Prophet, Farag finds Biblical persons and events to sing of: the tragic figure of the aged King David, who mourns for his son Absalom despite the fact that the latter, in his lust for power, had sought to slay his own father; or the enormity of Cain's fratricide, the first murder on earth and the harbinger of man's unnatural thirst for the blood of his own kind. Occasionally Farag touches a modern and personal theme, as when he asserts his loyalty to his native land of Egypt, in answer to an inquirer who presumably questioned his patriotism, if not that of all non-Muslim citizens.

In any case, Farag's poetical output is surely a valuable addition to the rather scanty (compared with Rabbanite poetry) known corpus of Karaite poetic literature in general, and Karaite-Arabic poetry in particular.

PLATE 5a: The last page of a treatise written about Murād Farag by Leon Nemoy and published in the *Jewish Quarterly Review*, New Series, Volume LXXIV.

— ٤٣ —

وما برحوا فيه مختلفينا   قد اختلف الناس فى أمره

وأما اليهود فمنتظرونا   فقال النصارى لقد جاءنا

صلبًا وأنكره المسلمونا   وقال النصارى اليهود أماتو

على غرةٍ للعباد اليقينا   فيا معجزات السماء أبينى

43 (ibid.) (meter: *mutaqārib*)

Qad ikhtalafa 'l-nāsu fī amrihi
Wa-mā barihū fīhi mukhtalifīnā
Fa-qāla 'l-Naṣārā la-qad jā'anā
Wa-ammā 'l-Yahūdu fa-muntaẓirūnā
Wa-qāla 'l-Naṣārā 'l-Yahūdu amātū-
-hu ṣalban wa-ankarahu 'l-Muslimūnā
Fa-yā muʿjizāti 'l-samā'i abīnī
ʿAlā ghirratin lil-ʿibādi 'l-yaqīnā

Mankind has (long) disagreed about his (the Messiah's) career,
And they still continue in their disagreement.
The Christians say he has already come to us,
While the Jews still await him.
The Christians say the Jews had put him
To death by crucifixion, while the Muslims deny it.[8]
O miracles from heaven, pray surprise the servants (of God) [9]
by revealing to them the truth!

[8] The denial of the crucifixion of Jesus goes back to the Prophet himself, who reproached the Jews for "their saying, 'Verily, we have slain the Messiah, Jesus the son of Mary, an apostle of God.' Yet they slew him not, and they crucified him not" (Koran 4:156). Cf. al-Bayḍāwī's comment on this verse (ed. Fleischer, I, 240).

[9] That is to say, mankind.

PLATE 5b: A sample of Murād Farag's poetry. L. Nemoy: *Jewish Quarterly Review*, New Series, Volume LXXIV.

— ٥٤ —

وطني مصر فهي مسقط رأسي وبها نشأتي وفيها ربيت
وهي استاذتي ومورد رزقي ومقرّي أضحو بها وأبيت
ليس لي غيرها ملاذاً فيحبي شكرها قدر ما بها قد حبيت
فلتعش حرةً ولو أنني من فرط حبّي استقلالها قد سبيت

54 (II, 47) (meter: *khafīf*)

Waṭanī Miṣru fa-hya masqaṭu ra'sī
Wa-bihā nash'atī wa-fīhā rubbītu
Wa-hya ustādhatī wa-mawridu rizqī
Wa-maqarrī aṣḥū bihā wa-abītu
Laysa lī ghayruhā malādhan fa-yuḥbā
Shukruhā qadra mā bihā qad ḥubītu
Fal-ta'ish ḥurratan wa-law annanī min
Farṭi ḥubbī 'stiqlālihā qad subītu

My [14] homeland is Egypt. She is my birthplace,
In her was I brought up, and in her was I educated.
She is my mistress and the source of my livelihood.
She is my abode—in her I come awake and spend the night (in sleep).
I have no other refuge, and the gift
Of (my) gratitude is (owed) to her, according as I have been favored (by her gifts) in her.
May she live free, even though I have been enslaved
By the intensity of my love for her independence.

[14] Footnote: "(Written) in reply to a certain person's query," who presumably questioned the loyalty of non-Muslim citizens in Egypt's struggle for independence from Britain.

PLATE 5c: A few months after World War I had ended Egyptians revolted against the British calling for independence. It was not until February 1922 that Egypt was declared an independent state. During the struggle Muslims and Christians (Copts) fought hand in hand while Jews were not so active. Their allegiance to the country was questioned. For this reason Murād Farag wrote these verses.

LXXXVI. 1901-1902. A BLOOD-LIBEL IN CAIRO

... Mon enquête a mis à nu la coupable indifférence du Grand Rabbin du Caire, dont le devoir était de prendre franchement position dans l'affaire en réclamant dès le début contre la prétention monstrueuse du ministère public d'échaffauder tout un acte d'accusation sur la dénonciation d'une femme imbue du préjugé du sang et le témoignage d'une fillette de 6 ans à qui on avait fait la leçon. Il a laissé faire et il a eu le coeur d'aller passer l'été en villégiature au Liban pendant qu'un pauvre Juif se défendait en vain contre une accusation dont l'infamie rejaillissait sur tous ses coreligionnaires. Les chefs temporels de notre communauté ne se sont pas montrés plus jaloux de leur dignité de Juifs que leur chef spirituel. Ils ont cru avoir beaucoup fait en renvoyant l'infortuné Kahana, qui était venu implorer leur assistance, à un des administrateurs de la Communauté, Mosséry Bey, colossalement riche il est vrai, disons celà à son honneur, mais dont j'ai eu l'autre jour l'occasion d'éprouver la sécheresse de coeur et l'outrecuidance aristocratique. Ce richard avait eu la charité de charger son avocat de s'occuper de l'affaire de l'inculpé. Il s'en est si bien occupé que le tribunal condamna son client. J'ai fait quantité de démarches pour m'aboucher avec cet avocat. On m'a toujours répondu qu'il était absent. Je me suis contenté de voir son premier employé et j'ai acquis la certitude que le Juif n'avait pas été défendu ou il l'avait été très mollement par le correspondant de l'avocat de Mosséry Bey. Ce qui est effrayant, c'est que ni au rabbinat ni à l'office de l'avocat on ne possède de données exactes sur cette affaire attristante. J'ai pu toutefois obtenir la copie de l'acte d'accusation qui date du mois d'octobre de l'année dernière.[1] Je vous enverrai la traduction de cette pièce par le prochain courrier ainsi qu'une relation authentique de cet incident dramatique à l'usage de votre bulletin mensuel. En attendant, je suis allé au plus pressé. J'ai chargé un avocat caraite[2] à défaut d'un avocat israélite de plaider l'affaire en appel. L'avocat est convaincu que le tribunal d'appel acquittera le Juif à moins qu'une pression étrangère ne pèse sur son jugement.

Vous savez que la justice indigène est loin de briller par son intégrité. L'acte d'accusation est tellement inepte que je partage aussi l'optimisme de l'avocat. Je lui ai promis 4£ pour ses honoraires. Je suis sûr que le Comité Central[3] approuvera mon initiative dans cette circonstance et qu'il me remboursera les honoraires de l'avocat ....[4]

> AIU, Egypte, X.E.182.e. This is a letter from S. Somekh in Cairo to the President of the AIU in Paris, dated October 17, 1902—extract.

1. October 1901.
2. Murād Faraj, well-known as a writer and poet.
3. Of AIU.
4. The accused was found innocent only in December 1902 in the Court of Appeal, after having been in jail for 14 months. Not less appalling is, if one is to believe Somekh, the total indifference of the Jewish community in Cairo.

PLATE 6: In October of 1901 a Rabbanite Jew, Ḥayyīm Kahānah, from Port Said, Egypt, was found guilty of trying to kidnap a six-year-old Christian girl. Kahānah was sentenced to one year at hard labor. At the request of a concerned Rabbanite, Murād Farag appealed the ruling and proved Kahānah's innocence. The judge also ordered the Egyptian Government to bear all expenses.

Dā'ūd Ḥusnī (1876-1937)*

Dā'ūd Ḥusnī is considered one of the foremost composers of Arabic music in Egypt, indeed in the entire Arab world.

His full name was David ben Khiḍr (Elīyāhū) Ḥayyīm Levi. He was born in 1876 in Ḥārat al-Yahūd, where most of the Karaites at the time used to live.

He attended "Les Ecoles des Frères" in Khurunfish where, at the age of 12, he directed the religious choir of the school. But Dā'ūd soon left the school to work as a bookbinder in a printing shop. The shop, as it happened, was owned by 'Alī Sukkar, a lyricist. In his shop many political leaders, writers, and musicians used to meet. One night, while working, Dā'ūd started to sing, and was heard by Muḥammad 'Abdū.[43] He was so impressed that in the presence of Dā'ūd he told those who were around him that Dā'ūd would be a great musician if he chose to follow that career. That prediction had a strong impact on the mind of Dā'ūd. While it strengthened Dā'ūd's feeling to pursue this career, it also awakened him to start reading and educating himself to make up for what he had missed in school.

Torn between pursuing his career and obeying his father, who himself was a well known 'ūd player and who opposed his son's decision to be a musician, Dā'ūd finally decided to leave home. In a sailboat, he escaped to the bride of the Nile, the city of al-Manṣūrah. There he met Muḥammad Sha'bān, an expert in Arabic music, its notes, beats, and harmony of sounds, but more importantly its modes *(maqāms)*. Within a short time he learned to play the 'ūd. Dā'ūd stayed two years with Sha'bān absorbing from him his considerable knowledge of music. Following Sha'bān's advice, Dā'ūd decided to return to Cairo, as there was nothing more to be offered to him in al-Manṣūrah.

In Cairo Dā'ūd started to sing songs by famous singers like 'Abdu al-Ḥāmūlī,

---

*. My deep gratitude to my friend since 1933, 'Abd al-Qādir Ṣabrī of Cairo, Egypt, who provided me with all names of the various maqams and reviewed this part before printing.

43. Muḥammad 'Abduh was an Egyptian thinker, writer and leader. He was one of the most respected leaders in the Arab world in the late 19th century. He died in 1905.

al-Sanṭūrī, al-Manyalāwī, and others. But soon he felt that he was capable of composing music, and so he wrote his first song, *"al-ḥaqq lak 'Andī yallī gharāmak zāyid"* ("You Whom I Love Very Strongly, I Owe You an Apology"). When Muḥammad 'Othmān heard him he quickly recognized Dā'ūd's potential and made his famous statement, "After I go, listen to Dā'ūd, for he is my successor in the realm of music." 'Othmān was so fond of Dā'ūd that he treated him as his son and let him borrow his orchestra, *takht,* whenever he wanted to celebrate a party. In 1906 Dā'ūd felt that his music was strong enough to stand competition with the music of other countries — and he was right. His song *"Asīr al-'Ishq,"* "Prisoner (or Captive) of Love," earned him the first prize at the Music Convention in Paris in 1906.

The death of 'Othman and al-Ḥāmūlī in the very early years of the 20th century left a void in the world of Arabic music that was felt all over. Dā'ūd considered that it was his responsibility to fill that void. He was able to continue the renaissance that was begun by his predecessors.

Although at the time, Dā'ūd felt that Arabic music was rich, yet he also felt that it was time to enrich it further.

Dā'ūd was the first to insert new *maqāms* into Arabic music, such as *Ḥugāz Kārkurd, 'Agam 'Ushayrān, Bāstanikār, Nakrīz,* and *al-Zingrān.* In the *qaṣīdah* "Let me hear your sweet graceful voice," Dā'ūd was the first to insert new and different *maqāms* in Arabic music.[44]

With this creative blend Dā'ūd composed hundreds of songs for the well known singers of the time, such as Laylā Murād, Fatḥiyyah Aḥmad, Ragā' 'Abdū, Asmahān, Nagāt 'Alī, Muḥammad 'Abd al-Muṭṭalib, Fāyed Muḥammad, and others. He also composed eleven songs for the "super-star of the East," Umm-Kulthūm.

That blend gave Dā'ūd's tunes a style that no one but Dā'ūd could create. His style of composition was deep, expressive, simple and most delightful. When asked to comment on Dā'ūd's music, Zakariya Aḥmad — the well known Egyptian composer — said, "The sweetness of Dā'ūd's tunes, the fineness of his songs, the depth of their expressions and engineering of their construction show the purity of his soul and that he is a capable artist." Aḥmad Shawqī, "the prince of poets," wrote: "Dā'ūd Ḥusnī is a precious and priceless art treasure. He is a valuable gem in Arabic music."

Dā'ūd was raised as an Egyptian with true Egyptian feelings and sensitivity: feelings toward the quiet nature of the country, the beauty of its countryside, the purity of the Nile and the dream of every Egyptian to end the British occupancy. All this shaped and affected Dā'ūd's music. That feeling was clear in the music he wrote in the *dōr,* the *qaṣīdah* or in the *ṭaqṭūqah,* and for years he infused in the

---

44. *al-Fann* (The Art) No. 26 (25 December 1950).

ears of the people light, sweet, merry, frivolous songs. That is, of course, along with national music that suited the time. Muḥammad Fatḥī, Professor of Criminology in the School of Law of the University of Cairo, and the chairman of the "Institute of Arabic Music" wrote: "Dā'ūd's music and melodies were pure Arabic because he was noble, faithful to his country and to his art, proud of his Arabic customs and traditions. In the history of the 'Renaissance of Pure Arabic Music,' Dā'ūd has reserved for him and for his country a page of glory and honor that will last for ever."[45]

After the Egyptian Revolution of 1919 Dā'ūd started more seriously to write operettas. Dā'ūd wrote eleven operettas which began and strengthened a new movement, called at the time the "singing theatre."

The success that Dā'ūd encountered in the operettas prompted him to direct his energy toward the opera. In his opera "Samson and Delilah," Dā'ūd surpassed himself with his descriptive music that suited the words and the scenery of every part of the opera. Dr. Ḥusayn Fawzī, in this regard, wrote: "Dā'ūd Ḥusnī has set the foundation of a complete opera in the East. If this is all that he has done, then that would be, for him, more than enough for glory and splendour." After that, Dā'ūd wrote the music for the opera "Cleopatra."

Sayyid Darwīsh, who also wrote music for the operetta, wrote about Dā'ūd: "Whenever a new opening in the music appears to me, I find that Dā'ūd has already preceded me to it, and that increases my admiration for this true artist and researcher."

When Sayyid Darwīsh died before finishing his operetta, *"Hudā,"* Dā'ūd undertook the responsibility of finishing it. It was not an easy task, as he had to follow the spirit and the style of Darwīsh. Dā'ūd decided to change it into an opera of two parts. He enriched each part with his style, and he succeeded fully in his enterprise — to the point that the audience was unable to detect more than one opera of one style.

Dā'ūd's last opera was "Semiramis," for which he wrote only the music of Act 2. Act 1 was written by Kāmel al-Kholaʿī, and Act 3 was written by Riyāḍ al-Sunbaṭī.

During the Music Congress held in Cairo in 1932, Dr. Zax, the Chairman of the Congress, listened to and accepted Dā'ūd's suggestion that it was possible to elevate Egyptian music using only national and oriental tunes. Dā'ūd was quoted as saying, "Our Arabic music is rich in melodies. It has the quarter *maqām,* which imbues it with beauty and delight. It is useless to ignore these melodies."

At the same congress Dā'ūd was entrusted with recording all the musical heritage of the old school. With the help of another musician, Dā'ūd completed his work on time.[46]

---

45. *al-Kalīm* No. 196 (16 December 1953).
46. He was ʿazīz Ṣādiq.

Dā'ūd never commercialized his art. He chose instead to devote himself and his efforts to his art. He was well known for his generosity and kindness towards colleagues less fortunate than himself.

Dā'ūd was well known as a family man who cared about his wife and children. In this regard 'Abd al-Raḥmān Sāmī, head of Programming Department of the Egyptian Broadcasting system, wrote: "Dā'ūd never led a private life that would defame him, as others did. His family life was an example and a model of conjugal life, love and mercy. It affected his art and radiated to the people. Without knowing its source, people were singing Oh Mariya without knowning that Mariya was Dā'ūd's wife and the mother of his children."[47]

Dā'ūd died in poverty on 10 December 1937, at the age of 67, before he could achieve his ultimate goal: composing new settings for almost all the Karaite prayers.

Since his death, and down to this day, the Institute of Arabic music commemorates Dā'ud's memory each December.

About Dā'ūd's Work:

* Dā'ūd's style evolved with the daring innovation of blending different *maqāms*. He was the first to insert Persian, Turkish and Andalusian *maqāms* into Egyptian music.

* The evolution of his style of singing caused the widening of the field of Arabic music.

* In his composition he was known for blending "sweet freshness" with the harmony of "architectural construction."

* Dā'ūd formed and shaped the new school of singers for men and women alike.

* He was the first to start a new trend of music to convey his art to the people. His music was heard in all neighborhoods, alleys, streets, and even at the nearby palaces of the rich.

* His creative music spread all over the country and beyond the Mediterranean. Some of these songs, which were called *Ṭaqṭūqah* are:
  Amar luh layālī — "The Moon Has Particular Nights."
  Yā 'Arūsah yā riqqah — "Oh, Sweet Bride."
  Ya tamr-ḥinnah — "Oh, Tamr-ḥinnah."[48]
  Yā maḥla al-fusḥah fī ras al-Barr — "How Enjoyable Is the Promenade in Ra's

---

47. *al-Kalim* No. 177 (16 January 1953).
48. Tamr-ḥinnah: a flower with a very attractive fragrance.

al-Barr."⁴⁹

Hatīlī 'Asfūrī yammah — "Bring Me my Sparrow, Mother."

* Some of Dā'ūd's work was chosen by the Military Music Corps and was played in the parks during national holidays and on other occasions:
  Laylah fī al-'Umr — "One Particular Night in a Life-Time."
  Farragīnī 'Alā shagar al-mangah— "Show Me the Mango Trees."
  'Adī al khudrah wa-'Adī al-mayyah — "Here Is the Green and Here Is the Water."

* As part of his outstanding contribution, he composed *tawāshih*;⁵⁰ some of these are:
  Ramānī bi sahm hawāh — "He Struck Me with the Arrow of His Love."
  Udhkurū al-ḥobb — "Mention Love."

* Dā'ūd also became involved in the *qaṣīdah*:⁵¹
  Yōm al-Widā' ada'tu rushdī — "The Day We Said Goodbye I Lost my Mind."
  'Uyūn al-Muhā — "The Eyes of the Deer."

* Not satisfied with his accomplishments, he started to write music for what was known then as the "Singing Theatre," and thus he started writing music for operettas. His first one, *"Ṣabāḥ,"* is distinguished by its descriptive music picturing the beauty and natural life of the countryside. He wrote the music for many operettas such as: *Ma'rūf al-Iskāfī, Nāhidshāh, al-ghandūrah* — all taken from The One Thousand and One Nights — besides many other operettas.

* Dā'ūd's goal was to write music for the opera; in this field he was the first and in it he reached his ultimate success. His first opera, "Sampson and Dalila," was among his best, followed by others like "Night of Cleopatra," "Semiranis," etc.

* It is a fact that Dā'ūd wrote the music of more than 500 songs and 30 operas and operettas.

* Towards the end, Dā'ūd's work bore the trait of mystical music, carrying the enlightening melodies whose effects lift up the soul of the listener to unconquered domains beyond man's conceptions.

---

49. Ra's āl-Barr: Summer resort near the city of Damietta.
50. Tawāshih: plural of tawshīḥ. Poem sung by two groups or choirs.
51. Qasīdah: a poem written in literary Arabic.
    NOTE: this part about Dā'ūd's work is taken from an article written by Joseph Sabbagh (a friend of mine) who translated a book written in Arabic about Dā'ūd by his son, Ibrāhīm Ḥusnī.

Quotations from Dā'ūd

On many occasions Dā'ūd was quoted talking about himself, his country, his music and his art. Here are a few of these quotations.

يا الهي اصغ الى عبدك الفقير اليك . اصغ الى الذي ائتمنه واودعت في قلبي عاطفة تشدد
الهمتني الفن ، في الفن عبادة ورسالة روحية . وحرمتني المادة وفي المادة فناء

My lord listen to your slave who needs you. Listen to me whom You have entrusted with an ever-strong sentiment.

You inspired me with art. In art there is worship and spiritual message. You deprived me of the material — and in it there is exhaustion.

اني اوتيت من الايحاء ما استطيع ان احجب قرص الشمس انغاما والحانا

I was given revelation with which I can cover the sun with tunes and melodies.

الموسيقى علم وفن وهندسة ، والعاطفة والوجدان الصادق يضفي عليها جمالا ما بعده من جمالك

Music is science, art, and engineering. Sentiment and true intuition add to it all beauty.

لا شك ان الطبيعة مرتبطة باسرار الانغام في العالم .. فطبيعة مصر الهادئة وسماؤها الصافية ونيلها الجاري يوحي بنغم رقيق حالم . كأنه ينساب به غدير ماء او جدول صافي

No doubt there is a connection between nature and the secrets of music in the world. The quiet nature of Egypt, its clear skies, and its vivid Nile inspire the musician with a fine dreamy tune as though running from a pure brook or a rivulet.

PLATE 5: "The Sailors' Song" from the operetta *Ma'rūf al-Iskāfī*

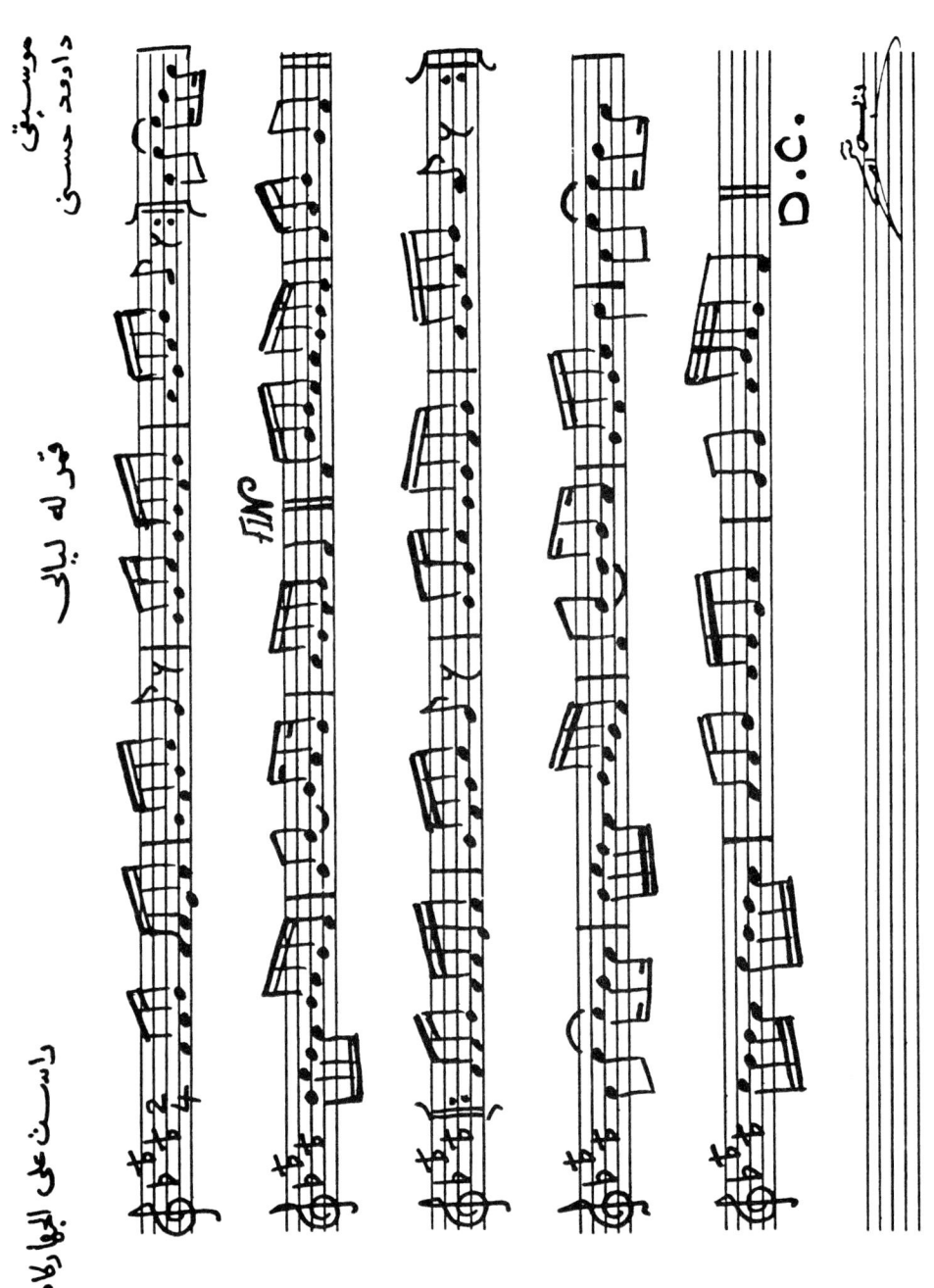

PLATE 6: Amar Luh Layālī: The Moon has Particular Nights

Chapter VIII

Chief Rabbis

The head of the Karaite community was its chief rabbi, or as he was called in Arabic, al-Ḥākhām al-Akbar or *ḥākhām-basha*. The following is a list of the chief rabbis, *"Ḥākhāmīm,"* who headed the community from 1856 to 1956.

Ḥākhām Mosheh al-Qudsī the second (1810-1905; served 1856-1872)

Mūsā ben Abrāhām ben Mūsā ben Samuel ben Abrāhām ben Elīyāhū ha-Levi al-Dimashkī was born in Jerusalem in 1810, the son of the ḥākhām-akbar of the small Karaite community in that city. He had an older brother, David, who took his father's place after his death.

Mosheh was a scholar in the Mosaic Law, *al-Sharī'ah al-Mūsawiyah,* in general, and in Karaite law in particular. Unfortunately, he was not concerned with writing his own works, and put all his efforts into copying works by others which he considered to be important.[1]

We do not have accurate information about the date when Mosheh became ḥākhām akbar for the Karaite community in Cairo.[2] We do know that he left Egypt in 1872 to head the Karaite community in Jerusalem after his brother David had

---

1. A list of the works of Mosheh, as well as of his father Abrāhām, may be found in the British Library in London. I donated to the Jewish Theological Seminary in New York 16 manuscripts copied by Mosheh. (Report of 1977 / 5735.) In 1877-1878 Mosheh copied in Jerusalem parts of Yefet b. Saghīr's *Sepher Miṣvot* and al-Qirqisānī *Katāb al-Anwār*. Mann, *Texts and Studies,* Vol. I, p. 325.
2. Ḥākhām Tobiah Levi Babovitch (who served from 1934 to 1956) wrote an article in *al-Kalīm* No. 8 (1 June 1945), in which he indicated that he found marriage records signed by Mosheh in the years 1863-1867. On my visit to Cairo in 1982, I found a real estate deed, dated 1859, in which the name of Ḥākhām Mosheh ben Abrāhām al-Qudsī was mentioned (Pl. 1).

died.³ He kept that position until he too died in 1905.

In his lifetime, Ḥākhām Mosheh mastered the Hebrew and Arabic languages, and also spoke English, French, Turkish, Greek, and the Tatar dialect spoken by the Russian Karaites.⁴

When Ḥākhām Mosheh left Egypt in 1872, his duties were carried out by two very well-informed Ḥākhāmīm, Nissīm al-Muṣaffī⁵ and Abrāhām Yomtōb.⁶

Ḥākhām Shlomoh Kohen (1831-1893; served 1873-1875)

Born in Istanbūl in 1831, he became the cantor *(ḥazzān)* of the Karaite community in Istanbūl after he had been ordained ḥākhām in 1855. He taught Mosaic Law in the Karaite Institutes in Turkey, and later became head of this community.

His abilities to inspire youth and to captivate an audience, and his good character, for which he was well known, earned him the love and respect of the members of the Karaite community. He came to Cairo in 1873, and held the position of ḥākhām akbar until 1875. Then he left for Istanbūl where he lived until his death in 1893 at the age of 62. He was buried in the Karaite cemetery in Istanbūl.

Well known as a poet and philosopher. Did his best to educate the younger generation. He lectured on a regular basis, and wrote a number of books about the Hebrew language and about the faith,⁷ the most important of them *Yerī'ōt Shlomoh.*⁸

Ḥākhām Shabbethāi Elīyāhū Mangūbī (1836-1906; served 1876-1906)

He was born in Istanbūl,⁹ and studied under well known Ḥākhāmīm there. He was both ḥazzan and ḥākhām of the Karaite community in Turkey.

---

3. There was no comparison between the Karaite community in Jerusalem and the Karaite community in Egypt. The latter was more important and wealthier; yet, Mosheh considered the appointment as head of the Karaite community in Jerusalem as the greatest honor.
4. One of the Arabic works that he copied was *Kitāb mā lā yasa' al-Ṭabīb gahluhu,* "The Book That a Doctor Should Know," or "The Book that the Doctor Cannot Afford Not to Know." Mosheh's niece and daughter-in-law, Naḥamāh (1859-1955), stated that the Karaite community in Jerusalem was poor and depended for its survival on the financial help from the Karaite community in the Crimea. Ḥākhām Mosheh traveled to the Crimea to get that help, so knowing the Karaite-Tatar language was of great help, as it was the common language of the Russian Karaites.
5. There is still, to this day, a lane called "Ḥārat al-Muṣaffī" in the old Ḥārat al-Yahūd al-Qarrā'īn, in Cairo.
6. When Ḥākhām Mosheh died in 1905, his son Rafael became the head and the ḥākhām akbar of the small Karaite community in Jerusalem. He was to be the last member of the al-Qudsī family to hold that position, which the family had held in Damascus, Jerusalem, and Egypt for over 200 years. Today many members of the al-Qudsī family from the branch of the Mosheh live in Israel, Egypt, France, Brazil, and the United States.
7. This information was given to *al-Kalīm* No. 128 by Isḥac Kīrīmī of Turkey.
8. The manuscript is now in the library of the Karaite community in Ramlah. (See Literary output.) It is printed in Hebrew. Its English translation will follow.
9. Some members of his family, now in the U.S.A., say that he was born in Mangūb, in the Crimea.

Ḥakhām Mangūbī came with his family to Cairo in 1876. The leader of the community at that time, Isḥāq Yūsuf Līshaʻ, appointed him ḥakhām.

In 1890 the authorities acknowledged his position, and also confirmed the Karaite community as a separate unit from the Rabbanite community.

Ḥakhām Mangūbī was a well known administrator. It was he who called for elections and formed the first religious council in the Karaite community. The first meeting of that council took place on 3 March 1901 (12 Adar 5611). It was also thanks to Ḥakhām Mangūbī's efforts that the community began to keep records of births, engagements, marriages, divorces, and deaths. He spoke many languages well: Hebrew, Arabic, Turkish, Greek, and Spanish.

He had good relations with the Khudaywī of Egypt, Twafīq and ʻAbbās Ḥilmī II, and was a friend of Lord Cromer, the British governor.[10]

Ḥakhām Mangūbī kept his position until his death on 2 April 1906. He was buried in Egypt. Delegates from the government and all local and foreign communities attended his funeral[11] (Pl. 2).

After Ḥakhām Mangūbī's death Dāʼūd Isḥāq Līshaʻ was elected deputy ḥakhām until another ḥakhām could be appointed (at that time, the ḥakhām akbar was considered the official head of the community and of the religious council). A letter was sent to Russia asking for a ḥakhām; in the meantime, Farag ʻAbd-Allah carried out the religious responsibilities until 1907.

Ḥakhām Ahārūn Kefīlī (1907)

He was born in the town of Kremenchug, in Russia, and completed his education at Eupatoria Theological Karaite Center. He was appointed to the Karaite High Religious Organization in Eupatoria, and had many badges and medals of honor bestowed upon him by the Tsar.

His application for the position of ḥakhām akbar of the Karaite community in Cairo was accepted, and on 1 February 1907, he was appointed for a three-year term.

Ḥakhām Kefīlī wanted to introduce many reforms, but found it impossible.[12] He was ultimately asked by the religious council to accept Yūsuf ʻAbd-Allah al-Gamīl as a companion, to accompany him wherever he went and to serve as a guide, *qawwāṣ*.[13]

---

10. In late September 1883, Lord Cromer visited Ḥakhām Mangūbī in his office at the Karaite bēt-dīn in Khunrunfish.
11. Among the delegates were the son of Ṣidqī Bāshā, representing the Khudaywī ʻAbbās Ḥilmī, the ḥakhām akbar of the Rabbanite community of Cairo and of Alexandria, the Assistant Wekils of the Patriarchs of the Coptic Orthodox Church and of the Greek Orthodox Church. (Minutes of the religious council of 13 April 1906.)
12. Many stories were told about the hecklers who annoyed him continuously.
13. Minutes of 27 April 1907.

His term ended, however, after a difference of opinion over the legal question of inheritance by the wife of Lieto Isḥāq Levi from her brother, Yūsuf Abū Qamar. A committee appointed to look into the matter disagreed with Ḥākhām Kefīlī, and his appointment was terminated. He left for Russia on Tuesday, 27 August 1907.[14]

Ḥākhām Kefīlī was a scholar and a man of reforms, but he would not accept compromise. He kept a diary, which he later published in Russia, and in which he recorded the details of his stay in Cairo. He called Cairo the "Mother of Wonders," *Umm-al-'agā'ib*.

Upon his return he became head of the Karaite community in Melitopol in the Crimea. He died in 1910.

Ḥākhām Berākhāh Isḥāq Kohen (1845-1915; served 1908-1915)

He was born in 1845 in Istanbūl, the son of Isḥāq Kohen, a well-known ḥākhām.

He completed his education under his father, and then worked at first as a merchant before becoming interested in religious matters. In 1902, he left for Jerusalem, where he later became ḥākhām akbar.[15]

After Ḥākhām Kefīlī left Cairo in 1907, the religious council wrote a letter to Ḥākhām Kohen, offering him the position of ḥākhām akbar in Cairo (the General Assembly having accepted his nomination for the post). Ḥākhām Kohen demanded a written letter of appointment; in case things went wrong in Cairo, he did not wish to put his Jerusalem position in jeopardy.

First, a letter of conditions was drafted by the religious council.[16] Ḥākhām Kohen accepted it, and the religious council delegated Dā'ūd Isḥāq Līsha' to write a letter of appointment and sign it.

Ḥākhām Kohen assumed his responsibilities in February 1908, and continued in office until his death in 1915.

One month after Ḥākhām Kohen was appointed, he asked the religious council to appoint an assistant for him. The council agreed, and gave him a list of names to choose from.

In 1911 some members of the community tried to pressure the religious council to terminate the services of Ḥākhām Kohen, but the religious council insisted that the rules of the Internal Code must be followed, and thus refused to yield.

After the death of Ḥākhām Kohen, the religious council appointed Abrāhām

---

14. Ḥākhām Kefīlī was given one full year's salary plus travel expenses to return to Russia. The story of his struggle with the religious council is very interesting and is recorded in the minutes of 5 September 1907. He kept in touch with well-informed men of the Karaite community until his death. (*Al-Kalīm* No. 166, 16 June 1952.)
15. Ḥākhām Mosheh al-Qudsī died in 1905. His son, Rafael, replaced him as ḥākhām akbar of the Jerusalem community. Rafael must have died in 1906 or in early 1907; I was unable to verify this. When the religious council in Cairo wrote to Ḥākhām Kohen in 1907, he was ḥākhām akbar in Jerusalem.
16. Minutes of 10 December 1907.

Mangūbī deputy in all religious and administrative matters. He assumed his position officially on 1 December 1915. In October 1916, Yūsuf Farag Ṣāliḥ became administrative deputy and Farag Mūsā Rāṣōn became religious deputy.

Ḥākhām Abrāhām Kohen (1860-1933; served 1920-1933)

He was born in 1860 in Istanbūl, where he completed his education. Considered a scholar in the Hebrew language, he had a fine writing style and wrote many books.[17]

In addition to Hebrew, he mastered Turkish and French. He used to speak French to members of the community who knew the language, but in all ceremonies he spoke only Hebrew.

He was appointed ḥākhām akbar for the community in Instanbūl in 1907, keeping that position until 1920. In December 1920, he came to Cairo, and assumed the responsibilities of ḥākhām akbar there.

Four months later, his wife and two daughters joined him.

On 20 January 1921, the religious council offered him a contract, which he accepted.

On 31 March 1921, a letter was received from the governor of Cairo indicating that the Ministry of the Interior had accepted Kohen as the "Head," *Ra's,* of the Karaite community.[18]

Ḥākhām Kohen kept his position until his death on 6 May 1933. His twelve-year period of service was filled with events and controversy about several important matters:

1. The Internal Code: The religious council under pressure from members of the community, decided to rewrite the Internal Code, which was considered outmoded. At the same time, efforts were made to codify the Personal Status Code and submit it to the authorities.

The Internal Code and the Personal Status Code were the center of dispute throughout the community. Everyone had a point of view, and tried to argue for it. At that time the most common thing to do was to print leaflets and pamphlets, and to distribute them throughout the community, sometimes literally to everybody.

2. Polygamy: According to the Torah, a Jew may have two wives, as long as he treats them fairly: "If he take him another wife, her food, her raiment, and her duty of marriage shall he not diminish" (Exodus 21:10); "If a man have two wives" etc. (Deuteronomy 21:15).

---

17. In the summer of 1979, I saw one of Ḥākhām Kohen's handwritten books in the Magnes Museum of San Francisco. On both my visits to Cairo, in 1979 and 1982, I could not find any of the books, nor a list of the books he wrote.
18. The authorities in Egypt did not offer recognition to Ḥākhām Kefīlī nor to Ḥākhām Berākhāh Kohen. Perhaps the community leaders neglected to inform the authorities of the change, or perhaps there were political reasons. (*Al-Ahrām* No. 1171, 15 August 1917; *al-Ittiḥād* No. 3, 18 May 1926.)

During the time of Ḥākhām Kohen, there were more than five requests from Karaites to marry a second wife. Ḥākhām Kohen and Murād Farag agreed on the legality of such a union, but both fought it as undesirable. Each case was examined separately to find a way out. (Minutes of 22 September 1921—3 March 1925).

3. Changing faith from Rabbanism to Karaism: The minutes of the religious council recorded many requests for changing faith to Karaism, mostly to marry Karaite girls. *Al-Ittiḥād* once again argued strongly against any change in the Eupatoria ruling of 1910. Ḥākhām Kohen advised the community that a different decision could be reached; Murād Farag advocated the legality of such action. Many leaflets were published against him. The problem lingered, and in 1936, Ḥākhām Tobiah declared that he would do nothing unless all Karaite communities reached agreement on this problem (Pl. 3).

Under such pressure, the religious council had to refuse all requests for affiliation with the Karaite faith.

4. As far as relations with the Rabbanite community were concerned, Ḥākhām Kohen and Ḥākhām Ḥayyīm Naḥūm, Chief Rabbi of the Rabbanites, enjoyed a good relationship and mutual respect (both were born in Turkey).

During this period of time efforts were made to narrow the gap between the two communities, but these efforts were unsuccessful because only the rich and the élite were involved. As usual, *al-Ittiḥād* left no room for compromise and therefore for success.[19]

5. In 1899, a woman named Sitaytah al-Muṣaffī donated a piece of land in 'Abbāsiyah and also a sum of money to build a synagogue and a school. It took the community 27 years to begin building the synagogue. On Sunday, 23 May 1926, Ḥākhām Kohen led the ceremony of laying the foundation stone for it; it was completed in 1931.

Ḥākhām Kohen died in May 1933. He left a library that included 70 rare books, as well as books that he himself had written. The religious council built a fine memorial for Ḥākhām Kohen, taking in return the treasures that he had left.

After Ḥākhām Kohen's death, Yaʻqūb Farag ʻAbd-Allāh took over his religious duties, while Yūsuf Ibrāhīm Marzūq became acting deputy for the community.[20]

It is interesting to examine Ḥākhām Abrāhām Kohen's contract and compare it with the one given to Berākhāh Kohen. Ḥākhām Abrāhām Kohen was offered more than double the salary of his predecessor, and better lodging, at least as far as location in 'Abbāsiyah is concerned — all this indicating that the community at that time was in better financial condition. It is also possible that Ḥākhām Abrāhām Kohen, as ḥākhām akbar in Turkey, was able to ask for more, before

---

19. *L'Aurore* No. 42 (5 December 1924). This is a French-language Egyptian newspaper (Sam Levi, *Sam's Guide,* 1925). *Al-Ittiḥād* (28 December 1924).
20. Minutes of 6 May 1933.

agreeing to accept a similar position.

There was no mention of his duties as ḥazzān. Perhaps someone else carried out those duties; he was asked to be in the bēt-dīn for only four days, and even then for only three hours each day.

Ḥākhām Tobiah Levi Babovitch (1879-1956; served 1934-1956)

Born in Russia, in Bakhtchisarai, he studied under many scholars, among them Isaac Sultansky, to whom he later became an assistant. He worked as a teacher in Karaite schools in Bakhtchisarai and Theodosia, where he later became ḥākhām akbar in 1911. That same year he became ḥākhām akbar in Sebastopol.

Ḥākhām Tobiah wrote to the Karaite community in Cairo offering his services.

The offer was discussed in the religious council on 21 March 1933, and it was decided to petition the Minister of the Interior for permission to allow Tobiah to enter Egypt. On his way, Tobiah was asked to inspect the Karaite settlement in Jerusalem. It was also decided that Elie Bārūkh Mas'ūdah would meet him in Jaffa and return with him.[21]

On 26 June 1934, the religious council appointed Tobiah Levi Babovitch ḥākhām akbar of the Karaite community in Cairo, on a temporary basis pending royal decree. He was given free lodging near the 'Abbāsiyah synagogue despite strong opposition from the "Organization for Social Reforms" to having the Ḥākhām living in al-Ḥārah.

The royal decree, however, did not arrive until 1941. Tobiah was given Egyptian nationality on 19 March 1941.

When he arrived in Egypt, relations between Karaites and Rabbanites were at their best, which he accepted as a pleasant fact. He tried in vain to end many customs among the Cairene Karaites. Unfortunately the opposition to his efforts came, as usual, from those who knew little about the faith.[22]

During his time many legal questions were raised, and Tobiah, along with a number of those knowledgeable in the faith, had many discussions, which were published in al-Kalīm.[23]

Ḥākhām Tobiah quickly learned Arabic and spoke it fluently, although with a Russian accent.[24]

Tobiah was well known to the Karaite community of Cairo even before he became ḥākhām. In Russia, around 1921, he had published a small book contain-

---

21. Elie Bārūkh knew Russian well.
22. Karaites in Cairo would not allow marriages during certain months of the year. Some residents of al-Ḥārah used to drink ouzo during Passover. They used to visit the cemeteries and spend one night with the dead on certain occasions.
23. The participants in the talks were Murād Farag, Yūsuf Marzūq, Yūsuf Ḥayyīhah, David Līsha', Yūsuf Yomtōb and others.
24. As early as 1937, I found his signature in Arabic on the minutes of the religious council.

ing three articles. These three articles, with an introduction, were published in Arabic in *al-Ittiḥād* from July 1927 to February 1928. In 1926 he sent a letter to the religious council asking for financial help to publish a book he wrote, *The Rise of the Karaite Sect*.

While in Egypt, he wrote many articles for *al-Kalīm*. He also published a small book in Hebrew *Rosh Penah*, "The Corner Stone."

Tobiah spent some time organizing the community library in Khurunfish; unfortunately, his efforts were not matched by the community or the religious council. Consequently, many valuable books and manuscripts in that library disappeared.[25]

In the 1940's Tobiah felt that the community was wealthy and could afford many reforms if everyone would pay the tithe, as called for in the Torah. He was hoping to surround the synagogue in 'Abbāssiyah with a hospital, a school, a library, offices, and apartments for members of the community.

For the community it was a beautiful dream, but for Tobiah it was almost a reality. To encourage the people to pay their tithe, he declared that he had received $2,500 from an anonymous member. This was followed by $2,200. Everyone knew then that the donor was Ḥākhām Tobiah himself. Unfortunately, his generosity was never matched.

According to the contract between Tobiah and the religious council, it was his duty to teach ten interested members to become ḥazzanīm and ḥākhāmīm. He began to do this, but how it ended, no one knows.

Tobiah kept a low profile, yet he was well known among the other minority leaders, as well as among Islamic leaders (Pl. 4). He was invited to, and participated in, all national events.[26] Shortly after World War II ended, however, many Islamic movements began to display open hatred toward Jews and other minorities.

The Muslim Brothers *(al-Ikhwān al-Muslimūm)* constituted the strongest of these groups. Their hatred and animosity reached a climax during the 1948 war. Many Jews were attacked in the streets and in their homes. In some cases, the police could do nothing.

In all fairness, one must admit that casualties were at a minimum. Many tolerant Muslims defended their Jewish neighbors and friends. Yet many Jews started to leave the country, and Karaites were no different. Tobiah did his best to stop this, insisting that things would improve, and the Jews would find no better place to live than Egypt.

---

25. After 1956, the ḥākhām's office and the library were rarely used. No inventory was ever taken. In the late 1960's, the library contents were placed in the Synagogue of Mosheh al-Darʻī. From that time on its treasures were everyone's prey.

26. All the ceremonies held during the reigns of King Fu'ād and King Fārūq, and the terms of Muḥammad Nagīb and Nāṣir. See "How the Community was Governed."

On 23 July 1952, the Free Officers, headed by Muḥammad Nagīb, overthrew King Fārūq. In October 1952, Tobiah met with Nagīb, accompanied by Lieto Bārūkh Masʿūdah, vice chairman of the religious council and Murād al-Qudsī, a member of the religious council, who himself had earlier arranged this meeting.

The visit was so successful that Nagīb promised to visit the Karaite synagogue in ʿAbbāsiyah. On October 25th, the visit took place and was the talk of the city and the main news.[27]

Soon afterward, Tobiah's health began to deteriorate. He was deeply saddened by the emigration movement, seeing that such events put an end to his beautiful dream: building a Karaite city around the main synagogue. He was hospitalized more than once,[28] during which time ʿAbdū Bārūkh Mūsā Ṣaliḥ was appointed acting ḥākhām.

On 25 July 1956, Ḥākhām Tobiah died. He was to be the last ḥākhām of one of the oldest Karaite communities. Literally the whole community attended his funeral.

Amīr Alāi (Colonel) Muḥammad Riyāḍ represented President Nāṣir; Qāʾim Maqām (Lieutenant-Colonel) Muḥammad Murād represented the Minister of the Interior; Elie Shamʿūn (a Karaite) represented the governor of Cairo. Arch-Metropolitan Yūsuf Tawīl represented the Roman Catholics; Ḥākhām Ḥayyīm Duwayk represented the Rabbanite community. The Shaykh al-Azhar and the French amabassador sent telegreams of condolence.[29] Saʿd Munīr represented Ḥākhām Ḥayyīm Nāḥūm, the chief Rabbi of the Rabbanite community (Pl. 5).

Murād Hārūn, a well-educated member of the faith, replaced Tobiah as acting ḥākhām. He kept this position until he left for Switzerland in 1967. His brother, Bārūkh Hārūn, took over the position. In September of 1984 he left for Israel.

The Karaite community, which, during the Fatimid reign was more numerous and more influential than the Rabbanite community, is now something of the past.[30] Its members number no more than 20, and there are no services held of any kind.

---

27. A full account of this meeting is found in the section "How the Community was Governed."
28. The second time Tobiah was hospitalized, the religious council delegated David Līshaʿ, Murād al-Qudsī, and the *shammas* (beadle) of the main synagogue to take an inventory of Tobiah's apartment and belongings. They were surprised to find boxes of donation receipts from an "anonymous" donor.
29. A full account of the funeral can be found in the local press of the day, or in *al-Kalīm* No. 235 (15 August 1956).
30. Graetz, *History of the Jews*, Vol. III, J.P.S.A. 1894, p. 444.

Ḥākhām Shlomōh Kohen (1873-1875)

Ḥākhām Mosheh al-Qudsī the second (1856-1872)

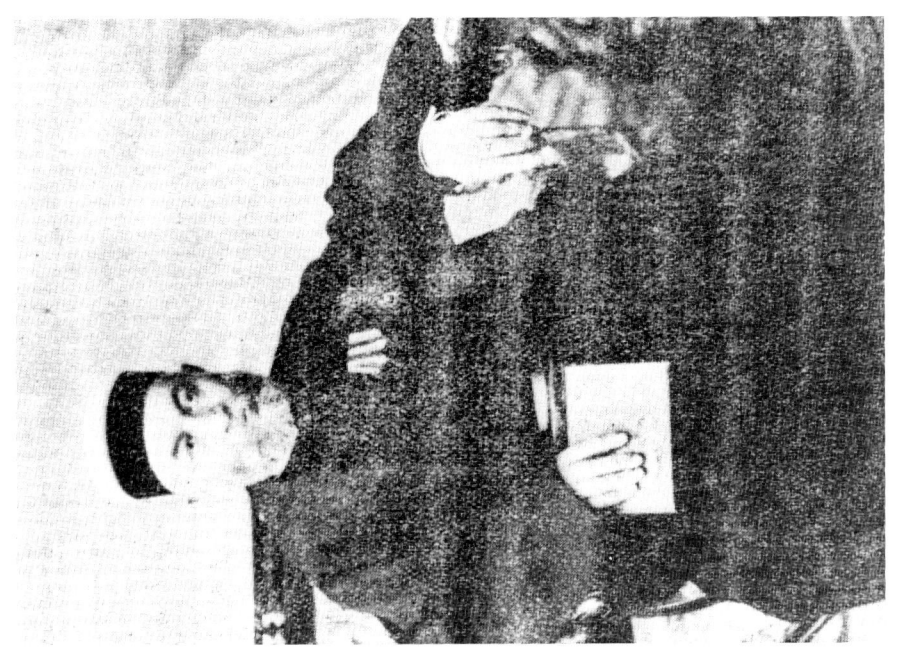

Ḥākhām Ahārūn Kefīlī (1907)

Ḥākhām Shabbethāi Mangūbī (1876-1906)

Ḥākhām Berākhāh Isḥāq Kohen
(1908-1915)

Ḥākhām Abrāhām Kohen
(1920-1933)

Ḥākhām Tobiah Babovitch (1934-1956)

Ḥākhām Tobiah Babovitch in the procession of King Fu'ād (1936)

Representatives of the three religions. Ḥākhām Tobiah Babovitch, al-Shaykh 'Isā Manūm, al-Anbā Tomās in the procession of the Unknown Soldier (May 1953)

PLATE 1: Part of a deed issued in 1276 Hijrah (1859 A.D.) in which the name of Ḥākhām Mosheh al-Qudsī, "the pride of his colleagues, and the treasure of his associates," the son of Ibrāhīm al-Qudsī, appeared as a witness for a sale of real estate that involved some members of the Karaite community.

وثيقة زواج تاريخية

An old Karaite act of marriage dated 1803 A.D.

From its contents we understand that the act was executed at the Karaite Bēt-Dīn, between Elīyāhū Fīrūz, the groom, and ʿAzīzah (the virgin) daughter of al-Shaykh Menashah.

ترجمة حياة المرحوم الحاخام شبتاى منجوبى
حاخامباشى الطائفة سابقاً

نشأ الفقيد في الاستانة العلية واقام فيها الى سن الاربعين وكان هناك الرئيس الديني لجماعة القرايين ثم استحسن الانتقال الى مصر فلما وفد ومكث مدة شهر من الزمان استصوب اعيان الطائفة تعيينه حاخاماً لما رأوه فيه من غزارة العلم ومحاسن الصفات والكفاءة لهذا المنصب الكبير . وقد لبث المرحوم في وظيفته مدة ثلاثين سنة كان في خلالها مثال التقوى والورع ونموذج الصلاح والاستقامة وقد جذب اليه قلوب افراد الطائفة بما اوتيه من مكارم الاخلاق ورقة الطباع والتواضع والبشاشة واللطف . وكان رحمه الله ذا منظر مهيب ووجه وقور تبدو على محياه الرزانة والحلم . اذا جلس اليه اي انسان شعر بجاذبية اليه واحسّ بسمو روحه . وكان رحمه الله معضداً ومسموع الكلمة لدى اعيان الطائفة المتوفين كالمرحوم اسحاق ليشع والمرحوم يوسف مرزوق وغيرهما كما كان محبوبا ومحترما لدى اعيان اخواننا يهود الطائفة الثانية وكانوا يدعونه في حفلاتهم الرسمية وغيرها وقد كانت بين الفقيد وبين حاخامباشى الطائفة الثانية الحالي صلات مودة عظيمة وكثيراً ما تبادلا الزيارات والمباحثات . وقد حظي رحمه الله بمقابلة المرحوم الخديوي توفيق عدة مقابلات خصوصية وذلك لان الخديوي المذكور كان يحبه ويحترمه كثيراً وكذلك كان يقابل اللورد كرومر معتمد انكلترا السابق في مصر لامور تختص بالطائفة فقد سعى رحمه الله لدى اللورد في حمل الحكومة على الاعتراف رسمياً بالطائفة فنجح في مسعاه . وكذلك حظى رحمه الله بمقابلة سمو الخديوي الحالي في اوائل جلوسه مقابلة خصوصية لقي فيها كل حفاوة واحترام وكان يذهب في ايام الاعياد للمعايدة على سموه وعلى عطوفة ناظر النظار . وقد تأسس في ايامه المجلس الملي للطائفة فكان رأس جلساته ويباشر تنفيذ قراراته كما كان يقوم بجميع اعمال الحاخامخانة والوقف وكذلك كان هو وحده القائم بتأدية جميع الشعائر الديدية من صلاة وزواج وختان ومأتم وكان لفرط تواضعه رحمه الله لا يتأخر عن الذهاب الى افقر فقير في الطائفة . وكان

رحمه الله يحسن التكلم بعدة لغات كالعبرية والعربية والتركية واليونانية والاسپانيولية

توفي رحمه الله في ٢ ابريل سنة ١٩٠٦ عن سبعين سنة وكان ذلك أثر مرض الزمه الفراش عدة اسابيع فحزنت عليه الطائفة باسرها حزناً شديداً وبكى عليه الشيوخ والشبان والعقائل والاوانس واحتفل بتشييع جنازته احتفالا مهيباً لائقاً بمقامه العظيم وقد مشت فيه الطائفة بأجمعها وجميع الرؤساء الروحانيين ومندوب من قبل سمو الخديوي وكثيرون من اعيان وافراد الطائفة الثانيه وجميع اساتذة وتلامذة مدرسة الطائفة. وقد عطل جميع افراد الطائفة اشغالهم في هذا اليوم حدادا عليه وقد احتفل بتأبينه في الكنيس في احد الايام فألنه كثيرون نثراً وشعراً، ولا تزال للآن ذكرى الفقيد في قلوب افراد الطائفة وما برحوا يترحمون عليه في كل آن ذاكرين ايامه الطيبات وصفاته الحسنة تغمده الله برحمته، واسكنه فسيح جنته

PLATE 2
A biography of the late Ḥākhām Shabbethāi Mangūbī

He grew up in Istanbūl and lived there until he was 40 years old. There he was the ḥākhām akbar of the Karaite community. Then he wished to move to Cairo. A little later, the leaders of the Karaite community appointed him ḥākhām because of his good character and high education. He occupied this post for 30 years.

The article goes on to describe the relationship between Mangūbī and the leaders of the community, such as Isḥāq Lishaʿ and Yūsuf Marzūq, as well as others.

The article also mentions that there was mutual understanding and respect between Ḥākhām Mangūbī and the ḥākhām akbar of the Rabbanite community.

It also mentioned that Ḥākhām Mangūbī met privately with Khudaywī Tawfīq, the ruler of Egypt, who liked Mangūbī and respected him. He met frequently with Lord Cromer, the British governor, to discuss with him matters of concern to the Karaite community. Lord Cromer successfully persuaded the Egyptian government to recognize the Karaite community as an independent one.

The articles goes on to mention that Ḥākhām Mangūbī spoke many languages fluently: Hebrew, Arabic, Turkish, Greek, and Spanish. Ḥākhām Mangūbī died on April 2, 1906 and was mourned by all members of the community.

اقرار حضرة الحاخام طوبيا سمحاه ليڤى

الى جميع ابناء افراد طائفة اليهود القرائيه
مصر

لتكن سلوماً لدى جميع افراد الطائفه امد سائله
تقرير الانضمام والزواج ممن لا عكست ابن ينى على
يدى الاسرائلفت من افراد الطائفة مصر وكذا جميع طوائف
القرائية فى الخارج لان هذه المسألة مبدائى لن لو
خوى الاسرائلفت الجميع مؤتمرات عالمية
القاهرة فى ١٠ يناير ١٩٣٦

جمعية الدفاع عن مصالح الطائفه

١٠ يناير سنة ١٩٣٦

PLATE 3: A note appeared in a bulletin published by *Gam'iyat al-Difā' 'an Maṣaliḥ al-Ṭā'ifah* regarding the subject of intermarriage, especially with Rabbanites.

To all members of the Karaite Community in Egypt:

It should be known to all members of the community that the question of accepting non-Karaites converting to our faith and marrying them will not be executed by me unless all members of the community in Egypt, as well as all Karaite communities abroad, agree to this, because such a matter can only be resolved by a total consensus of the Karaite communities meeting in an international convention.

Signature in Hebrew of Ḥākhām Tobiah Babovitch.
January 10, 1936

زيارة الحاخام الأكبر لفضيلة الأستاذ الأكبر

زار سيادة الحاخام الأكبر طوبياه سمحاه ليفى بابوفيتش فضيلة الأستاذ الأكبر عبد المجيد سليم شيخ الجامع الأزهر فى مكتبه ظهر الأربعاء ٢٥ الماضى مهنئا فضيلته بالمنصب الجديد .. وقد مكث سيادة الحاخام مع فضيلة الأستاذ الأكبر زهاء نصف ساعة تبادل الرئيسان الروحانيان خلالها حديثا شائقا .. ومما قاله فضيلة الأستاذ الأكبر لسيادة الحاخام فى معرض حديثه : ــ وانه يعمل وسيعمل على توثيق روابط الألفة والتعاون بينه وبين جميع الرؤساء الروحانيين للطوائف المصرية جميعا .

PLATE 4: Al-Ḥākhām al-Akbar visits al-Ustādh al-Akbar.

Last Wednesday afternoon, the 25th of October 1959, Ḥākhām Tobiah Levy visited his excellency 'Abd al-Magīd Salīm, the Dean of al-Azhar University, in his office to congratulate him on his new post. The two spiritual leaders had an interesting talk for half an hour during which the Dean said, "I am trying and I will always try to strengthen the relationship between all spiritual leaders."

al-Kalīm, no. 130, 1 November 1950

PLATE 5: Minutes of the Karaite Religious Council meeting in a special session in Mosheh al-Darʿī synagogue.

Dignitaries who attended the funeral of Ḥākhām Tobiah Levy Babovitch

1. Saʿd Munīr — Representing Ḥākhām Ḥayyīm Nāḥūm.
2. Ḥākhām Ḥayyīm Duwayik — Representing the Rabbanite Community.
3. Archimandrite Yūsūf Tawīl — Representing the Western Catholics.
4. Colonel Maḥmūd Riyād — Representing President Nāssir.
5. Lt. Colonel Maḥmūd Murād — Representing the Minister of Interior
6. Elie Shamʿōn (a Karaite) — Representing the Governor of Cairo
7. Both representatives of the Catholic Copts and the Armenian Catholics did not sign.

Shaykh al-Azhar, the Ambassador of France in Egypt, and many others sent telegrams.

Chapter IX

Karaites and Zionism

By his faith every Jew is a Zionist, in the sense that one day all the Jews will be assembled in the Holy Land. Karaites were no exception. In his book, *The Return to Zion,* Aryeh Rubenstein wrote:

> The Karaites, who proclaimed to their faithful, "Be assembled in the holy city and gather your brethren," began their Aliyah as early as the 9th century. In the 10th century, there was a cultural efflorescence among the Karaites in Eretz Israel, and the Karaite community spread to Ramleh. The Karaites used to bestow the title Yerushalmi ("Jerusalemite") on every immigrant and this event was the occasion for great celebration for the entire community.
>
> Most of the Karaites who settled in Israel in the 9th century ordered their lives according to the customs of the Avelei Zion ("Mourners of Zion"). These were groups of Jews devoted to mourning the destruction of Jerusalem and to praying for the redemption of Zion. The customs of this group — such as abstention from meat and wine — can be traced to the period immediately following the destruction of the second Temple in 70 c.e.[1]

Karaite scholars throughout the centuries wrote urging 'Aliyah. Daniel al-

---

1. *Popular History of Jewish Civilization: The Return to Zion,* compiled by Aryeh Rubenstein, (New York, Paris: Leon Amid Publisher)

Qumīsī, at the beginning of the 10th century, wrote a message to the Karaites in all countries urging them to make ʿAliyah. "In this message, he defended the idea that the Karaites should return before the coming of the Messiah and not wait for an act of God for their return."[2]

Japheth ben Eli, at the end of the 10th century, wrote a poem in Hebrew urging the Karaites to remember Zion.[3]

It must be remembered that the Karaites never forgot Zion in their writings, in their prayers, and in their hopes to live there.

There were always Karaites in Jerusalem. In the early years of the movement, they had a Karaite Academy there. The first crusades, in the year 1099, however, put an end to the Karaite community in Jerusalem. But the Karaite community as a whole has always tried to maintain a settlement in Jerusalem to mourn the destruction of the Temple.

In modern times there has always been a Karaite community in Israel, albeit a very small one. Its members depended for their livelihood on financial help from Russia, Poland, and Egypt, until the establishment of the state of Israel.[4]

Before the establishment of the state of Israel, however, Karaite participation in the Zionist movement was relatively limited. When modern Zionism started in the late 19th century, Jews in Egypt were in a transitional period. Their conditions had just begun to improve socially and financially. They were relatively secure, and did not foresee the need for such a movement. The Karaite community, too, was not in a situation that permitted it to get involved.

After World War I, this situation changed completely, and gradually the Jews of Egypt recognized the importance of such a movement, and in the 1920's the Zionist movement gained momentum, especially among Sephardic Jews.

In 1925, Chaim Weizmann visited Cairo to promote his ideas. Hayyīm Nahūm, the Chief Rabbi of the Rabbanite community, along with members of the Jewish community active in the Zionist movement, invited Weizmann to visit "Bēt Yisrael," the headquarters of the movement. There, they were welcomed by the executive chairman of Bēt Yisrael, the well-known Karaite attorney Yūsuf Bārūkh Masʿūdah, and they heard Weizmann express his gratitude to the Jewish community for their efforts in the movement (Pl. 1).

Included among those active in the movement was the chief Rabbi of the Karaite community, Ḥākhām Abrāhām Kohen, and Murād Farag, the well-known writer and poet, as well as other wealthy members of the community (Pl. 2). In fact, the book *Al-Qudsiyāt (ha-Qudisyot),* prose and poetry in Hebrew and Arabic, was dedicated to defend the Jews in Jerusalem in the 1920's.

---

2. Leon Nemoy, *Karaite Anthology,* pp. 34-38.
3. Nemoy, pp. 107-108.
4. See "How the Community was Governed," Chapter 2.

The Karaites themselves never formed any Zionist association of their own, nor did they have an affiliation with the Zionist movement. Yet the pages of *al-Ittiḥād* in the years 1924-1930 bore witness to the true feelings of the Karaites toward Zionism. In any case, it is a fact that in the early 1940's some Karaite high school and university students used to attend Zionist meetings, where they were recruited by Zionist girls, who at the time were working as A.T.S. in the British forces stationed in Cairo. After the 1948 Israeli War of Independence, the first Arab-Israeli war, Zionist activities were completely outlawed in Egypt.

The fact that Karaites did continue to become involved in Zionist activities, however, was suicidally demonstrated by one young Karaite doctor, Mosheh Lieto Marzūq, who joined a Zionist group which, among other things carried out anti-government activities. Mosheh, together with a Rabbanite engineer and others, was caught and tried, and condemned to be hanged. He was executed in January 1955.[5]

---

5. The Levon affair.

الدكتور روزمن زعيم الصهيونيين
في «بيت اسرائيل» بالقاهرة

رغب الدكتور وزمن بمجرد وصوله الى القاهرة في زيارة هذا البيت وشاركه في هناه الرغبة سيادة حاخام أكبر اخواننا وحددا لها يوم الاربعاء الذي سبق الماضي فاقامت اللجنة الاداريه لهذا البيت حفلة شاي تكريمية للزائرين الكريمين شرفها الكثيرون من كبار اخواننا المشتغلين بالحركة الصهيونية بمصر

وقد القى الافوكاتو يوسف باروخ مسعوده رئيس اللجنة الادارية خطبة بليغة رحب فيها بالزائرين الكريمين ثم خطب الدكتور وزمن عن واجب يهود مصر نحو الحركة الصهيونية منوها عن المساعي المشكورة التي يبذلها سيادة الحاخام الاكبر لاخواننا ناحوم افندي في سبيل الحصول على مؤازرة كبار أعيان يهود مصر للصهيونية

ثم القى سيادة الحاخام الاكبر خطبة بليغة للغاية أعلن فيها رغبته الاكيدة في الاشتغال للحركة الصهيونية في مصر

PLATE 1: Dr. Weizman, the Zionist leader in "Bēt Yisrael" in Cairo

As soon as Dr. Weizman arrived in Cairo he expressed his wish to visit "Bēt Yisrael." Ḥayyīm Nāḥūm, the chief rabbi of the Jewish community, joined him. On Wednesday a tea party was held for both and for all interested in the Zionist movement in Egypt.

Attorney Yūsūf Bārūkh Masʿūdah, the chairman of the executive committee, gave a speech welcoming the two dignified visitors.

Dr Weizman talked about the responsibility of the Jews in Egypt towards the Zionist movement. He thanked the chief Rabbi for his effort to solicit the help of rich members.

Ḥayyīm Nāḥūm gave an eloquent speech in which he affirmed his willingness to help the Zionist movement in Egypt.

al-Ittiḥād, no. 2, 5 May 1925.

زيارة وفد
من رجال التعليم اليهود فى فلسطين لمصر

وفد على مصر فى أوائل الاسبوع الماضى وفد من المعلمين والمعلمات اليهود فى مدارس فلسطين بقصد زيارة مدارس مصر ودور الآثار والمتاحف التى بها وهو مكون من ستين رجلا و ثلاثين سيدة وقد اهتمت حكومتنا المصرية بزيارة هـذا الوفد اهتماما دل على حسن تقديرها للعلم ورجاله وقامت بعمل كل ما رأته فيه تسهيلا للوفد فى تحقيق الغرض من زيارته وقد نزل أعضاء الوفد فى ضيافة وزارة المعارف العمومية بمدرسة الاورمان الثانوية بالجيزة وخصصت لهم طاهيا يهوديا لاعداد طعامهم احتراما لتقاليدنا

وكان فى استقبال الوفد عند وصوله الى محطة مصر كبار رجال التعليم بوزارة المعارف وكبار رجال الطوائف الاسرائيلية بمصر وكان بينهم مندوبا عن طائفتنا وهما سيادة حاخامنا الاكبر ابراهيم كوهين وحضرة صاحب العزة مراد بك فرج المحامى رئيس مجلسنا الملى

وقد زار الوفد معظم مدارس القاهرة العالية والثانوية والخصوصية والابتدائية والجامعة المصرية وسر أعضاؤه من تقدم التعليم ونظمه فى مصر وكانوا يشكرون ناظر كل مدرسة زاروها ومعلميها على حفاوتهم بهم وحسن استقبالهم لهم

وقد زار رئيس الوفد ووكيله وسكرتيره حاخامخانتنا يوم الثلاثاء الماضى دون سابق علم لشكر سيادة الحاخام على تفضله باستقبال الوفد عند وصوله الى محطة مصر وقد لغوا كل حفاوة من سيادته ومن حضرة وكيل الحاخامخانة

وفى يوم الاربعاء الماضى اقامت الطوائف الاسرائيلية حفلة شاى بهوتيل الكونتننتال فى الساعة الخامسة مساء تكريما لاعضاء الوفد شرفها بالحضور حضرة صاحب المعالى وزير المعارف وكبار رجال التعليم والدكتور وزمن وأعيان الطوائف الاسرائيلية كما شرفها بالنيابة عن طائفتنا حضرة صاحب السيادة حاخامنا الاكبر وحضرة صاحب العزة رئيس مجلسنا الملى وجناب الوجيه الكبير الخواجه باروخ ليتو عضو مجلسنا الملى وقد القيت فى الحفلة الخطب المناسبة باللغات العبرية والعربية والفرنساوية وكان ضمن الخطباء حضرة الحبر الجليل حاخامنا الاكبر الذى القى كلمته باللغة العبرية وقد اعجب بها رجال الوفد اعجابا حتى انهم رجوه أن يتفضل عليهم بأخذها وتسمح لهم بالاصل معه لكى يكن محتفظا بصورة منه وقد وصل البنان الخطبة كانت بليغة للغاية وحوت ما يملى من قدر طائفتنا ويزيدها مكانة وخضب أيضا باللغة العربية حضرة صاحب العزة مراد بك فرج رئيس مجلسنا الملى وكان لخطابه وقع طيب فى نفوس السامعين

وفى يوم السبت الماضى زار اعضاء الوفد احياء اليهود باقسام الموسكى والجمالية والكنائس التى بها

واليوم ظهرا يقيم لهم حضرة صاحب المعالى وزير المعارف مأدبة غذاء بمدرسة الاورمان بالجيزة وفى نفس يوم يبرحون القاهرة بقطار الساعة السادسة مساء ليتمكنوا من قضاء أيام عيد الفصح المبارك بفلسطين فندعوا لهم بسلامة الاياب إلى بلادهم ولا يسعنا الا أن نتقدم على صفحات هذه المجلة بواجب الشكر الوافر وفرض الامتنان العاطر لحضرة صاحب المعالى على باشا ماهر وزير المعارف على العناية التى شمل بها الوفد وكذلك رجال التعليم الذين رافقوا اعضاءه فى زيارتهم ولا يفوتنا أن نذكر بالثناء حضرة صاحب العزة ناظر مدرسة الاورمان احمد خيرى بك الذى بالغ فى اكرام اعضاء الوفد ومدة نزولهم بمدرسته بالجيزة وأينما سار اعضاء الوفد فى مصر كانوا محلا للتكريم والتبجيل فدل ذلك على ان المصريين حقيقة « كرماء لضيوفهم »

PLATE 2: A delegation of Jewish educators from Palestine visits Egypt

During the second week of March, 1926, a delegation of 90 Jewish educators (60 men and 30 women) arrived in Cairo to visit its universities, schools and museums.

The Egyptian government did its best to accommodate the visitors and to facilitate their stay.

Members of the delegation were lodged in the dormitories of the Orman Secondary School as guests of the Egyptian Ministry of Education. A Jewish "chef" was assigned to prepare Kasher meals.

Among those who welcomed the delegation at the Main Railway Station was the Karaite Ḥākhām Akbar Abrāhām Kohen, and Murād Farag, the chairman of the Karaite Religious Council. A delegation visited the Karaite Bēt-Dīn a few days later to thank Ḥākhām Kohen for welcoming them.

The Jewish community of Egypt held a reception for the delegation in the Continental Hotel (among the best at the time).

Murād Farag gave an eloquent speech in Arabic. Ḥākhām Kohen gave a speech in Hebrew which caught every one by surprise. Ḥākhām Kohen had to give the delegation the only copy he had of his speech when they asked for one.

Last Saturday members of the delegation visited both Jewish neighborhoods (Rabbanite and Karaite) and the synagogues there. Today the Minister of Education, 'Alī Māhir Bāshā, invited members of the delegation to a luncheon to be held in the Orman Secondary School at Gizah. In the afternoon all the members will leave Cairo at 6:00 P.M. so that they can spend Passover in Palestine. We wish them all a safe trip.

We take this occasion to extend our gratitude to 'Alī Māhir Bāshā and to Aḥmad Khayrī Bey, the principal of the Orman Schools. Indeed we can say that the Egyptians are truly hospital to their guests.

Chapter X

The Twentieth Century Exodus

Where Did the Karaites Go?

The Future of the Karaites

The Karaites in Israel

The Twentieth Century Exodus

    The Jewish community in Egypt in the 1940's was very strong, rich, and influential. Many commercial banks were run by them. Imports and exports of certain items were in their hands. Wealthy Rabbanite families[1] carried out industrial and agricultural reforms in many parts of the country, especially in upper Egypt. This activity, of course, was in addition to that of the many small businesses which served the country very well indeed.
    Most Jews were honest in their feelings towards the country and its future. They felt that they were as much a part of it as the Muslims and the Copts. The economic boom of World War II was a strong factor in uniting the various elements of the nation, Muslims, Christians, and Jews. Yet soon after the war ended, the various national and international movements gained strength, and true feelings towards non-Muslim communities came to the surface.
    No organization showed as much hatred to non-Muslims, especially Jews, as

---

1. These families included the Cicurel, Suarez, Qaṭṭāwī, Mosseri, Bitchotto, Farhī, Menasha, Nacamuli, Ades, and others.

the young and well-organized "Muslim Brothers." In the late 1930's their leaders used the "Palestine Question" as a tool to help spread hatred of the Jews all over the country and even all over the Arab World (Pl. 1). The Egyptian authorities never tried to stop such activities. At least (as the authorities felt), it kept millions from attacking the government policies of the time. They acted behind the scenes, but everyone was well aware of their involvement. During the Arab-Israeli war of 1948, they joined the Egyptian forces and fought fiercely. After the war they carried out a virulent national campaign against the Jews. At times anti-Jewish feeling swept the country, especially in rural areas. It was this popular anti-Jewish feeling that caused the greatest concern to the Jewish community.

Each Friday, after noon prayers, Muslim worshippers in some areas took to the streets and demonstrated against the Jews. On 20 June 1948, bombs exploded in both the Karaite and Rabbanite neighborhoods, killing 34 and wounding 80 from both communities.[2]

Between July 17-20, bombs were placed in the Rabbanite Jewish quarter, killing and wounding over 200 people.[3]

Jews, feeling less safe, began to leave. At first, however, the number of such emigrants was not noticeable. One of the first Karaites to leave the country was Solomon Shabbethāi Nōnō,[4] a dedicated Hebrew teacher in the Karaite schools. It was through his efforts that the Karaites arriving in Israel were settled together. This later helped them to form communities in different parts of Israel. Nōnō became the Chief Ḥākhām for the Karaites in Israel, and kept that position until his death on 8 March 1976.

In Egypt, life returned almost to normal after the first Arab-Israeli war ended. There was a feeling that the Arabs, led by Egypt, could work out a peace treaty with Israel. Still, the Muslim Brothers continued their violent campaign against the Jews. On Saturday, 26 January 1952, the center of Cairo was set on fire. The Shepard Hotel, the jewel of local hotels, Barclay's Bank, all the theatres, all stores owned by foreigners or Jews, all casinos and cafes, even the Rabbanite school in 'Abbāsiyah, were looted and then burned[5] (Pl. 2).

Efforts were quickly made to restore confidence in the government. It was felt that the sooner this terrible situation was eliminated, the sooner things would return to normal. That is precisely what happened. Cicurel reopened as an ultra-modern

---

2. *Al-Kalīm,* No. 82, 1 July 1948. The list of people killed was censored, but was later published in No. 103, 1 July 1949.
3. Hayyim J. Cohen, *The Jews of the Middle East,* 1860-1972, p. 50.
4. He left in January 1949.
5. *Al-Kalīm,* No. 158, 16 February 1952; all evening newspapers of 26 January 1952 *(al-Muqaṭṭam),* all morning newspapers of 27 January 1952 *(al-Ahrām).*

store[6] (Pl. 3). The Rabbanite school reopened after being completely repaired and refurbished.

Six months later, the "Free Officers" succeeded in putting an end to the Egyptian monarchy and established a military government. At first the Jews were uneasy, since the Royal Family had always looked favorably upon Jews and minorities. But Muḥammad Nagīb, the head of the Free Officers, called for equality and unity, and visited many churches and synagogues. This helped ease some of the tension caused by the fact that some of the Free Officers were members of the Muslim Brothers.

The Egyptian government, in an operation aimed at "cleansing" the government machinery of all undesirable personnel, *al-Taṭhīr,* forced most of the Jewish government employees to leave or take early retirement.[7]

It should be noted here that as early as 1948 many small Jewish communities in small towns and villages chose either to move to larger cities or to leave the country. Hostile feeling against the Jews in those towns and villages was very strong.

In 1956 the British, French, and Israelis invaded Egypt to put an end to Nāṣir's rule. Nāṣir retaliated by deporting all foreign Jews. Many Egyptians and stateless Jews were put into protective custody. The remaining Jews understood; they felt it was a matter of time before all the Jews were forced out.

Life became more difficult for Jews and foreigners. High school graduates were unable to continue their higher education. New doctors and lawyers had extreme difficulties in obtaining licenses to work. While the authorities did not force anyone to leave the country, the personnel in each occupation became gradually narrower through attrition. To make matters worse, some police officers took the opportunity to intimidate members of the Jewish community into leaving so that they could replace them in their better apartments.

After the invasion, many Jews preferred to leave, and they left by the thousands.[8] The Rabbanite Bēt-Dīn, in cooperation with the International Red Cross and many international Jewish organizations (especially HIAS), helped many to leave.

The Karaite Bēt-Dīn did whatever was necessary to help those who decided to leave. Of the community, those who left before 1956 constituted a little over 1%; between October 1956 and March 1957 about 40% left.[9]

After the withdrawal of the invading armies, Nāṣir began to rebuild his army,

---

6. Circurel was the largest department store in the country, in fact in the Middle East, owned by a Jewish family.
7. It should be mentioned here that some of these retirees are still receiving pensions, although they are living in other countries, such as the United States.
8. The Rabbanite Bēt-Dīn, in order to give Jews easier access, moved its headquarters to Les Ecoles Juives du Caire in November 1956.
9. The Karaite Bēt-Dīn estimates that, before the invasion, less than 100 people had left the country.

in line with a national movement to prepare the Egyptians for the "Liberation of the Holy Land." Anti-Jewish feeling was at its peak, and many Jews continued to leave.[10] When I left in 1959, there were less than 2000 Karaites in Cairo.

Those who stayed the longest hoped that the conditions would improve. When it was clear that they would not, they, too, left. In 1966 Jacques Mangūbī, chairman of the Karaite religious council for 15 years, left. A few months later all members of the wealthy Līsha' family left. About six months after the third Arab-Israeli war of 1967, acting Ḥākhām Murād Hārūn left Egypt.

In 1967, Nāṣir felt that he was ready to throw the Israelis into the sea, and ordered the United Nations peace-keeping forces out of Sinai. But in the Six-Day War (sometimes known as a mini-war), the Israelis, under Dayan, smashed Nāṣir's forces and occupied the Sinai Peninsula.

Nāṣir, beaten and humiliated, put hundreds of young Rabbanites and Karaites in jail. They were badly treated, suffering humiliation and sexual assault. They were kept in prison for two years, and when allowed to leave, were not permitted to take their money with them. That was in June 1969, when there were no more than 500 Karaites in Cairo. By April of 1970 that number was reduced to 300.[11]

When I visited Cairo in 1979, there were only 50 Karaites there, and when I returned in the summer of 1982, there were only 35 — in the summer of 1984, only 24.

Where Did the Karaites Go?

The majority went to Israel. Others went to France, Italy, Switzerland, and England. A little less than 1000 came to the United States. A few went to Australia, Brazil, and Canada.

The Future of the Karaites

All of the Karaites who left Egypt did so because they were Jews. Most of those who immigrated to countries other than Israel preferred to say they were simply Jews. Since they came from Egypt, it was assumed that they were Sephardic. Most, if not all, left it at that.

Those with children, however, found it more practical to be affiliated with a congregation, be it Reform, Conservative, or Orthodox. On that basis, their children became Bar or Bat Mizvah, and married.

Some, especially older people, did not affiliate with any Rabbanite congrega-

---

10. In September 1956, there were 1500 students in Les Ecoles Juives du Caire. When the school reopened, in March 1957, there were 500.
11. In the minutes of 16 March 1969, a little before the prisoners were freed, ther religious council ordered 3500 maṣṣōt to be made. In the minutes of 3/10/70, only 2000 maṣṣōt were ordered. (A member consumes about 7 maṣṣōt during the feast.)

tion, either because they felt there was no need for it, or because they could not afford the membership dues, or both.

The same situation exists with Karaites living in Australia and Canada. In France and Switzerland, the case is similar, except that in these countries Karaites gather during the High Holy Days to hold Karaite services.

It is my judgement that 80 percent of the Karaites who came to the United States have already been assimilated into the Jewish mainstream. They are scattered in many states: about 400 in California; 150 in New York; 150 in Boston and its suburbs; 200 in Chicago; and about 200 in other states, including New Jersey and Rhode Island.

In 1976, Jacques Mangūbī was able to form a non-profit organization in Chicago under the name of "The Jewish Karaite Community in America," registered under No. 27431. Shortly afterward, he died and that marked the end of any activity on the part of this organization.

During the years 1982-83 some young members of the Karaite community in San Francisco were able to form a non-profit organization registered under No. 758 (Los Altos) (Pl. 4). The Peninsula Sinai Congregation, a Rabbanite congregation, was so helpful to the new organization, that they offered the members a suitable room in the temple building to meet and hold services.

Because of the physical difficulties, the services are held there on the first Sabbath of each month. At other times they are held in the homes of members of the organization. The organization has published, so far, many bulletins in English and a little Hebrew stating their goals and activities, and of course, articles about the faith and its history.

Letters were sent to most of the Karaites living in the United States asking for financial help. They were asking for funds to build a synagogue, a Sunday school, and a library. Time alone will give its final assessment to the efforts and dedication of the members of this organzation.

The Karaites in Israel

In the early years of the state of Israel, 1949-60, life for Eastern Jews, including Karaites, was very difficult. Yet the Karaites managed to remain together, and to live in communities of their own in Ramlah, Beersheba, Ashdod, Jaffa, Jerusalem, and other places. They have a well-organized system of representation, and a Central Higher Committee. Their headquarters is in Ramlah, where they have built a modern center that includes a library, offices for the rabbis and the chief rabbi, courtrooms, and a large hall to serve many purposes. In 1984, another synagogue was built for the Karaites in the south of Ramlah. Their synagogue in Ashdod was completed in 1982; the president of Israel, Yitzchak Navon, attended the opening ceremony and delivered a speech. They have also built a beautiful synagogue in Beersheba, and a smaller one in Moshav Ranīn. There are also small synagogues in other places. As of this writing, a new one is being built in Moshav Maṣliyaḥ.

In Jerusalem, the Karaites still have the underground synagogue built more than one thousand years ago by the "founder" of the movement, 'Anān ben David.

The Karaites in Israel face two major problems:

1) Each year, hundreds of Karaite youths, like all Israelis, are drafted into the army. There, they are totally surrounded by a Rabbanite environment, where it is not easy to remain a minority. Many of these youths marry Rabbanite girls, and are lost to the Karaite community.[12] This also happens, of course, when a Karaite woman marries a Rabbanite man; she has to join the Rabbanite community. Some members are trying to relate the children through their mothers. Others are trying to accept mixed marriages, but opposition is strong.

2) A similar problem surfaces in education. All children, including Karaites, attend public schools. This means that they are under constant influence from Rabbanite children and educators. The Karaite community has Sunday schools to teach the faith, but is that enough?

Karaite children are also under the influence of Rabbanite literature and cultural songs, history, different customs, traditions and holidays that do not fall on the same day as theirs. The Karaites in Israel are a minority within a Jewish majority and that is the major problem.

"The foremost problem which faces minorities in their struggle for survival in the turbulent ocean of the majority is that of finding a way to preserve the cultural values and customs common to their group and to transfer them to their children. Such a problem is much more serious in the case of a Jewish minority within a Jewish majority."[13]

Karaite children, like any others, are looking for identity. They are torn between two identities; the one of their own country, the country where they were born, Israel, which is very strong; and the one of their own faith, which has thousand-year-old roots. It is not easy! Another problem facing the Karaites of Isarel is that of leadership, especially religious leadership. So far, all the Karaite rabbis were born in Egypt, self-educated rabbis. None of them graduated from a theological school. That does not make them less knowledgeable than rabbis with diplomas, but in this century college degrees mean a great deal. One way of solving this problem is to build a Karaite Yeshiva where Karaite children can receive the needed education and where the influence of the majority is less. In the meantime they can

---

12. The Karaites do not accept any converts to their faith.
13. Jehoash Hirshberg, "Preservation vs. Acculturation in the Musical Tradition of the Karaites in Israel," a paper presented at the ICTM conference, August 1983.

send educated members to Rabbanite theological schools to graduate as rabbis with additional graduate studies of their own in the Karaite faith.

Dedicated Karaites are doing their best to keep the community strong and active. I visited Ramlah and Ashdod four times within a seven-year period, and talked with many responsible members of the community there, as well as with members in other places. Progress is noticeable, enthusiasm is unlimited, but there is no solution in sight to the aforementioned problems.

Another major problem is that the Karaite community is threatened from within by the independent policy of the community leadership and their way of problem-solving. The elected leaders of every community, and the members of the higher committee in Ramlah, continue to follow their own policy of dealing with problems as they occur. Those responsible leaders should realize they are now part of the country whose majority practices a faith substantially different from that of the Karaites, and they should work within that framework. Isolation does not serve any purpose. On the other hand, a successful community must always use the present to plan for the future, and always learn from the past.

Outside the Karaite synagogue of Beersheba.

Inside the Karaite synagogue of Beersheba.

The Karaite Cultural Center in Ashdod

The Karaite synagogue of Ashdod.

Inside the Karaite synagogue of Ashdod.

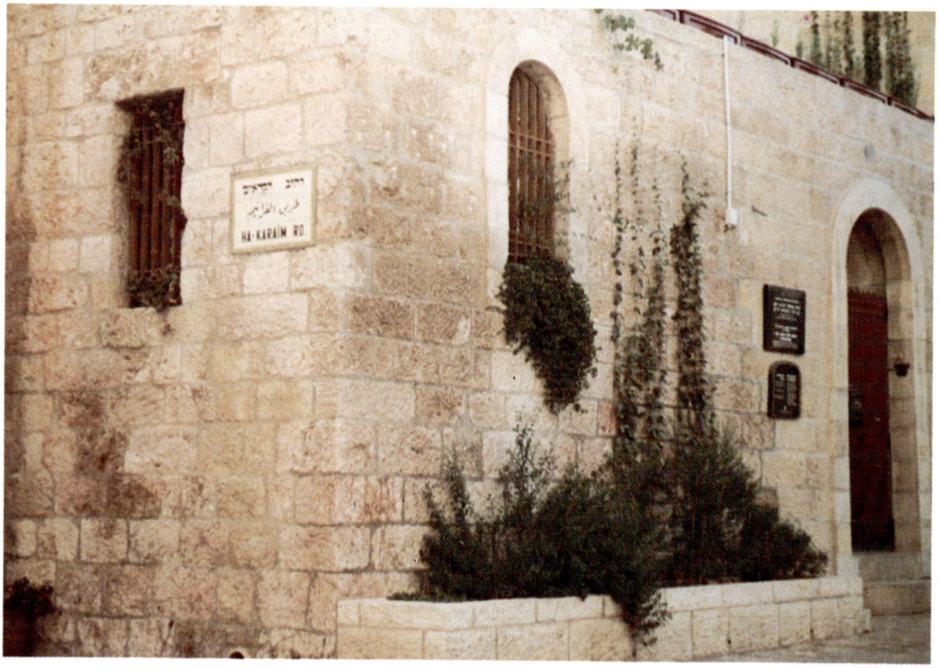

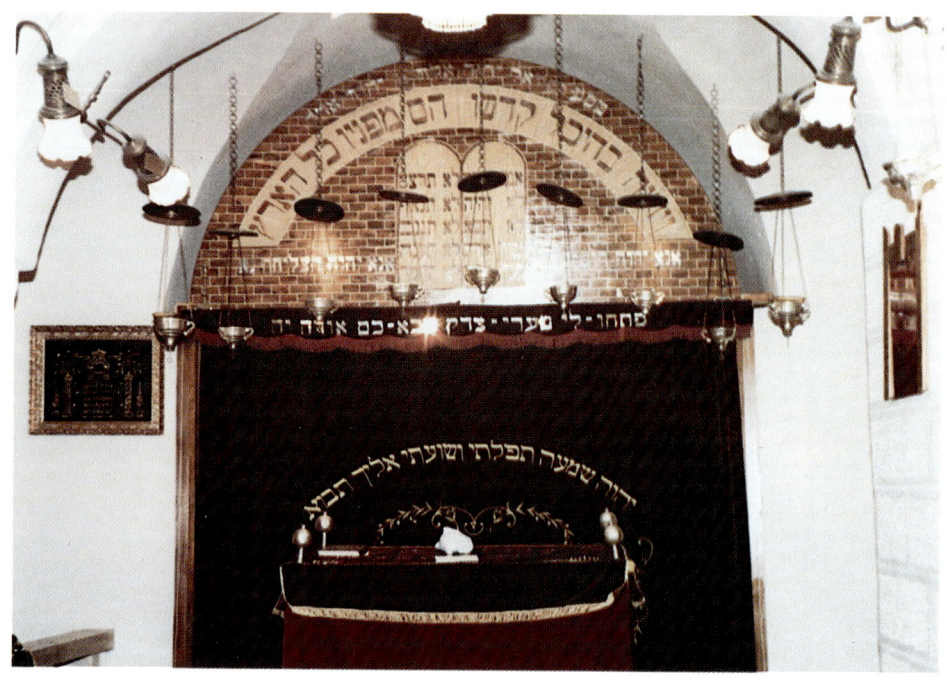

Outside the synagogue of ʻAnān.

Inside the old Karaite synagogue of ʻAnān in Jerusalem

Scrolls in different kinds of boxes

The headquarters of the Karaite Community in Israel - Ramlah

Inside the synagogue of Ramlah

Since leaving Egypt, Mūrad 'abd al-Wāḥid and his wife (to his left), Sarine (al-Qudsī), have entertained most of the Karaites who arrived and stayed in Paris on the way to their final destination to the U.S.A.

Lighting the candles, during a festival celebrating Yom Purim in San Francisco, March 1987

خطر اليهود على مصر

اليهود مسئولون عن نكبة مصر المالية

حقائق تاريخية مجهولة بقلم دكتور في الاقتصاد السياسي

لو عرف المصري أي خطر يهدده من فوز اليهود بامتلاك فلسطين وإنشاء دولة يهودية في ربوعها لأسرع إلى نجدة إخوانه الفلسطينيين الذين إنما يكافحون عن مصر قبل أن يكافحوا عن فلسطين.

قليل من المصريين من يعرف أن اليهود يسيطرون على اقتصاديات مصر وتجارتها وثرواتها ومواردها ويمتصون دماءها وأنهم قد تغلغلوا في جميع الشئون المصرية وقبضوا على كل شيء فيها تقريبا.

-b-

وقف لله تعالى

نرجو كل من يطلع على هذه الرسالة أن يطلع عليها غيره ويذيعها بين الناس بكل الطرق الممكنة وأوسعها احتسابا بالله والله لا يضيع أجر المحسنين

١٣٥٨ هـ ــ ١٩٣٩ م

-a-

The danger of Jews in Egypt

The Jews are responsible for the Egyptian economic disaster.

If the Egyptian knew the extent of the danger if the Jews succeed in acquiring Palestine and creating a Jewish state, he would not hesitate to rescue his brothers, the Palestinians, who in fact are defending Egypt before defending Palestine.

Very few Egyptians know that the Jews dominate the Egyptian economy, its commerce, and its resources, that they are "sucking its blood," that they have penetrated into all Egyptian affairs, and that they own almost everything in the country.

An Endowment to Allah

We beg of everyone who reads this article to pass it to others, and to circulate it among the people by all possible and most widespread means. For Allah's sake.

May Allah reward the benevolent.

PLATE 1: During the 1930s certain organizations used the "Palestinian Problem" to agitate feelings against the Jews. Above (a) is the front page, and (b) is page 1 of this circular dated 1939.

LIGUE INTERNATIONALE CONTRE L'ANTISÉMITISME

(SECTION D'EGYPTE)

COMITÉ CENTRAL:

Président :
LÉON CASTRO (LE CAIRE)
Vice-Présidents :
ABRAMINO MENASCE (LE CAIRE)
JOS. BOUBLI (ALEXANDRIE)
Secrétaire Générale :
R. H. BAKAL (LE CAIRE)

Pour la Paix
Pour la Justice
Contre le Racisme
Contre toutes les formes de l'Antisémitisme

Le Caire, le 25 Décembre, 1936. 193__
4, RUE EL MANAKH

Monsieur le Président;
de la Communauté Karaite,
En Ville.

Monsieur le Président,

   Nous avons l'honneur de vous communiquer, ci-inclus, le procès-verbal de la Réunion plénaire des Associations Juives du Caire, tenue le dimanche 20 ct. à la Salle des Fêtes du Temple d'Ismailieh.

   Nous espérons recevoir dans le délai fixé l'assurance de l'exécution par votre Organisation, des résolutions votées à cette Réunion, et nous comptons sur votre présence indispensable à la Réunion du 10 Janvier, 1937.

   Nous regrettons que vous n'ayiez pas estimé utile de vous faire représenter à cette Réunion du 20 ct. et ne pouvons croire que vous puissiez, en tant qu'Association Juive, vous désintéresser de la lutte contre l'Antisémitisme.

   Quel que soit le but principal de votre Association, il est manifeste que vous ne pourrez l'atteindre sans que les droits des Juifs soient maintenus et sauvegardés.

   Veuillez agréer, Monsieur le Président, nos salutations distinguées.

R. H. BAKAL,
Secrétaire Général

Le. Léon CASTRO,
Président

1 annexe.-

Since World War I anti-Semitism started to gain momentum in the Arab World. In Egypt some members of the Rabbanite Community formed a committee to fight back. This is a letter to the president of the Karaite community, informing him of the results of the meeting of the committee that took place in the Ismāʻiliyah temple (the headquarters of the Rabbanite Community).

عن الأهرام الغراء

مأساة القاهرة في ٢٦ يناير

تدمير فندق شبرد وبنك باركليز وصفوة المتاجر الكبرى ومعظم المحال التجارية

الحريق يندلع في ٢١٧ مؤسسة عامة مصرية وأجنبية ويلتهم بعض موظفيها ونزلائها

لم تشهد القاهرة في تاريخها الحافل الطويل يوماً أفجع من يوم السبت ٢٦ يناير الماضي ، فقد تعرضت فيه لفتنة جامحة هوجاء ، تألبت خلالها على عاصمة البلاد عناصر الشر والإجرام ، فأشعلت النار في مختلف أنحائها ، وأشاعت الخراب والدمار في أجمل أحيائها ، وتركتها طوال النهار وطرفا من الليل طعمة للنيران .

لقد امتدت الأيدي الأثيمة في ذلك اليوم المشئوم إلى أمن القاهرة فأحالته إلى فوضى واضطراب ، وامتدت إلى كثير من مؤسساتها الكبرى فأنزلت بها أبشع ألوان الخراب ، ولولا عناية من الله أدركتها فأنقذتها حين نزل رجال الجيش لاستحالت كلها كومة من تراب .

ونشر اليوم ما تيسر من وصف تلك الحوادث وفيه أية على ما تعرضت له البلاد من خطر ، ولحق بمالها ومعنوياتها من ضرر ، فقوبل بالسخط على الآثمين ، من جميع المواطنين . وإنا لنرجو أن يسفر التحقيق الذي يجري الآن في شأنها عن نتيجة حاسمة يندمل بها ما أحدثته في قلب هذا الوطن العزيز من جراح ، ويكون النار أوفى النار لما ذهب ضحيتها من أموال وأرواح .

تلك الحوادث المشئومة ، التي حولت وسط مدينة القاهرة وقلبها النابض وزهرتها اليانعة إلى خرائب وأطلال ينعق فيها البوم والغربان .

فقد دك فندق شبرد ، وأصبح أنقاضا من الطوب والحجارة ، بعد أن كان علما يرمز إلى حضارة مصر ورقيها وبستقبل آلاف من الزائرين والسائحين الأوروبيين والأمريكيين وغيرهم من مختلف بلاد العالم .

واندثرت مخازن شيكوريل ومحال شملا والأمريكيين . مرآة شارع فؤاد ، وأصبحت حطاما تدل على الخراب والدمار .

وكان شارع الأهرام يزدان بثلاثة كازينات كبيرة هي : الأوبرج وصوفر وكوفن جاردن ، فأصبحت أثراً بعد عين .

وكانت تشرف على ميدان الإسماعيلية عمارة شاهقة تتخذ فيها شركة الخطوط الجوية البريطانية مقراً ، فامتدت أيدي المجرمين نحو بيوتها ، وأتى الحريق على ما كانت تضم من أثاث ورياش .

أما المشارب والملاهي فكانت أول هدف للمجرمين الذين اندسوا بين المتظاهرين . نحربوها ودمروها ، ولم يبقوا على شيء فيها .

ومحال جروبي في سليمان باشا وعدلي باشا لم تنج من التخريب والتدمير والسلب والنهب .

ووكالات السيارات كانت هدفا للحريق فقد عمدت

العناصر الخبيثة إلى إخراج ما في هذه الوكالات من السيارات ثم إشعال النار فيها على قارعة الطريق .

والمتاجر الكبيرة كبزيون وداود عدس وشالوم ومحل ليون كوهين بشارع عبد الخالق ثروت باشا ومحل إخوان أيوب ثماس الساعاتية بميدان محمد علي الكبير وبقالة موسى مرزوق الشهير بفلفل بالعباسية وبقالة ثابت عبد الله بالقبيسى وبوفيه رأس البر بشارع عماد الدين وغيرها من متاجر مختلف البضائع كانت ميدانا للسلب والنهب ، ثم طعمة للنيران .

وأما دور السينما في وسط المدينـــة فلم ينج منها من التخريب والتدمير إلا عدد قليل منها وراحت الدور الجنية الأنيقة مترو وريفولي .

كما حرقت ونهبت مدرسة الطائفة الاسرائيلية بميدان فاروق .

ولقد خيم الخراب والدمار على منطقة كبيرة ، تعد أرقى مناطن المدينة ، وأكبرها روعة وجمالا ، وأكبرها ازدهاراً بالتجارة ، وازدحاما بالرواد وظلت رائحة الدخان تنبعث منها أياماً ، ومنع مرور السيارات والترام في شارع فؤاد حتى يوم ١٠ فبراير . فعسى أن يكون هذا مقدمة يعقبها أن تدب الحياة من جديد في جميع المحال والمتاجر والمنشآت ، التي أصيبت بالتلف .

~~~~~~~~~~~~~~~

PLATE 2: On Saturday, January 26, 1952 — or as it is called, "Black Saturday" — the best hotels, stores, cafes and cinemas were burnt to the ground.

al-Kalīm, no. 159, 16 February 1952.

PLATE 3: An ad about "Cicurel," one of the best department stores in the Orient, which was burnt to the ground on 26 January 1952. In less than a year the store reopened.

A MESSAGE FROM THE PRESIDENT

NOVEMBER 1983/KESLEV 5744

JACOB MASLIAH
PRESIDENT

At this beginning of the New Year 5744 let me take this opportunity to thank you for your continued support of our community. I sincerely hope the new year will be a prosperous one for you and your family

It is our duty to teach our children the Hebrew language and our old sacred traditions in order that we all, hand in hand, save our Sect and follow the high, heavenly constitution.

We may stop a moment and deeply think in our mind 'How can we save our religion?' The answer is so simple. First of all, we have to seek mercy from God. He is close to our hearts, especially to those who have true faith.

In addition, we have to be proud of our religion and never to deny it, no matter what may be. And we must teach our children to be the same because we are the most ancient sect in the world.

Here is a message about the forthcoming Board Election for 1984. As stated in the Charter of the KJA, the Election Committee, headed by our member Joe Abel, prepared the necessary preliminaries for mailing. We thank the Election Committee for their diligent efforts. Your own personal vote in this election will be an important one!

As we progress, we pray that God may keep us on the Right Track.

May God Bless You,

Shalom Rab

PLATE 4: The Karaite Jews of America

Epilogue

After World War II, the Karaite community in Egypt was among the few flourishing Karaite communities in the whole world. That community could have played a major role in reviving some of its dying sisters in Europe, or in Asia, but it failed to do so.

The many Karaite communities that once dotted parts of Europe, Asia, Africa, and at times made up 40% of the Jewish population in the world are now history, a history that is little-known to few. But their treasures and their contribution to Judaism and to the whole world in literature, science, philosophy, medicine, astronomy, music, etc., recorded in thousands of books and documents, still exist. Many museums, universities, and institutions in Europe, Asia, Africa, and the United States guard the treasures that have not yet been fully studied or discovered.

We hope that the day will come when everyone, especially the Jews, will learn more about this Jewish sect.

In Egypt, Jews in general were very well established, and many of them belonged to the élite. Although Judaism was a way of life for its believers, little by little, Jews, including Karaites, started to lose even that. The strength that Jews enjoyed was due to their unity and adherence to Judaism, as well as to their strong economic status. Rabbanites and Karaites were becoming richer, but their attachment to their religion and to the real Jewish way of life began to weaken. Religion became more or less a kind of social affiliation and not a basic practice.

In the period covered, the Karaite community progressed and grew in number. There is no comparison between their status at the end of the 19th century and that of the period after World War II. The Karaites grew richer and more secularized. Fewer people knew much about their faith and even fewer attended the daily services. In both communities, certain old people were paid to attend the daily services. Even Saturday services were attended by fewer people. The further the Karaites lived from their synagogue, the less they were attached to the community and to the Jewish way of life.,

I hope that this book, in recording the history of the Karaites in Egypt during the last 100 years, will offer something from which we may gain wisdom for the future.

Appendix A

The difference between the Karaites and the Rabbanites

(1) Calendar

The Karaites use lunar observation, hence their months are not of predetermined length, neither full nor defective. The Rabbanites use mathematical calculation.

(2) Removal of leaven at Passover

The Karaites insist on actual elimination of the leaven. The Rabbanites permit its fictitious sale *(bayʻ Ṣūriyyan)* to a Gentile. [10]

(3) *Twilight* (Exod. 12:6; literally "between the two dusks")[11]

The Rabbanites say that the first dusk begins when the sun inclines towards the West, six and one-half hours after sunrise, and that the second dusk is the time when the sun is "veiled" *(iḥtigāb)* by the horizon; the period between these two positions of time constitutes twilight. The Karaites define the first dusk as the time of the "veiling" of the sun, and the second dusk as the time when sunlight disappears from the face of the earth, twilight thus lasting approximately one and one-third hours, far shorter than the Rabbanite twilight.[12]

---

10. Cf. Maimonides, *Mishneh Tōrāh*, III, V, iv; Aaron ben Alijah, *Gan ʻEden* (Eupatoria, 1866), 45bb; Bashyatchi, 63bb.
11. The time of the Passover eve sacrifice.
12. Cf. Maimonides, III, I, v. 4; Aaron ben Elijah, 58a-59ba; *idem, Kēter Tōrāh* (Eupatoria, 1866-67), II, 29a, Bashyatchi, 55ab-ba. Six and one-half hours after sunrise is a little after high noon.

(4) Prohibition of having another (Gentile) person perform forbidden work on the Sabbath

The Karaites maintain this interdict absolutely, while the Rabbanites employ legal technicalities to evade this prohibition under certain circumstances.[13]

(5) *Eye for eye* (Exod. 21:24)

The Rabbanites interpret this precept metaphorically as referring to blood money or monetary fine, whether the mayhem was deliberate or accidental. The Karaites see no reason to regard mayhem as different from murder, for which the law is *life for life* (Exod. 21:23), with no monetary ransom permitted (Num. 35:31). They too, however, permit a monetary fine if the mayhem was accidental, or if the avenging kinsman is willing to accept it, or if the perpetrator of the mayhem is in such physical condition that retaliation is likely to result in his death or in excessive maiming (as when he has only one good eye).[14]

(6) Bailment (Exod. 22:9-14)

The Karaites, unlike the Rabbanites, do not allow the use of legal technicalities in order to absolve the bailee from responsibility for loss or damage to the bailment, as for example, by the bailee asking the bailor for a drink of water while simultaneously asking him for the loan of the bailment, and thus creating the fiction of having asked for the bailor's personal services as well, in which case Scripture exempts the bailee from responsibility for the bailment (Exod. 22:14).[15]

(7) Meat with milk ("seething a kid in its mother's milk," Exod. 23:19, 34:26; Deut. 14:21)

The Rabbanites, unlike the Karaites, extend this prohibition to cover all meat and all milk, including meat of birds, even though these are not mammals.[16]

(8) Menstruant woman (Lev. 15:19ff.)

The Karaites observe a seven-day purification period (Lev. 15:19). The Rabbanites extend it to fourteen days.[17]

---

13. Cf. Maimonides, III, I, vi; Aaron ben Elijah, 30ab-bb; Bashyatchi, 43bb-44ba.
14. Cf. Maimonides, XI, IV, i, 1-6; Aaron ben Elijah, 179aa-180bb; *idem, Kēter Tōrāh,* 72a-73a.
15. Cf. Maimonides, XIII, II, ii, 1; Aaron ben Elijah, *Kēter Tōrāh,* II, 75b.
16. Cf. Maimonides, V, II, ix, 1-4 (the prohibition of eating meat or fowl seethed in a mammal's milk is of Scribal, not Scriptural, origin); Aaron ben Elijah, *Kēter Tōrāh,* II, 79 a-b; Bashyatchi, 121bb-122aa.
17. Cf. Maimonides, V, I, xi, 4; Bashyatchi, 129aa; J. Preuss, *Biblisch-Talmudische Medizin* (Berlin, 1911), pp. 142-143.

(9) Incest (Lev. 18)

Some (early) Karaites who had embraced the so-called catenary theory of forbidden relatives *(al-murakkibīn* or *aṣḥāb al-tarkīb)* regarded the Scriptural statement *And they (man and wife) shall be one flesh* (Gen. 2:24) as equivalent to the statement in the Koran (16:74), "God has appointed for you of yourselves spouses,"[18] thus implying that the wife's relatives become the husband's relatives in the same degree. They also found indirect Scriptural support in the verse *The nakedness of thy father's wife shall thou not uncover — it is thy father's nakedness* (Lev. 18:8), implying that one's stepmother, upon her marriage to one's father, becomes *one flesh* with him, and violation of her chastity is as much an injury to him as to her. The error of this theory has been exposed by later authorities.[19] Recently (1910) Karaite scholarly opinion *(al-ijtihād al-'ilmī)* at a conference in Eupatoria (in the Crimea) has expressed itself in opposition to the rule forbidding a widower to marry his late wife's sister, two brothers to marry two sisters, and two (unrelated) men to marry each other's sister.[20] This narrows somewhat the dividing line between Karaite and Rabbanite law.

The terms of relationship in Lev. 18 should be understood literally and not metaphorically. Thus "uncle" refers only to a true *(ṣaḥīḥ)* uncle, meaning the son of both grandparents or of only one of them;[21] it cannot refer to a metaphorical *(majāzī)* uncle, meaning the son of the stepgrandmother or of the stepgrandfather by a previous marriage, whose ex-wife is therefore permitted in marriage. The same applies to the term "aunt." Likewise the term "brother" refers to the brother by both parents or by one of them, and not to a stepbrother.

Equally mistaken is the view that a subsequent unlawful marriage vitiates the previous lawful marriage; for example, that the moment a man marries his wife's daughter by a previous marriage, or her sister's daughter, he ipso facto invalidates his marriage to his wife. The latter rather remains essentially lawful, and the issue thereof legitimate, and it is neither logical nor fair to tarnish a perfectly lawful marriage with the taint of a subsequent unlawful marriage.

The chief point of divergence between Karaites and Rabbanites in the matter of incest is marriage to one's niece and to one's stepsister — the Karaites have always forbidden it, while the Rabbanites have permitted it.[22] As for the niece, the Karaites

---

18. "Of yourselves" is variously interpreted as "of your own [i.e. human] kind" and as "out of your own bodies," alluding to the creation of Eve out of Adam's rib (Bayḍāwī, *ad loc.*).
19. Cf. Aaron ben Elijah, 130aa-131aa; BAshyatchi, 148ba-149bb.
20. All of which were heretofore held to be forbidden, since marriage that has taken place first vitiates the marriage that follows. The reasoning for the abolition of these prohibitions is given in Farag's translation of Bashyatchi (listed above), p. 168ff.
21. That is the father's brother by both grandfather and grandmother, or by either one alone.
22. Cf. Maimonides, V, I, ii, 3, 14. The stepsister referred to is the stepmother's daughter by a previous or subsequent marriage.

regard her as analogous to the aunt, who is scripturally forbidden (Lev. 18:14), the relationship between uncle and niece being, in their view, no different from the relationship between aunt and nephew. As for the stepsister, the Rabbanites interpret *begotten of thy father* (Lev. 18:11) as indicating the sister sired by one's father out of one's stepmother, that is one's half-sister, which excludes one's stepsister; to which the Karaites reply that the half-sister is already mentioned previously in Lev. 18:9, *thy sister, the daughter of thy father, or the daughter of thy mother,* and hence verse 11 cannot refer to her.[23]

(10) Delivered woman

The Karaites adhere to the Scriptural rule (Lev. 12) that a delivered woman must observe seven days of uncleanness and thirty-three days of purification for a male child, and double that for a female child, and may not be approached by her husband through each full period of time. The Rabbanites forbid her husband to approach her only during the days of her uncleanness.[24]

(11) Slaughtering of a pregnant dam

The Karaites forbid it on the basis of *Ye shall not kill it (the dam) and its young both in one day* (Lev. 22:28) The Rabbanites permit it on the ground that an unborn young is the same as a member of its dam's body, and therefore the flesh of both dam and young is permitted for consumption. To this the Karaites retort that if the unborn young is alive to begin with, the killing of the dam kills it also, hence the rule in Lev. 22:28 must apply; if the unborn young is dead at the outset, not only is it itself unclean as *carcass (nebēlāh),* but it automatically renders the dam also unclean.[25]

(12) False dealing and fraud

The Karaites forbid it absolutely on the basis of Lev. 19:11, while the Rabbanites maintain the principle of *caveat emptor.*[26]

---

23. Cf. al-Qirqisāni, XI, xii (ed. Nemoy, V, 1134-1136); Ibn Ezra to Lev. 18:11; Aaron ben Elijah, *Kēter Tōrāh,* III, 47b-48a.
24. Cf. Aaron ben Elijah, 114ab-115ab, Bashyatchi, 130ab-131aa; Maimonides, V, I, iv, 5.
25. Cf. Aaron ben Elijah, 83bb-84ba; Bashyatchi, 113aa-ba; Maimonides, V, II, v, 13-14.
26. The author refers for details to Mordecai ben Nisan's *Lebūsh* and to Firkovitch's *Massāh,* which accounts for this highly prejudiced summation of the Rabbanite legislation concerning fraud (*'ōnā'āh, hōnā'āh;* cf. *Lev. 25:14),* for which see Maimonides, XII, I, xii-xiii. If the overcharge is 1/6 (16.66 percent) of the fair price, the sale is valid, but the vendor must refund the difference to the vendee; if more than 1/6, the sale is void, and the vendee may return the article to the vendor and recoup his money; if less than 1/6, the sale is valid, and the vendee has no recourse; this being a matter of "general custom" (Maimonides, XII, I, xii, 3). The claim of fraud must be filed within a reasonable time after the sale (no longer than it takes to have the article appraised by a competent expert); further delay presupposes the vendee's acquiescence in the price paid by him.

(13) New Year's Day

The Karaites interpret the term *terū'āh* (Lev. 23:24; Num. 29:1) as "shout (of prayer)," and therefore do not blow the ram's horn on that day, whereas the Rabbanites interpret it as "blast of the ram's horn."[27]

(14) Festival of Tabernacles

The Karaites celebrate it for seven days (Lev. 23:34-36), the Rabbanites outside of Palestine for eight, in accordance with their custom of adding a day to all holy days save the Day of Atonement, on account of their reliance on mathematical calendation, in disregard of lunar observation. Also, the Karaites interpret *And ye shall take you on the first day the fruit of goodly trees, branches of palm trees,* etc. (Lev. 23:40) as referring to the festal booth, and not to the ethrog and lulab, as do the Rabbanites.[28]

(15) Husband as wife's heir

Acknowledged by the Rabbanites, disacknowledged by the Karaites. The Rabbanites assert that the phrase *we-yārash ōtāh* (Num. 27:11) should be understood to mean *he (the husband) shall be her (the wife's) heir,* to which the Karaites retort that there is no explicit mention of either wife or husband in the whole account of the daughters of Zelophehad (Num. 27:1-11), and that the phrase should be understood to mean *he (the next nearest relative) shall inherit it (the deceased's estate).*[29]

(16) Tefillim

Used by the Rabbanites on the basis of their literal interpretation of Exod. 13:9 and Deut. 6:8. The Karaites do not use tefillin and interpret these passages as metaphorical admonitions to keep in mind and observe Scriptural ordinances; they point to similar passages in Scripture, e.g., *Circumcise [...] the foreskin of your heart* (Deut. 10:16) and *Bind them (the teachings of thy father and thy mother) [...] upon thy heart* (Prov. 6:21), which obviously cannot be taken literally.

---

27. Cf. Aaron ben Elijah, 58aa-bb; *idem, Kēter Tōrāh,* III, 67a; Bashyatchi, 73ab-bb; Maimonides, III, VI, i, I. The Karaites claim that where *herī'a* ("to shout"), or its derivatives, refers to the blowing of the horn, it is accompanied by the term *shōfār* ("horn"), e.g. Ps. 98:6.
28. This interpretation was disputed by some Karaite authorities; al-Qirqisāni, IX, xviii, 4 (ed. Nemoy, IV, 925-926); Ibn Ezra to Lev. 23:40; Aaron ben Elijah, 64ba-65ba; *idem, Kēter Tōrāh,* III, 67b; Bashyatchi, 76bb-77ab.
29. Cf. Aaron ben Eliljah, 170bb-171bb; *idem, Kēter Tōrāh,* IV, 42a; Bashyatchi, 174a. Some early Karaite authorities, however, sided with the Rabbanite view; cf. al-Qirqisāni, XIII, ix (ed. Nemoy, V, 1274-76).

(17) Obedience to those in authority (judges, magistrates, etc.)

Both Karaites and Rabbanites require obedience to constituted authorities, but the Rabbanites exaggerate the matter to the extent of asserting that the authorities must be obeyed "even when they call right left and left right."[30] The Karaites, on the other hand, require obedience to the authorities only when their instructions are in conformity with Scripture.[31]

(18) Captive alien women (Deut. 21:10-14)

The Rabbanites allow the Israelite captor to go in unto her prior to the expiration of the statutory month of her mourning, when he may marry her. The Karaites allow it only after the month's interval, upon the captor's marrying her.[32]

(19) Divorce

The Karaites interpret the particle *kī* in Deut. 24:1 as meaning "because," so that the husband must have a valid cause to divorce his wife. The Rabbanites, however, interpret *kī* as "or," implying that he may divorce her at will, "even if she does no more than burn his supper for him, or if he finds another prettier woman."[33] The objections to this interpretation are, first, that *kī* is nowhere else used in the sense of "or," the regular Hebrew word for the latter being *ō;* second, were *kī* to be understood as "or," the preceding statement, *if she find no favor in his eyes* (Deut. 24:1), would have been sufficient, and there would have been no need to add *or if he hath found some unseemly thing in her (ibid.),* since loss of attraction is the easiest and simplest excuse to get rid of an unwanted wife; third, the logical sequence would have been to list the more serious cause, the discovery of *some unseemly thing,* first, and the less serious one, the mere loss of attraction, second, not vice versa. Indeed the Mishnah states expressly that Shammai regarded adultery as the only valid cause for divorce.[34]

(20) Bill of divorcement *(gēṭ)*

The Rabbanites have elaborate rules governing the form of the *gēṭ,* supposedly meant to discourage divorce; for example, "it must consist of exactly twelve lines,

---

30. P. Hor. 1:1; Sif. Deut. 154 (rather a figure a speech, and not meant literally). The source is Deut. 17:11: *Thou shall not turn aside from the sentence which they (the priests and the judges) shall declare unto thee, to the right hand, nor to the left.*
31. Cf. Aaron ben Elijah, *Kēter Tōrāh,* V, 21a.
32. B. Qid. 21b; Aaron ben Elijah, *Kēter Tōrāh,* V, 24a.
33. *Giṭ.* 9:10; *B. Giṭ.* 90a and Rashi, *ad loc.,* cf. Ibn Ezra to Deut. 24:1. Divorce without the wife's consent is forbidden by Rabbi Gershom's (11th century) decree.
34. Cf. Aaron ben Elijah, 154bb-155ab; *idem, Kēter Tōrāh,* V, 27a-b; Bashyatchi, 163ab-bb.

no more and no less."³⁵ The Karaites have no such rules, just so the document fulfills its legal purpose.³⁶

(21) Compulsory divorce

"There are many cases where the wife should have the right *(ḥaqq)* to demand divorce, or where the law should have the right to impose a dissolution of the matrimonial bond," and both Rabbanism and Karaism acknowledge this fact. Sometimes, however, the husband refuses his consent to the divorce. What then is to be done, seeing that it is the husband who by Scriptural law has the prerogative of executing the bill of divorcement and having it delivered to the wife, thus legally consummating the dissolution of the marriage? "Should the law," in the face of such refusal on the part of the husband, "stand impotent ('freeze,' *yajmud)* before its own or the wife's right? [...] Here is the basic difference *(majāl al-khilāf)* between the two denominations: Rabbanite law is rendered impotent and helpless by its own shackles, whereas Karaite law makes right victorious *(naṣarū al-ḥaqq bil-shar')*." The Rabbanites say that divorce may be effected only at the husband's behest, whereas the Karaites say that this is indeed so, but if he wrongfully refuses to effect it, the law must admonish him and give him time to comply; if he still persists in his refusal, the law must step in his place and effect the divorce. It is for this reason that the Rabbanites question the legitimacy of the issue of any remarriage following such imposed Karaite divorce.³⁷

(22) Witchcraft

The Rabbanites, unlike the Karaites, believe in all sorts of superstitions, such as lucky and unlucky days and stars, the intercession of defunct saints, etc.³⁸ Yet this is expressly forbidden in Scripture (Deut. 18:10-11).

(23) Marriage

According to Rabbanite law marriage is effected publicly by marriage contract or by act of sexual intercourse, or privately by payment of token money, "be it

---

35. Corresponding to the numerical value of the letters of the word *gēṭ* (*gṭ* = 3 + 9 = 12); a thirteenth line, divided into two lines, is taken by the signatures of the two witnesses (*Enṣiql. Talmūdīt*, V, 613).
36. Cf. Aaron ben Elijah, 155ba.
37. Cr. Bashyatchi, 163bb; Maimonides, IV, II, ii, 20; D. W. Amram, *The Jewish Law of Divorce* (Philadelphia, 1896), p. 54 ff. While Rabbanite law insists on the husband's executing and delivering, personally or by agent, the bill of divorcement, the court may command him to do so if the wife produces valid grounds for it: refusal of conjugal rights, impotence, repulsive physical blemishes, nonsupport, cruel and offensive treatment, etc. If he refuses to comply with the court's order, the court may have him flogged until he consents.
38. These are, of course, popular superstitions not sanctioned by Rabbanite law or approved by the Sages and the scholars.

even a farthing *(bārah=pārah,* Turkish small coin) or its equivalent," provided that the transaction is duly certified by qualified witnesses; and if the bride is of age, her father's consent is not necessary. Karaite law, on the other hand, requires in all cases both marriage contract *('aqd)* and nuptial gift *(mahr),* as well as the bride's father's consent.[39]

(24) Degradation of women in prayer

In the Rabbanite ritual the male must pronounce the blessings "Blessed art Thou, O Lord, our God, King of the universe, who has not created me a bondsman," and "who has not created me female," while a female must bless God "who has not created me a bondswoman," and "who has created me according to His will."[40] None of this is in the Karaite ritual. It is not seemly to degrade bondsmen and bondswomen in prayer, since they too are God's creatures, and anyway slavery has long been abolished; nor to degrade females,[41] since every male is the son of a female and may be brother of a female, husband of a female, and father of a female. Moreover woman is man's rib, and is flesh of his flesh in marriage. Several women were prophetesses (Miryam, Deborah, Huldah) and matriarchs (Sarah, Rebekah, Rachel), while Esther's heroic service is commemorated by the festival of Purim. "I do not know how one can thus honor and degrade [a woman] at the same time."

(25) Wife's property rights

In Rabbanite law, the wife may not dispose of her own property without her husband's permission; in Karaite law this permission is not necessary.[42]

---

39. Maimonides, IV, I, i, 2; iii, 11-12; Aaron be Elijah, 141bb-142aa, 143ba; Bashyatchi, 155b, 156bb.
40. *B. Men.* 43b; Maimonides, II, II, vii, 6; A. Z. Idelsohn, *Jewish Liturgy* (New York, 1932), pp. 75-76.
41. The traditional reason assigned for these blessings is that women are exempt from the "yoke of the precepts," whereas men are favored with the duty and privilege of strict adherence and observance of them.
42. In Rabbanite law, the husband has the usufruct of his wife's property as a quid pro quo for his obligation to ransom her if she is taken captive (*B. Ket.* 47b). Distinction must be made between the wife's dowry (so-called "iron sheep property"), which is almost entirely under the husband's control for the duration of the marriage (although he may not sell it without her consent), and her private estate (so-called *"melōg* property"), of which the husband has only the usufruct. If she sells the latter without his consent, the sale is valid, but he may recover his continuing usufruct from the purchaser, and he may not sell it without her consent. Cf. L. M. Epstein, *The Jewish Marriage Contract* (New York, 1927), pp. 91 ff., 107 ff. Maimonides, IV, I, xvi, 1-2; xxii, 7 ff.; Aaron ben Elijah, 152ba; Bashyatchi, 161b.

(26) Levirate marriage

The Rabbanites still interpret Deut. 25:5-10 as enjoining levirate marriage.[43] The Karaites interpret the term "brother" in that passage as referring to a brother by the larger family (clan or tribe), not by blood, since Lev. 18:16 expressly forbids marriage to one's brother's wife, which must include one's brother's widow, even if he died childless.[44]

(27) Witnesses in judicial proceedings

The Scriptural requirement of at least two witnesses (Deut. 19:15) is interpreted by the Rabbanites as referring only to males, on the ground that the words used in that passage are in the masculine gender. The Karaites retort that the masculine gender is merely a linguistic custom, and that women too are qualified to offer judicial testimony.[45]

(28) Effect of husband's apostasy upon marriage

The Rabbanites hold that the husband's apostasy does not automatically dissolve the matrimonial bond, since it can be dissolved solely by formal divorce; if he subsequently returns to the Jewish faith, however, he must execute a new marriage contract for his wife. In Karaite law apostasy is equivalent to death, and the apostate's wife is free to remarry just as if she were his widow.[46]

(29) Effect of apostasy upon inheritance

In Karaite law, apostasy invalidates a person's inheritance rights.[47] Rabbanite law, on the other hand, does not cancel these rights legally, but the authorities are

---

43. Already the Mishnah (*Bek.* 1:7) urges the statutory refusal of levirate marriage in preference to submission to it. In the West, after Rabbi Gershom's edict which outlawed polygamy, levirate marriage became impossible if the levir already had a wife. In 1950 the Chief Rabbinate of Israel made refusal mandatory for both Western and Eastern (Ashkenazi and Sefardi) communities.
44. Cf. Aaron ben Elijah, 149ab-ba; *idem, Kēter Tōrāh*, V, 28a-b. His explanation is that the purpose of the Scriptural precept was to prevent the deceased's landed property in the Holy Land from passing, in case of his widow's remarriage to an outsider, out of the deceased's clan (cf. Ruth 4:5, 10); hence in the Dispersion such marriage has become unnecessary and invalid.
45. Cf. Maimonides, XIV, II, ix, 1-2; Aaron ben Elijah, 194aa. Rabbanite law permits women to act as witnesses in matters known to be within their particular knowledge and competence.
46. In Rabbanite law, an apostate Jew remains a Jew, albeit a sinful one (*B. Sanh.* 44a), hence his marriage remains valid, even though his Jewish wife may not abide with him so long as he persists in his apostasy (Maimonides, IV, I, iv, 15). Cf. Bashyatchi, 160ab (first count; in the foliation of the 1870 edition, 157-160 are repeated).
47. Cf. Bashyatchi, 174ab (the apostate's son, however, if he remains a Jew, takes his father's place as heir).

empowered to divert the inheritance to the apostate's Jewish children.[48]

(30) Unnatural sexual intercourse

The Rabbanites interpret the expression *lyings of womankind* (Lev. 18:22) as signifying that there is more than one legitimate mode of sexual intercourse with one's wife, since *lyings* is plural.[49] The Karaites forbid any mode of intercourse that cannot result in procreation.[50]

(31) Ransoming the wife from captivity

Karaite law obligates the husband to ransom his wife so long as he has the means to do so, even if she is captured more than once. Rabbanite law obligates him to ransom her only once; if she is captured a second time, he may divorce her and pay her the amount of her marriage contract, and she must then ransom herself.[51]

(32) Sexual intercourse during the Sabbath day

Rabbanite law not only permits it but even recommends it (on the basis of Isa. 58:13, *Call the Sabbath a pleasure*). Karaite law forbids it as a variety of forbidden "labor," and interprets *pleasure* as spiritual pleasure in the Sabbath's sanctity. "One of the Rabbanites told me that in their view it is merely permitted *(ḥill)* and is not compulsory *(wujūbī)*, except for scholars, so that they may be free to attend to their scholarly business *(a'mālihim)* during the rest of the week."[52]

---

48. Cf. Maimonides, XIII, V, vi, 12 ("such is always the custom in the West").
49. Cf. Maimonides, V, I, xxi, 9 (while unnatural coition with one's wife is lawful, one should nevertheless abstain from it).
50. Cf. Aaron ben Elijah, *Kēter Tōrāh*, III, 49a-b: the plural *lyings* may mean only normal coition, "either for procreation or for mere pleasure" (e.g., when the wife is unable to conceive); Bashyatchi, 167a. Farag refers to Koran 2:223: "Your wives are your plowed field; go in, therefore, to your field as *(annā)* ye will;" some interpret *annā* as "from whatever direction" (Bayḍāwī, *ad loc.*: *min ayyi jihatin)*; other take it to mean "how."
51. Cf. Aaron ben Elijah, 152bb; Bashyatchi, 161ab-ba (the husband may, however, divorce his wife after ransoming her); Maimonides, IV, I, xiv, 18-20. If the husband is away on a journey, both Karaite and Rabbanite law empower the court to sell as much of the husband's property as is necessary to pay the wife's ransom. Note the expression *wa-hiya wa-sha' nuhā* "she may do as she pleases"; cf. II, Wehr, *Dictionary of Modern Arabic* (Ithaca, 1961), p. 450.
52. Cf. Aaron ben Elijah, 27aa; Bashyatchi, 45ab-ba, citing the pun "this (Rabbanite custom) is not *pleasure ('ōneg)* but pother *(yega')* and plague *(nega')*": Maimonides, III, I, xxx, 14.

(33) Recapitulation of the status of women

	Rabbanite law	Karaite law
(a)	Apostasy of husband does not terminate matrimonial bond	Does terminate matrimonial bond
(b)	Captive alien woman may be subjected to sexual intercourse once, before her Jewish captor marries her	May not be subjected to sexual intercourse prior to marriage to her Israelite captor
(c)	May be divorced "even for burning her husband's supper, or in order to free him to marry a prettier woman"	May be divorced only for a serious malfeasance in character, behavior, or religious belief
(d)	May not be divorced without husband's consent	May be divorced by the court, even against husband's wish
(e)	Humiliated by the blessing "who has not created me female"	Not so humiliated
(f)	Cannot dispose of her property without her husband's permission	May dispose of it at will
(g)	Childless widow is in duty bound to marry her levir; if she refuses she is branded as a rebellious wife, and may not marry any other man until released by the levir from her obligation to him	Levirate marriage has been abolished[53]
(h)	May not act as witness in court	May so act
(i)	Wife may be subjected to unnatural sexual intercourse	May be subjected to natural sexual intercourse only
(j)	Husband is obligated to ransom his wife only once	Husband must ransom her even if more than once

---

53. Maimonides, IV, III, i, 2-3 (if the deceased has issue by another wife, the childless widow is not subject to levirate marriage); ii, 10 (the rebellious widow must be compelled to perform the ceremony of release from levirate marriage (ḥalīṣāh, Deut. 25:7 ff.), and is then dismissed with forfeiture of her marriage contract monies; she may thereafter mary any other man); Aaron ben Elijah, 159aa-160ba; idem, Kēter Tōrāh, V, 28a-b; Bashyatchi, 157aa-158aa (second count).

(34) Circumcision

In Rabbanite law, circumcision involves two acts: the amputation *(mīlāh, hittūk)* of the foreskin with the knife, and the tearing *(perī'āh)* by the operator's finger of the underlying mucous membrane; (also a third act, the suction—*meṣīṣāh*—of the oozing blood by the operator's mouth directly, or in recent times through a tube). Karaite law required only one act, the amputation of the foreskin.[54] "Nevertheless the Karaites, as a matter of custom, practice both amputation *(qaṭ')* and the tearing *(shaqq waṭarḥ).*" In the case of a proselyte who is already circumcised, (or of an infant born circumcised), Rabbanite law prescribes the drawing of a drop of blood from him; if he is not already circumcised, he must be circumcised not immediately but on the eighth day. Karaite law requires no drop of blood in the former case, and immediate circumcision in the latter.[55]

(35) Festival of Deliverance *(al-fawz,* i.e. Purim)

Rabbanite law prescribes the drinking of wine during that festival "until one is rendered incapable of distinguishing between blessing Mordecai and cursing Haman."[56] Karaite law never advocates inebriation, "either overt or covert."

(36) Wine

Rabbanite law forbids wine touched by a heathen, because wine used to be employed in the ritual of heathen worship.[57] Karaite law has no such prohibition.

(37) Holy days

The Karaites observe holy days for one day or seven days, respectively, exactly as prescribed in Scripture (Lev. 23). The Rabbanites extend them to two days (with the sole exception of the Day of Atonement) or eight days, as a precaution against possible errors in their mathematical calendation.[58] They also observe several postponements: New Year's Day cannot fall on Sunday, Wednesday, or Friday; Passover cannot fall on Monday, Wednesday, or Friday; Pentecost cannot fall on

---

54. Cf. Aaron ben Elijah, 162ba-163aa; Bashyatchi, 169ba-170aa; Maimonides, II, VI, ii, 2; J. Preuss, *Biblisch-talmudische Medizin, op. cit.,* p. 281 ff.
55. Cf. Maimonides, II, VI, i, 3-7; V, I, xiv, 5; Aaron ben Elijah, 163bb-164aa; Bashyatchi, 169aa. The eight days' delay applies in Rabbanite law only to an infant born while his mother is in bondage to an Israelite master. An adult proselyte or a purchased bondchild must be circumcised immediately, the former after he has passed the required examination as to his sincerity (Maimonides, V, I, xiv, 5).
56. B. Meg. 7b. Not all commentators take this sentence literally; for example, Maimonides (II, X, ii, 15) softens it into 'one should [:::] drink wine until it overcomes him and makes him fall asleep." In general, complete intoxication is strongly disapproved of throughout Jewish literature.
57. Cf. Maimonides, V, II, xii-xiii.
58. Cf. Maimonides, III, VIII, v, 6-12.

Tuesday, Thursday, or Saturday; and the Day of Atonement cannot fall on Sunday, Tuesday *(sic!)* or Friday.[59]

(38) *Be fruitful and multiply* (Gen. 9:7)

The Rabbanites generally regard this as a command making marriage obligatory, whereas the Karaites regard it as no more than a blessing.[60] "I believe, however, that the former is more correct, for several reasons" —the wording of the Scriptural sentence is imperative, not benedictory; benediction of propagation is already spoken of in Gen. 9:1, and there is no close connection between verses 1 and 7; verse 7 is directly connected with the preceding verse 6, which is an obvious command to execute the shedder of blood, implying that the executed murderer is to be replaced by a newborn child—"not to speak of the harm to the Karaites which arises out of the legalizaton of celibacy or platonic love with the intention aforethought of avoiding issue *(istiḥlāl al-'uzūbah aw al-mukhālalah ma'a qaṣd man' al-nasl)*, by contributing to their paucity. Yet the Karaites say that their sect is two thousand years old—when then will they increase in number?

(39) Lost and found property

Found property cannot but have an owner, namely the person who has lost it, which is why Scripture (Deut. 22:1-3) commands its return to him immediately, if he is known, or its storage until he is identified. The Karaites therefore obligate the finder to deposit the found property with the High Priest *(al-kāhin al-a'ẓam)* or the magistrate *(al-ra'īs)*. The Rabbanites, however, declare finders keepers, and if the finder is a married woman, what she finds reverts to her husband.[61] "The present day state law is that found property must be surrendered forthwith at the nearest police station, otherwise the finder is liable to the charge of theft."

(40) Synagogue

The floors of Karaite synagogues are entirely covered with mats and carpets, and worshippers remove their shoes before entering; in Russia some are so covered, and some are not. Rabbanite synagogues are totally uncarpeted, and worshippers keep their footwear on.

---

59. Cf. Maimonides, III, VIII, vii, 1 (New Year's Day); E. Mahler, *Handbuch der jüdischen Chronologie* (Leipzig, 1916), pp. 493, 495, 497.
60. Cf. Rashi to Gen. 9:7; Maimonides, III, I, xv, 1-16; Aaron ben Elijah, *Kēter Tōrāh*, I, 38b.
61. Cf. Maimonides, XI, III, xi-xviii; IV, I, xxi, 1; Aaron ben Elijah, 185a. In Rabbanite law, finders are keepers only if the original owner is not ascertainable or has definitely abandoned all hope of recovery, or if the lost object bears no marks by which the claimant might identify it as indubitably his property.

(41) Prayer

Karaites genuflect and bow down in the course of prayer, whereas Rabbanites merely bend down a little, on account of the bare floors of their synagogues. The prayers themselves also vary between the Karaites and the Rabbanites, "which is no wonder, seeing that within the Rabbanite liturgy there is a variance between the Sefardi and the Ashkenazi rites."

(42) *Thou shall not follow a multitude to do evil, neither shall thou bear witness in a cause to incline, after a multitude to turn* (Exod. 23:2)[62]

The Karaites interpret this precept as a single interdict of blindly following the majority in violation of true justice. The Rabbanites, however, interpret it as two interdicts followed by a command: *(a)* do not follow the majority in obvious miscarriage of justice; *(b)* do not offer prejudiced testimony; *(c)* follow the majority in everything else. And that is why the Mishnaic Sages did indeed rule after the majority.

---

62. I have translated the Biblical verse literally, to fit the context. Cf. M. M. Kasher, *Tōrāh shelēmāh,* XVIII, 154 ff.; Aaron ben Elijah, *Kēter Tōrāh,* II, 77b.

Mourad El-Kodsi

Appendix B

Some of the common blessings: *Karaite Prayer Book,* Vol. IV, pp. 20-79

BEFORE EATING:

Before eating followed by wine blessing

ברכת היין בחול

הוֹדוּ לַיהוָה כִּי־טוֹב ׀ כִּי לְעוֹלָם חַסְדּוֹ: הוֹדוּ לֵאלֹהֵי הָאֱלֹהִים ׀ כִּי לְעוֹלָם חַסְדּוֹ ׃
הוֹדוּ לַאֲדֹנֵי הָאֲדֹנִים ׀ כִּי לְעוֹלָם חַסְדּוֹ ׃ בָּרוּךְ אַתָּה יְהוָה אֱלֹהֵינוּ מֶלֶךְ
הָעוֹלָם אֲשֶׁר בָּרָא עֵץ הַגֶּפֶן וּמֵיָּינוֹ מְשַׂמֵּחַ לְבַב בְּנֵי הָאָדָם: כַּכָּתוּב וְיַיִן יְשַׂמַּח
לְבַב־אֱנוֹשׁ לְהַצְהִיל פָּנִים מִשָּׁמֶן ׀ וְלֶחֶם לְבַב־אֱנוֹשׁ יִסְעָד ׃ בָּרוּךְ אַתָּה יְהוָה
אֱלֹהֵינוּ מֶלֶךְ הָעוֹלָם הַנּוֹתֵן. לָנוּ שָׂשׂוֹן וְשִׂמְחָה וּבוֹרֵא פְּרִי הַגֶּפֶן • אָמֵן ׃

Bread

בָּרוּךְ אַתָּה יְהוָה אֱלֹהֵינוּ מֶלֶךְ הָעוֹלָם הַמּוֹצִיא לֶחֶם מִן הָאָרֶץ • אָמֵן ׃

Plants of earth

בָּרוּךְ אַתָּה יְיָ אֱלֹהֵינוּ מֶלֶךְ הָעוֹלָם בּוֹרֵא פְּרִי הָאֲדָמָה ׃

Food in general

בָּרוּךְ אַתָּה יְיָ אֱלֹהֵינוּ מֶלֶךְ הָעוֹלָם בּוֹרֵא מִינֵי מְזוֹנוֹת ׃

Any fruit

בָּרוּךְ אַתָּה יְיָ אֱלֹהֵינוּ מֶלֶךְ הָעוֹלָם בּוֹרֵא פְּרִי הָעֵץ ׃

The Karaite Jews of Egypt

Water or any drink

בָּרוּךְ אַתָּה יְיָ אֱלֹהֵינוּ מֶלֶךְ הָעוֹלָם שֶׁהַכֹּל נִהְיָה בִּדְבָרוֹ :

After eating

בָּרוּךְ מַאֲכִילֵנוּ בָּרוּךְ מַשְׂבִּיעֵנוּ בָּרוּךְ מַרְוֵנוּ : בָּרוּךְ מַשְׂבִּיעַ רְעֵבִים בָּרוּךְ מַרְוֵה צְמֵאִים : בָּרוּךְ הַנֹּתֵן לֶחֶם לְכָל־בָּשָׂר ו כִּי לְעוֹלָם חַסְדּוֹ :

Before wearing the ṭallīt

בָּרוּךְ אַתָּה יְיָ אֱלֹהֵינוּ מֶלֶךְ הָעוֹלָם אֲשֶׁר קִדְּשָׁנוּ בְּמִצְווֹתָיו וְצִוָּנוּ לִלְבֹּשׁ אַרְבַּע כַּנְפוֹת בְּצִיצִית :

When we see the rainbow

בָּרוּךְ אַתָּה יְיָ אֱלֹהֵינוּ מֶלֶךְ הָעוֹלָם זוֹכֵר הַבְּרִית קַיָּם בְּמַאֲמָרוֹ נֶאֱמָן בִּבְרִיתוֹ :

When we see the new moon

בָּרוּךְ אַתָּה יְיָ אֱלֹהֵינוּ מֶלֶךְ הָעוֹלָם מְחַדֵּשׁ חֳדָשִׁים בְּסִימָן טוֹב לְעַמּוֹ יִשְׂרָאֵל וּלְכָל הָעוֹלָם :

לא ראה הירח בחדושו או שכח לברך מברך עד מלאת אננה :

Any thing new

בָּרוּךְ אַתָּה יְיָ אֱלֹהֵינוּ מֶלֶךְ הָעוֹלָם שֶׁהֶחֱיָנוּ וְקִיְּמָנוּ וְהִגִּיעָנוּ לַזְּמַן הַזֶּה

ראהו אחר י"ב חדשים מברך :

When we hear about death

בָּרוּךְ אַתָּה יְיָ אֱלֹהֵינוּ מֶלֶךְ הָעוֹלָם דַּיַּן הָאֱמֶת

Prayer to get well

ברכה לחולה

יְהִי אלהי ישראל בר' הר' ובח' הג' והנ' הוא יחן וירחם ויחמל על טעלת (פלוני) שנפל בחלי: אלהי ישראל בר' הר' יחייהו מחליו וירפאהו מטכאובו ויסעדהו על ערש דוי וירחם עליו ויהיה חליו. כפרה לעונתיו: ויקימהו ויחלימהו מטחלתו: ויקים עליו מקרא שכתוב ויאמר אם שמוע תשמע לקול יהוה אלהיך והישר בעיניו תעשה והאזנת למצותיו ושמרת כל חקיו כל המחלה אשר שמתי במצרים לא אשים עליך כי אני יהוה רפאך: והסיר יהוה ממך כל. חלי וכל מדוי מצרים הרעים אשר ידעת לא ישימם בך ונתנם בכל שנאיך: רפאני יהוה וארפא הושיעני ואושעה כי תהלתי אתה: אל נא רפא נא לו: אל נא רפא נא לו: אל נא רפא נא לו:

Prayers after getting well

ברכת משלמי תודות
לחולי שנרפא

יְהִי אלהי ישראל בר' הר' ובח' הג' ובט' הנ' והנ' הוא יברך ויש' וינ' ויע' ויפ' ונ' ויר' וינ' את מעלת (פלוני) בעבור שהקדיש (כך וכך) לקפת הצדקה לשם תודה לה' אלהי ישראל שחייהו מחליו ורפאהו מטכאבו והקימהו על רגליו ובשכר זה אלהי ישראל יבר' ויש' וינ' ויע' ויפ' ויקים עט"ש זבח תודה יכבדנני ושם דרך אראנו בישע אלהים: ויאמר אם שמוע תשמע לקול יהוה אלהיך וב"ת וה"ל וכ"ח כ"ה אש"ב לא"ע כי אני יהוה רפאך: והסיר יהוה ממך כל חלי ומ"מ הא"י לי"ב ונתנם בכל שנא.אך: בצדקה תכננני ר"ם כל"ת וכ"ל ת"א: והיה מעשה הצדקה שלום ר"ה ה"ז ע"ע. אשרי שמרי מ"ע צב"ע:

Appendix C

A blessing for the New Moon. *Karaite Prayer Book,* Vol. I, p. 91

ברכה לברך ביום ראש חדש

מִי שֶׁבֵּרַךְ אֶת אֲבוֹתֵינוּ הַקְּדשִׁים אַבְרָהָם יִצְחָק וְיַעֲקֹב משֶׁה וְאַהֲרֹן דָּוִיד וּשְׁלֹמֹה ו וּשְׁאָר הַנְּבִיאִים וְהַצַּדִּיקִים וְהַתְּמִימִים וְהַיְשָׁרִים וְהַחֲסִידִים גְּמוּרִים ו הוּא בְּרַחֲמָיו הָרַבִּים וּבַחֲסָדָיו הַגְּדוֹלִים וּבְטוּבָיו הַנְּעִימִים וְהַנֶּאֱמָנִים ו יְבָרֵךְ וְיִשְׁמוֹר וְיִנְצוֹר וְיַעֲזוֹר וִיפָאֵר וִירוֹמֵם וִיגַדֵּל וִינַשֵּׂא אֶת מַעֲלַת וְחָכְמַת וּגְדֻלַּת כְּלַל קְהִלּוֹתֵינוּ הַקְּדוֹשוֹת יַחַד עִם אוֹתָנוּ שְׁאֵרִית יַעֲקֹב חֶבֶל נַחֲלָתוֹ. וְיַעֲלֶה וְיָבֹא וְיַגִּיעַ יֵרָצֶה יִשָּׁמַע יִפָּקֵד וְיִזָּכֵר זִכְרוֹנֵנוּ וְזִכְרוֹן אֲבוֹתֵינוּ וְזִכְרוֹן מְשִׁיחֵנוּ בֶּן דָּוִד וְזִכְרוֹן יְרוּשָׁלַיִם עִיר הַקֹּדֶשׁ וְזִכְרוֹן כְּלַל עַם בֵּית יִשְׂרָאֵל לְפָנֶיךָ. לְטוֹבָה וְלִפְלֵיטָה לְחֵן וּלְחֶסֶד וּלְרַחֲמִים לְחַיִּים וּלְשָׁלוֹם בְּיוֹם רֹאשׁ חֹדֶשׁ הַזֶּה. וְזָכְרֵנוּ יְיָ אֱלֹהֵינוּ בּוֹ לְטוֹבָה וּלְבְרָכָה. וּפָקְדֵנוּ בּוֹ לְשָׂשׂוֹן וּלְשִׂמְחָה. וְהוֹשִׁיעֵנוּ בּוֹ לִישׁוּעָה וּלְנֶחָמָה. וְרַחֲמֵנוּ וְרַחֲמֵנוּ בַּחֲנִינָה וְחֶמְלָה עֲצוּמָה. וְיִמְחוֹל וְיִסְלַח לַעֲוֹנוֹתֵינוּ וּלְחַטֹּאתֵינוּ. וִיכַפֵּר פְּשָׁעֵינוּ וְאַשְׁמוֹתֵינוּ. וִיהִי לְרָצוֹן אִמְרֵי פִינוּ מָקוֹם מוּסַף יוֹם רֹאשׁ חָדְשֵׁנוּ. וִיבִיאֵנוּ בְּרִנָּה לְצִיּוֹן עִירֵנוּ וְלִירוּשָׁלַיִם בֵּית מִקְדָּשֵׁנוּ. בְּשִׂמְחַת עוֹלָם. וְשָׁם נַעֲשֶׂה אֶת קָרְבְּנוֹתֵינוּ תְּמִידִין וּמוּסָפִין. וְאֶת מוּסַף רֹאשׁ הַחֹדֶשׁ נַעֲשֶׂה וְנַקְרִיב לְפָנֶיךָ בְּאַהֲבָה כְּמִצְוַת רְצוֹנוּ. כָּאָמוּר וּבְרָאשֵׁי חָדְשֵׁיכֶם תַּקְרִיבוּ עֹלָה לַיְיָ פָּרִים בְּנֵי בָקָר שְׁנַיִם וְאַיִל אֶחָד כְּבָשִׂים בְּנֵי שָׁנָה שִׁבְעָה תְּמִימִים וּמִנְחָתָם וְנִסְכֵּיהֶם. וְיִהְיֶה הַחֹדֶשׁ הַזֶּה רֹאשׁ וְהַתְחָלָה לִגְאֻלָּתֵנוּ וְקֵץ וְסוֹף לְגָלוּתֵנוּ. וְקוּמָה לְעֶזְרָתֵנוּ יְיָ תְּשׁוּעָתֵנוּ · אָנָּא יְיָ הוֹשִׁיעָה נָּא · אָנָּא יְיָ הַצְלִיחָה נָא · וְכַאֲשֶׁר הֱחֱיִתָנוּ וְקִיַּמְנוּ הַשֵּׁם עַד עַתָּה · כֵּן יְחַיֵּנוּ וִיקַיְּמֵנוּ וְיַאַסְפֵנוּ לְחַצְרוֹת קָדְשׁוֹ לִשְׁמוֹר חֻקָּיו וְלַעֲשׂוֹת רְצוֹנוֹ וּלְעָבְדוֹ בְּלֵבָב שָׁלֵם · וּמִי כְּעַמּוֹ יִשְׂרָאֵל אֲשֶׁר בָּחַר בָּנוּ מִכָּל הָאֻמּוֹת וְחֻקֵּי רָאשֵׁי חֳדָשִׁים לָנוּ קָבַע · בָּרוּךְ אַתָּה יְיָ מְקַדֵּשׁ יִשְׂרָאֵל וְרָאשֵׁי חֳדָשִׁים: וּבִדְבַר יְשׁוּעָה וְרַחֲמִים חוּס וְחוֹן וְרַחֵם עָלֵינוּ לְהוֹשִׁיעֵנוּ כִּי לוֹ לְבַדּוֹ נָשָׂאנוּ עֵינֵינוּ · כִּי אֵל מֶלֶךְ רַחוּם וְחַנּוּן הוּא · וְיִמְלוֹךְ יְיָ אֱלֹהֵינוּ עָלֵינוּ לְהוֹצִיאֵנוּ מִגָּלוּתֵנוּ בְּרִנָּה · וִיבִיאֵנוּ בְּשָׁלוֹם לִירוּשָׁלַיִם עִיר הַקֹּדֶשׁ · כְּמוֹעֵד הַמְיוּעָד · כִּי־בְשִׂמְחָה תֵצֵאוּ וּבְשָׁלוֹם תּוּבָלוּן הֶהָרִים וְהַגְּבָעוֹת יִפְצְחוּ לִפְנֵיכֶם רִנָּה וְכָל עֲצֵי הַשָּׂדֶה יִמְחֲאוּ כָף · אָמֵן וְכֵן יְהִי רָצוֹן: וְקָיָם הַשֵּׁם יִתְעַלֶּה עָלֵינוּ וְעַל כְּלַל קְהִלּוֹתֵינוּ הַקְּדוֹשׁוֹת הַבְּרָכָה הַכְּלָלִית הַכְּתוּבָה עַל יְדֵי מֹשֶׁה רַבֵּנוּ עָלָיו הַשָּׁלוֹם וְהָאֲמוּרָה מִפִּי אַהֲרֹן הַכֹּהֵן וּבָנָיו הַכֹּהֲנִים עַל עַם קָדְשֶׁךָ : יְבָרֶכְךָ יְהוָה וְיִשְׁמְרֶךָ : יָאֵר יְהוָה ו פָּנָיו אֵלֶיךָ וִיחֻנֶּךָּ : יִשָּׂא יְהוָה ו פָּנָיו אֵלֶיךָ וְיָשֵׂם לְךָ שָׁלוֹם: וְשָׂמוּ אֶת־שְׁמִי עַל־בְּנֵי יִשְׂרָאֵל וַאֲנִי אֲבָרֲכֵם : יְהוָה הוֹשִׁיעָה : הַמֶּלֶךְ יַעֲנֵנוּ בְיוֹם־קָרְאֵנוּ : בָּרוּךְ יְהוָה לְעוֹלָם ו אָמֵן ו וְאָמֵן :

Mourad El-Kodsi

Appendix D

The "lessons" and the "haftarōt" for the holy days.

[Table in Hebrew showing the lessons (פרשיות) and haftarot (הפטרות) for the holy days: פסח, סכות, כפור, תרועה, חגים ומועדים, מילה בשבת, שבועות, שביעי עצרת, ר' חדש בשבת, שמיני עצרת, חגים ומועדים — content not transcribed in detail due to image quality.]

333

Appendix E

Two parts from the Haggadah for Passover: the first and the middle pages.

THE BOOK OF THE HAGGADAH
FOR PASSOVER

****_____***

BY THE NAME OF THE DELIVERER
OF ISRAEL
WHO COMES TO THE RESCUE OF
THOSE WHO PRAY TO HIM.

Praise ye the Lord, I will praise the Lord with my whole heart, in the assembly of the upright and in the congregation. The works of the Lord are great, sought out of all them that have pleasure therein - His work is honorable and glorious; and his righteousness endureth for ever. He hath made his wonderful works to be remembered: The lord is gracious and full of compassion. He hath given meat unto them that fear him: He will ever be mindful of his covenant. He hath showed his people the power of his works, that he may give them the heritage of the heathen. The works of his hands are verity and judgement; All his commandments are sure. They stand fast for ever and ever, and are done in truth and uprightness. He sent redemption unto his people; He hath commanded his covenant forever, holy and reverend is his name. The fear of the Lord is the beginning of wisdom: a good understanding have all they that do his commandments: his praise endureth for ever. (Psalm 111:1-10)

I will meditate also of all thy work, and talk of thy doings. Thy way, O God, is in the sanctuary: who is so great a God as our God ? Thou art the God that doest wonders: thou hast declared thy strength among the people. Thou hast with thine arm redeemed thy people, the sons of Jacob and Joseph. Selah. - (Psalm 77:12-15)- Thou art the Lord the God, who didst choose Abraham, and broughtest him forth out of Ur of the Chal'-dees, and gavest him the name of Abraham. -(Nehemiah 9:7)- And you informed to him that his sons will be enslaving in a country that will not be to them.

סֵדֶר הַגָּדָה
שֶׁל חַג הַפֶּסַח
בְּשֵׁם גּוֹאֵל יִשְׂרָאֵל
הַנִּדְרָשׁ לְכָל־שׁוֹאֵל

הַלְלוּ יָהּ אוֹדֶה יְהֹוָה בְּכָל לֵבָב ׀ בְּסוֹד יְשָׁרִים וְעֵדָה: גְּדוֹלִים מַעֲשֵׂי יְהֹוָה ׀ דְּרוּשִׁים לְכָל־חֶפְצֵיהֶם: הוֹד־וְהָדָר פָּעֳלוֹ ׀ וְצִדְקָתוֹ עֹמֶדֶת לָעַד: זֵכֶר עָשָׂה לְנִפְלְאוֹתָיו חַנּוּן וְרַחוּם יְהֹוָה: טֶרֶף נָתַן לִירֵאָיו ׀ יִזְכֹּר לְעוֹלָם בְּרִיתוֹ: כֹּחַ מַעֲשָׂיו הִגִּיד לְעַמּוֹ ׀ לָתֵת לָהֶם נַחֲלַת גּוֹיִם: מַעֲשֵׂי יָדָיו אֱמֶת וּמִשְׁפָּט ׀ נֶאֱמָנִים כָּל־פִּקּוּדָיו: סְמוּכִים לָעַד לְעוֹלָם עֲשׂוּיִם בֶּאֱמֶת וְיָשָׁר: פְּדוּת שָׁלַח לְעַמּוֹ ׀ צִוָּה לְעוֹלָם בְּרִיתוֹ ׀ קָדוֹשׁ וְנוֹרָא שְׁמוֹ: רֵאשִׁית חָכְמָה יִרְאַת יְהֹוָה ׀ שֵׂכֶל טוֹב לְכָל־עֹשֵׂיהֶם ׀ תְּהִלָּתוֹ עֹמֶדֶת לָעַד:

אֲזַכֵּר מְהַלְלֵי יָהּ ׀ כִּי אַגָּדָה מִקֶּדֶם פֶּלֶא ׀ וְהָגִיתִי בְּכָל פָּעֳלֶךָ ׀ וּבַעֲלִילוֹתֶיךָ אָשִׂיחָה: אֱלֹהִים בַּקֹּדֶשׁ דַּרְכֶּךָ ׀ מִי אֵל גָּדוֹל כֵּאלֹהִים: אַתָּה הָאֵל עֹשֵׂה פֶלֶא ׀ הוֹדַעְתָּ בָעַמִּים עֻזֶּךָ: גָּאַלְתָּ בִּזְרוֹעַ עַמֶּךָ ׀ בְּנֵי יַעֲקֹב וְיוֹסֵף סֶלָה: אַתָּה הוּא יְהֹוָה הָאֱלֹהִים ׀ אֲשֶׁר בָּחַרְתָּ בְּאַבְרָם וְהוֹצֵאתוֹ מֵאוּר כַּשְׂדִּים ׀ וְשַׂמְתָּ שְּׁמוֹ אַבְרָהָם: וְכֵן הוֹדַעְתָּ לְאַבְרָהָם אָבִינוּ אֲנִי זֶרַע בָּאָרֶץ לֹא לָהֶם כַּכָּתוּב:

Those are the ten plagues that God hit Pharaoh and Egypt with:

The first	BLOOD	The second	FROGS
The third	GNATS	The fourth	FLIES
The fifth	MURRAIN	The sixth	ASHES
The seventh	HAIL	The eight	LOCUSTS
The ninth	DARKNESS	The tenth	FIRST BORN

to smote and to slain as written.

At midnight the Lord smote all the first-born in the land of Egypt, from the first-born of Pharaoh that sat on his throne to the first-born of the captive that was in the dungeon, and all the first-born of the cattle -And Pharaoh rose up in the night, he and all his servants, and all the Egyptians, and there was a great cry in Egypt, for there was no house without a dead. - (Exodus 12:29-30) - They are dead, they will not live, they are shades, they will not arise, To that end thou hast visited them with destruction and wiped out all their remembrance. Let them be blotted out of the book of the living. Let them not be enrolled among the righteous. But I am afflicted and in pain, let thy salvation, O God, set me on high - I will praise the name of God with a song, I will magnify him with thanksgivings. - (Psalm 69:29-30) - Sing unto the Lord, praise ye the Lord: for he hath delivered the soul of the poor from the hand of evildoers. (Jeremiah 20:13) And God recommended through our prophet, Moses, to tell the story to our sons and grandsons - as written -

And that thou mayest tell in the ears of thy son, and of thy son's son, what things I have wrought in Egypt, amd my signs which I have done among them; that ye may know how I AM the Lord. (Exodus 10:2)

וְהֵם עֶשֶׂר מַכּוֹת אֲשֶׁר הִכָּה יְהוָה בָּהֶם ׀ פַּרְעֹה וּמִצְרַיִם:

רִאשׁוֹנָה דָם:	שֵׁנִית צְפַרְדְּעִים:
שְׁלִישִׁית כִּנִּים:	רְבִיעִית עָרוֹב:
חֲמִשִׁית דֶּבֶר:	שִׁשִּׁית שְׁחִין:
שְׁבִיעִית בָּרָד:	שְׁמִינִית אַרְבֶּה:
תְּשִׁיעִית הַשֶׁךְ:	עֲשִׂירִית בְּכוֹרוֹת:

לְהַכּוֹת וּלְהָמִית כַּכָּתוּב:

וַיְהִי בַּחֲצִי הַלַּיְלָה וַיהוָה הִכָּה כָל־בְּכוֹר בְּאֶרֶץ מִצְרַיִם ׀ מִבְּכוֹר פַּרְעֹה הַיֹּשֵׁב עַל כִּסְאוֹ ׀ עַד בְּכוֹר הַשְּׁבִי אֲשֶׁר בְּבֵית הַבּוֹר ׀ וְכֹל בְּכוֹר בְּהֵמָה: וַיָּקָם פַּרְעֹה לַיְלָה ׀ הוּא וְכָל עֲבָדָיו וְכָל מִצְרַיִם ׀ וַתְּהִי צְעָקָה גְדֹלָה בְּמִצְרָיִם ׀ כִּי־אֵין בַּיִת אֲשֶׁר אֵין־שָׁם מֵת: מֵתִים בַּלֵּילוֹת רְפָאִים בַּל־יָקוּמוּ ׀ לָכֵן פָּקַדְתָּ וַתַּשְׁמִידֵם ׀ וַתְּאַבֵּד כָּל־זֵכֶר לָמוֹ: יִמָּחוּ מִסֵּפֶר חַיִּים ׀ וְעִם צַדִּיקִים אַל־יִכָּתֵבוּ: וַאֲנִי עָנִי וְכֹאֵב ׀ יְשׁוּעָתְךָ אֱלֹהִים תְּשַׂגְּבֵנִי: אֲהַלְלָה שֵׁם אֱלֹהִים בְּשִׁיר ׀ וַאֲגַדְּלֶנּוּ בְתוֹדָה: שִׁירוּ לַיהוָה הַלְלוּ אֶת־יְהוָה ׀ כִּי הִצִּיל אֶת־נֶפֶשׁ אֶבְיוֹן ׀ מִיַּד מְרֵעִים: וְכֵן צִוָּנוּ יְהוָה אֱלֹהֵינוּ עַל יְדֵי מֹשֶׁה רַבֵּנוּ לְסַפֵּר לְבָנֵינוּ וְלִבְנֵי בָנֵיוּ ׀ כַּכָּתוּב:

וּלְמַעַן תְּסַפֵּר בְּאָזְנֵי בִנְךָ וּבֶן־בִּנְךָ ׀ אֵת אֲשֶׁר הִתְעַלַּלְתִּי בְּמִצְרַיִם ׀ וְאֶת־אֹתֹתַי אֲשֶׁר שַׂמְתִּי בָם ׀ וִידַעְתֶּם כִּי אֲנִי יְהוָה:

Appendix F

The service to take out the Torah

Nothing is nearer to the heart of a devout Jew than reading from the scroll, carrying it or even just touching it.

In Egypt it was the custom among the Karaites that after reading the blessings *(berakhot)* and the memorials *(zikhronot)*, the *shammās* of the synagogue start calling for donations for the following:

1. The right to open the Ark; 2. The right to read the *Shemā'*, and to take out the Torah; 3. The right to read one or more than one part from the seven parts of the lesson; 4. The right to read the *hafṭarah*.

The shammās then calls for donations to read אָנָא יְהֹוָה חֻשִּׁיעָה נָּא אָנָא יְהֹוָה הַצְלִיחָה נָּא and יְ מֶלֶךְ וגו' and other readings for the following Saturday.

The service to take out the Torah starts immediately after that.

The person who has donated to take out the Torah goes to the pulpit, stands next to the *ḥazzān* and reads the *Shemā'* (part 1). The worshippers repeat the *Shemā'* after him and after each line in part 1, but when he reads part 2 the worshippers repeat each line read.

The *ḥazzān* reads then the first part of 3 and the worshippers respond to him with the second part.

The person who has donated to open the Ark comes forward and opens it while the *ḥazzān* reads part 4. The *ḥazzān* takes out the Torah and hands it to the person who read the *Shemā'* while everyone reads part 5.

---

*. Among the Karaites in Israel the same practice is followed with minor modifications.
The Karaites have no official reader. If someone does not know how to read his part, then the *Somekh* reads it. In this case the *ḥazzān* acts as the *Somekh*.
There are cases when more than one scroll is taken out. On Saturday, 31 January 1948, 7 scrolls were taken out (*al-Kalim* No. 74, 1 March 1948). Volume 1 of the Karaite Prayer Book has all the *hafṭarot*, all the poems that go with the lessons.

Mourad El-Kodsi

1-

	ויענוהו העם	שְׁמַ֣ע יִשְׂרָאֵ֑ל ׀ יְהוָ֧ה אֱלֹהֵ֛ינוּ יְהוָ֖ה ׀ אֶחָֽד :
שמע		אֶחָד אֱלֹהֵינוּ גָּדוֹל אֲדוֹנֵינוּ ׀ קָדוֹשׁ וְנוֹרָא שְׁמוֹ לְעוֹלָם וָעֶד :
שמע		יְיָ אֱלֹהֵינוּ אָבִינוּ בֹּרְאֵנוּ גֹּאֲלֵנוּ דֹּרְשֵׁנוּ ׀ יָחִיד בְּעוֹלָמוֹ אֱמֶת :
שמע		יְיָ אֱלֹהֵינוּ הוֹדֵנוּ וַהֲדָרֵנוּ זָנֵנוּ ׀ יָחִיד בְּעוֹלָמוֹ אֱמֶת :
שמע		יְיָ אֱלֹהֵינוּ חָנְנֵנוּ טוֹבֵנוּ יְדִידֵנוּ ׀ יָחִיד בְּעוֹלָמוֹ אֱמֶת :
שמע		יְיָ אֱלֹהֵינוּ כַּבִּירֵנוּ לַחֲמֵנוּ מְשַׂגְּבֵנוּ ׀ יָחִיד בְּעוֹלָמוֹ אֱמֶת :
שמע		יְיָ אֱלֹהֵינוּ נֶאֱמָנֵנוּ סוֹמְכֵנוּ עוֹזְרֵנוּ ׀ יָחִיד בְּעוֹלָמוֹ אֱמֶת :
שמע		יְיָ אֱלֹהֵינוּ פּוֹדֵנוּ צוּרֵנוּ קְדוֹשֵׁנוּ ׀ יָחִיד בְּעוֹלָמוֹ אֱמֶת :

יְיָ אֱלֹהֵינוּ רוֹמְמֵנוּ שׁוֹמְרֵנוּ תּוֹמְכֵנוּ ׀ יָחִיד בְּעוֹלָמוֹ אֱמֶת :

מַלְכוּתְךָ מַלְכוּת כָּל־עוֹלָמִים ׀ וּמֶמְשַׁלְתְּךָ בְּכָל־דּוֹר וָדֹר :

יְהוָה שִׁמְךָ לְעוֹלָם ׀ יְהוָה זִכְרְךָ לְדֹר־וָדֹר :

2-

יְיָ מֶלֶךְ ׀ יְיָ מָלָךְ ׀ יְהוָה ׀ יִמְלֹךְ לְעוֹלָם וָעֶד :

3-

יְהוָה עֹז לְעַמּוֹ יִתֵּן ׀ יְהוָה ׀ יְבָרֵךְ אֶת־עַמּוֹ בַשָּׁלוֹם :

פִּתְחוּ־לִי שַׁעֲרֵי־צֶדֶק ׀
אָבֹא־בָם אוֹדֶה יָהּ : זֶה־הַשַּׁעַר לַיהוָה ׀ צַדִּיקִים יָבֹאוּ בוֹ : אוֹדְךָ כִּי עֲנִיתָנִי ׀ וַתְּהִי־לִי לִישׁוּעָה :

4-

5-

בָּרוּךְ שֶׁנָּתַן לָנוּ תּוֹרָה אֱמֶת

The *ḥazzān* and the worshippers then read part 6 followed by part 7 which they read part by part while they raise their hands when the scroll is being raised with each part.

-6 וַיְהִ֣י בִּנְסֹ֣עַ הָאָרֹן֮ וַיֹּ֣אמֶר מֹשֶׁה֒ קוּמָ֣ה ׀ יְהֹוָ֗ה וְיָפֻ֙צוּ֙ אֹ֣יְבֶ֔יךָ ׀ וְיָנֻ֥סוּ מְשַׂנְאֶ֖יךָ
מִפָּנֶֽיךָ ׃ יָק֣וּם אֱלֹהִ֔ים יָפ֥וּצוּ אֹויְבָ֑יו ׀ וְיָנ֥וּסוּ מְשַׂנְאָ֗יו מִפָּנָֽיו ׃ וְעַתָּ֣ה קוּמָ֣ה
יְהֹוָ֣ה לִנוּחֶ֑ךָ ׀ אַ֝תָּ֗ה וַאֲר֥וֹן עֻזֶּֽךָ ׀ כֹּהֲנֶ֥יךָ יְהוָ֖ה אֱלֹהִ֥ים יִלְבְּשׁוּ־תְשׁוּעָ֑ה ׀ וַחֲסִידֶ֥יךָ
יִשְׂמְח֥וּ בְטֽוֹב ׀ בַּעֲב֖וּר דָּוִ֣ד עַבְדֶּ֑ךָ ׀ אַל־תָּשֵׁ֗ב פְּנֵ֣י מְשִׁיחֶֽךָ ׃ הַשָּׁמַ֗יִם מְֽסַפְּרִ֥ים
כְּבוֹד־אֵ֑ל ׀ וּֽמַעֲשֵׂ֥ה יָ֝דָ֗יו מַגִּ֥יד הָרָקִֽיעַ ׃ י֣וֹם לְ֭יוֹם יַבִּ֣יעַ אֹ֑מֶר ׀ וְלַ֥יְלָה לְּ֝לַ֗יְלָה
יְחַוֶּה־דָּֽעַת ׃ אֵֽין־אֹ֭מֶר וְאֵ֣ין דְּבָרִ֑ים ׀ בְּ֝לִ֗י נִשְׁמָ֥ע קוֹלָֽם ׃ בְּכָל־הָאָ֨רֶץ ׀ יָצָ֥א
קַוָּ֗ם ׀ וּבִקְצֵ֣ה תֵ֭בֵל מִלֵּיהֶ֑ם ׀ לַ֝שֶּׁ֗מֶשׁ שָֽׂם־אֹ֥הֶל בָּהֶֽם ׃ וְה֗וּא כְּ֭חָתָן יֹצֵ֣א
מֵחֻפָּת֑וֹ ׀ יָשִׂ֥ישׂ כְּ֝גִבּ֗וֹר לָר֥וּץ אֹֽרַח ׃ מִקְצֵ֤ה הַשָּׁמַ֨יִם ׀ מֽוֹצָא֗וֹ ׀ וּתְקוּפָת֥וֹ עַל־
קְצוֹתָ֑ם ׀ וְאֵ֥ין נִ֝סְתָּ֗ר מֵֽחַמָּתֽוֹ ׃

-7 תּ֘וֹרַ֤ת יְהֹוָ֣ה תְּ֭מִימָה מְשִׁ֣יבַת נָ֑פֶשׁ ׀ עֵד֥וּת יְהוָ֥ה נֶ֝אֱמָנָ֗ה מַחְכִּ֥ימַת פֶּֽתִי ׀
פִּקּ֘וּדֵ֤י יְהוָ֣ה יְ֭שָׁרִים מְשַׂמְּחֵי־לֵ֑ב ׀ מִצְוַ֥ת יְהוָ֥ה בָּ֝רָ֗ה מְאִירַ֥ת עֵינָֽיִם ׀

The scroll is then opened facing the congregation and the *ḥazzān* reads part 8 while the scroll is being placed over the *tevah*. He covers it with a special piece of velvet *(kepporet)*. Everyone kneels and prostrates himself with the forehead touching the floor. Then they stand up and read part 9.

וַיִּפְתַּ֨ח עֶזְרָ֤א הַסֵּ֨פֶר֙ לְעֵינֵ֣י כָל־הָעָ֔ם ׀ כִּֽי־מֵעַ֥ל כָּל־הָעָ֖ם הָיָ֑ה ׀ וּכְפִתְח֖וֹ
עָֽמְד֥וּ כָל־הָעָֽם ׃ וַיְבָ֣רֶךְ עֶזְרָ֔א אֶת־יְהוָ֥ה הָאֱלֹהִ֖ים הַגָּד֑וֹל ׀ וַיַּעֲנ֣וּ כָל־
-8 הָעָ֨ם אָמֵ֤ן ׀ אָמֵן֙ בְּמֹ֣עַל יְדֵיהֶ֔ם ׀ וַיִּקְּד֧וּ וַיִּשְׁתַּחֲוֻ֛ לַיהוָ֖ה אַפַּ֥יִם אָֽרְצָה ׃

וישתחוו כל הקהל ואחרי כן תאמר :

יְהוָ֞ה חָפֵ֤ץ לְמַ֣עַן צִדְק֑וֹ ׀ יַגְדִּ֥יל תּוֹרָ֖ה וְיַאְדִּֽיר ׃ תּוֹרָ֥ה צִוָּה־לָ֖נוּ מֹשֶׁ֑ה ׀ מוֹרָשָׁ֖ה
קְהִלַּ֥ת יַעֲקֹֽב ׃ וְזֹ֣את הַתּוֹרָ֑ה ׀ אֲשֶׁר־שָׂ֣ם מֹשֶׁ֔ה ׀ לִפְנֵ֖י בְּנֵ֥י יִשְׂרָאֵֽל ׃ כִּ֚י
הַמִּצְוָ֣ה הַזֹּ֔את אֲשֶׁ֛ר אָנֹכִ֥י מְצַוְּךָ֖ הַיּ֑וֹם ׀ לֹא־נִפְלֵ֥את הִוא֙ מִמְּךָ֔ ׀ וְלֹ֥א רְחֹקָ֖ה
הִֽוא ׃ לֹ֥א בַשָּׁמַ֖יִם הִ֑וא ׀ לֵאמֹ֗ר מִ֣י יַעֲלֶה־לָּ֤נוּ הַשָּׁמַ֨יְמָה֙ וְיִקָּחֶ֣הָ לָּ֔נוּ ׀ וְיַשְׁמִעֵ֥נוּ
אֹתָ֖הּ וְנַעֲשֶֽׂנָּה ׃ וְלֹא־מֵעֵ֥בֶר לַיָּ֖ם הִ֑וא ׀ לֵאמֹ֗ר מִ֣י יַעֲבָר־לָ֜נוּ אֶל־עֵ֤בֶר הַיָּם֙
וְיִקָּחֶ֣הָ לָּ֔נוּ ׀ וְיַשְׁמִעֵ֥נוּ אֹתָ֖הּ וְנַעֲשֶֽׂנָּה ׃ כִּֽי־קָר֥וֹב אֵלֶ֛יךָ הַדָּבָ֖ר מְאֹ֑ד ׀ בְּפִ֥יךָ
וּבִֽלְבָבְךָ֖ לַעֲשֹׂתֽוֹ ׃ ותאמר
-9

The ḥazzān addresses the Kohen with part 10 and calls on him by name with part 11 after which all the worshippers respond with part 12.

כִּי־שִׂפְתֵי כֹהֵן יִשְׁמְרוּ־דַעַת ׀ וְתוֹרָה יְבַקְשׁוּ מִפִּיהוּ ׀ כִּי מַלְאַךְ יְהוָה־צְבָאוֹת
10- הוּא : ותקרא לכהן ותאמר לו :

וְאַתָּה אָחִי הַכֹּהֵן עֲטֶרֶת רֹאשִׁי תֵּן כָּבוֹד לַתּוֹרָה ׀ וּקְרַב לִקְרֹא בְּסֵפֶר הַתּוֹרָה ׀
בִּכְבוֹד קְרָב : -11

12- אוֹ בֵּית אַהֲרֹן בָּרְכוּ אֶת יְהוָה :

The Kohen goes to the pulpit, kneels, stands up and reads part 13 responsively with the worshippers (they read the underlined part). When he finishes reading his part he — along with the worshippers — reads part 14 which also every reader after that will read when he completes his part.

יְהוָה בְּצִיּוֹן גָּדוֹל ׀ וְרָם הוּא עַל־כָּל־הָעַמִּים: בָּרוּךְ יְהוָה אֱלֹהֵי יִשְׂרָאֵל מֵהָעוֹלָם
וְעַד־הָעוֹלָם : אָמֵן וְאָמֵן ׀ כִּי־יָשָׁר דְּבַר־יְהוָה ׀ וְכָל־מַעֲשֵׂהוּ בֶּאֱמוּנָה :
13- צִדְקָתְךָ צֶדֶק לְעוֹלָם ׀ וְתוֹרָתְךָ אֱמֶת ׀ בָּרוּךְ יְהוָה לְעוֹלָם ׀ אָמֵן וְאָמֵן :

בָּרוּךְ יְהוָה אֱלֹהִים אֱלֹהֵי יִשְׂרָאֵל ׀ עֹשֵׂה נִפְלָאוֹת לְבַדּוֹ : וּבָרוּךְ שֵׁם כְּבוֹדוֹ
14- לְעוֹלָם ׀ וְיִמָּלֵא כְבוֹדוֹ אֶת־כָּל־הָאָרֶץ ׀ אָמֵן וְאָמֵן :

The next reader must be a Levi. The ḥazzān calls on him by name while reading part 15 to which all the congregation respond with part 16. Before reading his part the Levi reads part 17 responsively with the worshippers. (They read the underlined part.)

וְאַתָּה אָחִי הַלֵּוִי תֵּן כָּבוֹד לַתּוֹרָה ׀ וּקְרַב לִקְרֹא בְּסֵפֶר הַתּוֹרָה ׀ בִּכְבוֹד
קְרָב : והעם יענו לו -15

16- אוֹ בֵּית הַלֵּוִי בָּרְכוּ אֶת יְהוָה :

יְהוָה חָפֵץ לְמַעַן צִדְקוֹ ׀ יַגְדִּיל תּוֹרָה וְיַאְדִּיר : תּוֹרָה צִוָּה־לָנוּ מֹשֶׁה ׀
מוֹרָשָׁה קְהִלַּת יַעֲקֹב : וְזֹאת הַתּוֹרָה ׀ אֲשֶׁר־שָׂם מֹשֶׁה לִפְנֵי בְּנֵי
יִשְׂרָאֵל : צִדְקָתְךָ צֶדֶק לְעוֹלָם ׀ וְתוֹרָתְךָ אֱמֶת ׀ בָּרוּךְ יְהוָה לְעוֹלָם ׀ אָמֵן וְאָמֵן :
17-

The same procedure is followed with the rest of the readers with one change, i.e., the ḥazzān calls on each one by name using the word *Israel.*

When reading the lesson is completed, the ḥazzān closes the scroll and hands it to the person who read the *Shemaʻ* and who has been present while the lesson was being read. The ḥazzān does that while reading part 18 after which the person who is carrying the scroll sits down on a special chair (in the side of the pulpit) facing the congregation.

תְּנוּ עֹז לֵאלֹהִים | עַל־יִשְׂרָאֵל גַּאֲוָתוֹ | וְעֻזּוֹ בַּשְּׁחָקִים : נוֹרָא אֱלֹהִים מִמִּקְדָּשֶׁךָ |
אֵל יִשְׂרָאֵל הוּא נֹתֵן | עֹז וְתַעֲצֻמוֹת לָעָם | בָּרוּךְ אֱלֹהִים :
-18

It is the custom that those who want, among the worshippers, approach the scroll, put their right hand on it, read whatever psalm that best expresses their wishes and supplicate to the Lord. That usually takes no more than 10 minutes.

It is time then to read the *hafṭarah*. The ḥazzān reads part 19 as a preparation for that, and then calls on the person who will read the *hafṭarah*. Before reading the *hafṭarah* the reader must read part 20 and when he finishes it he reads part 21.

מַפְטִיר הַנְּבוּאָה כִּי יְהוָה יִתֵּן חָכְמָה | מִפִּיו דַּעַת וּתְבוּנָה . שְׁמַע בְּנִי מוּסַר
אָבִיךָ וְאַל תִּטֹּשׁ תּוֹרַת אִמֶּךָ . שְׁמַע בְּנִי וְקַח אֲמָרָי | וְיִרְבּוּ לְךָ שְׁנוֹת חַיִּים :
ויאמר המפטיר וְדִבַּרְתִּי עַל הַנְּבִיאִים . ומפטירים הפטרת היום וחותמים : גֹּאֲלֵנוּ יְהוָה
צְבָאוֹת . וברכת הקהל : יִשְׂמְחוּ הַשָּׁמַיִם וְתָגֵל הָאָרֶץ . ככתוב לעיל בסדר שבתות
-19

וְדִבַּרְתִּי עַל־הַנְּבִיאִים | וְאָנֹכִי חָזוֹן הִרְבֵּיתִי | וּבְיַד הַנְּבִיאִים אֲדַמֶּה : כִּי לֹא
יַעֲשֶׂה יְהוָה אֱלֹהִים דָּבָר | כִּי אִם־גָּלָה סוֹדוֹ | אֶל־עֲבָדָיו הַנְּבִיאִים :
אַרְיֵה שָׁאָג מִי לֹא יִירָא | יְהוָה אֱלֹהִים דִּבֶּר | מִי לֹא יִנָּבֵא :
-20

גֹּאֲלֵנוּ יְהוָה צְבָאוֹת שְׁמוֹ | קְדוֹשׁ יִשְׂרָאֵל : וּבָא לְצִיּוֹן גּוֹאֵל | וּלְשָׁבֵי פֶשַׁע
בְּיַעֲקֹב | נְאֻם יְהוָה : וַאֲנִי זֹאת בְּרִיתִי אוֹתָם אָמַר יְהוָה | רוּחִי אֲשֶׁר
עָלֶיךָ | וּדְבָרַי אֲשֶׁר־שַׂמְתִּי בְּפִיךָ | לֹא־יָמוּשׁוּ מִפִּיךָ וּמִפִּי זַרְעֲךָ | וּמִפִּי זֶרַע
זַרְעֲךָ | אָמַר יְהוָה מֵעַתָּה וְעַד־עוֹלָם :
-21
בָּרוּךְ יְהוָה לְעוֹלָם | אָמֵן | וְאָמֵן :

After finishing reading the *hafṭarah,* the reader reads an appropriate poem according to the lesson read. He reads the poem after he reads an introduction to it (part 22). To make this point clear, if for example the lesson read was *Bereshīt,* the reader will read part 22, then he reads a few lines from the top and a few lines from the end of a poem for the lesson *Bereshīt* (part 23). There is a poem for every lesson and they all end with the same line. When the reader reaches that line all the worshipers join him in reading it.

אֲדוֹן עוֹלָם עֶלְיוֹן בְּלִבִּי שִׂים הִגָּיוֹן וְחַזֵּק הָרַעְיוֹן לְהָבִין הַיְקָרִים:
נְתִינַת תּוֹרָתוֹ לְאַנְשֵׁי תִפְאַרְתּוֹ וְלֹא גוֹי זוּלָתוֹ לְבַד אֶל הָעִבְרִים:
צוּרְךָ אֲשֶׁר הוּא מַלְכֵּנוּ וְאֶחָד בְּרָאָנוּ וּבוֹרֵא הַיְצוּרִים:
יְסוֹד הַגּוּף אֵין לוֹ וְלֹא אַחֵר אֶצְלוֹ לְאֶפְשָׁרֵי מִכֹּל יָכוֹל וְהוּא עֶלַּת הַכֹּל אֲדוֹן כָּל אַדִּירִים:
הֱיוֹת קַדְמוֹן מִכֹּל יָכוֹל וְהוּא עֶלַּת הַכֹּל אֲדוֹן כָּל אַדִּירִים:
וְנָתַן הַתּוֹרָה תְּמִימָה וּטְהוֹרָה בְּיַד צִיר נֶאֶטְדָה בְּרָאשֵׁי הֶהָרִים:
דְּבָרָיו נוֹדְעוּ וּמֵרוֹם נִשְׁמְעוּ בְּסִינַי נוֹשְׁעוּ בַּעֲשֶׂר הַדְּבָרִים:
הֲיָקוּם עוֹד נָבִיא כְּנֶגֶד הַמַּעֲרָבִי תְּמוּנַת אֵל הֵבִיא אֵלָיו הָעִבְרִים:
בְּהַר סִינַי רָאָה תְּמוּנַת צוּר נָאָה בְּקוֹל שׁוֹפָר נִרְאָה לַאֲשֶׁר הָעִבְרִים:
נְבוּאָתוֹ רַבָּה וְצֶדֶק כָּה יָלִין בְּעֵת רָצָה נְבָא כְּאַחַד הַחֲבֵרִים:
אָדוֹן נָתַן צִדְקוֹ לְכָל דָּבָר חֻקּוֹ לְצַדִּיק חֵן עֶרְכּוֹ וְרֶשַׁע לִקְבָרִים:
לְקֵץ יָמִים יִשְׁלַח אֱנוֹשׁ בַּכֹּל יִצְלַח עוֹנֵינוּ יִסְלַח וְיִרְוַח בִּמְאוֹרִים:
יִחְיֶה אֵל אֶחָד מֵתַי עַמּוֹ יַחַד בְּמוֹרָא וָפַחַד לְדִרְאוֹן זָרִים:
הֱיוֹת לִקְצָת נִמְנָע וְדַעְתָּם לֹא יִכְנַע וְחָכְמָה לֹא יִצְנַע בָּאֵל הָעִקָּרִים:
וְהוּא אֵל חַי נוֹרָא לְבַדּוֹ הַגְּבוּרָה וְנִצַּח תִּפְאָרָה לְאֵל עוֹשֵׂה אוֹרִים:
גְּדֻלָּה אֵין חֵקֶר בְּעֶרֶב וּבַבֹּקֶר וְאִם אַתָּה חֵקֶר רְבָבוֹת מֶחְקָרִים:

22-

פרשת בראשית

בְּרֵאשִׁית אֵל בָּרָא עֲרָבוֹת תִּפְאָרָה וְכֻלָּם בִּגְבוּרָה כְּמֶלֶךְ עִם שָׂרִים:
וְאֶרֶץ שָׁמַיִם וְרוּחַ עִם מַיִם וְאֵלֶּה בֵּינְתַיִם לַהֲווֹת הַדְּבָרִים:
וְהָאוֹר אָז נִבְרָא וְחֹשֶׁךְ לֵיל נִקְרָא בְּיוֹם חַד נִגְמְרָה מְעוֹנָה עִם הָרִים:
וְרָקִיעַ נִבְרָא וְשָׁמַיִם נִקְרָא בְּיוֹם שֵׁנִי אָמְרָה לַמַּיִם וּנְהָרִים:
וְהָאָרֶץ תַּדְשֵׁא וּמַזְרִיעַ דֶּשֶׁא וְזַרְעוֹ בּוֹ עָשָׂה הֱיוֹת מִין נִשְׁמָרִים:

23-

וְכָל הַדּוֹר נִשְׁחַת בְּלִי מוֹרָא פַּחַד נְפִילִים גַּם יַחַד וְכָל הַגִּבּוֹרִים:
וְשַׁדַּי מַה בּוֹחֵן בְּנֶפֶשׁ יְבָחֵן וְנֹחַ מָצָא חֵן וְצַדִּיק מִגְּבָרִים:
זְכוֹר דַּת בֶּן עַמְרָם אֲשֶׁר עַל כֹּל הוּרָם וּבָהּ אָנוּ עַם רָם לְדוֹרֵי הַדּוֹרִים:

The person who has the scroll stands up, approaches the Ark while the ḥazzān reads part 24 to which the worshippers respond with part 25. The ḥazzān and the worshippers read responsively Psalm 145 "Tehilla le-David" after which the scroll is returned to the Ark while everyone reads part 26. The Ark is then closed and the curtain is drawn.

24- **אַשְׁרֵי** הָעָם שֶׁכָּכָה לּוֹ ׀ 25- אַשְׁרֵי הָעָם שֶׁיהוָה אֱלֹהָיו:

26- וּבְנֻחֹה יֹאמַר ׀ שׁוּבָה יְהוָה רִבְבוֹת אַלְפֵי יִשְׂרָאֵל:

Glossary of Terms

As this book deals with a subject not familiar to everyone, it contains certain words that need clarification.

I used the Sepherdic pronunciation with all Hebrew words. I used the Egyptian way in the pronunciation of the G, which is always hard.

'Aliya: literally "ascent" or "going up," refers to visiting or immigrating to the Holy Land, specifically to the sacred city of Jerusalem, the site of the old temple.

'Arīkhāh: monthly dues paid by able men of the Jewish communities (Rabbanite, Karaite) to help run the community affairs (equivalent to membership dues of a congregation).

Bēt-Dīn: the headquarters of a Jewish community where there are offices for the rabbi(s), the secretaries and all other employees. It is also the place where members of the religious council and the religious courts hold their meetings. All records of the community, old and new, are kept there. Starting from 1940, it became known as *Dār al-Shar',* which is the Arabic translation of Bēt-Dīn.

Gabalāh: taxes levied on each pound of kasher meat sold. The taxes were charged by both Jewish communities: the Rabbanite, and the Karaite in Cairo. Because each community had its own regulations about kasher animals, each had its own ritual slaughterers.[1]

Gabbāy: treasurer. The holder of this office is responsible for looking after a synagogue.

---

1. In the minutes of December 2, 1909 the religious council decided not to slaughter any animal for butchers who were delinquent in paying the *Gabalāh* to the Karaite Bēt-Dīn. In the minutes of February 9, 1911 it is mentioned that the kasher butchers used to pay 2' millièmes (about 5 cents) on each pound sold, except what was sold to needy people.

Genizah: a place where all discarded papers with Hebrew writing on them are kept. Among the famous genizahs is the one discovered in old Cairo (Fusṭāt) in the late 19th century. It contained more than 240,000 documents.

Ḥākhām: a term used by all Eastern Jews instead of rabbi.

Ḥākhām Akbar: or ḥākhām Pāshī or Bāshā. The chief rabbi or the chief ḥākhām of a Jewish community. During the period under consideration there were two ḥākhāmim akbar, one for the Rabbanite community and another for the Karaite community.

Ḥākhāmkhānah: another word for Bēt-Dīn. Bēt-Dīn is Hebrew, and came into usage since the rise of Islam. Ḥākhāmkhāhah is of two parts: ḥākhām which is Hebrew and khānah, which is of Persian origin, indicating the office of, the department of, the housing of. During the Turkish rule in Egypt many such combinations were used: Baṭrakhānah — the headquarters of a Christian community (Patriarchate), Kotobkhānah — library ... etc.

Ḥabarah: a type of women's clothing. It is of two parts: both are black; the bottom one is like a skirt, the top part is a plain piece of cloth that covers the head, the shoulders and the back. It may also be used to cover the face. Was the common dress for middle class women in Turkey and in Egypt, especially the Jews and the Copts (the Egyptian Orthodox Christians).

Ḥārat al-Yahūd: the neighborhood where most of the Jews lived until the end of the 19th century. Until 1970 A.D. there were *Ḥārat al-Yahūd al-Rabbāniyyīn* and *Ḥārat al-Yahūd al-Qarrā'īn*.

Ḥazzān: cantor. Karaites in Egypt did not have official ḥazzāns. Any one with good voice and musical ability could be a ḥazzān. In many cases the ḥākhām used to be also a ḥazzān.

Higriyah: Muslims start their calendar in the year when the prophet Muḥammad immigrated from Mecca to al-Madīnah. So if we say "Higriyah" or "lil-Higrah" we mean so many years after Muḥammad had immigrated. The Arabic -A.H.- is its abbreviation.

Ḥōsh: the courtyard of a house. Most of the houses until the 1920's used to have a *ḥōsh*. It also indicates a special burial place for a family. *Ḥōsh al-Qudsī*, for example, indicates the place where all members of al-Qudsī family bury their deceased.

Internal Code: a code drafted by elected members of the non-Muslim community and then approved by the Egyptian Ministry of Interior. The code defines the rights and the responsibilities of the head of the community, members of the religious council, of the religious courts, as well as all other members of the community. It also defines the rules for electing members of all bodies that govern the community.

Kanīs: kanis (masculine) is the place of worship for Jews, the synagogue.
kanīsah (feminine) is the place where Christians worship.

Khudaywī: the official title of the governor of Egypt from the time of Ismā'īl (June 1867) until it ended in 1914 when Britain terminated the Turkish rule of Egypt.

Mamelukes: Dynasties of military men who ruled Egypt from 1250 to 1517. Originally they were Turkish slaves or young Christian prisoners of war. They were trained militarily and schooled in Islam. The first to use them in his army was the Fatimid caliph al-'Azīz (975-996). From that time on, it became a tradition for every ruler to have his own trained slaves as personal guards. In 1250 they were able to sieze power in Egypt and ruled the country until the Ottoman sultan, Salīm I, conquered Egypt in 1715. Yet they remained powerful until 1811 when Muḥammad 'ALī, the governor of Egypt put an end to them.

Mohel: a qualified and certified Jew to perform circumcision, a ritual circumciser.

Muḥtasib: a government employee responsible for the supervison of the monetary system, the weights and measures, all the markets, and the streets and the roads. The position was eliminated during the last quarter of the 19th century.

Personal Status Code: during the first half of the 20th century (until 1956) all the non-Muslim communities followed the laws of their own religion in matters of marriage, divorce, and inheritance. These laws were compiled in a book, called the Personal Status Code, approved by the Ministry of Justice.

Qawwāṣ: guide. An attendant to the ḥakhām or to the patriarch, dressed in very decorative uniform and armed with a decorative sword. After 1937 the *Qawwāṣ* no longer carried a sword. A few years later the position was eliminated.

Religious Council: a body of 12 members or more of a non-Muslim community. Members of the religious council were elected by the members of their own community to run the community's affairs for a period of time specified in its Internal Code.

Religious Court: A court of three or more judges headed by a qualified ḥakhām or patriarch to look into matters of marriage, conciliation or divorce, and inheritance among members of a non-Muslim community.

Sēfer, Sefarīm: scrolls handwritten by qualified members of a Jewish community. They are written according to certain rules and regulations to ensure their correctness. In the East the *Sefarīm* are kept in special boxes of olive wood covered with velvet and silver or gold leafs, or with inlaid mother-of-pearl.

Shammās: a person in charge of a synagogue, responsible for cleaning and maintenance. He also bears certain religious responsibilities, such as preparing the synagogue for the holy days, lighting the candles and the chandeliers for memorial services, while reciting certain prayers, etc.; a beadle.

Shoḥēt: a qualified and certified Jew who is responsible for slaughtering kasher animals; ritual slaughterer.

Wālī: governor. A term used by the Arabs since the beginning of their Islamic Empire in the 7th century.

Bibliography

Arabic:

Al-Irshād. Karaite magazine. 1908-1909.
Al-Ittiḥād. Karaite magazine. 1924-1930.
Al-Kalīm. Karaite magazine. 1945-1956. Besides several issues published to cover important events.
Al-Masarrah. Revue mensuelle: Organe du Patriarcat Grec-Catholique Harissa (Liban), 20th year, Vol. V, May 1934.
Al-Qirqisānī. *al-Anwār wal-Marāqib.* New York: The Alexander Kohut Memorial Foundation, 1939. Vol. I, edited by Leon Nemoy.
Al-Tahdhīb. Karaite magazine. 1901-1904.
Al-Shubbān al-Qarrā'īn. Karaite magazine. April to November 1937.
"The Census of Egypt, 1927." Ministry of Finance. Government Press, 1931.
Farag, Mūrad. *al-Aḥkām al-Sharʻiyah fī al-Aḥwāl al-Shakhṣiyah lil-Isrā'īliyīn al-Qarrā'īn.* Cairo, Egypt, 1935.
Farag, Mūrad. *al-Qarrā'ūn wal-Rabbānūn.* Cairo, Egypt, 1918.
Farag, Mūrad. *Shiʻār al-Khiḍr.* Egypt, 1917.
Līshaʻ, David, and Yūsuf Yomtōb. *Al-Murshid al-Amīn* (a manual in the Karaite faith). Cairo, Egypt, 1948.
"Minutes of the Karaite Religious Council of Cairo, 1901-1972." The six volumes are now in the library of the Karaite Community in Ramlah.

French:

Carré, Olivier, et Gérard Michaud. *Les Frères Musulman (1928-1982).* Paris: Edition Gallimard/Julliard, 1983.
Clot-Bey, A B. *Aperçu Général sur L'Egypt.* 2 vols. Paris: Fortin & Masson, 1840.

"Communauté Israélite du Caire. Rapport et Comptes pour L'Année 1934." Le Caire: Imp. H. Urwand & Fils, 1935.

Szyszman, Simon. "Compte rendu de L'ouvrage de Naphtali Wieder. The Judean Scrolls and Karaisme." *Revue de l'Histoire des Religions,* Tome CLXVIII, No. 451.

Szyszman, Simon. "La redécouverte du Karaisme à lumière de nouveaux documents." *Revue de L'Association des Médecins Israélite de France,* No. 281 (1979) 283-1980.

Szyszman, Simon. *Le Karaïsme.* Lausanne: L'Age D'Homme, 1980.

English:

Adler, E.N. *Jews in Many Lands.* Philadelphia: J.P.S.A., 1905.

Avrin, Leila. *The Illumination in the Moshe Ben-Asher Codex of 895 C.E.,* Vols. I and II. Authorized facsimile by Ann Arbor, Michigan, 1980. University Microfilm International U.S.A.

Birnbaum, Philip. *Karaite Studies.* Edited and with an introduction by Philip Birnbaum. N.Y.: Hermon Press, 1971.

Chazan, Robert. *Medieval Jewish Life.* Selected and with an introduction by Robert Chazan. N.Y., 1976.

Cohen, Hayyim. *The Jews in the Middle East, 1860-1972.* Israel University PR.

Cohen, Mark R. *Jewish Self-Government in Medieval Egypt.* Princeton University Press, 1980.

Dubnow, S. *The History of Jews,* Vols. II and III. H.S. Barnes and Co., 1969.

Goitein, S.D. *Jews and Arabs.* New York: Schocken, 1955.

Goldberg, S. *Karaite Liturgy.* London: Manchester University Press, 1957.

Graetz: *History of Jews,* Vol. III. Philadelphia: J.P.S.A., 1894.

Hirshberg, J. "Preservation Versus Acculturation in the Musical Tradition of the Karaites in Israel." A paper presented at the I.C.T.M. conference, 1983.

Landau, J.M. *Jews in the 19th Century Egypt.* N.Y.: New York University Press, 1976.

Lane, E.W. *An Account of the Manners and Customs of the Modern Egyptians,* Vols. I and II. London, 1836.

Mann, J. *The Jews in Egypt and Palestine under the Fatimid Caliphs,* Vols. I and II. Oxford University Press, 1920.

Mann, J. *Texts and Studies in Jewish History and Literature,* Vol. II. New York: Ktav Publishing House, 1972.

Nemoy, Leon. *Karaite Anthology.* New Haven and London: Yale University Press, 1952.

Nemoy, Leon. "Qumisian Sermon to the Karaites." Reprinted from Proceedings of the American Academy for Jewish Research, Vol. XLII, 1976.

Nemoy, Leon. "The Karaites and the Rabbanites." (from Arabic by Murād Farag). *Revue des études juives,* Janvier-Septembre, 1976.

Nemoy, Leon. "A Modern Karaite Arabic Poet. (Murād Farag)." *The Jewish Quarterly Review,* new series, Vol. LXXIV.

Nemoy, Leon. "A Modern Egyptian Digest of the Karaite Divorce Law. (Murād Farag)." *Henoch,* 3 (1981) 350 - 368.

Rubenstein, A. *The Return to Zion.* Popular History of Jewish Civilization. New York: Leon Amid Publishers.

Rustum, Saad. *The Royal Archives of Egypt and the Disturbances in Palestine 1834.* Birut, 1938.

Stillman, N. *Jews of Arab Lands.* Philadelphia: J.P.S.A., 1979.

Zajaczkowski, A. *Karaism in Poland.* Paris: La Haye, 1961.

Index

All Karaite proper names under family name.
All Karaite Ḥākhāmīm (rabbis) under Ḥākhām (H).
All districts, streets lanes under places (P)
All Karaite organizations under Associations (A).
All Karaite magazines under Periodicals (P).

A

'Abbās Ḥilmī II (Khudaywī), 51, 269
'Abd Allah (family name), 222
   'Abd Allah Barakāt 'Abdu, 216
   Abd Allah Farag, 53, 63, 222, 269
   'Abd Allah Ya'qūb, 60, 222, 272
'Abd al-Magīd (Sulṭan), 19
'Abd al-Raḥmān Sāmī, 261
'Abd al-Wāḥid (family name), 15, 16, 223
   'Abd al-Wāḥid 'Abd al-'Azīz, 223
   'Abd al-Wāḥid Benoit, 213
   'Abd al-Wāḥid Leon (Murād), 223
'Abdū al-Ḥāmūlī (composer/singer), 258
Abū-Ya'qub, 214
Adler, 13
Adon 'Olām, 138
Adonai Mēlēkh, 151, 152
Ahl al-Kitāb referring to Christians, 25
Ahl al-Dhimmah referring to Jews, 25
Aḥmad Shawqī (Prince of poets), 259
Alexandria, 14, 20, 28, 61
Alfred Yaluz, 27
American University of Cairo, 23
Ampus Var (Region in France), 23
Anna Adonāi, 151
'Anān ha-Nāsī, 147, 219, 299
'Anān (Synagogue in Jerusalem), 24, 56, 299

Anti-Semitism, 24
Arab Israeli War(s), 1948/1956/1967, 22, 61, 62, 66, 99, 214, 215, 217, 289, 295
'Arīkhāh, 55, 58, 59, 64, 65, 66, 102, 222
Asfé Kayez, 218
Ashdod, 298, 300
Aṣlān (family name), 222
   Aṣlān Elīyāhū Ya'qūb, 13, 14, 15, 222
   Aṣlān Farag Ya'qūb, 222
   Aṣlān Jaques Ibrāhīm, 214
   Aṣlān Shalōm Ibrāhīm, 23
Asmahān (singer), 259
Associations:
   Gam'iyat al-Difā' 'An Maṣāliḥ al-Ṭā'ifah, The Association for Defending the Community Interest, 212
   Gam'iyat al-Ikhwān al-Qarrā'īn, Karaite Brothers Association, 134, 215
   Gam'iyat al-Irshād, The Association for Guidance, 211
   Gam'iyat al-Iṣlāḥ, The Association for Reforms, 211
   Gan'iyat al-Ittiḥād al-Isrā'īlī, The Israelite Union Association, 56, 211, 213, 245
   Gam'iyat al-Shubbān al-Isrā'īliyīn al-

Qarrā'īn, Israelite Karaite Young Men's Assocaition, 213, 215, 223
Gam'iyat al-Shubbān al-Qarrā'īn, Karaite Young Men's Association, 27, 212, 222
Gam'iyat Musā'adat al-Adhārā al-Faqīrāt, The Association for Helping the Poor Maiden, 134, 216
Gam'iyat Musā'adat al-'Adhārā al-Faqīrāt 'alā al-Zawāg, The Association for Helping the Poor Maiden Get Married, 216, 221, 222
Gam'iyat Musā'adat al-Marḍā, The Association for Helping the Sick, 134, 210
Gam'iyat Shubbān Ḥubb al-Tawrāh, The Love of the Torah Association, 100, 216, 223
Kashāfat wa Gawwālat al-Isrā'īliyīn al-Qarrā'īn, Israelite Karaite Boy Scout and Explorers, 214, 215
Mashghal al-Banāt al-Khayrī, The Benevolent Workshop for Girls, 100, 215
Maṭ'am al-Faqīr, Kitchen for the Poor, 215
Mugtama' al-Akhā', Brotherhood Associaiton, 211
Aswan, 14
Australia, 297, 298
Austrian, 218
Aveli Zion, 287
'Ayn Shams Company, 108
'Azīz Ṣādiq (Musician), 260

B

Barclay's Bank, 295
Bakhtichisarai, 273
Bar Mizva, 297
Basātīn, al-, 108, 182
Bat Mizva, 297
Beershiba, 298
Benevolent Home for Elderly, 60
Bereshīt (lesson/sefer), 151, 152
Bēt-Dīn (Karaite), 13, 14, 15, 27, 54, 62, 65, 66, 104, 108, 134, 135, 145, 146, 147, 152, 154, 175, 178, 187, 224, 244, 296

Bēt-Dīn (Rabbanite), 28, 296
Bēt Yisrael, 288
Bi'āh, 156, 173
Balāgh, al- (newspaper), 13
Bikkurīm, 148
Bilād al-Quds, 245
Brazil, 297
Bridesmaids, 156
British, 217
British Royal Navy, 23
Bughāshah (food), 152

C

Cairo, 13, 14, 19, 20, 23, 24, 25, 28, 53, 56, 58, 59, 60, 61, 62, 65, 99, 103, 104, 107, 108, 137, 142, 145, 148, 218, 223, 240, 258, 267, 268, 269, 270, 271, 273, 289, 295, 297
California, 298
Canada, 297, 298
Central Higher Committee of the Karaite in Israel, 300
Chicago, 222, 298
Christians, 20, 22, 28, 52, 99, 143
Cicurel (Department Store in Cairo), 295
Circumcision, 153, 154, 211, 224
Clot Bey, 13
Coconut, 147
Codex: Ben Asher, 107
Cohen Hayyim, 13
Coffin, 179, 182
Copts, 28, 60, 294
Co-Wife, 176
Crimea, 23, 219, 270
Cromer, Sir Evelyn Baring, 51, 269
Crusades, 288

D

Daniel al-Qumīsī, 219, 287
Dar'ī, al Mosheh (poet), 106
Dar'ī, al-Mosheh 'Abbāsiyah, (Synagogue), 61, 105, 106, 107, 145, 220, 275
Darwīsh (family name), 15, 16
Dayan Mosheh, 297
Days of Fast and Mourning, 153
Death, 178
Delta (Nile), 23

Divorce, 52, 175 to 178

E

Education, 59, 66, 96
Egypt, 12, 19, 24, 25, 51, 56, 57, 61, 62, 63, 64, 65, 133, 142, 145, 147, 174, 218, 258, 288
Engagement, 53, 154, 155, 224
England, 23, 297
Ephraim Deinard, 245
Eupatoria, 296
Eupatoria Karaite High Organizations, 296
Eupatoria Convention of 1910, 57, 244, 272
Eupatoria Theological Karaite Center, 296
Exodus, 294

F

Falakh or Falashas, 60
Faddān, 108
Farḥi Hillel, 27, 212
Fārūq, 61, 219, 275
Fatḥiyah Aḥmad (singer), 259
Fāyid Muḥammad (singer), 259
Fiancé, 155
Finacée, 155
Firkovich Abraham, 104, 105, 219
Firūz (family name), 15
Firūz Bank, 103
Food, 142, 185 to 188
France, 23, 297, 298
Free Officers, 61, 275, 296
French, 27, 53, 102, 155, 159, 213, 218, 223, 271
Fringes, 138
Fu'ād, 247
Fūl (fava beans), 17

G

Gabalāh, 59, 65
Gabbāy, 64, 108, 151, 219, 220, 221, 224
Galabiyah, 18, 143, 150
Gamīl, al- (family name)
    Gamīl, al- 'abd Allah, 269
    Gamīl, al- Amīn Barakāt, 219, 224

Gēfen ha-Adderet, 218
General Assembly, 51, 55, 59, 270
Geniza, 107
Gibbah, 143
Glodberg Selvin, 137
Gold Kings, 16, 223
Gōs we Tōm (food), 186, 187
Greek, 218, 223, 269
Gymnastics, 101

H

Ḥabarah, 143
Habdalāh, 144, 150
Haggadah, 148
Ḥākhāmīm, 52, 267 to 286
    Abrāhām Kohen, 27, 53, 55, 57, 218, 245, 271, 272, 288
    Ahārūn Kefīlī, 54, 269, 270
    Berākhāh Kohen, 54, 270
    Mosheh al-Qudsī, 105, 267, 268
    Shabbethāi Elīyāhū Mangūbī, 21, 27, 50, 51, 52, 58, 98, 268, 269
    Shlomoh Kohen, 218, 268
    Tobiah Levi Babovitch, 21, 52, 57, 58, 60, 61, 106, 218, 219, 244, 273, 275
HIAS, 296
Ḥamechi (fast of)
Ḥames, 146
Ḥāmiḍ (food), 186, 187
Hārūn (family name), 275
    Hārūn Bārūkh Lieto, 275
    Hārūn Murād Lieto, 275, 297
Ḥusayn 'abdul Ṣamad, 212
Haskoy, 25
Ḥilwān, 101, 142, 150
Hebrāt Qaddishah, 178
Ḥayyīm Duwayk (Rabbanite Ḥākhām), 275
Ḥayyīm Kahanah, 246
Ḥayyīm Naḥūm (Ḥākhām Akbar of the Rabbanite Community), 27, 272, 275, 288
Ḥayyīm Qīqī (Rabbanite Ḥākhām), 245
Ḥayyīnah (family name), 223
    Ḥayyīnah Yūsuf Farag, 63, 108, 223
Ḥazzān, ḥazzānīm, 52, 144, 145, 221, 223, 268, 273, 274
Heliopolis, 107, 108, 142, 214, 216

354

Hospital (Jewish Hospital), 26, 27, 151, 217, 221
Ḥusayn Fawzī, 260

I

I. A. Edham, 245, 256
'It Dodīm Kallah (song), 137, 270
Ikhwān, al- al-Muslimūn, 61, 270, 274, 295, 296
'Imām, al- al-Shāfi'ī 110
Internal Code, 50, 57, 212, 271
Italy, 297
Italian, 218, 223
Israel (country), 56, 174, 221, 287, 294, 298, 299
Israelis, 296
Istanbūl, 23, 25, 210, 268, 270, 271

J

Jaffa, 298
Japheth ben Eli, 288
Jerusalem, 23, 24, 25, 56, 136, 179, 267, 270, 287, 298

K

Kalé (Chufut Kalé), 219
Kāmil al-Khula'ī (musician), 260
Karaite Academy, 288
Karaite Creed, 136
Karaite Elements of Prayer, 138
Karaite Prayer, 107, 136, 137
Karaite Prayer Books, 137
Karaite Time of Prayer, 136, 137
Kasher, 17, 146, 148, 184
Ketubbāh, 147, 159, 175
Khawagāt, 22
Khaznī (synagogue), 105
Khaznī Nissīm Kohen (ḥākhām), 105
Ki Eshmerah Shabbāt, 137
Khidr (family name), 223
 Khidre Nagīb, 16, 223
 Khidre Thābīt, 16, 223
Kitāb (writ of marriage), 156
Khudaywī (title of governor of Egypt), 51, 246, 269
Kowwaḥ, ha- (sport club), 213

L

Lagnah, al- al-Milliyah, 51
Landau cars, 156
Law of Incest, 244
Laylā Murād (singer), 259
Laylat al-Ḥinnah (painting), 219
Leb Yahūdī, 19
Levi (family name), 220
 Levi Dā'ūd Ḥusnī, 19, 209, 218 (A complete biography and his work 258 to 266)
 Levi Ibrāhīm Ḥusnī, 220
 Levi Ibrāhīm Yūsuf (artist), 219
 Levi Kamāl Ḥusnī, 220
 Levi Salīm Ibrāhīm (M.D.), 220
 Levi Raḥmīn Farag, 220
 Levi Victor Ibrāhīm, 221
Linson, Dr., 51
Līsha' (family name), 16, 26, 65, 220, 244, 297
 Līsha' al-Kabīr, 13
 Līsha' Dā'ūd Isḥaq, 54, 108, 219, 269, 270
 Līsha' David Zakī, 63, 106, 108, 219
 Līsha' Elie Bārūkh, 219
 Līsha' Farag Samlīn, 211
 Līsha' Isḥāq Yūsuf (L. al-Kabīr), 269
 Līsha' Murād Farag, 27, 53, 56, 57, 60, 63, 106, 175, 177, 178, 209, 210, 211, 218 (A complete biography and all his work, 244 to 257), 272, 288
 Līsha' Raḥmīn, 60
 Līsha' Tawfīq Murād, 247
Lithuania, 24
Liwā', al (newspaper), 16
Los Altos, 298
Lottery, 53, 65, 66, 98, 102, 103, 104
Lozato, 147, 154
Luṭfī, 14

M

Ma'ādī, 108, 142
Maccabi (sport club), 213
Mc Gowan, 13
Maghribī, al- Samuel ben Moses, 136
Maḥallah, al- al-Kubrā, 14
Magīdī, al- (coin), 20

355

Magnus Museum, 218
Maimonides, 26
Mamzer, 244
Mangūbī (family name), 222
   Mangūbī Abrāhām Shabbethāı, 54, 63, 270
   Mangūbī Jacques Lieto, 62, 222, 297, 298
   Mangūbī Shabbethāi Elīyāhū (see ḥākhāmīm), 222
Manṣūr, 14
Manṣūrah, al-, 20, 258
Manyalāwī, al-, (musician), 259
Maqām, 258, 259, 261
Marriage (see Wedding), 224
Marriage Rituals, 161, 174
Marzūq (family name), 26, 221
   Marzūq Mattātiah Nissīm, 221
   Marzūq Mosheh (M.D.), 221, 289
   Marzūq Yūsuf Ibrāhīm, 59, 221
   Marzūq Yūsuf Mūsā, 63, 221
Maṣliyaḥ (family name)
   Maṣliyaḥ 'Abdū Bārūkh, 275
   Maṣliyaḥ Abrāhām (ḥākhām), 105
   Maṣliyaḥ Ibrāhīm Dā'ūd (artist), 219
   Maṣliyaḥ Isḥāq, 105
   Maṣliyaḥ Farag, 215
   Maṣliyaḥ Thābit, 100
   Maṣliyaḥ Yūsuf Farag, 271
   Maṣliyaḥ Zakī Ḥayyīm, 219
Mas'ūdah (family name), 16, 19, 26, 65, 220
   Mas'ūdah 'Abbās Yefet, 220
   Mas'ūdah Bārūkh Yūsuf (D.D.S.), 23
   Mas'ūdah Elie Bārūkh, 273
   Mas'ūdah Farīd Yefet (M.D.), 220
   Mas'ūdah Ḥabīb Yūsuf, 23
   Mas'ūdah Ibrāhīm Elīyāhū, 105, 106, 220
   Mas'ūdah Ibrāhīm Elīyāhū (artist), 219
   Mas'ūdah Khidr Yefet, 220
   Mas'ūdah Lieto Bārūkh (Odéon), 61, 275

Mas'ūdah Yūsuf Bārūkh, 220, 288
Maṣṣah, Massōt, 14, 21, 145, 146, 147, 222
Matfūnah (food), 185, 186, 187
Me'alliyah (food), 186
Melitopol, 270
Memorial, 184, 185, 216, 286
Menashah (family name), 26, 221
   Menashah Ibrāhīm Mūsā, 221
   Menanshah Mūsā Ibrāhīm, 63, 108, 221
   Menashan Zakī, 219, 221
Merorīm, 147
Mezuzah, 139
Mini-War (six days war) (see Arab-Israeli War)
Mishnah, 26
Miṣr (newspaper), 16
Mizvah, 154
Mohār, 156, 175, 221
Mohel, Mohelim, 52, 154, 221, 223
Mordokh (family name), 16, 223
   Mordokh Mūsā Murād, 223
   Mordokh Yūsuf Murād, 223
Morello cherry, 147
Mourners, 182, 183, 184
Muḥammad 'Abd al-Muṭṭalib (singer), 259
Muḥammad 'Abdū, 258
Muḥammad 'Alī, 20
Muḥammad Fatḥī, 260
Muḥammad Murād, 275
Muḥammad Nagīb, 61, 275, 296
Muḥammad Riyāḍ, 275
Muḥammad Sha'bān (musician), 258
Muḥammad 'Othmān (musician), 259
Muḥtasib, 20
Murshid, al- al-Amīn, 219
Muṣaffī (family name)
   Muṣaffī, al- Nissīm, 268
   Muṣaffī, al- Sitaytah, 105, 272
Mushav Maṣliyaḥ (Israel), 299
Mushav Ranīn (Israel), 298
Muslims, 18, 19, 21, 22, 52, 62, 99, 137,

143, 185, 274, 294
Muṣṭafā Ṣadiq, 60

N

Nagāt 'Alī (singer), 259
Naḥamōt, 153
Nāsī (family name), 105
Nāsīr, 18, 61, 62, 275, 296, 297
Nāṣiriyah (school), 99
Nemoy, Leon, 26, 175, 246
New Jersey, 298
New York, 298
Nile, 110, 131

O

Odéon, 16
Old Testament, 137
Oriental rug, 155
Oriental tent, 156

P

Palestine Question, 295
Paris, 23, 25
Passover, 15, 19, 21, 22, 55, 145, 146, 147, 148, 185
Peninsula Sinai Congregation, 298
Periodicals:
   al-Irshād, 211
   al-Ittiḥad al- Isra'īlī, 13, 21, 212, 219, 222, 224, 244, 245, 272, 274, 289
   al-Kalīm, 14, 58, 66, 99, 104, 214, 219, 220, 223, 224, 244, 246, 273
   al-Shubbān al-Qarrā'īn, 59, 213, 219, 220, 224, 246
   al-Tahdhīb, 16, 210, 211
   al Shams (Rabbanite magazine), 246
   Israel (Rabbanite magazine), 27
Pessaḥ (famiily name)
   Pessaḥ Maurice Yūsuf, 224
   Pessaḥ Shalom Mūsā, 17
Personal Status Code, 50, 60, 61, 212, 271
Places: Districts and also streets
   'Abbāsiyah, al-, 15, 61, 63, 65, 99, 102, 105, 142, 145, 210, 212, 214, 216, 217, 172, 195
   Azhar, al-, 19, 28
   Dāhir, al-, 15, 65, 105, 142
   Faggālah, al-, 60
   Gamāliyah, al-, 15
   Ghamrah, al-, 26, 65, 105, 142, 217
   Garden City, 142
   Gudriyah, al-,
   Ḥamzāwī, al-, 28
   Ḥusayn, al- 119
   Khurunfish, al-, 51, 99, 224, 274
   Muskī, al-, 19, 28
   Ṣāghah, al-, 12, 15, 17, 18, 28, 144
   Sakākīnī, al-, 15, 65, 142
   Wazīr, al-, 108
   Zamālik, 142
Streets, only, or lanes
   'Aṭfit al-Dabbāḥ, 18
   'Aṭfit al-Miṣriyīn, 18
   'Aṭfit al-Muṣaffī, 18
   'Aṭfit Menashah, 18
   Darb al-Furn, 105
   Ḥārat al-Ṣayārifah, 19
   Ḥārat ('Aṭfit) al-Yahūd al-Qarrā'īn known as al-Ḥārah, 12, 15, 17, 18, 19, 51, 63, 99, 145, 146, 152, 210, 211, 214, 215, 216, 217, 224, 258
   Ḥārat al-Yahūd al-Rabbāniyīn, 17, 18, 19, 217
   Ḥārat Zuwaylah, 119
Poland, 24, 25, 288
Polygamy, 57, 271
Port Sa'īd, 15
Psalms, 137, 181, 182, 216
Purim, 'Id al-Maskharah, 15, 19, 155 146, 152, 153, 155

Q

Qānūn al-Maglis al-Milly (The Religious Council Code), 54
Qaṭṭāwī Yūsuf Basha, 27
Qawwās, 269
Qiblah, 136
Qinyān, 176
Qinnōt, 153
Qirqisānī, al-
Qudsī, al- (family name), 26, 222
   Qudsī, al- Murād Mūsā Yūsuf, 61, 62, 222, 275
   Qudsī, al- Murād Yūsuf Mūsā, 211

Qudsī, al- Mosheh Abrāhām
(ḥākhām), 222, 267, 268
Qudsī, al- Yūsuf Lieto Yūsuf, 105
Qudsī, al- Yūsuf Mūsā Abrāhām, 222
Quftān, 18, 143
Qurbān (sefer), 107, 152

R

Rab-Simḥāh (synagogue), 19, 52, 104, 105, 106, 108, 142, 224
Ragā' 'Abdū (singer), 259
Ra'īs, al- 'Am, 55
Ramlah, 287, 298, 300
Raphael Ahārūn Simon (ḥākhām akbar of the Rabbanite Community), 27
Ra's, 271
Red Cross, 296
Religious Councils, 24, 50, 53, 54, 55, 56, 58, 59, 62, 63, 99, 101, 104, 105, 108, 109, 133, 134, 177, 178, 210, 211, 212, 217, 222, 223, 244, 270, 273, 274,
Religious Courts, 27, 50, 59
Reshtah we Tagarīnes (food), 185, 186
Rhode Island, 298
Ritual slaughterer, 52, 100, 185, 217
Riyāḍ al-Sunbāṭī (composer), 260
Rome, 23
Rosh Penah, 218, 274
Rosh ha-Shannan, Yom Terū'āh, 144, 145, 149
Rubenstein, Aryeh, 287
Rue (herb), 145, 155, 156
Russia, 24, 54, 104, 219, 269, 270, 273, 288
Russian, 24, 57, 218, 273

S

Sa'ādiah al-Fayyūmī, 26
Sabbath, 144, 145, 149, 151, 187
Sa'd Munīr, 275
Sa'd Zaghlūl Basha, 21
Safāh Berorāh, 214
Samaritans, 18, 26
Samm Baladī, 187
Samuel Ḥasīd, 106
San Francisco, 218, 298
Sanṭūrī, al- (musician), 259

Sayyid Darwīsh (composer), 260
Schools
  Karaite, 53, 61, 63, 65, 66, 98 to 103, 215, 216, 222, 223
  Rabbanite, 26, 27, 63, 99, 104, 134, 217, 220, 222, 295, 296
  Others - Les Ecoles des Freres, Khurunfish, 258
Sebastopol, 273
Seliḥot, 149
Sephardic, 288, 297
Shabu'ōt (feast of),
  Ḥamishīm Lisfirāt, 145, 148
  ha-Omer'
Shamuel (family name), 18
  Shamuel Salīm Farag, 108, 223
Sham'ūn Elie, 275
Sharikat al-Gamal al-Miṣriyah, 16
Sharqiyah, al-, 23
Shaykh al-Ḥārah, 19, 20
Shemā', 138, 139, 151
Shepard Hotel, 295
Shoḥēt, Shoḥetīm, 52, 185, 187, 223
Shofar, 139
Simḥat Torah (feast of), 27, 145, 151, 152
Simīṭ, 17
Sinānī, Marco (M.D.), 210
Sirgānī (family name), 223
  Sirgānī, al- Farag Mūsā Rāsōn, 63, 223
  Sirgānī, al- Mūsā Farag Rāsōn, 218, 223
Ṣiṣit, 138
Six days war, Mini war (see Arab-Israel War)
Siyāḥū (family name), 15
Solomon Shabbethāi Nōnō, 295
Spanish, 218, 223, 269
Stuffed Chicken, 186
Stuffed Pureed Potatoes, 186
Stuffed Turkey, 185
Stuffed Vegetables, 186
Sukkah, 150, 151
Sukkot, 150, 151, 185
Sukkar 'Alī, 258
Sūq al-'Aṭṭārīn, 144

Synagogues, 104 to 108, 138, 143, 144, 150
Szyszman Simon, 25, 26

T

Table Tennis, 101, 210
Ṭafl, 144
Ṭallīt, 138, 139, 159, 170
Talmud, 26
Talmudic, 137
Ṭanānī, al (family name), 224
    Ṭanānī, al- Yūsuf Farag, 224
Ṭanṭā, 20
Taṭhīr, 296
Tawfīq (Khudaywī), 51, 269
Tefellin, 139
Temporary Committee, 58, 220
Tevah, 152
Theodosia, 25, 273
Tishri, 138, 149
Tithe, 274
Trousseau, 155, 156
Tuhmat al-Damm, 22
Turkey, 24, 51, 268, 272
Turkish, 25, 218, 269, 271

U

Umm al-'Agā'ib, 270
Umm Kulthūn, 16, 259
United States, 23, 297
Usher's, 156
'Ūd, 254
Uziel (family name), 219
    Uliel Zakī Amīn, 219

W

Wālī, 20
Waq̄'i', al- al-Miṣriyah
Warshah, al-, 60
Wedān, Haman, 152
Wedding, 155, 156
Wedding Ceremony, 156, 175
Weizmann, Chaim, 288
World War I, 24, 102, 188
World War II, 14, 22, 25, 109, 188, 270, 274, 288, 295, 296

Y

Yalūz Alfred, 27
Year book, 102
Yeshiva, 299
Yeri'ōt Shlomoh, 218, 268
Yidish, 218
Yitzhak Navon, 298
Y.M.C.A., 213
Y.M.M.A., 213
Yogurt, 183
Yom Kippur, 106, 144, 145, 149
Yom Shebe'i 'Aseret, 148
Yomtōb (family name), 223
    Yomtōb Ibrāhīm Yūsuf, 268
    Yomtōb Yūsuf Ibrāhīm, 63, 108, 223
Yūsuf Tawīl (Catholic Arch-Metropolitan), 275

Z

Zagal, 219, 224
Zakariyā Aḥmad (musician), 259
Zakariyā Ḥāmid Bey, 60
Zayt, al- al-Faransāwī, 187
Zax, Dr., 261
Zion, 287, 288
Zionism, Zionist, 212, 214, 221, 247, 287, 288, 289
Zot ha-Berakhah, 151